The Temperament of Generations

For those who have told the truth as they see it
and their cantankerous editors

THE TEMPERAMENT *of* GENERATIONS

Fifty years of writing in *Meanjin*

Edited by
Jenny Lee, Philip Mead
and Gerald Murnane

MEANJIN / MELBOURNE UNIVERSITY PRESS
1990

First published 1990
Typeset by Bookset Pty Ltd, Melbourne
Design by Mark Davis
Cover image by Peter Lyssiotis
Printed in Australia by Brown Prior Anderson Pty Ltd, Burwood
for *Meanjin*, and Melbourne University Press,
Carlton, Victoria 3053

This publication is assisted by the Australia Council, the
Australian Government's arts advisory and support organization.

Arts for Australians
Australia Council

National Library of Australia Cataloguing-in-Publication data

The temperament of generations

Includes index
ISBN 0 522 84448 0

1. Australian literature — 20th century. 2. Australian
literature — 20th century — history and criticism.
3. Australia — Popular culture. 4. Australia — Politics
and government — 1945- . I. Lee, Jenny, 1953- .
II. Mead, Philip, 1953- . III. Murnane, Gerald, 1939- .
IV. Title: Meanjin.

A820.8003

Contents

Part Five: The Temperament of Generations

Part Six: The New Brigade

Part Eight: Pressure Points

ACKNOWLEDGEMENTS

Most of the material appearing in this anthology has been reproduced by the authors' permission. The following people have also assisted in tracing authors and arranging permissions for the reproduction of various works:

Pacita Alexander
Carol Brown
Penelope Buckley
Suzanne W. Baker
Margaret Donald
Maurice Elkin
Dorothy Fitzpatrick
Miranda Manifold
Miss V. Murdoch
Leonie Sandercock
Marea Symes
A. Waten
Mrs N. Whitlock
Mrs M. Wright
Tim Curnow and Margaret Connolly (Curtis Brown (Aust.) Pty Ltd)
T. J. Glen (Equity Trustees Executors and Agency Co. Ltd)
Janet Burke (Thomas Nelson Australia)
Margaret Craddock (Longman Cheshire)
Heather Cam (Hale & Iremonger)
Annette Renshaw (Angus & Robertson)
Elizabeth Clare (Murray Pollinger)
Peg McColl (Penguin Australia)
Auriol Milford (Oxford University Press, Oxford)
Margaret Dowling (Oxford University Press, Australia)
Nicola Evans and Eileen Sneath (University of Queensland Press)
John M. Slattery (Corrs)

Among all these it might seem invidious to single anyone out, but I would like to give special thanks to Margaret Connolly of Curtis Brown, without whose careful help it would have been almost impossible to track down permissions for many of the earlier writers.

I also have to acknowledge a more general intellectual debt to Lynne Strahan, whose book *Just City and the Mirrors* (Oxford University Press, Melbourne, 1984) has been an invaluable source of information on *Meanjin*'s first twenty-five years.

PREFACE

There is an axiom in the publishing trade that any anthology is worth a hundred enemies. By that yardstick I reckon that anthologizing *Meanjin* should be worth at least a thousand, so perhaps at the outset I should explain something of how this book has been put together.

This selection does not pretend to be the 'best' of *Meanjin* in any absolute sense. If anyone ever believed in such transcendent standards, a few weeks' experience of the arbitrary, contingent process of editing a magazine would soon disillusion them. What we have tried to do here is to construct a narrative of some of the major developments in Australian cultural and intellectual life over the last fifty years as they have been refracted through the prism of an aggressively eclectic 'little magazine'. To tell the story of *Meanjin* in the words of those who worked and wrote for it is also to tell another story — or, to be more accurate, many other stories.

If *Meanjin* has been a hardy perennial among cultural magazines, this is partly because it has been in a state of more or less perpetual revolution. Most literary magazines have a distinct life-cycle; they start with a rush of enthusiastic idealism, but gradually peter out as their stable of contributors becomes ossified and their views predictable. *Meanjin*, by contrast, has provided a forum for several generations of Australian writers (a literary generation being far shorter than a biological one). Much of the credit for this must go to Clem Christesen, who founded the magazine in Brisbane in 1940 and remained at its helm until 1974. It was the breadth of his vision, and his sheer bloody-minded determination, that kept the magazine alive against substantial odds. Under his guidance *Meanjin* not only served as a training-ground for successive generations of Australian poets and novelists, but also promoted interdisciplinary intellectual work long before the term came into currency. Perhaps most importantly, at a time when Australia was still pretending to be a British island that had somehow been misplaced off the coast of Asia, *Meanjin* acted as a vital link with other cultural traditions, not only publishing significant works by writers from other countries, but also providing a much-needed space for the work of Australian writers of non-British origin.

We have tried to give an indication of *Meanjin*'s wide range of concerns in this book. Eclecticism, however, is the bane of the anthologist. Our initial forays yielded a selection of about 1200 pages. From this we have whittled the book down to its present length by a series of stages, each more painful than the last. After much soul-searching, we decided that we simply did not have the space to offer a reasonable representation of *Meanjin*'s extensive coverage of the visual arts, a field that would warrant a volume in itself, or of the vast array of overseas material that has appeared in the journal over the years. Among the remainder, when in doubt we have tended to select writings that address large questions in preference to those with a more specific orientation; but even here the constraints of space have made it impossible to republish a number of remarkable long essays. In some cases essays and letters have been abbreviated; excisions are indicated by spaced ellipses (. . .). We have taken the liberty of correcting obvious typographical errors, and in a few cases have accepted authors' corrections to the original text.

One theme that constantly recurs in the *Meanjin* correspondence is the dearth of resources to sustain the magazine. In this respect times have changed less than one might wish. The *Meanjin* office at present has two staff: an editor (nominally working two-thirds time) and an assistant editor (nominally working half-time). Without special assistance it would have been impossible to compile this volume. I would therefore like to thank the Australian Research Council for its financial support. We are also grateful to the Literature Board of the Australia Council for their assistance.

Like anything associated with a literary magazine, however, the compilation of this volume has had to rely on the voluntary assistance of a small army of individuals. Philip Mead and Gerald Murnane have put a lot of care and thought into the formidable task of selecting the poetry and fiction. Chris Wallace-Crabbe read a penultimate draft, and tactfully pointed out some of my blind spots. Charles Ferrall tackled both the archival research and the mass of administrative work with an initiative and patience far beyond the call of duty, and Lisa Jacobson helped us to steer the book through the crucial last stages.

Above all, I would like to thank Clem Christesen, Jim Davidson and Judith Brett, the past editors of the magazine. *Meanjin* has been very much their creation, and I am acutely conscious that it is a trying experience to have someone else taking a snippet here and there from the pages of a magazine over which one has laboured long and hard. That all three former editors have been prepared to spend long hours working through the initial, tentative selections and suggesting alternatives is a tribute to their patience and their commitment to *Meanjin*.

Any errors and idiosyncrasies in the editorial commentary, however, are entirely my responsibility.

Jenny Lee

Part One

Expanding from Within

The first issue of the *Meanjin Papers* appeared in Brisbane in December 1940. This was hardly the ideal time or place to establish a literary magazine. Australia was in the throes of what is now described as the 'phoney war'. There were no large-scale hostilities in the Pacific, but contingents of Australian troops were being despatched to Europe and the Middle East, and every second country town seemed to have become an army camp. The daily press was full of strident Empire nationalism and, with the banning of the Communist Party in June 1940, the Menzies government had made it clear that internal dissent was not to be tolerated.

Brisbane was hardly at the centre of Australian cultural life. A sprawling provincial city with a small population, it was conservative and inward-looking. Reflecting on his Brisbane years a decade later, *Meanjin*'s founding editor, Clem Christesen, bluntly described the city as 'a deadly place for an aspiring writer to live in'. Various attempts to establish a literary magazine in the city had already foundered, and Christesen's first approaches to other writers met with apathy and scepticism. But he was not easily dissuaded. Lacking the capital to launch a 'fully fledged' magazine, Christesen decided to start small and 'expand from within'.

The first edition of 250 copies was printed for £4 10s. It was an eight-page booklet, its beige cover bearing the legend 'Meanjin Papers No. 1. CONTEMPORARY QUEENSLAND VERSE' above a design of four black footprints, one for each of the poets whose work was represented: Brian Vrepont, James Picot, Paul Grano and Christesen himself. The issue was entitled 'Traditionalist Number' and prefaced with a brief statement by Christesen.

Number 1, December 1940

Foreword

'Poetry's unnat'ral; no man ever talked poetry 'cept a beadle on boxin' day, or Warren's blackin' or Rowland's oil, or some o' them low fellows; never you let yourself down to talk poetry, my boy.' But we have disregarded Tony Weller's advice to his son, Samuel. In an age governed by the stomach-and-pocket view of life, and at a time of war and transition, we still strive to 'talk poetry.' For we believe that it is our duty to do so. We believe that it would be a grave error to suppose the nation can drop its mental life, its intellectual and aesthetic activities for three or five or more years, neglecting them and those trained to minister to them, and then pick everything up again as though nothing had happened. Literature and art, poetry and drama do not spring into being at the word of command. Their life is a continuous process growing within itself, and its suppression is death. Therefore we determined to commence publication of the *Meanjin Papers*. Media for similar expression are sadly lacking in this country. It is hoped to continue publication of this brochure throughout the war period — and perhaps well into the Peace. Prose, as well as verse, will be included.

The name of the magazine was intended to emphasize its regional character. Readers of the first issue were informed that 'Meanjin' was the Aboriginal word for 'spike' and was the name given to the finger of land bounded by the Brisbane River and extending from the city proper to the Botanic Gardens. Nevertheless, from the first Christesen harboured ambitions of establishing a national presence for the magazine. A twenty-nine-year-old native son who had worked in newspapers and radio and now held a Cabinet appointment as publicist for the Queensland government, Christesen threw himself into publicizing his new venture. He distributed his early issues, unsolicited, to literary people in all corners of Australia, with a request that they either forward 2s. payment or return the copies.

Critical response was mixed. The Brisbane *Courier-Mail*'s regular literary critic, Firmin McKinnon, wrote a brief review that lumped the first issue of the *Meanjin Papers* together with two other recent publications from the perfervidly nationalistic Jindyworobak school. McKinnon's comments expressed a common complaint: harking back to the romantics, he deplored the signs of incipient modernism in poetry. 'This is not an age of good poetry,' he intoned,

> and Australian poetry certainly should not be judged by that of 1940 . . . [T]he contemporary poetry of Australia, perhaps, like much of the national consciousness, stands irresolute at the crossways, without a signpost. Much of it, pretending to be lyrical, is merely impressionist prose cut into poetic lengths.

In literary circles, however, the unprepossessing little booklets met an overwhelming response. Extracts from the flood of correspondence that ensued were published in the third issue. One of the strongest reactions (though by no means the most favourable) came from Randolph Bedford, veteran writer, journalist and Labor parliamentarian.

Randolph Bedford to C. B. Christesen

Parliament House, Brisbane
3 March 1941

Dear Mr. Christesen,

. . . Your 'Meanjin' papers are plucky for the time, but what a waste of good type, paper and ink. Just imagine such lines as these

'The ego fruitful in collective peace,'

and

'I suffer, not you; you suffer, not I;
Let States declare a dividend
Earned of such separate end,
Let States try, and die.'

GOOD GOD! If I tackle this ridiculous stuff I would have to make your paper a slaughter house. Alleged to be new, it is as old as stupidity. Gilbert got on to an equally ridiculous racket in 'Patience,' and as a youngster on the 'Bulletin,' I wrote of the soulful poem in derision. It began —

'In grim and lonely silence disarrayed,
Fate turned a handspring on the closet roof.'

I suppose this nonsense finds a recrudescence as a result of the last war — Gertrude Stein who wrote 'Tender Buttons' has even got an audience; and the other Stein, Ep, who makes an alleged statue like a swollen trunk and labels it 'Pregnancy.' These alleged poets should be forced to do something useful, such as digging post holes. . . .

Sincerely,
Randolph Bedford

More favourable responses came from outside Queensland. Nettie Palmer sent congratulations from both herself and husband Vance, and R. D. FitzGerald wrote: 'I believe myself to be in complete disagreement with what I believe to be your aims, but loudly applaud you for having such aims in a time somewhat aimless mentally and completely chaotic physically.' The older generation of Queensland writers seemed to share these sentiments. In particular, James Devaney, a Queensland poet and prominent member of the Queensland Authors and Artists' Association, took an avuncular interest in Christesen's activities. Devaney had the wisdom to know that this raw new venture should be encouraged, whatever his own reservations about it. He offered Christesen a willing ear, and a lot of well-judged advice. And in 1941 he secured a small scoop for the novice editor: a sharp-edged poem by his old friend, John Shaw Neilson.

Number 5, October 1941

To Norah McKinney

JOHN SHAW NEILSON

Your father is quick with the gun, and he long has been hating
The poor little sparrows who keep on their loving and mating.

Your father the keen man he is, and I see his face harden;
It costs him a lot for the poison he puts in the garden.

Your father has spite on the chin and the core of his marrow;
He says that the phosphorus burns, and is best for a sparrow.

The end of September it was and a patch of bad weather,
And you and the spawn of the enemy sobbing together.

Oh you with the love in your eyes and the smutch on your pinny,
It's a very good girl that you are, then, my Norah McKinney.

Your father the strong man he is, with the gloom in his marrow,
But the love that was deep in your heart it was poured on a sparrow.

All Sunday your father has hate that he hoards for to-morrow,
But you gave the mercy of God to a thief in his sorrow.

That mercy was up in your eyes and it fell on your pinny:
It's a very good girl that you are, then, my Norah McKinney.

The young thing had only one right — 'twas the right to be frozen,
But how for the mercy of God could he ever be chosen?

Your father the big man he is and his forehead is narrow,
But you had the pity of God and the tear for a sparrow.

I talk in the tongue of the asses, a fine thing for braying,
A fine thing for buying and selling, a fine thing for paying.

But I being wrong in the reason and dull over money,
It's love that I want to be telling, all in the green honey.

I saw you with spawn of the enemy, you two together;
The end of September it was, and a patch of bad weather.

Your father has gloom in his eyes and a gloom in his marrow,
But the pity of God that was in you, it fell on a sparrow.

It's love that I want to be telling of you in the pinny:
It's a very good girl that you are, then, my Norah McKinney.

Between the enthusiasm of the new generation and the tolerance extended by the old, the magazine's circulation expanded rapidly, as did its scope. The subtitle 'Contemporary Queensland Verse' was dropped after the first issue. For much of 1941 the magazine appeared with the subtitle 'Contemporary Queensland Prose and Verse'; then, at the end of the year, simply as 'Contemporary Verse and Prose'. By that stage the original eight pages had swelled to thirty-two, and the magazine was rapidly establishing an audience in all parts of the country.

In the interim the war had taken a new turn. With the rapid Japanese advance through South-East Asia, the hostilities were coming perilously close to home. The sharpening consciousness of war had contradictory effects on *Meanjin*. At one level, it posed many problems, both practical and personal. Paper rationing was introduced late in 1941. Christesen was left tramping the corridors of Paper Control, where an endless succession of bureaucrats passed his requests from hand to hand. He recalls: 'It was like a Kafka nightmare. I used to wonder whether I'd ever see the outside light again.' The nightmarish experience of war was sharpened by a deep sense of personal loss. Christesen sorely felt the departure of James Picot, who enlisted in March 1941. Though the two kept up a lively correspondence for some time, contact was severed after Picot's capture at the fall of Singapore. Picot died a prisoner of war on the notorious Burma–Thailand railway. Many years later, Christesen learnt that the crime for which his good friend had been killed was to address his captors in their own language, thereby branding himself as a spy.

At another level, however, the journal was buoyed up by the surge of patriotism that accompanied the intensification of the war effort; the question of defining what it meant to be Australian was given a new urgency. Christesen maintained a vigorous correspondence with various proponents of cultural nationalism, including Jindyworobak stalwart Rex Ingamells, and W. J. Miles and S. B. Hooper of the Australia First movement. During 1941 Christesen began soliciting material for a 'Nationality Number', which appeared at the end of the year with a declamatory preface by Rex Ingamells and a rambling polemic from P. R. Stephensen, the high priest of Australia First, proclaiming the necessity of 'developing here a distinctively-Australian culture'. One hoped-for contribution, however, did not eventuate: an essay on Australianism by Xavier Herbert.

Xavier Herbert to C. B. Christesen

Caloundra
19 October 1941

Dear Clement Christesen,

Forgive me for keeping you waiting so long for a reply. I received your first letter and packet of papers as soon as they arrived, and was grateful for your promptness. The reason for the delay is that I wanted to write that bit on 'Australianism' you asked for. I had several shots at it, the last only a couple of days ago. I had to give it up. It seems that I can write nothing of any value that is not in the nature of fantasy. Facts seem not to matter a bit to me. That, I suppose, is a great asset to one as a story-teller. At the same time it is a bit of a nuisance to one in one's practical work-a-day life.

Although I am madly patriotic, I am bored by talk of 'Nationalism'. What is Nationalism but the Football-team spirit? Actually, I hate Australians. I hate their faces, those long Punch noses (did you ever see the monster Punch in a Punch-&-Judy-Show?) & their cruel thin lips & moron's brows and hooded idiot's eyes. Yet I can turn to them with relief and love from contemplating the juicy faces of Pommies. I loathe Englishmen so much, that I can tell their foot prints (bare feet, of course); & about their tracks there is to me something obscene. Oh, I'm not a bit practical about my patriotism. Here's an example.

Some years ago, in the town of Darwin, I rushed out of my house in the middle of the night & attacked a number of drunken Pommy sailors (off a British warship) who were piddling in the street. I rushed upon them roaring: 'How dare you piss on my country!' They bolted.

Now, if Meanjin Papers would allow me to write an article on my contempt for a Pommy's tracks, or to recount the Darwin incident, I could make a lovely job of it. But I'm sure that's not what they want. Yes, I'm afraid that I must stick to fiction, as the only medium for expressing my fantastic ideas. . . .

Now, this is all I can write. I'm sorry I can't give you the article. It would have pleased me mightily to have appeared in 'the papers'.

Again I ask your forgiveness. I hope I shall see you again soon. If you should be coming here, would you let me know, so that I can get you to bring me some paper?

My wife sends her regards, and thanks you for *The Publicist.* I am posting all the papers back to you with this.

With best wishes,

Xavier Herbert

P.S. It has just occurred to me that I am no madder than the average person. I differ only in that I don't try to hide it.

In February 1942 the supposedly impregnable Singapore naval base fell to the Japanese army, and Darwin was bombed by Japanese aircraft. In March, amid an atmosphere of public panic, Christesen published a 'Crisis Number'. His editorial announced that 'we are faced to-day with a war on two fronts. Military victory alone will not save us, if we lose the intellectual battle.' It was the latter struggle that preoccupied most of the contributors to the issue.

Number 8, March 1942

Battle

VANCE PALMER

The next few months may decide not only whether we are to survive as a nation, but whether we deserve to survive. As yet none of our achievements prove it, at any rate in the sight of the outer world. We have no monuments to speak of, no dreams in stone, no Guernicas, no sacred places. We could vanish and leave singularly few signs that, for some generations, there had lived a people who had made a homeland of this Australian earth. A homeland? To how many people was it primarily that? How many penetrated the soil with their love and imagination? We have had no peasant population to cling passionately to their few acres, throw down tenacious roots, and weave a natural poetry into their lives by invoking the little gods of creek and mountain. The land has been something to exploit, to tear out a living from and then sell at a profit. Our settlements have always had a fugitive look, with their tin roofs and rubbish-heaps. Even our towns . . . the main street cluttered with shops, the million-dollar town hall, the droves of men and women intent on nothing but buying or selling, the suburban retreats of rich drapers! Very little to show the presence of a people with a common purpose or a rich sense of life.

If Australia had no more character than could be seen on its surface, it would be annihilated as surely and swiftly as those colonial outposts white men built for their commercial profit in the East — pretentious facades of stucco that looked imposing as long as the wind kept from blowing. But there is an Australia of the spirit, submerged and not very articulate, that is quite different from these bubbles of old-world imperialism. Born of the lean loins of the country itself, of the dreams of men who came here to form a new society, of hard conflicts in many fields, it has developed a toughness all its own. Sardonic, idealist, tongue-tied perhaps, it is the Australia of all who truly belong here. When you are away, it takes on a human image, an image that emerges, brown and steady-eyed from the background of dun cliffs, treed bushlands, and tawny plains. More than a generation ago, it found voice in the writings of Lawson, O'Dowd, Bedford, and Tom Collins: it has become even more aware of itself since. And it has something to contribute to the world. Not emphatically in the arts as yet, but in arenas of action, and in ideas for the creation of that egalitarian democracy that will have to be the basis of all civilised societies in the future.

This is the Australia we are called upon to save. Not merely the mills and mines, and the higgledy-piggledy towns that have grown up along the coast: not the assets we hold or the debts we owe. For even if we were conquered by the Japanese, some sort of normal life would still go on. You cannot wipe out a nation of seven million people, or turn them all into wood-and-water joeys. Sheep would continue to be bred, wheat raised; there would be work for the shopkeeper, the clerk, the baker, the butcher. Not everyone could be employed pulling Japanese gentlemen about in rickshaws.

Some sort of comfort might even be achieved by the average man under Japanese dominance; but if anyone believes life would be worth living under the terms offered, he is not worth saving. There is no hope for him unless a breath of the heroic will around him stirs him to come out of the body of this death. Undoubtedly we have a share of the decadent elements that have proved a deadly weakness in other countries — whisperers, fainthearts, near-fascists, people who have grown rotten through easy living; and these are often people who have had power in the past and now feel it falling away from them. We will survive according to our swiftness in pushing them into the background and liberating the people of will, purpose, and intensity; those who are at one with Australia's spirit and are capable of moulding the future.

I believe we will survive; that what is significant in us will survive; that we will come out of this struggle battered, stripped to the bone, but in a wider world than the one we lived in hitherto. These are great, tragic days. Let us accept them stoically, and make every yard of Australian earth a battle-station.

If patriotism was the order of the day, however, Australia First was not. In the very month in which the 'Crisis Number' appeared, the police swooped on the Australia First crew and their sympathizers, Ingamells included. Stephensen and several others were interned under the War Precautions Act. Nevertheless, the quest for a national sense of belonging, of identification with the land, remained an important motif in Australian intellectual and literary life. Often, as in the following essay, the search led back to Aboriginal culture.

Number 2, 1943

Steps into the Dream-time

A. P. ELKIN

The Port Jackson–Lower Hawkesbury region of New South Wales is famous for its aboriginal rock 'carvings.' Each of the numerous 'galleries' usually consists of a series of outline-engravings on a horizontal surface. These depict one or more marsupials, birds, fish or reptiles, native weapons and implements and ritual symbols. The most important figure, however, represents the cult-hero and culture-giver of the tribe. He it is who made the natural features of the region, gave life to its fauna and flora, endowed human beings with their implements and weapons, taught them their laws and instituted their rites and ceremonies. He is now in the sky, where he can be visited by the initiated men of the highest degree, the 'wise men,' generally called by us medicine-men. He takes an interest in what men do, especially in their ritual. Indeed, the ritual ground which is marked either by permanent or temporary symbols depicted on the rock, earth or trees, represents the sky-world, his world, that is, his presence.

Moreover, in the ritual, by appropriate 'dressing,' by chanting the myths, and by contemplating and even touching the representation of the hero and other symbols, the initiated man becomes identified with him, the source of life in the past, present and future.

One of the most interesting symbols on the rock galleries or 'trading boards,' consists of a series of foot-tracks. In some cases these are only small holes, heel or toe marks, but in others are obviously foot tracks. In a few 'galleries,' the latter, being larger than human feet, are referred to by some recorders as *mundowi*, spirit-tracks. Actually in all cases, be they large or small, definite foot-tracks or less determinate marks, they represent, or indeed are, the steps taken by the hero of the cult ('lodge') in that place, as he performed some act or endured suffering, perhaps death, which is now of ritual importance.

The significance of the tracks is associated with the pattern and function of all ritual. This is 1) to re-enact the past, that is an event in the life of the cult-hero; 2) to pre-enact the future, which the present actor desires for himself and which is the same future as that experienced by the cult-hero; and 3) to gain moral courage and life in the present and immediate future. The basis of these 'blessings' is the identification of the actor with the cult-hero; and the outward means and sign of the inward and moral identification is to perform ritually what the hero himself did, and which has become of ritual, that is, life-giving significance. This includes following literally in his steps towards, and across, and from, the ceremonial ground. In this way, the actions and thoughts of the 'actor,' the participant in the cult, follow the sequence of the occurrences in the hero's experience. Thus is the efficacy of the ritual ensured.

The footprints are frequently irregular, because the hero was suffering and stumbling blindly unto death when reaching his sanctuary. Moreover, the newly initiated, when being shown the 'gallery' for the first time, is led blindfolded and walks with uncertain and irregular steps like the hero in his sufferings. In fact, he is guided along the hero's tracks. They are the steps to death, or rather through death. For just as the hero was not holden of death, so, too, the candidate, being killed in the ritual, is raised to life, or born again. He is now a new creature, with strength to live a man's life, to obey the tribal laws, and to perform the life-giving rites on which the vitality of the tribe and of nature depends.

Every aboriginal sanctuary must be approached by the track made by the great hero or heroes of the 'dream-time.' This is so whether that track be marked by permanent foot-prints or not. The route is taught to the worthy, and to them, the cult-hero is, indeed, 'the way.' Although an aborigine knows quite well the direction and location of a site sanctified by the mythological and symbolical presence of the hero, he will, if necessary, spend much time looking for the landmarks, until he is certain that he can approach by the heroic and mythological path. By this approach, identification with the hero is begun. It becomes complete when the individual, having duly 'prepared' himself, takes his place in the ritual. For the time being, he is no longer himself. He is the hero himself. As a result, the life and power of the hero flows through him to the world around.

The ritual path leads the aborigine into the world of the past; from it come the sanctions for his behavior to-day and also his hopes for the future. In other words, they are not merely backward-pointing. The heroes were great adventurers, performers of great exploits, who were ready to cope with any emergency, including death. Consequently, those who become identified with them are endued with determination and courage to face new situations. Thus inspired, the tribal leaders have modified old customs and institutions or adopted new ones, and have led their groups now here, now there. But each change and migration has, in course of time, become sanctioned and sanctified by mythology, that is, by the cult-hero. The myth of this hero of the 'dream-time' is like an ever-lengthening chain, and those who provide the additional links are the custodians of the tribal mythology themselves. And why not? They are the representatives, even the 'incarnations' of the cult-heroes. They are the link with the 'eternal dream-time,' and on ritual occasions, are the myth in action.

To the aborigines, those foot-prints, those mythological paths, are not simply relics, fossils or memorials of an age long past. They are steps into a present, of which the past and future are but phases. In aboriginal philosophy, as in dreaming, the limitations of time and space do not exist. They live in the 'eternal now,' in all the richness of its experience and the inspiration of its conviction.

Our Steps?

What about ourselves? Have we any steps which lead us to our 'eternal dream-time,' to that sanctuary of thought, sentiment, and inspiration, whatever be its outward form, where the manifold streams of our country's past flow again in us — blood of our blood, thought of our thought; — and where, too, the future is already present, so that we may step out boldly even into the night, knowing that the 'heavenly city' with its perpetual light can be brought down to earth? If our answer be 'no,' it is obvious that we have not yet fashioned an Australian culture, with a tradition which is a ground of hope, and a goal which will sanctify our traditions. Perhaps we are not yet sure where our 'eternal dream-time' is, and our steps are uncertain, with no guiding hand to direct us to the place of vision! It may be that we are pondering whether it lies in the eastern Mediterranean in the sanctuary of Plato and Virgil, of Homer and Lucretius; or in the more northern lands, in the 'gallery' of Marx, Engels, and Lenin, or perhaps Trotski; or in a land across the Pacific, in the ledgers of business triumphant; or even in those small northern ancestral islands, in the pages of Shakespeare and John Bunyan, of the Areopagitica and the Authorized Version.

Culture, however, is a people's continuing response to its own environment — not to conditions of another time and place, however great and ennobling. We cannot fly with borrowed plumes nor run with artificial legs. Our literature and art in all its forms, like our ways of living, our politics and our religion, are vital elements in that complete whole we call culture. It must express *our* character, and not another's. It must be *our* response to Australia — the expression and means of our living together in our own land.

The elements of a great myth are in our heritage. Let the myth-makers arise and express them in such a way that they will become an integral and dynamic part of our life from childhood to death. We have our heroes and our epics, no less wonderful and inspiring because their setting is Australia and their period the past 150 years, or because, to the people of the time, there seldom came the vision that anything of cultural or national significance was being done in their midst.

Think of those simple but stout-hearted folk who ventured for four months and more across the world in sailing ships to begin life afresh in a strange land, not to fill a ready-made niche there, but to carve out one on plain or mountain, along the coast or in the interior, pushing out a little further than their predecessors, looking for a land of promise! Men and women, and even children; educated and uneducated; alike they ventured and toiled to reclaim a continent where we can plan a society of the just and good and free! Why are they not the subjects of epic-myths as powerful as those of Abraham and Lot, of Moses and the children of Israel? They, too, crossed Jordan and redeemed a land and a heritage for those that should come after them. But do we tell their deeds as a sacred duty, and seek to be one in spirit with them, so that we, following their examples, shall step out, ever onwards, beyond the confines of our material, social and intellectual settlement, seeking the new Jerusalem?

And what powerful symbols of determination, endurance, leadership and faith many of the explorers could be to us, if instead of 'debunking' them because of human frailties, we 'heroized' them for what they did, for the powers and virtues which they manifested, in cutting the tracks for us and seeking pastures for our flocks and herds. What great myths would grow up around these culture-heroes, if they had been aborigines! To them would be ascribed the making of the natural features which they discovered, and incident after incident would be preserved in myth and ritual and constantly conned over as inspiration for the present, thus making these heroes a potent cultural force. Surely we will do no less!

Of course, there are also other tracks into our 'dream-time' — tracks first blazed by men and women venturing and struggling for free institutions, for social and industrial justice, for knowledge and for art. They too, when the vision comes, will be seen to lead, as through gates of pearl, into our city of life.

And above all, there is Australia itself — Australia whom so few Australians know, for they have not crossed the Dividing Range — formerly the barrier and beckoning challenge to the discovery of unknown geographical and material possibilities, and which even now calls us to cross and experience for ourselves the spiritual riches of a vast quiet land, where in contemplation of the 'eternal dream-time,' strength, vision and contentment are found.

Finally, let us have no doubts. We shall know when we have found the path into our 'eternal dream-time,' with its life-giving myths and traditions. For we shall realize that we are not retreating into a time that is no more, nor into a phantasy, safe from the angular facts of daily life. On the contrary we shall be irresistibly drawn on by the vision of what has been and can be, and indeed, already is. Our task will be to express it, to work it into our national life, and to do so in the spirit of adventure and conviction. In that spirit we shall place our feet firmly in the heroic steps, and go forward to build an Australia, not only economically just, democratically free, educationally wise and morally strong, but also culturally alive — an Australia in which we shall live out our 'dream-time' myths, sharing them with all men of vision, courage and truth. Thus, from within, will come the 'new order,' the city of life.

Alongside this continuing search for a touchstone of national consciousness, *Meanjin* also evinced a sharp awareness of international developments, both political and cultural. Christesen was an eclectic reader, and often garnished the magazine with well-chosen quotations from his favourite authors. Perhaps his youthful nationalism was also tempered by the influence of Nina Maximov, a university tutor of White Russian background, whom he had married at the beginning of 1942. But there were also larger forces at work. By the end of 1942 the immediate military threat to Australia was over, and in spite of rationing and the presence of large numbers of American troops, for many Australians life had returned to something approaching normality.

Meanjin, too, began to settle down a little. From the beginning of 1943, the slim bi-monthly became a plumper quarterly. The crusading nationalism of the early issues was increasingly leavened by a closer attention to aesthetic questions. Here, Christesen was fortunate enough to bring into his stable a genuinely fierce literary critic, in the person of A. D. Hope, then a little-known lecturer at Sydney Teachers College. Hope's uncompromising literary standards and lively prose style quickly made a mark. Here he reviews four Jindyworobak publications: *Content are the Quiet Ranges* and *Unknown Land*, by Rex Ingamells, and *Their Seven Stars Unseen* and *The Australian Dream*, by Ian Mudie.

Number 2, 1944

From: Corroboree on Parnassus

A. D. Hope

The latest work of Mr. Ingamells and Mr. Mudie does not differ much from their earlier verse in theme, theory or method, though Mr. Ingamells is now writing a little better, and Mr. Mudie a little worse. I have the same feeling with Mr. Ingamells that I have when I see a man striving hopelessly to extricate a bogged car. Here is a fellow man in a fix. Let's give him a hand. Mr. Ingamells is plainly a decent man unequal to the task he has set himself. He has a small poetic talent which has grown with each volume he has published. He has a deep sympathy with the aboriginal of whom he writes and a considerable incapacity to understand the aborigines' world owing to the fact that he cannot understand his own. He has a great deal of genuine love for and observation of the country he lives in. He is capable, as many of the poems in these two volumes show, of pleasant and sometimes moving poems of observation and imagination on these themes. But his treatment of his subjects is at its best when it is merely ornamental. As soon as he begins to be an apostle of the cultural Renaissance, it becomes evident that his whole social doctrine is the produce of an uncritical and uninformed mind. *Unknown Land*, his latest analysis of Australia's cultural problem, shows Mr. Ingamells indulging in a kind of head-line thinking similar to that which solves all social problems by attributing them to the machinations of the Catholics or the Jews. For all that I enjoy Mr. Ingamells' verse when he is dealing with subjects within his capacity.

With Mr. Mudie, on the other hand, I have the feeling of watching a happy drunk lurching on the edge of the platform in front of an oncoming express train. Mr. Mudie is so intoxicated with his vision of the Australia that will be, that he pays no attention to the powerful sweep of that great machine as it is and to its real direction. All his poems have the one theme, the renaissance of Australian culture and the emergence of a self-conscious nation of Australians. Most of his verse is apt to be rhetorical and even oratorical, and the long prize poem, *The Australian Dream*, in spite of a few good images and in spite of its burning sincerity, is too full of versified political jargon. His shorter poems on the whole are better poetry — though like Mr. Ingamells in *his* worse moments, Mr. Mudie's obsession with culture makes it almost impossible for him to produce examples of it. This I think is the fundamental mistake of these two old men of the Jindy tribe. Culture is not produced by writing *about* it, and that is all they have done so far. They are liable to wake up one day and find that some Australian who never heard of culture in his life has jumped their claim and worked it while they were still marching round singing their Jindy version of Onward Christian Soldiers, and trying to organise a proper gold rush.

And, in a different mood, we have Nettie Palmer recognizing that the war is effectively over, and contemplating the future with remarkable prescience.

Number 1, 1944

From: Australia — an International Unit

NETTIE PALMER

When, as Bernard O'Dowd put it in a famous and unsuperseded sonnet, Sailor Time dredged up a new, last sea-thing, and it was Australia, did Time do well? Or would he have done better to sink this island back into its sea? This question has to be looked at every little while. What is the human value of this last Continent, which stepped straight into the age of industry, world-communications, world-wars, and accepted them all? Its very name is a synthetic product, not a hundred and fifty years old; so is its constitution, still newer. Australia as a white man's country lacks all antiquities of civilisation (ruined castles, primitive folk-songs, traditional law). Instead of these, we have had the possible benefits of a new start, virgin pages, and the future for our own to make or ruin. Can we use them?

These questionings haunt us in normal years. Perhaps any significant work in the arts, plastic or verbal, has been mainly an attempt to provide an answer, to meet this challenge. A new country that is merely an imitation of its predecessors, that discovers no new thoughts and forms, that contributes nothing to the meaning of the world — would it deserve to exist?

At the present time the questions do not so much haunt us as shout at us from the skies. This country of ours — how does she stand; where is the Napper Tandy to tell us the truth? We are in the fifth year of this war. Sometimes, as the war drags its slow length along, we see no breaks in our experience of it, even as onlookers; but this year, 1944, seems to make us take a long breath, even if it is the climax. We see now that this country of ours, this last sea-thing, has been virtually saved from invasion. The tide touched it, the fiery rain scorched it, and then incredibly withdrew. Ah, we know it was no accident, that withdrawal; we know that tide is still being held back as if by a human dyke made of the strength and agony of human bodies. But the fact is that the country is physically above the tide. And how does she stand?

It is time for stock-taking, as never before. In stock-taking, though, the auditors need the books to be produced. The 'books'? Yes, and in this case the significant examples of the written word, the spoken word, the collective thought and utterance of Australia in paint and sound and design. In no country could it be more difficult to get all the facts in these matters; each generation falls away and is in turn forgotten. Responsible historical summaries are now slowly appearing; patterns and periods are beginning to be discovered, such as the resurgent nineties, the complacent 1920's . . . All these have to be included in any current understanding, but there is much to impede this. There are among us, endemic, those who from their attitude have been described as cultured Philistines. Their culture is entirely a borrowed thing, their Philistinism is shown in regard to the world as they see it in Melbourne or Cairns — a contempt for all signs of mental or artistic vigour; a pride in knowing nothing of our past. To me this variety of pride is incomprehensible: to rejoice because the country you belong to has not contributed at all to the thought of the world, not done its 'bit' . . .

Those of us who are anxious that our country should deserve to float about the tide have various reasons for our belief in her present, and more important, her future. Each of us has a special experience, a special standpoint, a mental habit of our own. For a long time my own chief interests have been international literature, and, in consequence, our own literature and its contribution. At present I seem to see where the tributary meets the river. For many years Australians have been told they were isolated from the world, therefore unimportant, with nothing to be expected from them in the arts or literature. They were told their minds were full of great empty spaces; then to fill their minds a little they were offered only a fluid that came by pipe-line direct from London. Anyone who resented that restricted diet was forced to 'aggressive Australianism,' humorous or not. Refusing to accept or to revere English literary fashions that by the time they reached us were already old-fashioned, English reputations that were being made and unmade by the advertisements accompanying the weekly review columns, they were thrown back on an independence that amounted to literary isolationism. This was in some ways a healthy gesture — but a gesture sometimes becomes a rigid posture.

Yet all this time there was another course possible. We had only to admit we were part of mankind. Instead of the unhealthy attitude of 'England is writing pastoral poetry, therefore Australia is automatically reading pastoral poetry this season' (alternatively reading, 'therefore Australia is refusing to read pastoral poetry'), there was the third course — to find out mankind for ourselves. The strange turns of recent history have brought a large cross-section of mankind to us, in person; and have made the writings and thought of mankind more accessible. The fires that harried Europe, long before the present war began, burst open many a seed-pod and sent the seeds flying overseas. In recent decades we have become used to a variety of new citizens, with ideas and outlooks new to us. They have made it possible for us to know their literature a little. We have been more inclined to learn some of their languages, and we come to take for granted a more direct communication with countries in various stages of development — some of them, like the South American republics, being nearly as new as ourselves, and dealing with many of the same problems. We are no longer impelled to know what some coteries in London are saying about Russia or France before we begin to use our minds about Russia or France. With regards to the hopes of Free Italy or Greece, we have the direct means of access — no more or less — obtainable by all the free nations. We can be a little proud, I think, that in Australia such movements have been able to raise their flags for the future.

This stock-taking would not begin to be valid without including the refugees from Europe and elsewhere, who, at first in bewilderment and grief, have made this country their home. Instinctively, they have made their challenges to our monolingual speech and our remnants of Victorianism; more than that, in their natural mental curiosity, they have often posed questions about our past and our social purposes, have made us see how much more is needed to be known by so very many more of us.

The last great item in this assessment is the arrival and circulation here of overseas soldiers. The results are barely beginning to show. That is, we feel the real results will be incomparably vaster than what we see already: libraries of American books, University courses in Dutch, contacts with the literature of modern China — English, Canadian, American poets in *Meanjin*. Perhaps I have suggested enough. I was never good at addition. The international outlook of such an indubitably (if not aggressively) Australian organ as *Meanjin* seems, to me at least, a symbol of our cultural continuity, a ratification of Sailor Time's whimsical act. . . .

Part Two

From Ern Malley to Tom Collins

Perhaps it is a testimony to the Australian sense of humour that two pseudonymous authors should have been at the centre of local literary debate in the 1940s and early 1950s. Tom Collins, the 'author' and left-footed narrator of Joseph Furphy's *Such Is Life* (1903), was a standing parody of one of the staples of nineteenth-century Australian writing — the earnest treatise on life in the back-blocks, written in high literary style by some educated itinerant.

Ern Malley was constructed half a century later, and in a more cynical spirit. The target was Max Harris, then a young Adelaide writer and editor of a self-consciously avant-garde literary magazine called *Angry Penguins*.

One hectic afternoon in 1943, the poets James McAuley and Harold Stewart set out to parody everything they disliked about 'modern' poetry, and particularly the English 'Apocalyptics', with their free use of rhythm, their introspective bent, their paradoxical use of language. They then equipped the poems with a fictitious author — Ern Malley, a recently deceased mechanic and insurance salesman — and despatched them to Harris with a covering letter from Ethel Malley, sister of the deceased. Sure that he was onto a scoop, Harris published the poems in a special issue of *Angry Penguins* in Autumn 1944. At that point, all hell broke loose. The hoax was revealed; worse, Harris was dragged through the courts after the police decided that the poems were pornographic.

The hoax was gleefully reported to Clem Christesen by A. D. Hope, who was in on the plot.

A. D. Hope to C. B. Christesen

22 June 1944

. . . I suppose by now you have heard of the super-hoax played on Maxie Harris. Two pals of mine invented Ern Malley and led Max right up a tree. After you've read the latest A.P. *Ern Malley Special Number* and reflect that it was all done by two of the conventional poets whom Max particularly despises, you will indulge in a few moments serious reflection on the terrible danger in which the editor of a literary journal lives and then you will sit back on your heels and indulge in a good horse laugh. I've been sitting on the bank for the last six months watching Maxie played for sucker — but of course sworn to secrecy . . . How Max will roll those great big bed-room eyes! as one of the conspirators remarked. How angry was my Penguin! Do review it in your next number. It's the finest literary hoax since Bacon wrote Shakespeare.

Yore luvin frend
Jim the Penman.

25 June 1944

. . . As you will see a lot of fun has been had by all. I am rather pleased by the whole thing because, amusing as the hoax is itself, Stewart and McAuley have conducted it in a way which raises it above the level of a mere hoax and makes it a serious piece of criticism. I'm interested to see what Harris's reaction to the second article will be. He will wriggle, of course, but I don't think he can get off this hook. The method of composition is surely a final test. It was this which made it so much better than my own projected hoax which I gave up on learning of their scheme. I had planned to send him a number of similar poems but poems constructed on the surrealist plan. It was true that I wrote the whole ten in two sittings of an hour each, approximately, and that they were deliberately phoney constructions but Max could simply have replied that it only proved his point about composition — whereas with Stewart and McAuley he seems to be left with *no* appeal to the unconscious. The Ern Malley poems are complete artifacts and it will be very difficult for Max to unsay what he has said about them. The best touch from my point of view is his coupling Ern Malley and himself as author of The Vegetative Eye. The conclusion that if one is phoney so is the other is irresistible.

Well keep your spirits up and your head down. The bullets fly close to the ground these days.

A.D.H.

[Marginal addition:] I may say, in case you doubt the statement that the whole of Ern's works were composed at a sitting that McAuley and Stewart are both remarkably apt at improvised parody and have practised it for years on a number of subjects. They are in addition remarkable blokes.

29 June 1944

I've been thinking over your suggestions about the By-Now-So-Angry Penguins and those Cruel Boys. I don't want to review it myself. I've said my piece about gentleman Max and his Literary Confidence tricks. I suggest that in any case we might wait to see how things develop. Probably, as you say, by August the whole box of tricks will be out of date — in any case I suppose Meanjin's proper role is one of dignified restraint rather than a war-dance in the bowels of a prostrate rival. But it won't do any harm to point the moral even if we don't adorn the tale. Let me know your opinion. . . .

In the event, Christesen asked the Adelaide literary critic Brian Elliott to comment on the affair.

A Summing-Up

BRIAN ELLIOTT GIVES ERN MALLEY DECENT BURIAL:–

I think I may quite decorously begin by saying that I am heartily tired of Ern Malley, Ethel Malley, McAuley, Harris, Stewart, and everybody down that alley. But a summing up is certainly called for; and as I have been right at the centre of this flutter from the beginning perhaps I can do it more fittingly than anybody else at the present moment. What follows, therefore, though it may partake of a certain ennui, is at least not without the support of a considerable effort of critical thought, and I hope may do poetic justice to all the parties concerned. Whether Malley may then be allowed peacefully to rest in his urn is yet to be seen.

Everybody in Adelaide had been talking about the poems of the great new poet, but unfortunately (in a way!) I did not see them until *Angry Penguins* was out. I immediately sensed a very powerful *odeur de rat*. My first (and I still think, in the circumstances, natural) impression was that Harris was the author. The poetic line was much less foggy than Harris's commonly is, but I thought he was possibly trying out something new and . . . in effect, was doing just what Messrs. McAuley and Stewart set out to do, writing with his tongue practically bursting his cheek muscles to see if the fools would still crowd as before into the circle. I asked him — giving him full credit for Shakespearean allusion — whether the mystic word 'duc-dame' might be his motto. I was wrong: Harris was fooled along with the rest; genuinely sucked in. I was fooled too, by being a little over-subtle; but no more of that. Harris didn't write the poems, and the hoaxers declare that he was not intended to be their victim. Yet naturally, as the most vigorous voice of the Angry Penguin coterie, the parody falls most weightily on him. And as to that, it may fairly be said he deserved it thoroughly. I think they all did. What is so admirable about the whole hoax is its wonderful prophylactic value. A clean sweep with modern Australian poetry! Away with the humbug and the pretentious flutter which makes up nine-tenths of it! What can the Penguins do now, poor birds, but look about them and consider one of two other present realities besides the lilies of the psychological field?

But the hoaxers should not be permitted to have too absolute a triumph. As newspaper stuff it came off pretty well, and they won hands down. But there is a little more to Mr. Harris and his brood than they have allowed. I think the critical situation ought to be more thoroughly aired than it has been, and I should like to see justice done (or said) on both sides.

To begin with, the hoaxers declared that the only way to settle their doubts as to the goodness of the sort of eggs the Penguins were laying, was by experiment. If Mr. Harris had the discrimination to reject the poems they concocted, then they, and not he, would be placed in the ridiculous position. But is this so sure a test? A test of discrimination I think it is, and not a bad one; but not a test of the *poetic* judgment. Mr. Harris and Mr. Reed have acted with what seems to me incredible naivete in the matter of this publication, but they do not (in my opinion) stand convicted of insensibility. That is to say, I commit myself to the contention that in spite of what the authors say, the Ern Malley poems are *not* devoid of poetic merit. If there *is* merit in them, then the test was one of rational discrimination only, and was greatly confused by the presence of real poetic values to offset the absurdity of the story. This real value is something to be demonstrated, since the authors deny it; I shall come to it in a moment.

There is another aspect of this 'test' which ought to be examined. The authors claim that the poems are nonsense from beginning to end. But that is not so. They themselves describe the work in another phrase as 'a serious literary experiment.' It is that: it certainly is that. I think highly of what poems of Mr. McAuley I have read, and reasonably well of the one or two of Mr. Stewart's that I have seen. But nowhere else in their writing have they written (I feel) with the same genuine seriousness. There is a paradox to assimilate here, it is true: they wrote nonsense seriously. But that is definitely something that can be done, and the result is of the order of parody, literary parody.

I do not think that the authors' statement that they aimed at no coherent theme can therefore be taken at its face value. There is no coherent rational theme perhaps. (Actually I don't think that is quite true either. There is a constantly recurring motive of the young poet's frustration and sense of the obstacles to poetic realization.) But their poems are held together by the energies of their serious intention. To prove that upon the rational level they are nonsense, is not to demonstrate that they are meaningless on the poetic — unless the authors confuse the rational with the poetic. These things are not the same at all, though admittedly poetry that is rational is much easier to assimilate than poetry which is non-rational; and equally clearly, poetry of the non-rational kind is the easiest kind to imitate if (here's the rub) nothing more is aimed at than the avoidance of reasonable statement. I am inclined to wonder if Messrs. McAuley and Stewart did not commit themselves, in their published declaration, to more than they really believe. They began, and I take it they were sincere, from the doubt that 'we had really failed to penetrate to the inward substance of these productions.' That is, they were open to conviction; although from another part of their statement (that 'for some years now we have observed with distaste the gradual decay of meaning and craftsmanship in poetry') it would seem that they had in part already made up their minds. This was not so reasonable of them as they seem to pretend. Leaving aside the question as to whether there is any conflict of logic here, or even any latent malice, it seems that they set out to prove a deficiency in reason, but used a method that was not at all likely to approach the question which they meant to enquire into; namely, the 'inward substance' of the Penguin poetry.

I am here making a serious criticism of Messrs. McAuley and Stewart for their method, and for an implied lack of poetic sensibility. I am not, however, claiming that their censure was not deserved. The eggs in the

Angry Penguin basket are often enough addled, and it is time someone cracked a few and cried shame. But it is important that it should be done in a way which does not smack of the philistine; and this is unfortunately one of the inescapable implications of the hoaxers' method.

I really think that what this parody has done has not been to demolish the 'school' of Penguins as the authors hoped, but merely to emphasize the old rule which ought never to have been forgotten: namely, that poetry should never desert the truth of the heart. (That sounds a little sentimental, but I distrust the word 'sincere,' which might mean earnest only; and it is not enough for poetry to be earnest.) The Penguin 'school' has produced much verse which has been merely manufactured to formula (or haphazard). This is not true, I think, of Mr. Harris's own poetry at its best, but I should not care to commit myself to contending that it was never true . . . after all, he is still quite young and no doubt often foolish. But it does also seem to me that the Penguins (and Mr. Harris in particular) have a genuine aesthetic inspiration if they can only discipline themselves to interpret it in stricter emotional honesty. This is a severe provision. But they should realize that by electing to attempt to express the experience of beauty at a higher-than-rational plane, they have a much greater need of discipline than have the rationalists and the logicians.

As to the poetic literary quality of Ern Malley, it may most of it be due to the simple fact that the poems were written by two competent people with the inescapable implication of their good taste. If 'no care was taken with verse technique,' it is difficult to see how the two *Night Pieces* merely happened. These, in fact, could quite well have been two separate treatments of the same agreed set of symbols in an agreed metre — but as to that I make no hazard. But whether by the purest accident, or by design unacknowledged, both of these poems reach a high order of suggestibility (in crude terminology 'atmosphere').

Incidentally, the spirit of irrationality which produces two pieces so closely resembling each other in so many particulars seems to be an extremely careful and much considered irrationality; and as to the contention that the authors took no care with the verse technique, the test of that is in the ear.

What moves me to admiration in the poem is the *audacity* of it. 'The symbols were evident.' 'A frog makes guttural *comment*' — even to punning on the name of a magazine. The iron birds with their supercilious beaks suggest to me a humour which is almost Aristophanic. That was why I felt the newspaper statement to be an anticlimax: because it reduces the genuine Aristophanic hilarity of the parody to a kind of sour academic philistinism. The evidence of the poem itself, however, conflicts; and I dare say the newspaper publicity is really best ignored for the most part (if only it weren't so much more likely to stick than the good humour of the spirit within the poetry). . . .

There is no doubt that this hoax has been brilliant and successful. I have my fears that it may be too successful. Much of the poetical action which is attacked is perfectly genuine, and will suffer from being discredited. There is some hope though, that, as the effects balance out, more good than harm will have been done, if only because for the first time some elements of Australian poetry have come into sufficient prominence to be given the kind of close attention and scrutiny which is necessary before poetry can be written at all. I think the Penguins should welcome this, after their wrath has cooled a little. Because it may very likely be true that the element of falsity which Messrs. McAuley and Stewart aimed to denounce is partly there and partly not there. In other words, some of the poetry is perfectly genuine, but a great deal of it is confused and chaotic; and this condition has arrived largely because they have lacked the kind of attention which a poet *must* have before he can ever gain sufficient confidence in his audience really and genuinely to put himself into what he writes.

The hope that 'more good than harm will have been done' proved sanguine. The Malley affair cauterized the development of modernist poetry in Australia, which was precisely the project that Christesen and his associates had initially hoped to promote.

Yet there were lessons to be learnt from this brief tussle. After seeing Harris pilloried for an adventurous editorial decision, Christesen trod a careful path between the competing 'traditional' and 'contemporary' schools of poetry. He published many of the canonical poems of Hope and McAuley, but he also lent an ear to a large number of unknown writers, among them Judith Wright, who was *Meanjin*'s first secretary.

Number 2, 1944

For New England

JUDITH WRIGHT

Your trees, the homesick and the swarthy native,
blow all one way to me, this southern weather
that smells of early snow;
And I remember
the house closed in with sycamore and chestnut
fighting the foreign wind.
Here I will stay, she said; be done with the black north,
the harsh horizon rimmed with drought.
Planted the island there and drew it round her.
Therefore I find in me the double tree.

And therefore I, deserted on the wharves,
have watched the ships fan out their web of streamers;
those paper prayers reeled from the heart to London,
(thinking of how the lookout at the heads
leaned out towards the dubious rims of sea

to find a sail blown over like a message
you are not forgotten.)
Or followed through the taproot of the poplar . . .
But look, oh look, the Gothic tree's on fire
with blown galahs, and fuming with wild wings.

The hard inquiring wind strikes to the bone
and whines division.
                    Many roads meet here
in me, the traveller and the ways I travel.
All the hills' gathered waters feed my seas
who am the swimmer and the mountain river;
and the long slopes' concurrence is my flesh
who am the gazer and the land I stare on;
and dogwood blooms within my winter blood,
and orchards fruit in me and need no season.
But sullenly the jealous bones recall
what other earth is shaped and hoarded in them.

Where's home, Ulysses? Cuckolded by lewd time
he never found again the girl he sailed from,
but at his fireside met the islands waiting
and died there, twice a stranger.
                    Wind, blow through me
till the nostalgic candles of laburnum
fuse with the dogwood in a single flame
to touch alight these sapless memories.
Then will my land turn sweetly from the plough
and all my pastures rise as green as spring.

Number 1, 1945

Dust

JUDITH WRIGHT

This sick dust, spiralling with the wind,
is harsh as grief's taste in our mouths
and has eclipsed the small sun.
The remnant earth turns evil,
the steel-shocked land has turned against the plough
and runs with wind all day; and all night
sighs in our sleep against the windowpane.

Wind was kinder once, carrying cloud
like a waterbag on his shoulder; sun was kinder,
hardening the good wheat brown as a strong man.
Earth was kinder, suffering fire and plough,

breeding the unaccustomed harvest.
Leaning in our doorway together
watching the birdcloud shadows,
the fleetwing windshadows travel our clean wheat
we thought ourselves rich already.
We counted the beautiful money
and gave it in our hearts to the child asleep,
who must never break his body
against the plough and the stubborn rock and tree.

But the wind rises; but the earth rises,
running like an evil river; but the sun grows small,
and when we turn to each other, our eyes are dust
and our words dust.
Dust has overtaken our dreams that were
wider and richer than wheat under the sun,
and war's eroding gale scatters our sons
with a million other grains of dust.
O sighing at the blistered door, darkening the evening star,
the dust accuses. Our dream was the wrong dream,
our strength was the wrong strength.
Weary as we are, we must make a new choice,
a choice more difficult than resignation,
more urgent than our desire of rest at the end of the day.
We must prepare the land for a difficult sowing,
a long and hazardous growth of a strange bread,
that our sons' sons may harvest and be fed.

Number 2, 1945

The Incarnation of Sirius

James McAuley

In that age, the great anagram of God
Had bayed the planets from the rounds they trod,
And gathered the stars into a shining nation
Like restless birds that flock before migration.

For the millennial impulse of new flight
Resolved the antinomy that fixed their light;
And, echoing in the troubled soul of Earth
Quickened a woman there to bring to birth

What scarce was human: a rude avatar
That glistened with the enclosed wrath of a star.
The woman died in pangs, before she kissed
The monstrous form of God's antagonist.

But at its showing forth, the poets cried
In a strange tongue; hot mouths prophesied
The coolness of the bloody vintage-drops:
'Let us be drunk at least, when the world stops!'

Anubis-headed, the heresiarch
Sprang to a height, fire-sinewed in the dark,
And his ten fingers, bracketed on high,
Were a blazing candelabra in the sky.

The desert lion antiphonally roared;
The tiger's sinews quivered like a chord;
Man smelt the blood beneath his brother's skin
And in a loving hate the sword went in

And then the age sank, bloody and aborted.
The stars that with rebellion had consorted
Fled back in silence to their former stations.
Over the giant face of dreaming nations

The centuries-thick coverlet was drawn.
Still on the huddled shape Aldebaran
Glittered with its sad alternate fire:
Blue as of memory, red as of desire.

Number 2, 1947

Heldensagen

A. D. Hope

Pop-eye my hero, Everyman my refuge,
Ahab within mad master of my craft,
My instinct Noah, safest on his wet raft
And only bed-wrecked in the bibulous deluge.

My evening bus seeks out her northwest passage
And I my hero in the comic strip.
In every age the hero has taken ship
Away from the Newer Deal, the Nobler Message.

Commercial travellers' tales from a slick Munchausen;
Plastic milleniums of the technocrat;
The tribal psychologist pulling out of my hat
His portrait of Mansoul as a bottled abortion;

Admirals with power to organise my search
For Ithaca through this ten years monstrous dream:–
To all Messiahs the same reply: I am
Sinbad and on this Roc you build no church!

Number 3, 1948

On a Tapestry

ROSEMARY DOBSON

'And in whose eyes I drown,' the Lady said.
Her thoughts unspoken beat upon my ears,
Compounded of all elegance and grace,
Blown by the wind, she swayed, her hands entwined,
Viewing beyond the lilies and the trees
The limitless horizons of her grief.
The unicorn was pensive at her side,
The lion heraldic on a coral sea.

'And for whose words I die,' the Lady cried.
The longing turned her body half away
And in that curve was all her grief expressed.
Behind her reared the towers of all the world,
Hill upon hill of battlements and spires —
The disregarded riches of her life.
A bird above her preened its crimson beak
And apples hung like bells upon a tree.

'Whose I am utterly,' the Lady said.
The wind behind the arras stirred the folds,
I saw the truth of joy upon her lips,
The eagerness with which her body turned,
And in a dream it seemed she spoke to me,
'In loving is my sum of happiness.'
'Oh, all the sadness in the world —' I cried
Who loved not, whether loved or unbeloved.

Number 3, 1949

Waiting for a Train

BRIAN VREPONT

Looking from Milson's Point station
To Pyrmont, over a harbour water,
Pyrmont is a pastel of sleepy tones.
First to the eye the Sierra
Of glued terraces — weathered
Old umber in young sunlight,
Stretching uphill, and oil tanks
In a spread of mould;
These lead to a steep street-slope,

Deserted of movement save
The sunlight strolling;
Deeper and unurgent the dense
Houses pointed by a chimney stack
Breathing black in morning's face;
A distant church spire
Fingers the sky, on the horizon
A green pencil line of sea;
Sharp in the foreground of my train —
Three ships — one a mere curved smudge,
One scarlet bellybanded and funnelled,
The third with yellow,
The three tethered to a nebulous wharf.

Meanwhile, Christesen had also begun to publish short stories. Though fiction was no great feature of the magazine at this stage, the temper of some of the best short stories that appeared in its pages during the 1940s anticipated a theme that was to become very important in the following decade: a concern to engage with working-class life and culture.

Dal Stivens to C. B. Christesen

Department of Information,
Melbourne,
18 December 1944

. . . I must say I was disappointed you thought the two stories slight.
. . . Somewhere between mythology and reality the real Trumper is lost. The average Australian is very close to poetry when he talks of his sporting heroes — and kelpie dogs.

I don't think one should have preconceived lines into which the short prose work should be fitted. . . . The whole thing that matters is whether the short prose work succeeds in evoking an emotion economically. . . .

When I read a short prose work my only concern is not what I think the writer ought to do but what did he try to do and to what extent has he succeeded.

There! I've got it out of my system. But this word 'slight' is always guaranteed to set me off; I got it so much in my younger days from editors who turned down stories I knew to be good — and who, after London critics had approved and time had broadened their judgement, then wanted stories. These were largely commercial magazine editors and not over-intelligent.

You and your paper, of course, are in a different category.

Number 1, 1945

The Man who Bowled Victor Trumper

DAL STIVENS

Ever hear how I bowled Victor Trumper for a duck? he asked.

— No, I said.

— He was a beautiful bat, he said. He had wrists like steel and he moved like a panther. The ball sped from his bat as though fired by a cannon.

The three of us were sitting on the verandah of the pub at Yerranderie in the Burragorang Valley in the late afternoon. The sun fell full on the fourteen hundred foot sandstone cliff behind us but the rest of the valley was already dark. A road ran past the pub and the wheeltracks were eighteen inches deep in the hard summer-baked road.

— There was a batsman for you, he said.

He was a big fat man with a chin like a cucumber. He had worked in the silver mines at Yerranderie. The last had closed in 1928 and for a time he had worked in the coal mines further up the valley and then had retired on a pension and a half an inch of good lung left.

— Dust in my lungs, he said. All my own fault. The money was good. Do you know, if I tried to run a hundred yards I'd drop dead.

The second man was another retired miner but he had all his lungs. He had a hooked nose and had lost the forefinger and thumb of his right hand.

Before they became miners, they said, they had tried their hand at many jobs in the bush.

— Ever hear how I fought Les Darcy? the big fat man asked.

— No, I said.

— He was the best fighter we have ever had in Australia. He was poetry in action. He had a left that moved like quicksilver.

— He was a great fighter, I said.

— He was like a Greek god, said the fat man reverently.

We sat watching the sun go down. Just before it dipped down beside the mountain it got larger and we could look straight at it. In no time it had gone.

— Ever hear how I got Vic. Trumper?

— No, I said. Where did it happen?

— It was in a match up at Bourke. Tibby Cotter was in the same team. There was a man for you. His fastest ball was like a thunderbolt. He was a bowler and a half.

— Yes, I said.

— You could hardly see the ball after it left his hand. They put two lots of matting down when he came to Bourke so he wouldn't kill anyone.

— I never saw him, I said, but my father says he was very fast.

— Fast! says the fat man. He was so fast you never knew anything until you heard your wicket crash. In Bourke he split seven stumps and we had to borrow the school kids' set.

It got cold and we went into the bar and ordered three rums which we drank with milk. The miner who had all his lungs said:

— I saw Tibby Cotter at the Sydney Cricket Ground and the Englishmen were scared of him.

— He was like a tiger as he bounded up to bowl, said the big fat man.

— He had even Ranji bluffed, said the other miner. Indians have special eyesight, but it wasn't enough to play Tibby.

We all drank together and ordered again. It was my shout.

— Ever hear about the time I fought Les Darcy? the big fat man asked me.

— No, I said.

— There wasn't a man in his weight to touch him, said the miner who had all his lungs. When he moved his arm you could see the muscles ripple across his back.

— When he hit them you could hear the crack in the back row of the Stadium, said the fat man.

— They poisoned him in America, said the other miner.

— Never gave him a chance, said the fat man.

— Poisoned him like a dog, said the other.

— It was the only way they could beat him, said the fat man. There wasn't a man at his weight that could live in the same ring as Les Darcy.

The barmaid filled our glasses up again and we drank a silent toast. Two men came in. One was carrying a hurricane lantern. The fat man said the two men always came in this night for a drink and that the tall man in the rain coat was the caretaker at one of the derelict mines.

— Ever hear about the kelpie bitch I had once? said the fat man. She was as intelligent and wide awake as you are. She almost talked. It was when I was droving.

The fat miner paid this time.

— There isn't a dog in the bush to touch a kelpie for brains, said the miner with the hooked nose and the fingers short.

— Kelpies can do almost anything but talk, said the fat man.

— Yes, I said. I have never had one but I have heard my father talk of one that was wonderful for working sheep.

— All kelpies are beautiful to watch working sheep but the best was a little bitch I had at Bourke, said the fat man. Ever hear how I bowled Victor Trumper for a duck?

— No, I said. But what about this kelpie?

— I could have got forty quid for her any time for the asking, said the fat miner. I could talk about her all day. Ever hear about the time I forgot the milk for her pups? Sold each of the pups later for a tenner.

— You can always get a tenner for a good kelpie pup, said the miner who had all his lungs.

— What happened when you forgot the pups' milk? I said.

— It was in the bucket, the fat miner said, and the pups couldn't reach it. I went into the kitchen and the bitch was dipping her tail in the milk bucket and then lowering it to the pups. You can believe that or not, as you like.

— I believe you, I said.
— I don't, said the other miner.
— What, you don't believe me! cried the fat miner, turning to the other. Don't you believe I bowled Victor Trumper for a duck? Don't you believe I fought Les Darcy? Don't you believe a kelpie could do that?
— I believe you bowled Vic. Trumper for a duck, said the other. I believe you fought Les Darcy. I believe a kelpie would do that.
The fat miner said: You had me worried for a minute. I thought you didn't believe I had a kelpie like that.
— That's it, said the miner who had all his lungs. I don't believe you had a kelpie like that.
— You tell me who had a kelpie like that if I didn't, the fat miner said.
— I'll tell you, said the miner with the hooked nose. You never had a kelpie like that, but I did. You've heard me talk about that little bitch many times.
They started getting mad with each other then so I said:
— How did you get Vic. Trumper for a duck?
— There was a batsman for you, said the fat man. He used a bat like a sword and he danced down the wicket like a panther.

Number 3, 1946

Absentee

MONA BRAND

Now what does the clock show? Only three! Still two hours of it! Two hours that are like a hill you have to climb over with a ton on your back. Don't let the hours be piled into a hill — let them be a straight slope you can go running down fast. The machines are making the noise of a train, of an express train, streaming down the long, straight rails. You be a passenger — you be a girl riding on a fast train.

Of course there's no seat for you on the train, but you can walk up and down. As much as you like you can walk up and down. Certainly when you're on a train you don't have to be tying together the broken threads, and you don't have to watch the spindles and the bobbins with their whizz, whizz, whizzing rhythm. Don't you think about the spindles. You think of what's outside the train window — the trees and the green grass and the smoke coming up out of the chimneys.

Easily you can think of the smoke because of this fluff all about you — this fluff that comes up off the machines and floats through the mill and all around you, clinging to your face and your clothes and your hair — to your fine, free, shining, golden hair.

You're Lana Turner, and you're on a vacation — you're going down South. You're going deep down over the border to the orange groves and the palm trees and the long, full summer.

Oh, but there's a hand, and it's holding on to the time — it's a hard hand!

But you, you at the tall machine with your running and tying — why don't you snatch a fistful of life? Wrench yourself free of the whizzing and tying. You can creep out from under this roof that stoops down over your life. Go out into the free air, and walk over the yard slowly, to the tin shed, and the only haven. But you've got to ask the foreman, and he'll say, 'What, again?' Not that you mind what he says, the old fish-face.

Go now! But wait — don't go now — because, look at the boss coming through. His sad, tired face looks down, because he doesn't want to be coming through, but he has to and now he's talking to Fish-face. It's warm and smooth with a faster rhythm, and time leaps on. The boss drags down the big hand of the clock, because you can look at his clothes which are thick and grey and good. You can stare at the warp and the weft standing out in their squares. And he's got a broad back, and he's so close you can touch him.

He's gone now; there's a machine where he was, and time's like a sea that's closed over the place where he was. Oh, this isn't a job, this running and tying! It isn't a job because it hasn't an end. You can never say to yourself, 'Now I've done that much — that's good.' You just go on and you go on. You tie up the threads that get broken; that's all. Every thread you tie up is a bit of time you've tied up. All day you've been tying up time.

What a life! What a life for Lana Turner! What a life for the girl with the fine, free, shining, golden hair.

Why not go out and get yourself a drink now? Why not go out and put your mouth under the tap and turn on the sharp water? They can't stop you turning on water. Everybody turns on water. Everybody but Fish-face. And then when you've turned on the water, and come back, of course it will be a bit later, and a bit later, and a bit later. And the lateness will climb up in a high point, and stretch to five o'clock and touch the whistle. And a blast of the whistle will shatter the machines, and they'll murmur and stop, and then you can go home.

And now you can go home, because here it is — the whistle. This is what you wanted, isn't it? You wanted to go home. Off you go and punch the clock. Give it a hard punch — give it a punch to go on with. You're in a hurry, you are. You've got to catch a train.

Look at the night. The wind blows needles of rain in your face. It's cold and fast and it hurts and you rather like it. In the grey street, with the dark coming on, the lights look like moons. Misty and yellow they look, with a soft edge dimming out of them.

You'd better hurry, Lana. Remember who's calling at your apartment tonight? Of course there'll be Larry, and perhaps there'll be The Kid — poor Kid. You'll have to be putting them off, Lana. You've got a date with Someone Else. 'Now *please* don't be silly, Larry . . . and . . . I'm sorry, Kid.'

That noise you can hear — that's the train. It gets crowded down the line, and now there's all this mob from the mill getting on. Don't let them push you about, those boys. Don't look at the boys. Don't look at the boy with the oily hair and the pimpled face. You're shy when it comes to boys. Look the other way, get in another carriage; get on your own.

Now you're in and you're standing in a crowd, but you're on your own. The train swings and jerks so you'd better hold on. Now, where were you? Oh, yes — Larry. 'Larry, you're not to be stupid, *please*. Why, of *course* I like you, I've always said I *like* you — but not 'like that.' *You* know how it is, don't you, Kid — or do I have to *explain*?

Just down the hill and you'll be home. It seems years since you left home, and you're hungry. What is it for dinner tonight? But you don't have to wonder, do you? Sausages again. It's always sausages. There's something wrong with your mum, and she can only think of sausages. And she's left the gate open and the children will be up the street, and you'll have to go and get them. As if you didn't have enough to do without running all over the streets after a couple of kids. But they're not out after all; they're home. That's Stannie you can hear yelling. You'll give him something to yell for, won't you? You'd like to, anyway. You'd like to give Valerie a piece of your mind too. Valerie's getting a big girl, and nobody cares about Valerie. Your mum doesn't care. Your mum doesn't care about this family at all since your dad cleared out.

You'd better put your nose in the kitchen and say hello to your mum. You'd better ask if you can help dish up. You needn't wait to hear if she says yes — you'd better ask her, though.

She's thought of sausages. And it's full of steam and smell and frying, the kitchen is. Look at the sideboard mirror — it's clouded over. Wipe off the mist and the steam with your hankie. Wipe off a circle big enough to see yourself, wipe off a big circle.

Look at you. This is you. So you thought you were Lana Turner? What, with your straight black hair, and your face like a white pie, and your eyes like heavy grapes?

Turn your back on the mirror — it will get misted again, and then you can be Lana Turner — Lana with Larry coming, and The Kid; Lana with a date to keep — with Someone Else.

You ought to ask your mum if she'd like to go to the pictures too. You know she'll say yes. That's why you won't ask her, because you know she'll say yes. She'll interrupt you all the time. She won't let you be Lana Turner. Well, anyway, you'd better wash up. You'd better scrape up the dishes, and pour on the water, and watch the steam rise. Don't make yourself late with the dishwater and the grease and the steam rising.

You're not very late; they still have some single seats — and it's warm inside. It's dark and warm and the war's on the screen. The seats are soft and there's a carpet, and maybe your feet will dry off, and maybe when you go out, maybe it won't be raining.

It is, though; it's still raining. And you've seen yourself in the foyer mirror. Oh, what a blob you are with your black hair and your white face and your eyes like heavy grapes! Because, in America everybody is young and beautiful, and they wear furs and full gowns, and diamond flower-shapes are in their hair, and they live in white houses, and they go places, and everybody loves them. Yes, everybody loves everybody in America. And there's Uncle Sam, and he loves everybody, and everybody loves Uncle Sam, and nobody gets up to breakfast, because there's a black maid, and she brings it in on a tray.

But *you* have to get up for breakfast. Anyway, you have to get up. Put your key in the door, Lana, but don't turn the key. Don't turn it yet. Look, you haven't said goodnight. Someone Else wants to say goodnight to you.

— Goodnight . . . goodnight . . . goodnight.

It's warm in bed, Lana, and your fine, free hair is gold on the white pillow, and your arms are white, and you're so beautiful. 'Ah, it's no good, Larry, and I'm sorry, Kid. It had to end like this, didn't it? Don't take it to heart, Larry. You *knew* there was Someone Else. Who is he? Who is he? Well, he's . . . I'll tell you who he is. He's . . . he's . . . he's . . .'

He's not the foreman and he's not the boss. He's dressed like the boss and he's got that sort of a face. He's taller, though, and he's getting taller and taller. When you stretch up and try and touch him, then he's gone. Then he comes back, and he's not like the boss at all — no, he's the boy with the oily hair and the pimpled face. But you like him now, don't you? Yes, he's not so bad now, because now he's Someone Else. And you're riding with him on the train, and you're both near the door, and the train is swaying, and now you're swinging out of the door, and you're clinging on so hard to the boy with the oily hair, because you're going to fall. And he's holding on to you, and he's going to fall too, and you're both falling and falling and falling . . . and somebody's screaming. Who's screaming!

It's the alarm clock screaming. You'd better turn it off. You'd better get some sleep.

Wake up! You've overslept. You're late. Oh, you're late, you're late, you're late. Too late for breakfast. Get dressed and run for the train, that's all. You've just about time for the train. You'd better hurry.

Why should you hurry? You're late already. It's awful when you're late. The foreman looks at you. Not that he says anything — it's the way he looks at you. You'd better not go.

You're not a millionaire — you'd better go. Well, you'd better hurry if you're going. You'd better hurry and you'd better hurry and you'd better hurry.

You did hurry. It's because you live at the end of the hill that you've missed the train. It's because the station is at the top of the hill, and because there's a ladder of steps going up, and a bridge across and the steps going over. And the train was coming and you heard the train and you remembered the steps and the going up, and the longing to scream and fall down with the weight in your thighs . . . and the pain in your mind that goes up with the guard's green flag.

It's gone now. The train's gone and the day's gone. The day at the mill has gone with the train, because you'd rather not go than be late with the foreman watching, and not saying anything, but only watching.

Look, Lana, it's a lovely day! Look at the sky. Did you see the sky, Lana? It's blue like summer, and you can go down South. You can go down deep over the border to the orange groves and the palm trees, and the long, full summer.

So this is goodbye. Don't take it to heart, Larry; never mind, Kid. I said it had to end. And the end is always like this — it's the burnt-out cigarette, the lipstick on the cup, the way I wear my hair. Give me something to remember you by. I told you there was . . . Someone Else.

On the critical front, among the liveliest of the writings in the early issues of *Meanjin* were a series of 'Letters to Tom Collins'. Taking as its occasion the centenary of Joseph Furphy's birth, the series served a dual purpose: it was both a vehicle for remedying the neglect into which Furphy's work had fallen, and an opportunity for writers of various persuasions to reflect on the changes that had occurred since Furphy wrote his monumental novel, *Such Is Life*. Several of the 'correspondents' took this as an opportunity to write about literary matters in a direct, colloquial style.

Number 10, Spring 1942

The Case for Critics

Laurieton, N.S.W.
September, 1942

Dear Tom,

I am not an admirer of yours because I consider you a literary snob. For years I had been hearing about a classic called 'Such Is Life'; and prowling through the village library I unearthed a first edition of your great work. The librarian was only too glad to part with it for half-a-crown. He had, he said, been cleaning out a lot of old junk like that. 'Burnt a coupla hundred of them old books a month ago.' Incensed at the thought of an early Australian classic so narrowly escaping, I carried home 'Such Is Life' and settled down to digest it.

It was indigestible. Enormous sentences unrolled themselves like strips of fly-paper on which the mind dangled bumbling and bewildered. Those sentences were written by a word-intoxicated man, wallowing, positively wallowing, in print. All that magnificent material, all that humour and kindliness and observation, sicklied o'er with the pale cast of an elaborate prose style.

And the reason why your works are lost to the vulgar (meaning me)? You had to be literary, you had to show you could write like the big bugs! You wanted to let the reader know you had read Shakespeare, that you thought of setting up as a Shakespearian critic. One of Lawson's worst short articles (but how much better) showed he had the same low taste. Of course it adds in a way to your lovableness, but it is like meeting a man who has bellowed about the rights of the workers and tossed his last sixpence ('Tucker or tobacco: hooray it's tobacco') and camped with you and argued with you — meeting such a man, I say, all dressed-up and shiny, slicked up for a vice-regal party. Someone should have restrained you. Some friend should have led you aside and said: 'Look here. You don't need to dress your stuff up like that. The chaps who want to read it will never be able to wade through the long words.'

The curse of book writing in this country is largely pretentiousness. If stuff gets into print it automatically becomes Australian Literature in capital letters. The idea seems to be that if reviewers don't speak nicely to young Australian Literature it may go off in a huff and choke. So the critics encourage and encourage, they laud a good medium-quality book as an epic, and a classic, a mighty saga; and the faithful public (a few, anyway) buys the book and is naturally disappointed.

There is some reason for sympathy with the low-brow who 'doesn't like Australian books.' He has grown tired of having cat's-meat passed off on him as sirloin. A really cold ferocious critic is badly needed to prick the swelling conceit of self-styled 'Australian Literature.' A hopeful beginning has been made by 'Southerly,' whose critic goes about searching for small cracks in which he may insert his proboscis, a veritable hornet.

The trouble with most literary folk is that they huddle into warm little circles of mutual esteem. There is no bitter blast from a 'Quarterly' or 'Edinburgh Review' to break the heart of a Keats or set a Byron roaring. Not that the reviewers ever really did break Keats's heart or anyone else's for that matter. The vitality of a book, the actual percentage of life the author manages to spin out of himself like some shining ectoplasm, is what carries a book down the years. Your 'Such Is Life,' I admit it grudgingly, will probably float along on that vitality of yours, but its sails will be sighted far out to sea by a few, whereas its rich cargo might have fed multitudes if you had kept closer to the shores of common speech.

To revert to our discussion on critics and criticism. I think you would have agreed that until a writer learns to take punishment he hasn't much stamina. I am urgent in the cause of higher critics and higher criticism; men like Hazlitt who could say when he was dying: 'I have written no commonplace, not a line that licks the dust.' Nor any kindly lies, guaranteed to encourage second-rate writing, in the idea that it has only to persevere.

Yours sincerely,
Kylie Tennant

And in 1943 a young teacher at Geelong Grammar contributed his own letter on a subject that had come to be of central importance to Australian culture, particularly under the stress of war.

Number 3, 1943

Mateship

Geelong Grammar School Victoria

Dear Tom,

I feel embarrassed in addressing you by your Christian name — in this your centenary year; nor does your hatred of pretentiousness, your enthusiasm for intimacy put me at my ease. Australian writers have become more polite, more formal since your departure from human society; the drawing-room has replaced the drover's hut. I don't think you would like us if you came back to earth. We wince at the behaviour you approved of. Perhaps it is 'matey' or 'friendly-like' to call you Tom, to use the vernacular to communicate our experiences to you. You and Lawson almost canonised the word 'mate.' 'Mateyness,' I believe, made life bearable for you; it was your metaphysical comforter. A true mate was a 'dinkum Aussie,' a real pal. Please don't think that I disapprove of your sentiments, that I am ridiculing the ideal which warmed your heart. The French were the inspiration for all men of good will when they were the apostles of 'fraternité.' But . . . yes, you should see what has happened to your ideal — 'Dad and Dave,' 'having a good time,' and then the sneer of the upper 1000 at the vulgarity of things Australian. This hurts us, Tom, and I believe it would hurt you. So I ask you: what are we to do about Dad and Dave, about this ideal of yours which embarrasses the elite and sustains the vulgar? You see there is a rift in our society — the elite flee to the garret, to the polite drawing-room, to Europe, while the people ape the mate ideal, being bonzer sorts! I am not asking you to feel penitent, to take back what you said. I am addressing you because I believe you tried to do something worth while — to interpret Australian life.

I said you and Lawson gave us the ideal of being 'mates,' that it was your comforter. But I wonder whether either of you had the courage to say what you really felt about Australian life. Perhaps you were horrified, even terrified and thought that things would not be quite so bad with a mate, that if men huddled together, if they were as endearing to each other as little children they would repress the awful spectacle you saw. Yes, Tom, in Australia we are all afraid; and you and Lawson had a great chance to explain why, because by your time the excitement of the discovery was over: man had uncovered the woman he was to live with (queer, Tom, how expectancy distorts a judgment). Yet you do not seem to have noticed the queer relationship between man and earth in Australia: how he treated her as a harlot, frenziedly raped her for her wealth — wool, gold, wheat; no wonder his conscience was uneasy, no wonder he was restless. The monuments he erected, the houses he gave his fellow men, the entertainments he provided — vulgar, meretricious, pretentious. It was beginning even in your time. Yes, and the swaggering, and the sensitivity to criticism — this was the behaviour of guilty men. Yet you did not see how ill we were, nor how profound our despair was to become.

Even if life with the drovers was exciting, if their company warmed your heart, and made you feel glad, I still cannot understand how you repressed the painful sensations left by our countryside. It hurt Lawson — despair with it is always seeping through his mind. You may remember this passage from his story: '. . . plains like dead seas . . . scrub indescribably dismal — everything damp, dark and unspeakably dreary.'

Perhaps man's environment is always hostile; perhaps his works are always vile. But we cannot live by that faith. We spew it out. The queer thing is that we are tortured by doubt. Civilised life with us is *artificial*. It is a shock to see houses, churches, even towns in Australia. And because we are aware of a gulf between the acquired idea of what life could be, and what our environment insidiously suggests — was sun-bathing popular in your time, Tom? — we behave like guilty children, as though we were concealing some crime. So we must ask the dreadful question: do we belong here? I do not mean to imply that the country belongs to the aborigines, or that our sense of guilt is due to the crime our ancestors committed against those strange members of human society. In that we are disinterested. The emotions roused on that score are 'salon' emotions — not conducive to action! What I am saying is that this myth of 'mateyness' which you preached to your generation is just not enough: we want, curse us, the something more. I know that we have only vulgarised the ideal of the Europeans who believed that affection would bind men together when the old comforters were removed. And perhaps it is only over-refinement or squeamishness which makes us jib at being 'mates'; or perhaps it is the peculiar environment which rouses these cursed doubts in our minds, and makes us only half believers. Do we need a prophet to preach a new myth, or a sage to convince us that it is better to accept things as they are, better to forget the something more? If the dead stand by and help, we need you now, Tom, because the unhappy want us to confess our failure, to embrace the old faith. When we see Dad and Dave we feel angry with you and Lawson. When we contemplate the alternative we are thankful for you and your ideal. I wonder what we will do.

Yours ever,
Manning Clark

Another of Tom Collins' correspondents, Sidney J. Baker, author of *The Australian Language*, raised a contentious issue that was to receive consistent attention in *Meanjin* throughout the Cold War period: the state of the mass media, in this case the magazine that had once been a standard-bearer of Australian radicalism.

Number 4, 1946

Demise of *The Bulletin*

SIDNEY BAKER

You, Tom — the most prized of all *Bulletin* protégés — once saw a parallel between the railway line and human will. Life is like a railway track, you said. Every so often the track comes to a fork. Fate decrees that man must keep on travelling, but just for one moment he has the right of choice. He can choose which track he wishes to take. Beyond that he is a victim of the machinery of destiny.

Since *The Bulletin* has, not unjustifiably, prided itself on discovering and nurturing you and your writings, its failure to benefit from the wisdom of your somewhat homespun philosophy is a little baffling. Long ago *The Bulletin* came to a fork in its journalistic railroad track, but instead of turning one way or the other it jumped the points and has remained bogged down ever since. The fact that *The Bulletin* today is a lost and discredited journal is one of the saddest things any student of Australian culture and traditions is obliged to recognise. Perhaps even more tragic is *The Bulletin*'s failure to realise its own decline. . . .

As I write I have before me copies of *The Bulletin* for December 18, 1897, and for June 26, 1946. Superficially, they look similar. True, the colour of the cover today is a little less red than it used to be, but the size is the same and the format is the same. Both copies have 36 pages. Main features in both are: The Red Page, the editorial page, Plain English, Sundry Shows, The Wild Cat Column, Society, Woman's Letter, Personal Items, Aboriginalities, Sporting Notions and Political Points. A half century and no change? Surely a journal should grow up a little in half a century. Main evidence of *Bulletin* growth is a feature called Uncabled Additions (two pages of dull reprint from overseas papers), some notes for servicemen by that international expert on military affairs, 'Ek Dum,' and two pages of unsigned correspondence.

At the outset it becomes clear that *The Bulletin* is trying to live on its past history. It hasn't grown up. By retaining the appearance of the old, vigorous, nationally-revered *Bulletin* it is allowing itself to be deluded into the belief that it is still vigorous and nationally-revered. This self-hypnosis is conspiring to edge it out of the journalistic market. Look at the issue of December 18, 1897, again. Of 36 pages in that issue, more than 20 are devoted to advertising. More than 250 separate advertisers use its columns. But of the 36 pages in the issue of June 26, 1946, only 12 are given to advertisements — and the number of advertisers has shrunk to slightly more than 50. Two hundred fewer advertisers! No wonder *The Bulletin* is trying to keep up the pretence that it is as good as it ever was.

Why is it on the downgrade? Part of that question has already been answered. Same old format, same old features. But there is something equally important. *The Bulletin* no longer thinks progressively. The brand of political faith it espouses today is anything but the old brand of its political faith. Let us look at the issue of June 26, 1946, again. Pages 8 and 9: Eight extracts from overseas papers condemning Russia and Communism. Page 11: Anti-Soviet cartoon by Norman Lindsay. Page 12: Editorials attacking Russia, the Australian Labor Party and Communists. Page 13: Sub-editorials attacking Communists; cartoon attacking Russia. Page 14: Political Points — ten attacks on Communists and trade unions. Page 15: Cartoon attacking Labor Party and Communists. Pages 18 and 19: 'Ek Dum' attacks Labor Party and Communists.

So it goes on and so it has gone on in *The Bulletin* in every issue for years past, Tom. Now, no one will disagree with any journal's right to take a slap at the Labor Party, trade unions, Russia and Communists now and then. But there is a limit to the endurance of any reader. *The Bulletin* has lost its sense of proportion. It has become obsessed with the idea that anything pertaining to liberalism in general and to the workers in particular is unspeakably evil. Even when John Curtin died it could not resist unloading its spleen on his memory. A little of this goes a long way; and in these days it goes a particularly long way, since all but the blindest, most wooden-headed conservatives realise that Toryism is dead as a political faith. Any journal which vomits up this strange brew of discredited fanaticism is obviously going to alienate many liberal-thinking readers, even though they may not be trade unionists or overt Communists. This is certainly one reason why *The Bulletin* is not being read and quoted as widely these days as it used to be. Instead of attempting to stand at the head of sane progressive thought as it did 50 years ago, it is slopping around in a reactionary morass. Somewhere, in some small corner of Labor politics, trade unionism and Communist ideology, there must be some small grain of wisdom and truth. But *The Bulletin* cannot see it. It is paying the penalty for its blindness.

There is another reason why *The Bulletin* has lost caste. Its Red Page — once the literary forum of Australia — has been somewhat given of late to outbursts of self-adulation. Its principal contributor is Douglas Stewart, with an occasional article by Norman Lindsay. Personally, I hold both of them in high esteem as creative workers, but their efforts to prove that *The Bulletin* is the fount of all literary wisdom in Australia, the ardour with which they adjust facts to suit themselves, and their bouts of mutual backslapping, are scarcely calculated to earn the Red Page the approval of Australian writers and artists. This brings me to the reason why I chose the issue of June 26 last as an example of the modern *Bulletin*. The Red Page in this issue is devoted to a justifiable outburst against the iniquities of Australian censorship, with particular reference to Lawson Glassop's interesting but overrated *We Were The Rats*. *The Bulletin* says in the course of its argument: 'Force a writer to be false to his vision and the game's not worth the candle. . . . The sentence that shocks, the page that offends, the moment when the writer's analysis of life reaches its extreme — that is likely to be the absolutely vital moment of his book, when the whole truth is revealed. An honest writer cannot sacrifice that extreme moment of truth.

If he does — if censorship makes him a liar — the falsity will destroy his whole work.'

These comments are specially interesting to me, Tom. In July, 1945, following the publication of *The Australian Language*, *The Bulletin* protested to my publishers about a sentence which ran: 'We who see that journal today as a minor weekly can have little inkling of its once immense influence, not only upon the writers and would-be writers of Australia, but upon the nation's politics'. The publishers withdrew all copies of the book, excised the offending page, and glued in a new page with this sentence deleted. Result: In all but a few copies of my book which were sold before *The Bulletin*'s impertinent protest, I am made to appear a liar. This factual evidence immediately renders *The Bulletin*'s indignant protests against censorship so much misleading nonsense. With this type of intellectual dishonesty to support its ratbag outlook on life in general, it is little wonder that *The Bulletin* has become no more than a pale shadow of what it once was. It is suffering from all the disabilities that conspire to kill a journal: it is attempting to live on its past reputation; it backs discredited causes; it has cut itself adrift from the main stream of Australian thought. Where once it was quoted by the man in the street it is now ignored or condemned; where once it was a guiding light for progressive thought and a vehicle for vigorous, adventurous literary expression, it has become dull, repetitious, reactionary. Its spirit has been broken; it is dying tediously of an intellectual inertia.

Maybe, with your metaphysical outlook, Tom, you would say that such is life, but if you did I wouldn't think too (gerundive) highly of your (adj.) verdict.

When Furphy first sent *Such is Life* to A. G. Stephens at the *Bulletin*, the manuscript ran to 1125 pages. At Stephens' request, Furphy excised two large sections in an attempt to reduce the book to publishable length. One of the excised sections, titled *Rigby's Romance*, contained what Furphy himself considered to be the philosophical gist of his work: a sustained dissertation on socialism. The manuscript of *Rigby's Romance* lay on Furphy's shelf until 1905, when R. S. Ross published it as a serial in his left-wing Broken Hill newspaper, the *Barrier Truth*; but it was fifteen more years before an abridged edition was published in book form, and not until 1946 did Angus & Robertson finally produce a complete edition. To celebrate the occasion, Christesen invited Lloyd Ross, son of the original publisher, to review the new edition.

Number 1, 1947

Socialist Ideals

LLOYD ROSS

To (sheol) with commentators, critics and confusionists of Tom Collins and his works. To (sheol) with literary wisemen, who are building walls of theses between the people and a writer of the people. To (sheol) with *The Bulletin* that postdates its analysis of *Rigby's Romance* without recalling its judgment in the days when A. G. Stephens discovered Joseph Furphy . . . Let's have a close season for theorizers on *Such is Life!* What do they amount to, all these scholars who count the words, divide the number of words by the chapters and prove what a careful writer was this Joseph Furphy? Why didn't they recognise his genius when he was gazing quizzically at the unpublished manuscripts piling up on his shelves! How many of those who now praise him would recognise his greatness if he came among us today; and how many, who tear him apart and acknowledge his genius, know they are praising the humanitarian who wrote in the wild, turbulent, Utopian-minded, socialist, crazy 'eighties and 'nineties? And to hell with the Furphy cult — let's settle down and read *Rigby's Romance*, give our attention to advising the reader, who is attracted by the cult or trapped by the title.

It's a book in which intense political conviction on the ethical case for socialism is blended with the rich, deep humour of an open-air Australia; in which a group of rare characters sit fishing, yarning, stretching their minds and limbs, blending discussion on socialism and religion with a grand Australian night of scenery and talking. . . . But that sounds too prosaic a version of *Rigby* — let's cut out the cackle and take the book fishing with us, or on a long train journey; leave it on the seat as we go out for a beer; pass the book round with the bottle; swap a Rigby story for the latest; open the pages and read anywhere; stroll through the volume; yarn about Tom Collins with a few bosom mates; take endless time to enjoy its flavour and its friendship. No six o'clock serial rush with this book, but an experience to be enjoyed, deeply, humorously — determinedly. . . .

Tom Collins overflowed the wisdom of 'The Commodore' into the editorials of *Barrier Truth*; the 'Colonel' wrote 'pars'; Joseph Furphy's serial participated in every one of the interminable controversies that kept *Barrier Truth* and Broken Hill alive. Rigby and Ross believed in the same Romance; if only the people heard the truth of socialism, the world would be born anew! Said Joseph Furphy to Miles Franklin —

> Socialism is in the atmosphere just at present, and I flatter myself that *R's R* speaks the last word on the moral aspect of that movement; the Socialism being sugar-coated with the sweetest romance you ever struck.

Rigby went on talking his wisdom, deepened by humour and experience.

It was the year the miners of Broken Hill sent the idea of a Socialist Objective to a Labor Party Conference; the year the anarchist poet,

A. J. Andrews, died, defiant to the end; the year of drought and dust storms; the years of the great agitators — Tom Mann, Harry Holland, Scott Bennet, Jack Barnes, Josiah Thomas, Paddy Lamb, Harry Gray, A. K. Wallace, Miss Powell, Miss Ahern . . . For them the socialist struggle meant the development of literature, opportunities for the masses to express and to enjoy the best in literature today and under socialism. Deeply serious as they were, their agitation included joy in combat, warmth of fellowship, strength through solidarity. These are the qualities of *R's R* propaganda for socialism woven into a series of short stories and held together by the personality of the lovable Rigby.

What have they done to Joseph Furphy — the high-powered literary critics? Nothing nearly as destructive as Labor has been to Rigby's democratic equalitarian socialism! Oh (sheol)! Rigby saw ahead to the day — our day — when his message would be so desperately needed that this book should be passed around the workshops in a desperate attempt to revive the idealism of Labor . . . So let's drink to Angus and Robertson Ltd. for issuing this new edition and to R. G. Howarth for his honest and understanding foreword. And don't let's get cynical, or defeatist, or depressed, for Tom Collins warned us against these weaknesses. Another 'bob in' — and a round of drinks in honor of A. G. Stephens, R. S. Ross, Miles Franklin and Kate Baker, O.B.E. — she ought to have been Governor-General — and that's a good story for Tom Collins.

Ross's comments elicited a strong response from Frank Dalby Davison and Jim Cairns, who was then teaching economics at the University of Melbourne. Like many of his contemporaries, Cairns was intensely disillusioned by the Labor Party's failure to implement socialist objectives during its six years in power at the federal level.

Number 2, 1947

Wot, No Socialism?

J. F. Cairns

In his review of *Rigby's Romance*, Lloyd Ross wrote: 'What have they done to Joseph Furphy — the high-powered literary critics? Nothing nearly as destructive as Labor has been to Rigby's democratic equalitarian socialism.' Rigby's message is certainly needed in the 'workshops,' but any attempt to revive the 'idealism of Labor' would certainly be a desperate one and it is pretty certain that the 'workshops' will never hear about Rigby if it is left to the Labor Party to tell them.

The 'intense political conviction on the ethical case for socialism' has certainly gone from the Labor Party and likewise are gone its 'years of the great agitators.' Perhaps it is not unfair to Lloyd Ross to have expected him to 'cut the cackle' a bit earlier and tell us why this has happened. The other reviewers did not seem to notice the matter at all. If he had done so he might have told us that the Labor Party is now what the old Australian Socialist Party told us it would be — a party of opportunists, or old men, or men whose minds are full of abstractions about things which are incapable of proof or disproof. If he had tackled this question, he might have told us that those 'with an intense political conviction' about socialism are today found in the Communist Party. It may perhaps be said that this has damaged the prospects of socialism because in the Communist Party it has acquired a foreign association with Russia. It has been possible to stir up all the emotion of patriotism against socialism for this reason. If it had not been for this perhaps a virile socialism 'blended with the rich deep humour of an open air Australia' would today be found in the Labor Party . . .

It is very obvious that any socialist movement would have been painted in vicious foreign colors even if Marx had been born in Woolloomooloo. It was painted in these colors when the worst they could do was to call its leaders Irish and demand that they should be deported. Socialists are always called traitors as are most reformers — as John Balle was in 1381 — if they really mean business.

Why are there few real socialists in the Labor Party?

1) Because socialists have found it difficult or impossible within the Labor Party to make effective steps to bring about socialism. This seems to be because the Labor Party has adopted a policy of day to day objectives strictly within the capitalist status quo. In other words the Labor Party is the 'left wing' capitalist party and is not a socialist party at all.

2) Socialism has become associated with the 'materialist conception of history,' and this is not acceptable to many of the poorer classes whose religious beliefs demand an abstract subjective faith in the supernatural. These people support the Labor Party because of their economic position, but will not generally accept modern socialism because it is 'materialistic.'

Talking about religion: Dr. Ross asked, 'How many of those who now praise Joseph Furphy would recognise his greatness if he came among us today?' Perhaps this would also be true today of Jesus Christ — particularly if he were to proclaim, 'Think not that I am come to send peace on earth: I came not to send peace but a sword'; or, 'What does it profit my brethren, though a man say he hath faith, and hath not works? Can faith save him? . . . Ye see then how that by works a man is justified, and not by faith only.' It seems to me that in this Jesus was even more concerned about what happened in this world than what might happen in the next. It is surely not unfair to suggest that a bit of militant socialism would not be contrary to the traditions of either the Church or the Labor Party.

Part Three

Life in a Cold Climate

Number 1, 1945

Editorial

This issue of *Meanjin* marks a new development in the journal's history. Instead of being published in Brisbane, it now appears under the imprint of the Melbourne University Press.

Meanjin was first published in Brisbane in 1940, a handsel of twelve pages. Today it is a well-established quarterly of 80 pages with a circulation of 4000 copies per issue. As the magazine developed, editing and managerial problems increased proportionately. Conducted as a sparetime venture, publication under wartime conditions presented almost insuperable difficulties, and three numbers only could be distributed last year. It was then that an offer of assistance was received from Melbourne University. Subsequently arrangements were made for Melbourne University Press to publish the magazine, and the editorial office was transferred to the University. As the journal may fairly claim to have a nation-wide audience, we have retained the regional title *Meanjin*. The format and general character have remained unaltered, except for minor adjustments. It may be as well to point out, however, that *Meanjin* is not a university magazine: its policy and direction remain under the control of the editor.

The next number will be *Meanjin*'s twenty-first. Then a restatement of our aims, our 'policy' will be made. Meanwhile, we reiterate that our central aim is to publish a magazine of ideas, built around literature and art, to encourage discussion and criticism, to present advance-guard writing as well as the more traditionally-based creative work, to develop cultural contacts with other countries — a literary lend-lease . . . in short, to work for a healthy climate of opinion and literary activity.

No Australian concerned with literature and art can fail to feel that something new is stirring throughout the country. In the cities, in country districts, there is renewed activity, a quickening of interest, a fresh hope for the nation's future. This alertness, this heightened consciousness, is evident also in the cultural field. The role of a journal such as *Meanjin* is to present to the public examples of the country's present-day literary and art work, to record, interpret and discuss trends and problems associated with its life and growth. To do that to the best advantage we would of course need a much larger quarterly magazine, or else to publish monthly. Such development during the war would be impossible; and so we ask our readers to continue their interest and support until wartime restrictions can be eased.

In previous numbers we said that in so far as the determination of the Australian future depends on the Australian people, it depends upon their power to imagine such a future as they want and can believe in; that many have not to any notable degree imagined such a future, but seem rather to be unable or unwilling to consider what they wish their lives to be; that this failure of imagination, if continued, will tragically affect our victory in this war. But we feel the majority of the people understand very well that this war is not a war only, but an end and a beginning — an end of things known and a beginning of things unknown. They have smelled the wind blowing from the coast, noted the relative humidity, felt the sun's temperature: change of weather. They know that whatever the world will be when the war ends, the world will be different.

Now is the time for re-creation, the rebuilding not of the city or town but of the nation. Towards the achievement of that end the artist can make his significant contribution. Already there is heartening activity in various cultural fields — a vitality and expectancy which has not yet been noted by the popular (Mandrake) press. This new drive is coming mainly from the younger people — a generation which was largely untouched by the between-wars disillusionment. In the work of these young writers and artists a strong socio-political consciousness is evident. Their vision of a post-war Australia is radically different from that of their predecessors. To them art and politics are interlocked. They couple thought to action, and action to life, and life itself to all the highest manifestations of sense, feeling and experience: organic life for them does not merely culminate in man's superior cunning but in man's superior ideals. Man's existence does not stay at the biological level of organism, function, and environment, nor even at the tribal level of folk, work, place: man perpetually renews himself and transcends himself by means of that heritage of ideal values, of self-surpassing purposes, which are covered by the terms polity, culture and art. They challenge present-day education, advertisement and propaganda, which, as developed under capitalism, has helped to produce such criminal social disintegration.

To seize the moment and the means . . . To give an impetus and direction to this new adventure . . . It is a matter of some urgency . . .

In 1943 and 1944, Christesen had been struggling against the odds. The antics of Paper Control were a constant frustration, and the magazine was beset by mounting financial problems, especially after Christesen fell out with J. V. Duhig, who had promised to indemnify him financially, when Duhig showed an inclination to become more than a sleeping partner.

After working from an outpost within an outpost, the embattled young editor was understandably receptive when overtures came from the University of Melbourne. The university at that time had no literary or cultural magazine of standing, and elements within the university hierarchy felt that it would be better to take *Meanjin* on as a going concern than to start a new magazine from scratch. Their terms, at the time, seemed generous. It was informally agreed that Christesen would receive an annual stipend of £250 and retain his editorial authority, while the Press would relieve him of responsibility for physically producing and distributing the magazine. Nina Christesen, too, was offered a job as tutor with the University's Extension Board.

Yet, in spite of the high hopes expressed in the first editorial from *Meanjin*'s new home, there were worrying signs that something was amiss even before Christesen moved to Melbourne, as can be seen from the following letter to the general manager of MUP.

C. B. Christesen to G. J. James

Brisbane,
14 December 1944

Dear Mr James,

Thank you for your letter of December 1, which I received only a few days ago. I shall reply to it soon. First I wish to mention this matter.

Recently I was astounded to receive an order from Robertson & Mullens for 150 copies of Vol. 3, No. 3 *Meanjin* instead of for 1000 copies. I wrote seeking an explanation, mentioning that R&M took 200 copies of Vol. 3, No. 1 (which must have been sold, otherwise an order would not surely have been given for 1000 copies of Vol. 3, No. 2). Peters replied that you had advised him of the arrangement with the Melbourne University Press for 1945 and consequently it was not worth his while to handle the Victorian distribution for one issue only. Several letters have followed, explaining his position, which, from his point of view, is reasonable enough. But of course his belated decision has been a most severe blow to me. He left it very late to advise me of the changed arrangements, so late that I had already printed two forms of 4000 runs each. I am now likely to be landed with 1000 copies of this number. Melbourne bookshops take very few copies — 300 including Mullens' order of 150. No copies are distributed in the country, to my knowledge. I distribute more than that in Queensland.

I now wish to know whether your organisation can assist to dispose of these extra copies in Victoria — and elsewhere if possible. At this late stage I have decided to send copies of my contacts in Melbourne (about 300 copies), and the distribution list is very similar to that for Vol. 3, No. 2. It would seem to me that there would still be a fairly wide field available if contact could be made. If more than 1000 copies can be distributed in NSW surely a similar number could be distributed in Victoria.

Anyway, will you please let me know if you can assist? If M.U.P. cannot help in this matter, then I shall have to approach some other concern. For I shall take every possible step to prevent what threatens to be a most serious loss for me, and one which is likely to affect the whole future of *Meanjin*.

Relations between editors and production staff are seldom entirely smooth. Publishing is a closely interactive process, constantly performed under intense pressure of time; delays naturally tend to issue in mutual recrimination. In this case, there were special difficulties in adapting what had essentially been an amateur operation to the strict discipline of a professional press. The problems were compounded when, with typical high-handedness, Paper Control refused to give MUP a paper quota for *Meanjin*.

G. J. James to C. B. Christesen

7 June 1945

Dear Mr. Christesen,

Herewith my views on *Meanjin*.

(1) There are two separate issues to be discussed concerning the future of *Meanjin Papers*, (a) the remaining issues for 1945 and (b) the possible continuation of our association in and after 1946. In considering these issues, I am conscious of two things, namely, that no agreement has yet been signed, and that nothing that has so far been done by us for either the production or publication of *Meanjin Papers* has seemed to meet with your whole-hearted approval or satisfaction. I am quite confident, however, that no other publisher would have endeavoured to meet you to the same extent as M.U.P. and that no other publisher would have offered comparable terms.

(2) I now assume that you regard *Meanjin* primarily as a business venture. Our own attitude at the outset was not purely a business attitude; we wanted to assist in maintaining a journal which members of the Board and many other University people considered to be significant and valuable for Australian Literature. We also wanted to contribute something towards good typography in Australian publications, and to make *Meanjin* as good in its production as it had become in its content. What we cannot do, now or at any time, is sacrifice anything of our existing programme to this one item; nor can we make the association of M.U.P. with the journal so incidental as to reduce M.U.P to the status of a mere handy means to purely editorial ends.

(3) None of our proposals or actions in any way challenge or detract from the individuality of the journal. Your actions, however, are instantly entrenching on the field which we expressly reserved for ourselves from the beginning of negotiations — publication and distribution. . . .

(8) Your lay-out for an octavo letter-head refers to *Meanjin* as a 'National Journal of Literature and Art.' Elsewhere, and in the journal itself, it is referred to as a 'Quarterly of Literature.' Whatever arrangements may be made for building up the art side in 1946 onwards, when the problems of getting really suitable paper for half-tone insets have eased, I feel that it is unfair to the publishers to keep trying to push in the thin end of an art wedge during 1945. I am not complaining about four pages of pictures as in the current number. I am simply pressing for a definite acceptance of the present arrangement of copy until art work can be tackled properly. Even if D.I.P. approved of special paper for art work, remember that a permit to use paper is a vastly different thing from an assurance that it can be obtained when and as required.

(9) I could not recommend the Board to continue publication under our imprint in and after 1946 unless a much more detailed agreement is signed and adhered to without exception.

I am not satisfied that you have accepted even in principle any clear distinction between editing and publishing. You are obviously unwilling to leave distribution to our existing channels, otherwise you would not be worrying about 'copy' for newspaper advertising until opportunity had been given for reviews to appear.

Unless you will concentrate on copy for the journal, and produce it *all* cleanly typed and with all marks or instructions *carefully* indicated, and allow the future discussions of sales policy to be based on actual sales figures, then there will be constant friction. And in that case, it were better you went elsewhere. We have our hands too full to sacrifice everything to one item. We have pushed ahead with our plans for equipment and plant with the intention of building up *Meanjin* as No. 1 priority in our own printing programme. I think that this warrants some measure of appreciation, in a practical form. Otherwise the Press can be better employed handling the pocket editions that have been postponed for the time being while *Meanjin* is being established.

When all is said and done, there has been ample time for the full preparation of No. 2; but some of the items are written out in long-hand and the amendments to titles and so on are all done in a delightfully easy sweep of the pen which is understandable when seconds count, but which can and should be improved upon when fast, accurate and economical setting is sought after.

In general, I must frankly state that my own future interest in the journal depends entirely upon yourself. I feel that we have tried to meet you in a much more liberal and co-operative spirit than any commercial publisher would be prepared even to contemplate. Nevertheless, there are limits. *Meanjin* was not taken over simply and solely as a commercial proposition by the Press, but we cannot handle it other than on a clear, definite, and fully observed basis.

Either we publish and you edit or you are back to the Brisbane set-up. There's no half-way stage.

I am compelled to be blunt. Every time we offer an inch in concessions, a yard is seized as a first instalment.

Do not assume that I regard ourselves as beyond reproach. The first issue was late; this was partly due to the fact that copy was received later than expected and partly due to the job proving to be a bigger one than I had expected. Number 2 will not be delayed, but if *Meanjin* is henceforth to be produced on our newly-arrived equipment, then the points made in this letter must be noted and observed.

In 1945, for the second year in succession, only three issues of the magazine were published. Furthermore, the agreement between Christesen and the Press was still not finalized. Troubles continued to mount in the following year; the magazine's circulation declined to barely a thousand copies an issue, and the friction between the parties continued unabated. By the end of 1946 it had become clear that the relationship was simply not going to work, and Christesen abandoned the MUP association in favour of a distribution arrangement with Georgian House.

G. J. James to C. B. Christesen

14 February 1947

Dear Mr. Christesen,

I sincerely trust that the arrangements you have made for *Meanjin Papers* in 1947 will prove satisfactory. In order to make the change over as smooth as possible, I am having the subscription list checked over and brought right up-to-date. We should be able to hand this over next week, together with an analysis of the cards showing exactly how the current subscriptions stand. All moneys now received by us as subscription renewals are being held, and will be handed over with the cards so that there will be no confusion. . . .

The two years during which we have handled *Meanjin* were difficult years for all forms of publishing. And although the immediate future may not be what we would like it to be, I trust that M.U.P. did at least help *Meanjin* through and that your association with us may prove to have been a stepping stone to the final realisation of your hopes.

For once, the prognostication was probably correct, though finality in these matters is elusive. The association with the University of Melbourne gave *Meanjin* a physical base, a new authority and new connections. In particular, both Melbourne itself and the university community were far more cosmopolitan than Brisbane, and Christesen was able to secure a wide range of overseas contributions on literature and international affairs — 'London Letters' from Alex Comfort, a piece on 'The Intelligentsia' by Arthur Koestler, polemics by Sartre and, later, Arthur Miller, critical comments on literature and the war by Frank Kermode and Stephen Spender, to name only a few. At the same time *Meanjin* gave prominence to writing by Australians on world affairs, ranging from snippets of reportage by recently returned travellers to substantial articles that attempted to unravel the tangled political alignments of the postwar period as they affected Australia's position. The magazine's first peace-time issue included the following essay by Macmahon Ball, then professor of politics at the University of Melbourne.

Number 3, 1945

Australia in World Affairs

W. Macmahon Ball

During the last four years the Commonwealth Government has made a sustained and determined effort to ensure that Australia shall play an important part in world affairs. In particular, the Government has insisted that Australia must play a principal, not a subsidiary part, in deciding the terms of the peace settlement in the Pacific. There can be no doubt that during this period Australia has spoken with an independence, a clarity and an importunity that must have surprised other nations, and sometimes Australians themselves. And there is evidence that the Australian viewpoint has strongly influenced British and Allied decisions on a number of questions, some of which, such as the allocation of military forces to the Pacific, have been of extreme importance in maintaining the security of our mainland. Yet it seems equally clear that on other issues, issues which concern the basic pattern of the post-war world, Australia has failed to get her voice heard, still less to get it heeded.

At Cairo in December 1943 the American, British and Chinese leaders met to decide the essential terms of the peace-settlement with Japan. Australia was not consulted directly or indirectly, and the Commonwealth Government knew nothing of the decisions taken until they had been published in the press. Between the Cairo Conference and the Potsdam Conference of 1945, our Government constantly reiterated its claim to prior consultation on all matters directly affecting Australia. Yet at Potsdam, the Big Three formulated the terms of the ultimatum to Japan and published these terms to the world before Australia had received any offical advice about what was going on. In these circumstances, we can hardly refuse to recognise the measure of our present failure to exercise effective influence in international councils.

What are the causes of the failure? Do they lie outside our own control? Is it an inevitable failure, because our national ambitions have outstripped our national power? Or is the failure due, in great part, to weaknesses we can remedy? Perhaps nations, like individuals, do not grow evenly all over; perhaps while they grow to maturity in their capacity to make war and to organise industry, they may retain some of the characteristics of adolescence in their attitude to world affairs. There are some historical grounds for supposing that the conduct of foreign policy is the most difficult of all the arts for a young nation to master, and is usually the last to be acquired. . . .

For a people that claims the rights and privileges of independent nationhood, that is proud of its democratic traditions, we are singularly casual about our international responsibilities. I doubt whether there is any other country in the world controlling its own foreign policy, in which Parliament shows less interest in foreign affairs. On those rare and sporadic occasions on which the Commonwealth Parliament does discuss foreign affairs, the contributions to the debate, with few exceptions, are not well-informed, the atmosphere is generally listless, and the attendance generally poor. The Australian–New Zealand Agreement, which has set the course of our foreign policy these last two years, was not debated in the House of Representatives at all. When Mr. Menzies, the leader of the Opposition, was giving Parliament a searching analysis of the United Nations Charter, there were eleven members on the Government benches, and fourteen on the Opposition side; twenty-five members out of a total of seventy-four. . . .

No doubt the casual and perfunctory treatment that Parliament usually gives to international questions faithfully reflects a widespread lack of active interest among the Australian people. What is the use of complaining that the Great Powers ignore the Australian view if there is nothing here that can properly be called an Australian view? How many people in Australia, apart from a handful of officials and students, have tried to work out, on the basis of the most reliable information, the right line for Australia to take on any of the big questions that must be decided soon? Should the Japanese Emperor be retained, or should he be tried as a war criminal? Should Japan be deprived of her heavy industries? Or should Australia try to resume trade with Japan as soon as possible? Should we seek to encourage or oppose the Chinese 'Communists'? Should Australia subscribe to the Bretton Woods monetary agreement? The answers to these questions will have a great influence on Australia's future, and they are questions now being decided in the world's councils. What is the Australian view?

If Australia is to have a genuine public opinion on such major questions, we must do several things. We must organise and finance continuous research on world affairs, particularly Pacific affairs. This means a further extension of the Department of External Affairs. Dr. Evatt has made to Parliament a number of very able and careful statements, setting out the general line of Australian foreign policy. During the same period the Department of External Affairs has been considerably developed, and its senior officers are doing work of high quality. But these official statements in Parliament are not enough; they show activity at the Ministerial level, but not below it. Ordinary citizens know of these statements only through scattered snippets published by the press or radio. A Foreign Minister is not a foreign policy.

We must find a method to ensure that our voice will be heard in the right place and at the right time. This is partly a question of organisation, partly of manner and method. On the organisational side, the greatest present need is to establish smooth and continuously operating machinery for consultation between the British and Australian governments. The present methods of official consultation are unsatisfactory. Cairo and Potsdam are enough evidence of that.

Having decided what Australia wants to say, and having made sure that our voice is heard, brings us to the third and hardest question. We must develop the most effective manner and method to get our views accepted. We should recognise the importance of good manners in the conduct of our foreign relations. By good manners I do not mean that we should try to cultivate a merely superficial social technique, the polished insincerity of phrase that is popularly supposed to be the distinguishing mark of the successful diplomat. Good manners in a nation, as in an individual, must be rooted in a real respect for others, based on understanding and some sense of history. I think that one of our most serious weaknesses as a nation is not that we ourselves lack culture or character or intelligence, but that we lack sensibility about the culture and character and intelligence of other nations. We are dinkum Aussies, and don't set any great store by the Yanks or the Pommies or the Wops or the Chinks. The worst example of this is our attitude to our thousand million neighbours in the north. Most of us feel an instinctive superiority to people who can't speak English and whose skins are more heavily pigmented than ours. And if we are polite to these people our politeness has the insincerity of formal good manners and deceives nobody. If it were based on a real respect for their culture and their interests, we could afford to be quite blunt and frank in what we say. Verbal ineptitudes, such as the phrase 'White Australia policy' are always unfortunate, but they only do serious damage when they spring from lack of feeling and understanding, from pride and prejudice.

Having achieved the right manner we must go on to adopt the best method of getting Australia's view accepted. International politics is a tough game. A nation is not given influence and power in international negotiations as an expression of gratitude for its wartime services. We may regret this but it is no use being wistful about it. We must recognise the fact that a nation's influence in world affairs is in proportion to its power — its population, its physical resources, its industrial development. There are only three Great Powers in the world today — the United States, Russia and Great Britain. Hence Australia's influence will in the last analysis depend on the extent to which she can help shape the policy of one or several of the Big Three.

Recently Australia has been described as a leader of the small and middle Powers. At the San Francisco Conference Dr. Evatt was the most prominent spokesman of the 'Little Forty-five' against the veto powers of the 'Big Five.' It is sometimes claimed that if this Small Power leadership can be maintained it will bring great advantage to Australia, since it will mean that our policy will have the combined support of all except the Big Five. I think it important that we should get this question in true perspective. I believe that there are real and important advantages in the idea of Small Power solidarity, but it is a policy with very important practical limitations. Small Powers have much more to gain than the Great Powers by a system of collective security; by the rule of law in international life. Those who lack might will generally be the most sincere in their belief in right. For this reason the impetus towards a rule of right as distinct from a rule of might is likely to come from the smaller nations. Australia should take every opportunity to promulgate the ideal of collective security in the councils of the world and try to win the support of all small nations for this ideal. Meanwhile, we should not forget that, in present circumstances, the small nations are not a homogeneous group. Their ultimate interests may be identical: the rule of law. But their immediate interests are tied inexorably to the interests of their more powerful protectors. This came out very clearly at the San Francisco Conference. Czechoslovakia and Yugoslavia are small powers of Central Europe, but on issues Russia considered vital they voted with Russia. Norway and Denmark are small powers of Western Europe, but on issues Britain considered vital they voted with Britain. There is a number of small powers in Central and South America, and when the vote was primarily an opportunity for declaring their national faith, these Latin Americas voted with the Small Power bloc, together with Australia and New Zealand. But when it came to a show-down, when the policy meant something of concrete and immediate importance to the

United States, then the solidarity of the Small Powers was quickly dissolved and a sufficient number would swing over or abstain to give the United States policy the necessary majority. This means that today, and for the immediate future, the solidarity of the Small Powers tends to be ideological and abstract and is not based on tangible or immediate national interests. As a long term educational policy, the fostering of a sense of common interest among the small nations is important and valuable; but it is not likely to produce any immediate or tangible advantages.

This throws us back on the policies of the Big Three. That is the real centre of gravity. And of these three, it is through our influence on Britain that we have the best prospect of helping to shape the post-war world. It is true that in the early stages of the Pacific War, Australia was of great strategic importance to the United States. That however was partly due to the fact that the Japanese Mandated territories lay directly athwart the east-west approach of the United States to Japan, and enforced a south-north approach. If the United States retain the military control of all important islands in the north Pacific, this will considerably reduce Australia's value in United States strategy. From whatever way we look at it, I think we are forced back to the conclusion that Mr. Curtin reached after the British Commonwealth Prime Ministers' Conference in London last year: that it is as a member of the British Commonwealth that Australia can exercise most influence in world affairs.

The importance of maintaining the unity and strength of the British connection does not for a moment mean that Australia should passively acquiesce in British foreign policy. We should work out our own policy to meet our own needs. Our destiny lies mainly in the Pacific. England's destiny lies mainly in Europe. These geographical facts alone mean that Australian and British foreign policy will tend to emphasise different things. It is most desirable, for example, that we should get together with New Zealand in the effort to ensure that London is impressed with the vital importance of the South Pacific. In the past, Britain has tended to give rather a low priority to this area. But these are questions which we should try, as far as possible, to settle inside the British family.

We are an Australian nation with our own character and our own needs. But the power and dignity of our nationhood will be increased and not diminished if we show at every point our loyalty to those ideals which are not purely Australian, but which we share with all members of the British Commonwealth.

Ironically, just as Christesen's ambitions to develop the magazine as a forum for commentary on world affairs were within sight, the tide began to shift against him. During the war many writers and intellectuals had willingly lent their skills to the patriotic cause, but with the end of hostilities it was increasingly accepted orthodoxy that politics had no use for writers and intellectuals, and vice versa. One mechanism for policing

the separation was the Commonwealth Literary Fund. *Meanjin* succeeded in gaining a small 'emergency' grant of £100 from the fund in 1946, but this first experiment in assisting literary magazines was abruptly discontinued after Christesen published the following 'Trailer'.

Number 2, 1946

Elections in Europe

This is election year in Europe. The Dutch, the French, Belgians, Czechs, Hungarians, Italians — are all going to the polls. The odd thing is that, though our information about these elections is very sketchy, this does not deter the political sooth-sayers, the radio commentators and the press columnists from reaching strong conclusions. Of course, they do not all come to the *same* conclusion. Hell no! That would be bad for business. Some say the results are a victory for the Right, and some say they are a victory for the Left. Power over public opinion entails duties as well as rights. And surely, one of their duties is to give us the evidence on which they formed their opinions. But these gentlemen never try to make us well informed: their aim is to keep us well indoctrinated.

Here are some of the things we would need to know about these elections before we could gauge the trend of public opinion in any of the countries. 1) The distribution of the electorates: are they weighted in favour of any class or district, or are they divided on the strict principle of one man, one vote? 2) Which system of vote counting is being used — the 'first past the post,' the preferential system, or proportional representation? If either of the first two is being used, then the number of votes won by each party will tell us more than the number of seats gained. 3) What attempts were made to influence or intimidate electors by persons enjoying a privileged position in those countries? How did the British use their power in Greece? How did MacArthur use his power in Japan? People who are used to voting under duress may infer that the occupying power expects approval of its own political sympathies — even if the occupying power makes a fetish of 'impartiality.' But we do not know for certain the answer to any one of these questions. We do know that, despite the idle vapourings on 'Latin luminosity' and 'national character,' the central issue in Europe is still between the Left and the Right. We do know that they are the symbols for two distinct ideas on how society ought to be organised. We do know too, that the tradition of government by discussion is rather feeble in *all* of these countries, and this in itself should counsel caution and sympathy in our comments. But we cannot make these comments until we have more information. So, please, ye gentlemen of the press, ye men who handle the cables, give us this knowledge; or if it is not available here, request your representatives in Europe to send it.

ELECTIONS IN AUSTRALIA

It is also election year in Australia. Here too, the central issue will be between the Left and the Right — with a difference. Some of the believers in socialism are not convinced that the Labour Party intends to create a socialist society. This explains why some on the Left are sceptical about Labour, and why some of them are very angry. It also helps to explain the attitude of the owners of the big monopolies to a Labour government. It poses an awkward problem for them. The plain fact is that for them a Labour government which is not socialist is preferable to a non-Labour government. For two reasons: 1) It would be more efficient than its opponents, and big business likes efficiency; 2) there would be less industrial friction. The record of Labour in the industrial field since 1941 shows this pretty clearly, and big business is not slow to scent out the government which can preserve industrial peace, even if its principles are rather radical. The poser for big business to decide is how long they can rely on Labour not to carry out its socialist programme. So long as Labour soft pedals on the question of ownership, big business may continue to rely on working with Labour, and Labour may continue to ape the way of life of its opponents. Of course, the potential 'troopers' on the Right will go on ranting about the red menace, and the angry men of the Left will talk about traitors and wreckers. The people of Australia, however, do not have to choose between a socialist and a capitalist society this year.

This does not mean that all the main parties believe in the same type of society. Labour's society would be more humane, less ruthless than the opposition's. After all, there must be some reason for the anti-Labour propaganda barrage. Perhaps the most interesting thing will be popular reaction to this onslaught. If the people stand firm one's belief in human progress will be strengthened. One of the important differences between the Right and the Left is just on this question of human nature — the Right being pessimistic, and the Left optimistic. The judgment of the Australian people will probably provide evidence for both sides!

Christesen's comments won him no friends on either side of politics. With Labor running out of steam and struggling to hold onto power against the resurgent conservative forces, neither party was especially tolerant of criticism. The use of CLF money had also become a political hot potato after it was revealed that a grant had been given to J. N. Rawling, an ex-Communist, to write a literary biography. Christesen was informed of the dire consequences by Tom Inglis Moore, a Canberra literary critic and writer who was one of *Meanjin*'s staunchest allies. As Inglis Moore's letter makes clear, the decision to cut off *Meanjin*'s funding was not made by the CLF [Advisory] Board, which was drawn from the ranks of writers and scholars, but by the Parliamentary Committee that had ultimate authority for the disbursement of funds.

T. Inglis Moore to C. B. Christesen

16 April 1947

. . . I'm sorry, while on M[eanjin] P[apers] that some political comment in your 'Trailer' drew, inevitably, of course, unanimous objection from the C.L.F. Committee, overwhelming the Board. I did suggest that a random and minor piece of political comment shouldn't be stressed and put out of proportion as against the major literary subject matter and valuable aid to literature of M.P., but the Parliamentarians would have none of this, and it cut no ice whatever.

I'm particularly sorry that you entered the political field in this way in that the M.P. comment has killed all hope of the Literary Fund sponsoring literary magazines in the future, so that 'Poetry' and 'Southerly', for instance have been denied the aid given to 'M.P.' and there will be no more subsidies in future — or at least during the lifetime of the present members of the Committee. In principle, of course, they're right, that Government aid cannot be given to a magazine which is political not purely literary, in content, no matter what brand of politics. On the other hand, I've always felt strongly — and still feel — that financial aid to literary magazines is one of the most practical and fruitful ways of the Fund helping Australian literature. I feel it's a great pity that the first step in this direction will also be the last. The goose is killed. There will be no more golden eggs.

Australia has advanced, but not to the point, evidently, where we can combine Grant aid with social freedom of literary journals. In this respect Vance Palmer's prophecies have proved more correct than my hopes. Still, it was worth trying, and at least has given you a chance to develop M.P.

Support was again refused in 1948 and 1949. Privately Christesen canvassed the possibility of closing the magazine; to make ends meet, he took a position as Australasian manager for the British publishing firm Heinemann in 1948. In less than three years he trebled the business, but keeping *Meanjin* going while working at the new job imposed both physical and political strains. Almost as soon as Christesen arrived at his new office there was a move to sack him in retaliation for an unfavourable review by A. D. Hope of a Heinemann poetry anthology. In the following year, Christesen again encountered trouble on several fronts after *Meanjin* published an essay that struck hard at the politics of the mainstream press.

Political Bias of the Press

E. P. Dark

From all parts of the world the daily Press has been for some time clamouring about threats to its freedom; our own newspapers have taken their full share of the clamour, so it is opportune to examine critically just how free it is.

There are very definite standards to which a Press calling itself free should conform: Its news service should be unaffected by any political or racial bias; its correspondence columns should be open equally to all sides of any serious political or social discussion; they should also be open to reasoned criticism of any opinion expressed by the paper itself, and such criticism should have the same prominence as the original opinion. When any important news reported is later proved, or stated on reasonable authority, to have been incorrect, the correction should be as prominent as the original report.

These criteria are not mere foibles. The public importance of an unbiassed Press can hardly be exaggerated in a modern democracy, since in the democratic State policy should be shaped largely by the force of public opinion, which, in its turn, is shaped by what the public believes to be happening. Obviously, if its Press continually feeds it misstatements or untruths, the opinions it forms must be worse than useless; they must be dangerous, since they will be formed on a false view of events, and no policy based on an untruth can be anything but disastrous.

One example should be enough to illustrate this: before the last war practically all the world Press lied about developments in Russia, and particularly about the strength of her industry and of her armed forces. As a result the great mass of the public formed a quite incorrect idea of the value of Russia as an ally against the menace of Germany, which made it easy for the Chamberlain Government to follow its disastrous policy of appeasement during the Austrian and Czechoslovakian crises. If the people had been told the truth by their Press, public opinion might have been strong enough to prevent the tragedies that followed. The public could hardly form a just estimate of Russian power when it was constantly fed with statements like that of the Sydney *Bulletin* of 7.12.1938: 'Moscow and its panegyrists . . . perpetrated acres of mush about the Might of the Soviet War Machine. Their bluff was called in September. The impression left in impartial quarters was that the Russian Army would be hard put to it to beat the Salvation Army.' Of course, not much of the world's Press could equal such crude vulgarity, but the import was the same, and without question the responsibility for the unspeakable horrors of the last war falls largely on its political bias.

The present attitude of our Press to overseas news is well illustrated by the way in which it handled the crisis in the Hungarian Parliament in June,

1947. The headlines spoke constantly of a 'Communist Coup,' with sub-headings to the effect that Smallholder Premier Nagy was forced to resign by the Russians and the Hungarian Communists. The only reasonable interpretation would be that the Communists had violently seized power, and that was the suggestion of most of the Press. Then, on June 7, the *Sydney Morning Herald*, in heavy type, across two columns, says, 'Hungarian Premier's Son as Hostage in Communist Coup,' followed by the statement that 'Communists who carried out a coup in Hungary this week forced the Premier, Mr. Ferenc Nagy, to resign by threatening to kill his four-year-old son, according to Mr. Nagy's eldest son . . .' There was only one possible way to take the *Herald* headline, that is, as a statement of fact. But if we read further on into the smaller print we find that it was simply the reported ex-parte statement of a witness who was very likely to be biassed; and if we read further still we see that the eldest son was at the time in Washington, many thousands of miles away. Two days later the *Herald*, having already stated that Mr. Nagy had been forced to resign by Russians and Communists, says that he himself stated that he was asked to resign by M. Balogh, Secretary to the Smallholders Party, 'in view of feeling in the Cabinet and the Smallholders Party.'

During the period of the 'crisis' the Press consistently denied the report that there had been a threat to the safety of the Hungarian Republic from the Right, saying that it was only a Communist fabrication to excuse their coup, and conveniently forgetting what had been reported in their own columns just three months before. The *Sunday Telegraph* of March 9 had said: '. . . Thousands of reactionaries, former Horthyites, and even straight out Nazis, joined the Small Landholders because it was the only non-Marxist, national political organisation of any significance. Their plan was to infiltrate the party, to occupy key positions, and eventually grab the reins of government. Repeatedly the party had to purge members; although a genuine democratic political organisation, the scandalous political past of some of its members did it a lot of harm. To make matters worse, two Horthyite conspiracies were detected within three months. Former Army officers, members of the diplomatic staff of the Foreign Ministry, and others were involved. . .'

If, then, one takes the trouble to read carefully through all the small print, it becomes evident that what really happened was that Mr. Nagy was asked to resign by his own party, and was replaced by another member of the Smallholders; that there had been a Right-wing plot to seize power; that the balance of power in the Parliament was not affected, and that ordinary Parliamentary government continued. For the *Herald* reported, in a not very prominent place, on June 27: 'There was another violent scene in the Hungarian Parliament yesterday, but it ended in the rejection of a motion by the Communists and Socialists. They sought to have a non-party member of the House . . . brought before the Privileges Committee, because, in a speech in Parliament, he had called a former Socialist Deputy a traitor.' A party that had just seized power would not tamely submit to a democratic vote.

This brief examination of the Press handling of the Hungarian crisis shows one of the methods used for distortion — the view to be impressed on the minds of the public is given in heavy headlines; anything that conflicts with that view is put well down the column in small print; previous news that may negative the effect aimed at is ignored. The efficiency of this method depends on the well-known fact that most readers of a paper merely glance at the headlines, and do not remember news more than a few days old, unless the subject is of special interest to them; and unfortunately it is doubtful if any but a small percentage of readers is well enough educated to study foreign and political news with a critical eye. . . .

The Press reporting of the Melbourne tram strike of January, 1948 gives a fair indication of its attitude to Labour in general, and especially to the Left-wing. Practically all the papers ignored the background of the strike, picturing it as a wanton outrage on the public, engineered by Communists. The men, in fact, had a reasonable case; when the 40-hour-week became law, industry generally began to arrange its rosters for a five-day week. In November, 1947, the members of the Tramways Union, in a secret ballot, voted 5 to 1 for a five-day week, and notified the Victorian Premier and the Tramways Board. By this time most employers in transport and industry had arranged for the shorter week, including the management of the tramways in other Victorian cities, Tasmania, Queensland and N.S.W. The men offered to work 44 hours, six days a week, on the usual shifts, with pay for overtime, until the Tramways Board could take on enough extra men to permit the working of the 40-hour five-day week. But the Board was adamant, and the strike began. I did not see that background fairly stated in the Press, which pictured the strike as utterly irresponsible, provoked and led by Communists.

After 13 days it ended on these terms: the Board to apply the 40-hour week; 5-day rosters to be prepared and posted by April 1, but not later than April 15; the Board to pay overtime in excess of 40 hours; all meal breaks in excess of an hour to be paid as time worked. This was almost exactly what the men had claimed from the start, yet when they returned to work the Sydney Press wrote of it as a Communist rout. The *Daily Telegraph* had a leader and another long article eulogising the Liberal Government for the strong line which had led to this great victory over the subversive Communists. Any reader who had not heard the ABC news, which gave, with admirable impartiality, the terms of settlement, would have been completely deceived about the result of the strike (as well as about its causes), for I searched that issue of the *Telegraph* in vain for any mention of the terms of settlement.

To blame the Communists for the strike was as false as most of the other Press statements about it, seeing that the men decided to insist on a five-day week by an 80 per cent majority in a secret ballot. . . .

Finally, the Press constantly smothers discussion after some particularly biassed anti-Left article. Four times in the last two or three years I have written to the *Sydney Morning Herald*, temperately pointing out obvious inaccuracies in such articles; in no case was my letter, or any other critical letter, published; so the biassed statements went unanswered.

There is little doubt but that distortion and suppression would be far more blatant than they are now, if it were not for the objectivity of the ABC news service. It is easy to understand the tenacity of the fight waged by the proprietors of the Press to prevent the ABC from having an independent service, and their generous offers to make their own available at cut rates. If the independent news service of the ABC cost us ten times as much as it does, it would be well worth the price.

I have dealt mainly with the *Sydney Morning Herald*, because of its reputation as the most important, the most accurate, the most sober and respectable of all our papers; but any daily would provide similar examples.

We find that the inaccuracies and the bias all conform exactly to one pattern; they are all directed against the Left — against the USSR; against the Eastern European Democracies; against the Communists; against Labour (except the Right-wing).

The reason is obvious; the daily papers are all owned, or have their policy directed, by wealthy men, who fear the growing strength of socialism.

But the results of this policy of suppression and distortion are vitally important; it has already created artificial divisions, tensions and hatreds in our society and, if continued, may easily lead to civil strife. Further, all who depend on the Press for international news must have an utterly false picture of the world; a picture that will inevitably cause an irrational distrust, fear and hatred of the Soviet Union; emotions that can make a sane foreign policy impossible, and might well end by dragging us into an unnecessary and disastrous war.

Much has been said lately about the importance of a free Press. I agree that there can be hardly anything in the world more important, but unfortunately we have not got it; our Press is bound hand and foot to the interests of a group of men who for their own selfish purposes are using every device in their power to prevent their readers from knowing the truth. When one seriously considers the possible results of this policy one is justified in accusing those responsible for it of being the most deadly enemies of our country.

C. B. Christesen to Dr E. P. Dark

16 May 1949

Dear Eric Dark,

. . . The Autumn *Meanjin* has been well received in most quarters, but very badly in others. In fact it precipitated a first rate row with my printer. He ear-bashed, bulldozed and bullied me for about two hours, alleging I was a Communist and that the magazine was a Communist undercover organ. He refused in future to allow his press to be used for 'such shameful propaganda.' So I'll have now to find another printer — if I can; though there is just a chance that, with so much overset matter, I may get this next issue printed by

Speciality Press. There is just a remote chance. Anyway, I'm already looking round for a suitable printer. Not easy to find, for the printer, Allan McKay, warned me that he would see to it that none of the big printing houses took on *Meanjin*! It was not only your article that offended McKay — he also took exception to Manning Clark's and Jim Cairns's. The state of the nation. I have also been sacked from my job as book reviewer for the *Digest of World Reading* — a Speciality Press publication. McKay also warned me that I might lose my job with William Heinemann Ltd. Speciality Press is the chief printer of Heinemann books in Australia.

So you see I have had a very nice time of it lately. On top of everything, a large number of booksellers have cancelled their orders. We have lost about a thousand within the last few weeks. Obviously someone has got at McKay — and at some of the booksellers too. I was informed by a staff member that [Keith] Murdoch sent for a copy.

I'll keep going somehow — though the winter issue will be smaller and very late.

T. Inglis Moore to C. B. Christesen

Canberra University College,
17 March 1949

Dear Clem

. . . I've been going to write to you ever since the last disastrous meeting of the CLF committee, but have been entangled with College work. Temby told me he was writing to you, and by now you will have also seen Vance or Flora.

The Committee's decision is a bad blow, and I know how you must be feeling about it. When I heard the bad news from Temby straight after the meeting, I felt so sick about it over the whole week-end that I didn't feel like writing to you or anyone about it. It's been a bitter disappointment to me personally, since I believe so strongly in the policy of aiding the magazines and spent a lot of time, which I couldn't really afford, on trying to do something. The Board went through my memo thoroughly, after I made some changes in the original draft along the lines you suggested, and Flora wrote some extra material. The case was put as fully and strongly as possible by the Board in its recommendation to the C'ee, whilst Harold White, who was present at the C'ee meeting, put up a stout fight for it. At least the Board, therefore, did all it possibly could. Also Haylen did some personal urging with Chif, White with Fadden, and myself with Menzies. You might say, in best journalese, we left no stone unturned — except the hearts of stone beating under the breasts of the politicians!

Even before the meeting, it would seem, Chif and Menzies — since Fadden hardly counts — had made up their minds against the subsidy, for different reasons. Chif, I gather, has the current Labour movement prejudice against anything intellectual (I say 'current' since the original Labour stalwarts were keen on education, educated themselves, and respected knowledge and matters cultural in themselves). Chif feels that the literary magazines cater only for a small minority of intellectuals, that they offer nothing to the great masses of horny-handed workers, that they would be meaningless to the ordinary rank and file of trade unionists, and therefore he is out of sympathy with them. Also I suspect that he is doubtful lest something of a political nature might appear and lead to attacks on the Government similar to those made recently on Rawling and the Commonwealth Office of Education poster in Parliament. He wants no trouble in the House, and wants to play safe, especially as, again, the ordinary Labour member and his party rank and file would have no interest in, or sympathy with, the magazines.

Menzies, on the other hand, is against Government aid, a form of socialization, on political principle. He thinks the magazines should fight and survive — or perish — as examples of free and private enterprise. He, too, would want to play safe in the case of criticism in the House, since he is responsible for the CLF policy as a member of the C'ee, and doubtless wants to avoid the sort of awkward situation that arose when the Country Party attacked the Govt. on the Rawling issue, and he kept discreetly, if ignobly, out of sight. . . .

In December 1949, after a turbulent year in which the Chifley government had signalled its break with the left wing of the labour movement by sending troops to break a coal strike, Robert Gordon Menzies began his second term as Prime Minister of Australia. During his election campaign Menzies had pledged to ban the Communist Party. His accession to office marked the beginning of a protracted witch-hunt, directed not only against known Communists but also against 'fellow travellers'. The latter included many intellectuals who had been active in the peace movement and in civil liberties organizations. Christesen, who had campaigned vigorously for both causes, found himself in this category, along with a substantial number of *Meanjin* contributors.

The consequences were profound. The CLF was constantly under attack for funding 'Communist' writers, and the fact that several of the supposed offenders had published in *Meanjin* made the magazine a prime target for right-wing critics. There were parallel moves within the university. Sensitivities had been aroused by press attacks on the university for harbouring 'Red Professors', and the administration moved to restrict Christesen's editorial autonomy. In 1950 an Advisory Committee was set up to supervise the magazine, as a condition of *Meanjin*'s gaining a share of the Lockie Bequest for Australian literature. For the rest of the decade relations between *Meanjin* and the university were uneasy. In 1952 the magazine's support was halved, and the situation only improved in the following year after Christesen, in desperation, threatened to abandon the entire enterprise. Nina Christesen, too, came under pressure. She had moved from her original position at the Extension Board to become founding lecturer in Russian, only to find herself in the middle of a political minefield.

Like all good witch-hunts, the Cold War anti-Communist scare placed its victims in a conundrum: there was no surer way of proving one's guilt than to protest one's innocence, let alone to take a wider stand on civil liberties at a time when civil-liberties organizations were under a cloud. In response, Christesen trod a careful line between honesty and discretion. He restricted comment on political matters to a minimum (sometimes under pressure from the Advisory Committee), and cleverly opted to outflank his critics by focusing attention, not on the local political situation, but on the parallel McCarthyist moves in America.

Nevertheless, the influence of the Ministry of Fear was pervasive. A number of writers began to shy away from the magazine to avoid guilt by association. At times Christesen was driven close to despair. Unable to vent his bitterness publicly, he poured it out in his correspondence, as in this short note asking Miles Franklin to contribute to a fiction anthology that he was editing:

C. B. Christesen to Miles Franklin

8 May 1953

Have you a story for *Coast to Coast*? I'll be hard-pressed to find twenty or so suitable stories. Not writing now seems to be the occupational disease of Australian writers. As for *Meanjin* — I'm damned if I know why I bother to publish the journal. The list of those who no longer contribute, or have never contributed, grows . . . — I could fill a page.

Throughout the mid-1950s the magazine was embattled on several fronts. The Christesens were hauled up before the Petrov Commission, political opponents attempted to sabotage *Meanjin*'s CLF support, and the university, alarmed at the mounting financial deficit, threatened to refuse to pay the magazine's bills, sending Christesen on a frantic search for new sources of support.

C. B. Christesen to A. D. Hope

5 April 1955

. . . The office is pretty well at a standstill and the disorganization incredible. I'm beefing out this note myself because I no longer have a secretary — Pat [Excell] has married and gone abroad.

I understand from Ian [Maxwell, chairman of the *Meanjin* advisory board] that he wrote recently to [ANU Vice-Chancellor] Melville, asking whether it would be worthwhile to seek financial help for *Meanjin* from the National University. If Melville says there might be a chance of help, then an official approach would be made to him. If he says No, then that would be the end of that. I wish Ian had discussed the matter with me in some detail first. However, it was very decent of him to think of writing a personal unofficial note to Melville; and I most sincerely hope something comes of the tentative enquiry. I gather that Ian thinks, as you also know the Vice, you might consider having an informal talk to him.

A few weeks ago I was told that *Meanjin* finances are in a bad way. Ever since I came down here in 1945 I have sought but never obtained quarterly statements. There has really never been a manager, in anything like the proper sense of the term. Despite initial promises and undertakings by the University, I found that I made up the monetary loss each year, until the last two or three years. Once I was in a position to do that, though my household and personal affairs suffered gravely. From 1945 to about 1950 the yearly loss to me averaged about £400. My accountants, Messrs Gandy and Skate, now tell me that I have sunk well over £7000 into *Meanjin* — that is recorded in the books, but they point out that I paid cash for very many things and they can only surmise that the total expenditure was about double that figure since 1940 when I first published the damn journal. For instance, from about 1943 to about 1949 I paid some £800 to contributors out of my own pocket. Obviously *Meanjin* has been a most expensive 'hobby'. I lost £100 cold when old Capt Peters of Robertson & Mullens broke his promise regarding a firm order for copies of the journal — in 1944 or 1945. I lost another £100 when the late Walter Cousins also broke his promise — as a result of pressure from one of the Priors of *The Bulletin*, after I had published an article by S J Baker, 'The Demise of *The Bulletin*.' Cousins cancelled the whole of A&R's order. Then in 1947, as a result of the British Board of Trade's embargo on Aust books and publications — acting under Article 9 of the American Loan agreement — I lost in that year £400. Then another £400 loss resulted when the Department of Information abruptly cancelled its order for *Meanjin* — the time when the Chifley Govt was turfed out by Menzies. That sort of thing would not have been tolerated by a 'regular' publishing firm; but *Meanjin*, being a small venture, does not seek redress, etc. For one thing I hadn't the time, nor the experience, and so on. I footed the bill myself. Nina went without new clothes, we did not have holidays, we did not buy much new furniture, sheets, blankets, curtains, etc. Always she urged me to 'cover' *Meanjin* financially. But cost of living jumped so high that eventually I simply could not afford to do that. It was then that I was forced to make a desperate bid to obtain regular financial help from the University. Fortunately, through the good offices of Maurice Brown, I obtained aid from the Lockie Bequest, and later from the CLF. All most inadequate, though; and I still had to pay many of the running costs out of my own pocket. All book, periodical, magazine, newspaper expenses, for instance, running into at least £200 a year — plus subs to various literary and art societies, and so on. I also paid Betty Vassilieff £4.10.0 a week for editorial help, and a lass from the Phil dept whose name I can't recall — for extra typing help. Pat Excell came in at £200 a year, and she worked full-time — though she could have obtained, had been obtaining, more than double that figure elsewhere. Over the five years she was with me I gradually managed to get her salary increased to £550 a year. We could not cope with the amount of office work, however, and I continued to pay out of my own pocket for extra office help. The beginning salary for a young tissey without any experience at all is about £620 a year. . . .

Well, I am now informed that the *Meanjin* account is overdrawn about £1200. The Vice has written to say that no bills will be paid unless they receive his personal ok. The autumn issue is being printed, and will be ready for distribution next week or the week after. God knows how it will be distributed, for I can't make sense of the mess Pat has left. Most of the copy for the winter issue has been subbed, and some of it is in type. But it looks as though no further issues of the journal will be published unless the whole office is reorganised and we manage to obtain extra finance. Ian says that the University commitments — £650 from the Lockie estate and £50 from the General Fund — cannot be increased. However the Vice says that 'it is obvious' that extra money must come from the General Fund. I had a very courteous interview with him a few days ago. He agreed with me all along the line and was most co-operative and sympathetic. But in the past I have always had a similar reception — and yet nothing has been done. The humbug, year after year, has caused me a great deal of worry and anxiety and considerable financial loss. Fundamentally, the administration is not interested in what *Meanjin* is striving to achieve — though God knows I've talked long and often enough about the role or function of such a journal. To most people here, *Meanjin* is a 'good idea', vaguely worthy of support — but there the matter ends. I was brought down from Brisbane by Medley to do a certain job. My association with the English department was pleasant and close until Seccombe died. Then the situation changed. The journal was intended to act as a forum for published work by members of the Arts faculty, particularly the English dept. But over the years singularly little work has in fact come from members of the Eng dept. I'm not commenting on that — doubtless reasons can be given why that was so — but I have in the past objected to the kind of criticism levelled against *Meanjin*, often most ignorantly based. I've simply done the best possible, with the given material. Occasionally members of the English dept., including yourself and Ian, have kindly read manuscripts and commented; but no one has worked on the editorial side, no one has come in to give help as, say, assistant editor. . . .

During the past two years (I think) I have been receiving £100 a quarter 'out of pocket expenses.' Ian himself said recently that if I were a staff member that would be 'sweated labour.' But as I am not on the staff, seemingly it is not exploitation. NO ONE has even attempted to investigate my personal situation — to find out how on earth I manage to keep going, year after year, on such a pittance. NO ONE has thought of the psychological effect on me — quite deplorable, I might say. I have no *standing* in this university community, no *practical* help, no means of running the office or the affairs of the journal efficiently. I feel as though I'm trying to do a job with both hands tied behind my back. Yet seemingly I am blamed for letting the financial affairs get into a mess. It is an entirely impossible position. When I had a full-time job in the city I just about managed to keep the journal alive — by giving almost every evening and most week-ends to *Meanjin* affairs. The journal is larger now, the pattern of activity centring around it very much greater. Last year I was forced to give almost ALL my time to the magazine — for £400. I can no longer afford to do that. Unless I am paid to do a full-time job this year — and believe me it is more than a full-time job — I shall, whatever happens within the next week or so, be forced to concentrate on my own work. That means that I shall not be able to come into the office during the daytime, or scarcely ever, but shall try to come in for a few nights. Which will mean that unless I have daytime staff to carry out my instructions, the journal will simply not be able to continue. But to have staff will require money. . . .

But I can't write any more, Alec. The fact that I have written so much and at such speed is probably indicative of my state of mind. I'm worried ill by the whole rotten business. It looks as though 14–15 years of my life are about to go down the bloody drain. No money is available. Yet you and I know that in point of fact money *could* be available. Men of vision are extremely rare, in any community, I suppose. My few qualifications are not much, God knows; but at least I've tried to do what will in years to come prove to be fairly worth while. This journal will be remembered, and used, long after many people at this University will be forgotten. Its job, its usefulness is not done — indeed it has scarcely begun. To my mind it is now extremely important to keep it going — and not only to keep it alive but to place it on a regular and proper footing; to consolidate and then to extend its function, its activities. The editor should be paid, staff should be paid, and contributors should be paid. It's not decent to let the thing agonize like this year after year, just because the nominal owner is mug enough to continue making sacrifice after sacrifice. . . .

For Pete's sake have a word with Melville. Try to interest him in this suggestion. At least try to keep the door open, so that a proper proposal could be submitted later, details worked out, etc. But if he says No to Ian, then *Meanjin* is up the bloody creek. And pardon this long screed. I'm sitting amid piles of correspondence going back three weeks or more much of it still unopened. Nina and I have been coming in at night, and working here until 2:30 am and even later, trying to clean up the bloody mess. Without Nina's help and encouragement I'd have packed up long ago.

The proposal, however, came to nothing, and the magazine was also unsuccessful in gaining support from the Victorian State Cultural Fund; though the Premier, John Cain senior, had promised a grant on receipt of an official request from the Vice-Chancellor, the request never arrived. Through these times of tribulation, Christesen drew some sustenance from his relationship with Stephen Murray-Smith, who had founded *Overland* in 1954. Murray-Smith was generous in his support of *Meanjin* and its editor. Being a man with a flair for practical politics, he leapt to *Meanjin*'s defence on several occasions when its CLF funding was under attack. He also offered a sympathetic ear and personal reassurance to

Christesen when the elder editor was close to despairing of the whole enterprise.

C. B. Christesen to Stephen Murray-Smith

23 June 1955

. . . I suppose, to use Jacob Burckhardt's phrase, 'a man is only interested as long as he loves something'. I haven't many faiths; but one of them is a faith in the 'common man' to realize, ultimately, Bernard O'Dowd's dream of the Just City. I have always felt that Australia, my native country, has a better chance of making that dream a reality than have most other countries. I love this country, know more of it and about it than many other Australians. I began publishing *Meanjin* because I too had a Dream — an Idea. (I wrote in an early issue, '*Meanjin* is an Idea — and I'm hanged if you can wring the neck of an Idea'!)

But . . . fifteen years is a long period of time in a man's life. If I were myself creating, writing, perhaps I would not feel so browned off. Work begun has remained unfinished. There's the rub, I suspect. The daily slug at routine matters, the sheer physical and mental effort required to bring out even four issues a year under these inadequate conditions, seems to have drained me of any vital creative ability. It's got to the stage now when I doubt my ability to do any creative writing of my own. I feel I have for too long been a nurse-maid to other writers. Bob FitzGerald warned me of the danger long ago, and so did Jim Devaney. But what was I to do? Wring the neck of the Idea? Nina says that the production of *Meanjin* is in itself 'creative'; and so it is, in a sense — but not in my sense. Note that I am not alone in this feeling of failure. I know something of the effect of this work on others — on Howarth, for instance, on both Reed and Harris, on Hudson; and, particularly, read what Cyril Connolly had to say, when *Horizon* folded up! Similar bitterness was expressed by Lehmann upon the demise of *New Writing*, and by Leavis when *Scrutiny* ceased publication a year ago. This is not said by way of self-justification — I am merely pointing to similar phenomena.

All right. In this form of society one has to 'live' — one has to be able to earn enough money to pay for this, that and the other thing. Perhaps it is my bourgeois hangover — I want the wrong thing and am obsessed with a feeling of humiliation when I regard my more successful colleagues and old school mates. Perhaps I should say, with Socrates in the bazaars of Athens: 'How many things there are I do not want!' Fair enough. But my *wants* are not so many — though my *needs* might be greater, or less obtainable. Mainly, immediately, I want *not* to be a drag on Nina. Rather, it is high time things were made easier for *her*, after all the years of exceptionally hard struggle. And I can't do anything, materially, to alleviate the position. I can just about afford to come in and out of the city, pay for a few meals, pay for a few household expenses. More than £7,000 have gone into keeping this magazine alive — money from personal income, not inheritance. Now I'm flat; and fifteen years older. I have had extensive experience on newspapers, here and in England. But I'll never again work for salary on a newspaper. I have some knowledge of publishing, and a great liking for it. But I can't afford to set up my own business; and a publishing industry scarcely exists in this country. I do not possess the formal qualification necessary to secure a good teaching job; anyway I doubt whether I am temperamentally suited to that kind of work. Several recommended applications for Public Service jobs have come to nothing — not even an interview. Security, I am quite certain, on the information I have received, have seen to that. Last year I devoted two days a week to gardening, at £2-15-0 a day. I suppose I should stick to that kind of work. I've thought of various other jobs, but always I've lacked either the capital or the ability to see them through. But even if I obtained a fine full-time job next week, it would mean the end of this journal, unless I could find someone capable of taking over. For this job is in fact a full-time job — a fact that no-one seems to be able to understand. When I was in the city a few years ago I kept *Meanjin* alive by the skin of my teeth — by coming into this office night after night, after a hard day's work; and by taking work home every weekend. Since then the journal has developed, the pattern of activity has increased; and the office is only now beginning to be reorganised, following Pat's departure.

The Idea is still alive; but the psychological damage has been considerable. It *is* humiliating to find that this kind of work, this kind of national contribution, is held at such a low discount.

In the latter part of 1956 the university moved to take direct control over the magazine. Christesen had announced his intention of spending a large part of the following year overseas, as Nina was lecturing at Oxford. Various schemes were put forward — for the installation of a salaried academic editor (with an accompanying restriction of the magazine's scope); for a merger with another journal; and for the complete closure of the magazine. After endless negotiations, Christesen pre-empted his opponents with the announcement that Geoffrey Serle had agreed to act as editor in his absence in 1957.

The editorial voice in 1956 had been as strong as ever, but increasingly gloomy and self-absorbed, preoccupied with local troubles. The Suez crisis and the Russian invasion of Hungary were allowed to pass with barely a mention. The latter crisis profoundly shook the Australian left, and was the subject of the editorial in Serle's first issue as acting editor.

Number 1, 1957

Editorial: 'A Crisis of Conscience'

During the appalling events of the last five months, men have been forced to choose, to decide, as rarely in a lifetime, on momentous matters of conscience. As usual we in Australia only felt the backwash of world currents of opinion: even though on one of the great issues we were committed by our Government to a course of action which might have seemed quixotic, were it not so fateful, in its almost lone support for a hopeless and discreditable enterprise. In Britain, on the other hand, the nation was deeply and bitterly divided. In the House of Commons there was violence of speech and behaviour on a scale previously unknown in this century. In their comments on events in both Suez and Hungary, newspapers such as the *Manchester Guardian* and the *Observer* renewed the liberal tradition with noble and moving sentiments and language. Men were so stirred that one, Philip Toynbee, could make the suggestion — absurd only in this day and age — of a pilgrimage of youth to Hungary as a plea to the Russians, in the spirit of 'Ghandi and Christian humility' and as an 'act of penance for the crimes of the West' including the 'crime against Egypt.'

There have been many revolutions in Europe in which 'students and intellectuals' have played an important part. In none more than the Hungarian revolution of 1956, can the origins and driving-force be more clearly attributed to writers and students. The Hungarian Writers' Association and the Petöfi Club (Petöfi was a nineteenth century poet) were centres of bold criticism of the regime and ultimately gave the signal for open resistance. Leading members of the Writers' Association in the exhilarating moment of freedom acted as a brains-trust for Prime Minister Nagy. The last tragic appeal for help from Radio Kossuth was theirs. And now more than twenty leading writers have been arrested or executed; the fate of George Lukács, the marxist scholar whom Thomas Mann called 'the most important literary critic of today,' is uncertain — recently he was reported to be imprisoned in Rumania. We pay homage to those who have risked or given their lives for intellectual freedom.

Soviet communism is now completely discredited in the eyes of many in the west and in eastern Europe. As in 1948 the Czechoslovakian coup alienated the liberal left, so now after Hungary and the great majority of 'fellow travellers' and Communist intellectuals have passed the point of no return and look now to China, Poland and Yugoslavia, if they are not completely disillusioned. For the reaction of many of the marxist intellectual élite in Australia and Britain (and in Italy and France too) has been striking. They, like the liberal, are now uneasy in their quest for reason in human affairs.

Serle was assisted by Vance Palmer, A. A. Phillips, Brian Fitzpatrick and an expanded team of editorial advisers; together they produced a year's solid, if seldom spectacular, issues. Serle tended to act as mediator rather than as an aggressive editor. Occasionally, though, he was prepared to overrule his advisers; perhaps it was his historian's eye that led him to publish the following essay by Gwen Kelly, which is unique in giving a woman's perspective on the postwar housing crisis in Sydney.

Number 4, 1957

Portrait of a New Community
A Personal Impression

GWEN KELLY

As everyone knows, one of the legacies of war and depression throughout Australia has been a housing shortage unparalleled in our previous history. Nowhere has the lack of homes been more acute than in Sydney where a naturally expanding population has combined with a large migrant intake to produce a chronic discrepancy between the number of people and the number of homes. Even now in spite of the assurances of Federal politicians it is doubtful if the position has eased to any extent. Nevertheless the years between 1946 and 1954 were years of feverish activity on the part of the unhoused, resulting in the growth of new suburbs and in some cases what were, in effect, new communities. These mushroom growths slowly but steadily swallowed the green of little used golf-courses and river flats and swept away the gums of the bushlands that had fringed for long years the outer suburbs of Sydney. The golf-courses and river flats were largely the preserve of the Housing Commission and Council Housing schemes. Almost overnight tiny doll's-house settlements appeared, fenced, kerbed, guttered, with ready-made shopping centres and all the hallmarks of bourgeois society, except the gardens. In the brick centres they appeared almost simultaneously with the new tenants and owners, gardens created for the most part with the unerring lack of originality that marks the commuter with sufficient money for a deposit and payment from four to six pounds a week over a period of twenty-three years. The poorer settlements whose balloted tenants paid impossibly high rents for working men, to escape life with mother or crowded single rooms with children, remained box-like, uniform and comparatively gardenless.

The settlements hewed out of the bush on the fringes of Sydney were different and, in terms of human endeavour, the most interesting. The ballots of the Housing Commission left at every drawing a disappointed majority, and the deposits required by the better-class council settlements, plus the subsequent payments, meant that many people of small capital had no hope. From this class sprang the home builder in the literal sense, the man who decided to turn his own skill and endurance to creating his own dwelling. He watched the papers for the cheaper blocks of land, the division of old estates in outer Sydney, the release of areas within the green belt. Occasionally he took the risk of buying within the belt itself, hoping with the incurable optimism of certain Australians that the County of Cumberland Plan for Greater Sydney would never eventuate. Quite often the new blocks were bush without even a path, let alone a road, to penetrate the scrub. The home builders spent the first few months clearing ground, rooting up gum-trees, pushing back grevillea, trying in the case of the aesthetically minded to preserve the boronia and the wattle. Having cleared sufficient space to lay their foundations, they hacked through the undergrowth to reach the nearest road to ensure the delivery of materials. For the most part the ensuing houses were fibro constructions, with here and there one in brick or wood. They were unpretentious, even humble. They did not show the consciously contrived variation of the best housing settlement, or the wearying monotony of the worst. They were unique, individual, homes shaped from the owner's own design limited only by the restricting demands of money. Quite often the patterns were commonplace, lacking the structural magic of the creative architect, sometimes curious where the quirks of unorthodox human nature had been given full rein. These districts were also the paradise of the 'ready-cut' firms — the few who by 1949 could guarantee a definite, if tardy, delivery of goods to men too poor to afford a builder's contract and with no contacts within the building trade itself.

They became mixed communities, independent and proud. Many of the new citizens were skilled tradesmen, ex-soldiers who used their gratuities as a deposit, bought their block of land, ran up a temporary shack or garage and set to work in their spare time to make a home. While the newspapers ran articles on the iniquity of the forty-hour week, and the comfortably housed from the North Shore gave hurt little radio talks on the destruction of our green belts, they rose at five to travel the twenty-odd miles to work, arriving home again well after five in the evening to spend the hours between dinner and bed labouring on their own building. Nights and weekends were alive with the constant beat of the hammer, the whirr of the saw, the odorous skid of the plane. When they ran out of money they built cupboards and laid bricks for their wealthier neighbours, or their wives took jobs in the stores of the nearest suburb. Their babies were conceived in garages or unfinished back rooms, against the grand day when the whole family would move in. Sometimes two or even three children had appeared before this happened, and new bedrooms or sleep-outs were carefully tacked on to the original design. If they were bricklayers, they built in brick, the brown-red walls rising as a mark of their conscious superiority as tradesmen and by inference, as citizens.

These were, as I said, mixed communities. They contained as well the poorer professional classes, the teachers, the lecturers, the engineers, the £1000-£1500 a year community who had enough money to pay a carpenter to erect their walls and ceiling but no more. Their shell completed, they set about painting, fence-building, path-laying with their more gifted brethren, uneasily aware that the hieroglyphic patterns of their brushwork betrayed the amateur. In some cases, the precision of a good scientist was transferred to the mastering of a new craft, and a house slowly emerged in which every brick was hand selected and correctly laid, every cupboard a masterpiece of accurate construction. The wives of such perfectionists needed enduring patience, for their wait for a completed home was a long one.

On the outskirts were the get-rich-quick men who saw in the housing shortage the opportunity of a life-time. They dragged their wives and children from garage to house as each jerry-built structure was completed, from house to garage as each new building was sold. They progressed from shed to cottage, from fibro to wood to brick, hoping to catch finally the £6000 customer who would make their lifelong dream, 'a farm of their own,' a reality. With the houses came the taxi-trucks, the small businesses and finally the schools. . . .

In many new districts of this type, and also in the suburbs swollen by the addition of Commission or Council homes, the demand for new schools had been met by infants' schools, compact wooden buildings with verandahs jutting out from one or two rooms, usually painted a gay white, or portables notable mainly for the glassiness of their central walls. In general their air was ephemeral, and in the quick-growing communities extensions were added as needed so that some playgrounds were dotted with two or three or even four little buildings. In a central area such as Botany East, the infants' school progressed in the course of three or four years to a full primary section, but in the smaller centres the children continued to transfer at the age of eight to a larger school. Mount Colah, however, had become imbued with the pioneer spirit. They had built their own houses, they were not going to be fobbed off with any old school. They had the effrontery to demand a full primary, covering all grades from kindergarten to sixth class, the final primary grade in New South Wales. With the resolution that had tamed the scrub, they signed petitions, interviewed M.Ps and called public meetings to air their grievances. Maybe the pending State election helped matters, as for some reason, not quite clear, they got their school: a white wooden two-room affair no bigger than most of the new infants' schools but classed as a true primary school. There it stood, Mount Colah Public School 1952, the promise of the future. The people that had fought for it, loved it. They turned out to look at it, to admire it, and almost immediately they began to work for it, to make it 'the best school in the district.' When snakes were found next to the children's lunch benches, the parents and citizens came out in a body to clear the grounds. They raked, they hoed, they burned; one parent even supplied a council bulldozer to prepare a garden. The mothers raised money to buy pictures, curtains, paints. There was no kindergarten equipment, so they made it, aided only by the advice of the teacher. They painted cotton reels in the same gay assortment of colours as they had splashed across the walls of their houses. They made blocks, doll's-house furniture, they contributed books and rebound them. Slowly the school began to live, to grow. Within a year of its foundation, they ran a fete and from that tiny population extracted £500.

The first year of the school's life was not, however, an easy one. They could supply material goods, but they were soon faced with the one shortage they could not meet simply by enthusiasm or hard work — older children. There were a few in the district, but they belonged for the most part to the original inhabitants, a small conservative group. These people even resented the spate of building that was transforming the tiny bush settlement where they had lived in safe seclusion for a generation. Some of these children went to private schools. The others had started at Asquith or Hornsby. Their parents had been there themselves. The children were old enough to manage the roads. There they would stay. Some of the earliest of the new settlers took the same view. They hesitated, with reason, to transfer children who were already in third or fourth class.

The school as it stood then was weighted at the bottom end. Starting in September with ten to twenty children, the infant enrolments in the new year were sure to bring the total number to about 70. With the steady birthrate, the number of enrolling kinders was likely to continue at this rate for many years to come. In the initial twelve months, however, the true primary children, those aged from eight to thirteen, numbered less than ten. Headmasters and teachers with a knowledge of Departmental policy forecast the closing of the primary section. They predicted that the upper group was likely to remain minute for two or three years, and they knew the status of a school depended on present numbers, not future. But again the parents refused to be beaten. They received no co-operation from the heads of neighbouring schools, who had no desire to see their own numbers drop as this could entail a change in status and possibly a move for themselves. Nevertheless the new school did its best to prevent the issue of free train passes from stations north of Mount Colah to either Asquith or Hornsby. They reminded the local bodies that the new school was in existence, and they undertook an immense personal canvass. In this department the women proved they were the worthy partners of their constantly toiling husbands. Not for nothing had they raised babies in garages, painted houses, planted gardens. They put their babies into their prams or strollers, and they walked from door to door in the summer heat, trying to convince those with children elsewhere that they would be wise to transfer to the new school. In a limited way they were successful. Only a few children were won, but they were sufficient to stave off the threatened closure. And so the school survived; but the canvass brought to the surface a latent snobbery in the new community towards some of the less fortunate groups within its midst.

Most of these new bush settlements have grown on the fringes of an older community. This is true particularly of settlements along the main railway lines both north and south. As already mentioned, at the core of Mount Colah was an older, more comfortable, somewhat rural settlement. I doubt if it numbered more than ten to twenty families. These homes were usually wooden with wide verandahs and plenty of ground, or ivy-covered brick with slate roofs. Some had overgrown ancient gardens running along the edge of the creek, some were backed by the beauty of half-decayed orchards. This group remained and still remains, somewhat aloof from the recent settlers; but time will undoubtedly bridge the gap between the two.

There were, however, two poorer groups whose absorption into the new community was not welcomed by the newcomers themselves. On the outskirts of all settlements north of Hornsby are the farms. Many of them have been there at least twenty or thirty years, poverty-stricken, at times almost destitute. The barren, rocky, grotesquely beautiful Hawkesbury country gives very little change to these people whose hens and cows fight with the rocks and scrub for a bare existence. A little further south the land runs westward into the green flats and hills of the Dural and Windsor country where it is possible to farm with some chance of success, although even here there is poverty. But north of Asquith the land falls away into steep blue-gum gullies that offer no hope to civilized man.

Nevertheless a few families continued the attempt to wrest a living from the soil. In general they lacked the vigour and enterprise of their artisan neighbours, but they had at least the self-respect and status of freehold existence.

To these were added those too poor ever to build; they rented or owned land on the edge of the gully where it was cheap, and led a sort of hill-billy life in cement or fibro shanties. In one case as many as six children shared with their parents a single-roomed shack with a dirt floor. Some of these people were not popular with the newcomers, but the canvass did not ignore them. In this way a few of the children were brought into the new school and so into touch with the new population.

The contempt or pity of the community was reserved for the railway employees, who lived perforce within these settlements where there was a railway track. The Department of Railways solved the housing shortage simply. It had always been accustomed to house its fettlers along the side of the permanent way. It seemed a suitable place for the men whose profession was so essentially impermanent. Sydney people grew used to the little white tents dotted along the track to Newcastle or Wollongong. It was simple enough to extend this principle to cover the post-war situation. Forced to find accommodation for the men — drivers, firemen, etc. — whom they moved casually from country to city, they offered them a tent and about thirty feet of ground beside the line. So a haphazard community grew up, children whose lives were lived under 100 square feet of canvas to the accompaniment of the unbelievable din of the passing expresses, the coal-black chug of the slow goods trains, the oily purr of the new diesels. Occasional men made the best of it and fought desperately for respectable survival. Such men joined the P.& Cs and local Progress Associations even though they knew they were not welcome. The local citizens tended to look down on these people as a type of nomad, to consider them dirty, unfit to mix with their own neatly laundered children. The miracle is that so many were as clean as they were. Their washing was despoiled by every blast of soot that issued from the funnels of the passing steam trains, their water was limited to a small tank, filled by a little engine that trekked up and down the line once a month supplying water from its own tanks like a quaint prehistoric elephant. They could obtain electricity if they were prepared to pay for it, but the local councils refused to extend the town water supply to these dwellings. They argued it was not building land and the Railways knew it; but the theoretic correctness of their argument was little consolation to those who in the cases of big families could afford only one bath per person per week.

As indicated earlier, initiative was not lacking among these people. One man who appeared to father a new child every year, wrenched periodically a further twenty feet of land from the Department for extensions. By 1954 his tents sprawled between the railway and the highway along a good 30 to 50 yards of the permanent way. His wife, in between pregnancies, grew passionfruit to cover the canvas and spinach to feed the babies. These people were, however, the exception rather than the rule. Many families simply gave up the struggle for communal survival. Their tents became squalid: no passionfruit vines, no spinach; bare canvas and dirty stony railway ground. Even the spiky grass found it hard to survive. In one tent full of children, a boy struggled to pass his Intermediate with only a smoky oil lamp set in the middle of the table to light his books. Even this feeble illumination was constantly dimmed by the fumes of the kerosene stove running along the back of the tent only a few feet from the table. Needless to say he failed. His father accused him of not trying. In another case an electric train driver travelled on his motor-bike almost 25 miles daily to reach his depot on a line the other side of Sydney. For eighteen months, he could not obtain a slice of land within easy reach of his own route. If he had fallen asleep over his signals, and a collision had ensued, no doubt he would have been charged with negligence. His tent was named Yarralumla, whether by himself or some previous humorist I do not know.

For a short period during the Queen's visit there was a rumour that the tent people were to receive new homes. The Royal train would pass them on its way to Newcastle and it would never do for the Royal eyes to light on such sub-standard dwellings. For a time the community became quite enthusiastic. The new residents felt that they would lose at last this blot on their carefully constructed landscape; the tent-dwellers hoped for homes, except for the pessimistic few who feared rents beyond their means. But there was no need to worry. It was all a fairy-tale. It proved simpler to plant gardens around Sydney Town Hall and decorate Randwick racecourse than to renovate an entire population. The tents stayed and the Queen passed apparently undismayed by the spectacle. If she saw them at all, she probably thought they were maintenance workers.

The tents stayed, and with them the perpetual hazard to human life. The more careful families fenced the back of their land with wire netting and barbed wire, but the careless were content to leave a single strand of wire as the only barrier against destruction. In the four years we lived in the district, there were, I think, three children under five killed on the stretch of line between Cowan and Hornsby: children from the tents who had wandered on to the track running temptingly a few yards from their back door. When one of the Mount Colah babies was killed, the people of the district did their best to show the family involved they were sorry. Normally they resented the happy-go-lucky attitude of this particular group. In a curious way, they were even jealous of them. It seemed to them in some way unfair that every Sunday, this homeless set of beings should rattle off down the road in their old brown jalopy en route to the beach while they, the industrious, hammered and planed week in and week out. They adopted a somewhat pious attitude to the tent-dwellers and for the most part carefully kept their children away from them. They blamed them for all acts of vandalism and most of the thefts. They never asked them to birthday parties with the other children or invited them home after school. Yet with the death of the baby the people tried to show their sympathy in a practical way. They took up a subscription, and nearly everyone contributed even though none of them was rich. And so a gift of a few pounds was presented to the mother in an attempt to make money atone for human life. But with all their sympathy for the dead, they did not want the living children to attend the new school. By a sort of unspoken consent they were not included in the canvass, even though they could have supplied at least ten children within the required age group.

So the new self-created community evolved. Already some of the comradeship created by common struggle is being destroyed by the growing distinctions within groups. The P.& C. has lost some of its earliest and most enthusiastic members through its failure to cope with disagreements within its midst. Even so, much of the earlier vigour and communal spirit survives. The houses now number 600, a good 60 per cent. of them home-built; the school has between 250 and 300 pupils; and a woman from Mount Colah itself has been elected to represent the riding in the Shire Council. The tent problem looks as if it will be solved by the operation of natural causes. The Department, even though it has done nothing positive, seems at least to be allowing the situation to wear itself out. In Asquith and Mount Colah, transfer has removed some families, death others; and, this month of my writing, one tent was destroyed by fire. On the stretch between the two settlements, only one tent remains.

Mount Colah then has arrived; but on the fringes of this community and communities like it are newer settlements still, of men and women who are even now living in garages and on verandahs, fighting the bush in an attempt to create for themselves the homes they cannot find elsewhere. And an occasional tent or shanty still stands as a reminder that for some, even this solution is not possible.

At the end of 1957 Christesen returned to find that little advance planning had been done, the financial position was still critical and circulation was falling. Furthermore, there was an aggressive new competitor in the field. *Quadrant*, edited by James McAuley and backed by the Australian Committee for Cultural Freedom, had first appeared at the end of 1956, in the same month as Christesen went overseas, and had made great headway in his absence. McAuley had a wide-ranging network of contacts

and supporters within the literary community; furthermore, *Quadrant* was able to elicit support from the business community in a way that *Meanjin* had never been able to. Several former *Meanjin* stalwarts, including A. D. Hope, appeared on the *Quadrant* editorial board. Under McAuley, the magazine fused the campaign against literary modernism with the attempt to counter 'Communist' influence; its strategy for the latter, as Lynne Strahan aptly describes it in *Just City and the Mirrors*, was to 'manufacture . . . spells of equal potency from another mental sphere' (200). Within a year the crusade was in full swing. Not being supported by the CLF, *Quadrant* was free to publish political polemic in a way that *Meanjin* did not dare. Ironically, in a climate of political and aesthetic polarization, the liberal humanist critique was doubly hamstrung — treated with suspicion by critics of both left and right, and constrained by the magazine's dependence on the beneficence of a state funding agency that insisted on its own narrow definition of the 'literary'. Serle's letters to Christesen after one such foray encapsulated the dilemma.

Geoffrey Serle to C. B. Christesen

London,
4 May 1958

. . . A very decent letter from Tom: the bastards. I did not realise they stressed 'literary' so literally. It doesn't help, in some ways, the comparative figures against Quadrant, for if I remember rightly, our *art* content is about 20% whereas in Q it's nil. Make sure your purely literary content is over half each issue and *always higher than Quadrant's*. Print more stories and verse. Cut, i.e. edit down the wordage of all non-literary articles. . . .

30 June 1958

. . . As for bloody Quadrant, I can hardly bear to even look at it now. . . . What are we to do? They're winning all along the line . . . and we're all too gutless and spineless to do anything about it. Can the Quarterly or the Observer be used as a place to take them on? *You mustn't*. I know it's almost more than you can bear but *Meanjin* must keep out of it, you mustn't jeopardise your backing. I'm horrified to think how things are going in Australia (and, incidentally, really treasure the liberal intellectual atmosphere here, with all the hypocrisy and injustice of English society. One feels part of it, whereas at home one is an outsider). Are any of the apathetic liberals waking up? . . .

14 July 1958

. . . I had better point out that our enemies will seize on the amount of 'political' content. A rough break-down would be 42% literature, 42% 'affairs' and the rest — TV, art and architecture. But all the stuff is liberal rather than left-wing — OK with me. . . .

In the year after he returned Christesen published a number of substantial polemical essays on civil liberties themes. Here we see Brian Fitzpatrick applying his formidable scholarship and wit to the question of civil rights for Aborigines; this is followed by R. D. Wright's defence of academic freedom.

Number 4, 1958

Lesser Tribes without the Law

BRIAN FITZPATRICK

In *How Australia Is Governed* (Melbourne, 1939) Miss D. M. Davies offered some spirited observations upon anomalies and distasteful oddities of laws then existent. Many of these survive, including the provision of the Commonwealth Constitution by which half the membership of the Senate is elected every three years, all retaining their senatorial togas for six years. The object of the Fathers in this cunning device was to give the Senate continuity of existence — so that, as Miss Davies pointed out, the Government should be subjected to the pressure of a public opinion which had ceased to exist three years before.

Senate elections before 1949 used to provide a still more succulent dish — the system of evaluating preference votes was such that the party assembling a trifle more than half of the electors, in support of its No. 1 candidate, should fill all, or almost all, the vacant places. Thus in 1931 all senators elected were anti-Labor, in 1934 all but three; in 1937 all three returned were Labor, in 1940 all but three were anti-Labor — although in the electorate there was relatively little shift of party support, as shown in numbers of votes cast.

Even those peculiarities did not vie, as exercises in subtlety, with the federal 'dictation test', which lost caste only lately. The then Minister for Immigration, Mr. Townley, announced this to the Citizenship Convention at Canberra last January. We have had fifty-seven years of this — in the Minister's sober words — 'famous, not to say notorious, provision' (*Age*, Melbourne, January 22, 1958). The object of the test, which could be administered to any intending immigrant, was to keep Australia 'white' without saying so. So it was decided that the ostensible object should be to keep Australia literate. The device brought to bear was, accordingly, at first called an 'education test,' the then Prime Minister, Sir Edmund Barton, passionately pooh-poohing cynical suggestions from the Irishmen Higgins and McMillan that it was really intended to keep out anybody the Government did not wish to let in:

> I may say at once that there is no desire on the part of the Government to keep out educated or reputable Europeans . . . To put an illustration: if a Swede were asked to write a passage at dictation, I should not dream of instructing the officer to subject the immigrant to a test in Italian. That would be unfair . . .

And in fact there has not been any case, as far as I know the record, in which Barton's 1901 undertaking was dishonoured. No, subsequent Ministers exercised due care, so that a generation later it was an unwanted *English* lady who was required to take her test in Italian, an unwanted New Zealander his test in Dutch, and so on. (When about that time a Czech gentleman was required to pass a test in Gaelic, because apparently he was acquainted with every civilized tongue, in revulsion the High Court of Australia declared black the test which had been given him, deciding that Gaelic was not a language.)

There is a case, however, for the view that nothing in the Senate or the Immigration law and practice rivals, for breadth or variance from logical canons, the great range of federal and state statutes, ordinances, regulations and other learning regarding the aborigines. Some might find a sort of explanation for the peculiarity of this body of law in the undoubtedly peculiar character of the aboriginal people its subjects. (The pirate William Dampier, the first European to look us over in a careful way, concluded that the Hodmadods of Monomatapa, though a nasty people, yet were gentlemen to these.) But on investigation, the unprejudiced student must find more peculiarities in the law itself than in the subjects of it — by it variously styled 'aboriginals,' 'aborigines,' 'natives,' and (the latest locution) 'wards' or 'certain persons.'

In the circumstances of my own layman's understanding of the law relating to the indigenes, the hobby of many an idle hour since I learned that in the Northern Territory the Administration had powers of a miraculous nature, it seems to me temerarious in the extreme that the Victorian matriculation authorities should have set *The Aborigines* as a *must* among the topics on this year's British History syllabus. I think it particularly daring on their part to require study and exposition of 'later government policies, changes in attitude towards them, the situation in recent years.' For it is precisely in recent, post-war years that real ingenuity has been applied by draftsmen to the task of seeming to recognize aborigines as human beings, without doing so. Delicately trained men have sat down under green eye-shades in Canberra, Darwin, Brisbane, Sydney, Melbourne, Adelaide and Perth to grapple with a grave problem having two obvious aspects.

One of these, and that the less urgent, has to do with the ineluctable fact that Australia not only cordially endorsed the Universal Declaration of Human Rights which the United Nations adopted at Paris in 1948, but actually had an eighth part in drawing it up (if 'laying it down' be not the apter phrase). There was a Labor Government at Canberra then, and Dr. H. V. Evatt was busy, in his capacities as Australian Minister for External Affairs and Federal Attorney-General, and as President of the General Assembly of the United Nations, making things as hard as possible for Governments that would follow Mr. Chifley's. Under his coaching, there was to be on Australia's part no *Realpolitik* of the South African kind. . . .

A second vexatious aspect of the aboriginal problem, for officialdom, has had to do with the public safety; specifically, the defence of the country by testing long-range atomic weapons for the United Kingdom and, also, by discovering deposits of uranium and the like which might be sold to the United States and the United Kingdom. By a singular irony, desert areas are the most suitable for letting off atomic bombs, and desert areas seem richest in fissionable metal, and of course it is desert areas which have been set aside for the aborigines. 'Inviolable' reserves had been marked out for the tribes in South Australia, Western Australia and the Northern Territory; and over these spacious resorts the aborigines might wander at will, visiting their ceremonial sacred places at set seasons; and when not engaged in pursuing aboriginal fauna and plucking edible aboriginal flora, thinking longingly back to the Alchuringa or Dreamtime. Mineral prospectors had been prohibited from encroaching upon these reserves (until resources more valuable than gold were found there) and nobody had been permitted to drop bombs there (until it was found that plutonium and even hydrogen atoms could and ought to be split). But now the aborigines had to be shifted from the happy hunting grounds of tradition and, abandoning as it were the Julian calendar by which they had for millennia regulated their comings-in and goings-out, they must now conduct their walkabouts in a modern, Gregorian way. Such were the problems posed.

Nor were they the only ones. A mounting minor difficulty for all who had the best interests of the aborigines at heart was the proneness of many dark people, latterly, to pay less attention to Alchuringa — on the working principle that fine dreams butter no yams — and to set up as artists, clergymen, military officers, teachers of singing, professional boxers and footballers, and exponents of other white mysteries not to be spat upon. And what about aborigines who had fought for Their Country? Official horizons had to be extended to comprehend a veritable host of novelties, and officialdom was not found wanting. . . .

A New Deal for the aborigines was introduced by the Labor Government incidentally to purposes of section 10 — (1) of the Nationality and Citizenship Act 1948-1950. Dr. Evatt having failed in 1942-4 to obtain power for the Commonwealth Parliament to make laws with respect to aborigines in the states, his colleague Mr. Calwell four years later devised a fit punishment for the states that had promised and failed to coöperate. The punitive sub-section reads:

> Subject to this section, a person born in Australia after the commencement of this Act shall be an Australian citizen by birth.

In this manner — without fanfare or tattoo — were Jackadgery and Nimitybelle, born in 1949 or since, given status with your child and mine. The dark youngsters, being Australian citizens by birth, will at the age of twenty-one presumably appear on the electoral roll and vote, whatever the states' statutes provide. (Only in Victoria, where there are hardly any aborigines, is the aboriginal child vested at birth with the same rights as the white child.) But the implications of section 10 are a headache for *future* administrators; and even those people who expect to see the year 1970 will not anticipate that an issue of aboriginal enfranchisement will convulse it. No, difficulties of and for the future must not vex us; they matter less than preoccupations of the present. Now, these are tackled most forthrightly in the Northern Territory Welfare Ordinance No. 16 of 1953, and Ordinance to Provide for the Care and Assistance of Certain Persons. Of this momentous instrument its sponsors write appreciatively:

> In June 1953 the Northern Territory Legislative Council passed the Welfare Ordinance, considered to represent the most important single step yet taken in the approach to the aboriginal problem. This abandons the 'protective' approach represented by the Aboriginals Ordinance and substitutes the positive 'welfare' policy. It abandons the method of defining such terms as 'aboriginal' and making persons covered by the definition subject to special legislation unless they obtain exemption from it. Under the new legislation individuals only may be committed to the care of the State — and only on the grounds that they stand in need of special care and assistance. This legislation assumes that Aborigines as well as white Australians in the Territory have full citizenship as a right and that this right is to be withheld only in cases where an individual is in need of special care and assistance . . .

At this time the Native Welfare Department set about taking a census of Territory residents who might be in need of special care and assistance. This had never been done, the Fathers of the Constitution having dismissed the aboriginal problem, with memorable simplicity, in section 127, which states:

> In reckoning the numbers of the people of the Commonwealth, or of a State or other part of the Commonwealth, aboriginal natives shall not be counted.

But the new broom, it was clear, could not sweep clean without census details. These were at length forthcoming. A friendly commentator writes:

> The Welfare Ordinance met with considerable opposition from people who wished to retain the subject status of the Aborigines but raised the hopes of all those who believe that the best way to assist the development of people is to remove the discriminations against them and give them equal rights and opportunities. However, these fears and hopes were without foundation. After the adoption of the Ordinance the Native Welfare Department commenced the compilation of a census of all the Aborigines in the Northern Territory, giving full particulars of their blood groupings, identifications marks, stages of development, etc. This was not completed until early in 1957.
>
> After the census was completed (and four years after the adoption of the Welfare Ordinance) the Ordinance was gazetted on May 13, 1957. At the same time all the 16,000 full-blood Aborigines in the Northern Territory listed on the census, except 15, were declared wards.

That is to say: the welfare approach having been substituted for the protective — and the system abandoned whereby all aborigines except fifteen or so exempted persons were treated as aborigines — under the new legislation 15,985 individuals only were committed to the care of the state — and only on the ground that they stood in need of special care and assistance. The legislation assumed that aborigines as well as white Australians in the Territory have full citizenship as a right, and withheld the right only in the 99.99 per cent. of cases where the individual was in need of special care and assistance . . .

To doubt the good faith of the Minister, Mr. Paul Hasluck, responsible for the admission of the Territory aborigines to a Welfare State of their own, is not called for. During his eight years' term in Territories the aborigines' situation *has* been bettered in several important respects, and 'full citizenship as a right' *has* been ceded to part-aborigines, who may now drink in bars with anybody. Moreover, a determinedly liberal administration of the Welfare Ordinance, and of the Wards' Employment Ordinance (No. 24 of 1953) supporting it, may after many musters secure 'just and favourable conditions of work' for full-bloods, as enjoined in the Universal Declaration of Human Rights. All this is germane, and substantial or else full of promise. Still, it is hard to forbear from a wry grin when the mountain labours and brings forth a ward.

Mr. Hasluck's Welfare Ordinance is I think the most remunerative gleaning which a comparative study of the aboriginal rights laws yields. But, risking bathos, I do not refrain from acknowledgment of the *next* most important step in the approach to the aboriginal problem. Credit for this goes to the State of Western Australia, where more aborigines are believed to live — nobody just knows how many, because nobody has counted them — than live in the Territory.

The Native Administration Act 1905-1947 of Western Australia, section 2, defines 'native' as meaning any person of the full blood descended from the original inhabitants of Australia or from their full blood descendants excepting a quadroon under 21 years of age who neither associates with or [*sic*] lives substantially after the manner of persons of the full blood unless he is ordered by a magistrate to be classed as a native, or a quadroon over 21 unless ordered by a magistrate or requesting to be classed as a native or person of less than quadroon blood who was born before December 31, 1956, unless he applies to be brought under the Act and the Minister consents.

The Natives (Citizenship Rights) Act 1944-1951, section 4, liberalizes the treatment of persons whose birthstain is more than a quarter, by providing that if a native repudiates the other natives he may become a citizen. Such a one may make application to a district board for a certificate of citizenship supporting his application with a statutory declaration that he wishes to be a citizen and has for the previous two years dissolved tribal or native association except in respect to [*sic*] lineal descendants or native relations of the first degree and that he has served in the armed forces and earned an honourable discharge or that he is otherwise a fit and proper person to obtain a certificate of citizenship. But — let the applicant beware! — section 7 provides that upon complaint of the Commissioner of Native Welfare *or any other person*, a local Natives (Citizenship Rights) Board may suspend or cancel a certificate of citizenship if the Board is satisfied that the holder is not adopting the manner and habits of civilized life — whereupon he is deemed to be a native again. Finally, in this disconcerting history, note that in the last third of 1958 was introduced, and rejected, a bill to give Western Australian aborigines — except those declared 'protected natives' — full citizenship by birth. What, the legislature said, is the good of that? And, until there are equal opportunities for black and white, and one set of laws for both — what, indeed?

Number 3, 1958

The Academy and its Freedom

R. DOUGLAS WRIGHT

The number of universities and the variety of subjects taught by them have increased rapidly in Western countries in the last century. Many of these subjects, such as atomic physics, microbiology and economics, have become extremely important to the general public, to industry and governments. In their early stages, however, they did not appear important to the community, and the inspired individuals working in the universities were allowed to develop their experiments and ideas by free discussion and publication. Two world wars brought home the tremendous practical, material, intellectual and spiritual changes produced by these abstract studies. The universities have become recognized as a source of national power, and the other organs of the community, especially the governments, have sought to do the usual things to a source of national power — to encourage its extent, to direct its activities and to restrict its export. In these activities governments are frequently supported by legal, religious and political institutions so that consideration of the matter is often emotionally charged.

The essence of academic freedom is that an academic is free to discuss with his students and colleagues any matter whatever relevant to his subject and to publish to the world the results of discussions and experiments. Academic freedom is therefore mainly a matter of individual freedom. All academics will agree that these are the essential conditions for optimum development of knowledge. Such conditions permit everyone to confirm and advance the novel discovery and to refute the fallacy. Successful activity in the academy often implies continuous change of ideas and processes, which may disturb the religious, legal, industrial and political equilibria of the nation. Reactions occasionally lead to overt restrictions on the academy, as in the monkey trials in Tennessee, which stated what must not be taught, or the 1951 directive on medical research in the U.S.S.R., which restricted the manner in which research should be done, or the *Apartheid* Laws of South Africa, which state the company in which the discussions may take place. The pressure for restriction of academic freedom in British countries is usually insidious.

It is my intention to outline what seem to me to be the important aspects of the present position of universities in their communities and the sources of pressure to restrict the freedom of their members. My postulates of the problems involved and suggestions as to their approximate magnitude are in the line of academic enquiry: generalisations in this nebulous field are intended to be evocative, not authoritative; magnitudes are of the sort which might arise from thirty years' experience of phenomena for which standards of measurement have not been evolved.

My first proposition is that the university has, in this century, retained, or even increased, its prestige as a fountain of information and understanding in the western European civilizations and is growing in influence in the eastern civilizations. Further, this has happened in a period when religion, legalistic institutions, and political and economic instrumentalities have failed relatively to maintain their respected positions. One does not need to argue in 1958 that the discoverers of penicillin, of the chain reaction systems of atomic fusion and fission, and herd psychology are the important practical men of modern civilization. Our essential material civilization is built on industries, concepts and forms evolved from academic discoveries. Most of them have been inveighed against or resisted by the custodians of the *status quo ante scientiam*. The upholder of fundamental religion has been just as firm a brake on change as the owner of threatened industrial apparatus and thereby each has played his proper part in the community by compelling proof and adjusting rate of change to the rate of adaptation by the people. But the impetus of the university is increasing; its power is so great that modern nations compulsively seek to use it in their competitions: one has only to observe the perturbed soul-searching of Western civilization since *Sputnik assumptus est*.

My second proposition is that this power has arisen because at certain stages in evolving civilizations a peculiar social phenomenon arises and is tolerated. This phenomenon is the bonding together of 'academics' in micro-communities to carry out, in their fashion, the competitive play of human beings. The qualifications for this society are a high intelligence and a profound obsession that by the use of this intelligence one can learn what is known and improve upon it. Because the academic can read, sometimes in several languages, he builds on past knowledge or mistakes; he never regards the concept as complete, the equation as absolute or the phenomenon as totally elucidated. It is the disciplined hope of the academic that he will develop a synthesis of knowledge which will astonish his fellow academics and that such a synthesis will become part of human progress. These are the ambitions of men who seek to be academics. Like all other men they may not attain their ambitions: the psyche may be warped, the intellectual attitude too rigid, the cares imposed by their acceptance of social custom or emotional satisfaction too distracting. But the academy survives so long as significant numbers in it are successful and the majority cannot think of a better ambition.

In Western civilizations these people have, for centuries, had a special position in society. They are the rebels against orthodoxy. The children of each generation are essentially rebels against the previous generation; the academic is therefore the natural mentor of the highly intelligent young.

The ideal academic remains in sympathy with the disciplined rebel of all generations. Ideally, the university is the haven of all free spirits in a society. As such it could probably not sustain itself; even if it could for a period, it would lack stability. Most universities which used to sustain themselves have come to accept formal provisions from the society in which they occur. Many new universities in the last century have arisen from statutory powers and provisions.

My third proposition is that these statutory provisions of Western societies imply a surprising trust in the universities. I infer this from the fact that, in most societies, the university is entrusted with the instruction (and bestowal of registrable qualifications) for the chief professional callings in the society: Law, Medicine, Education, Dentistry are usually monopolies of the universities. Science, Architecture, Engineering, Music are not always registrable qualifications but the universities are the usual source of degrees. When one considers that Law, Medicine, Education and Dentistry affect the individual of society closely as a person, the conclusion that the academics enjoy exceptional trust is inevitable. Another indication of the trust placed in them is that they are given the power to admit to or exclude students from these courses. As a corollary, there is the danger that they may be saddled with the wrong sort of obligation along with the trust, namely to be the upholders of orthodoxy. To accept this would be contrary to my second proposition, that the essential characteristic of the university is refusal to accept authority without evidence. The university is therefore faced with a very straightforward *modus vivendi* with the society which supports it: energetic, inquisitive instruction of candidates for professions in exchange for the opportunity to give the intellect full challenge.

A consequence of this arrangement often occurs. Inevitably the teacher in the university feels sympathy for some intelligent students and not for others. Real antipathy is not uncommon and not unhealthy. For this, but mainly for other reasons, many highly intelligent graduates go into practice instead of becoming academics, which is the ambition of many students in a successful university. In practice of politics they may be very successful, but resentful of the intellectual dominance which the academics had over them. An anti-intellectual attitude is not uncommon among 'expatriate' graduates and frequently leads them to seek appointment on the governing body of universities with the (usually vain) objective of using power rather than intellect to dominate the academic. A majority of such people on the governing body of a university can lead to social and institutional discord. This attitude is sometimes accentuated when the graduate of this type is a judge who accepts the opportunity for unjudicial behaviour!

This proposition, that academics are trusted to run their own affairs, also raises the question of majority rule and individual and institutional freedom in democracies. The dilemma is most easily posed by an example: If the majority decides on abolition of alcohol nobody is permitted to consume this substance; but if the majority votes in favour of non-abolition nobody expects the consumption of alcohol to be compulsory. The example of abstainers being free to remain so in a community where the majority holds with drinking, is pertinent to the position of the academics. Experience has shown the benefit of allowing the individual to contemplate a heliocentric system even though the majority of his community holds strongly to the geocentric postulate.

Western countries have recently had two experiences of circumstances in which the individual has been subject to almost complete regulation of every phase of life. Nine years of war have given too many people a taste of authority over their fellows, and too many people, including academics, a taste for direction rather than independence. In democracies the tyranny of majorities can be just as irksome and stupid as that of tyrants.

My fourth proposition is that the only acceptable censors of each academic in his academic functions are his colleagues and students. It is clear from what has already been said that an academic would not accept a non-academic as fit to judge his intellectual attitudes and achievements. One does not have to be a horse to judge a horse show, but it is conceivable that horses might have a more comprehensive basis for judging other horses than have humans. Academics are not always humble or judicial and there is no doubt that many get carried away by popular feeling. A Professor of Physiology might unjustly say of a learned but at the moment unpopular Professor of Chinese that he could not read the inscription on a ginger jar, but the balance is usually re-established by a student who respects that professor or by a colleague who dislikes the accuser. Academies are not lotus gardens of mutual adulation. Academic behaviour would often scare Daniel even after his biblical experiences.

My fifth proposition is that the most fruitful material for academic intellectual enquiry is natural phenomena, including the behaviour of human beings. No academic feels that an ivory tower provides the best conditions for his work, though a lay group which is threatened by academic pronouncements will often assert that the academic is unpractical and should stay in his tower. Sound academic work is always potentially socially useful even if its relevance is not immediately apparent. Any finding which is new and true becomes in time socially useful. Galvani's study of the reason why frog-legs kicked when hung on an iron balcony by a copper hook gave rise to the electrical industry. Pavlov's study of salivation by dogs did not at first appear to be the fundamental contribution to sociology which it has become. Many people, in advocating socially useful work for academics, imply that the result should not upset the norms of society. A political leader of recent times has stated plainly that public funds should not be used to provide the salaries of academics who criticise the government. Many actual instances could be given of the holders of important public offices admonishing academics to keep out of public controversy. In Australia we have not had a full-grown McCarthy but there have been many adolescent aspirants.

Others feel that they have the authority to direct the socially useful work. If Galvani or Pavlov had been directed by a government or a senior scientist to restrict his work to the orbit of a director's imagination, the world might have been richer by only a trifle: it would have been poorer by the acceptance of a negative value — the right of the powerholder to subjugate the potentially powerful.

The academic also does socially useful work by training students. The real academy conveys instruction and evokes an academic attitude of mind, as defined under my second proposition. The academic must feel free to discuss anything whatever with his students. If the subject matter is intellectually relevant to the topic under discussion, the students will accept it as such, even if it disturbs their norms. The academic who introduces material solely for his own emotional titillation, be it moral, political or theological, will be quickly censored by his students. If he is insensitive to this he will soon find that his colleagues will act to prevent him becoming an excuse for society to limit their intellectual opportunities. All universities have statutory powers for dealing with such cases. So long as the academic conveys to his students, without bias, the information relevant to his synthesis of knowledge on matters appropriate to his subject, he will provide a satisfactory basis not only for practical but also for progressive adaptation of, and sometimes contribution to, advancing knowledge.

The freedoms outlined above, essentially to develop knowledge and to publish it, are not, however, sufficient basis for an academy at this time: a prime requirement is money. Ideally there should be enough money for good sound buildings, adequate furniture, superb libraries and equipment, and sufficient numbers of well-trained teaching staff to develop students to their maximum capacity. Financial assistance should enable intelligent students to study without distraction and provide salaries for staff which do not price them out of normal social activities. No Western community would contest these sensible suggestions, but no Western community has taken all the necessary steps to effect them. The steps required are quite simple: namely to find out what is required and then provide it.

At the present time the need in Western nations for increased 'expertise', both technical and mental, is obvious as a result of the progress of the other societies. The shortage of highly trained personnel is mainly due to the uncertainty of employment and low remuneration in the past. The technological faculties in the universities have only just become saturated. More universities will not increase the flow of graduates unless conditions of employment for graduates take account of the financial outlay, loss of earnings during training and high level of skill of graduates. The drive for more technical education must result from economic demand. This demand seems to have arrived.

So let us accept the proposition that a country wants to set up a high level contemporary standard of academic education in order to produce graduates suitable for administrative, pedagogical, legal, economic, medical, scientific and applied scientific fields. Who can assess the requirements? There is no one group of people qualified to do so. Many academics can assess the material provisions necessary for the students seeking to study their subjects, but few of them can assess either the structures required or the costs; in many cases it is necessary to forecast the future. Obviously a group of people with the requisite variety of special skills, including those of negotiation, is necessary. But such a group will be really effective only if each member believes that the advancement of universities is the job most worth doing.

These contentions imply that the universities occupy a political position as a charge upon the public purse. As such the university has the right to use political practices to publicise its aims, methods and needs. In a democracy this may be called pressure politics. Academics are academics because they believe deeply in the importance of their calling. It would be a queer democracy which denied a group of devoted people the opportunity to advance their claim on society. If, however, the university or its teachers wish to move into other political fields, they cease to be members of a privileged community and can expect normal social reaction to their activity. In these cases it is stupid to invoke the term 'academic freedom'. Academic freedom is a privilege which obtains within the academy or in the prosecution of the good of the academy as a group devoted to the search for universal truths. It does not obtain when the academy or members of it use the academy's letterhead to advance the prejudices of a majority or of individual members of the academy. When these are the purposes, the academy or the individual reverts to the unprivileged position of any other self-seeker.

One disadvantage of being an academic is the limitation of access to judicial proceedings. Many judges of the Courts of the States of Australia are on the governing bodies of the respective universities, and in any action between an academic and his university these judges would not therefore be suitable to preside. The academic may therefore have restricted access to justice.

Occasionally a member of an academic group is considered with regard to his fitness to carry out the high purposes of his office. Legalistically, he will be dealt with by the governing body, usually according to its statutes. Such bodies may contain a number of legally qualified members, some of whom escape the restraint of laws of evidence and impartiality without noticeable regret. There are standards of conduct, intellectual and moral, towards colleagues and students which can be easily derived from the consideration that an academy is a community devoted to the search for universal truths, by discourse, discussion and research. Such a community must, however, inevitably be composed of people with strong motivation, i.e. of strong emotions. These strong emotions can cause herd reactions, and academics do not always show judicial attitudes to their colleagues. Nietzsche's drawing of the characteristics of the academic is a cartoon rather than a photographic likeness, but he does point to two attributes which occur sufficiently often to constitute a danger to the freedom of colleagues of the academics who have them. 'The most dangerous thing of which the intellectual is capable stems from the mediocrity of his type . . . which instinctively labours to destroy any unusual man; which seeks to break every tight drawn bow, or better yet, to slacken it'. This attitude has been quite frequently seen: when an academic constantly belittles his colleagues, either within or outside the university, he does everybody a disservice. It is a sort of Gresham's law of academics — bad academics drive out the good ones.

In the last year the executive bodies of the academic staff in two Australian universities have proposed conditions of tenure of appointment which would have greatly reduced the existing freedom and privileges of the academic staff. And the previous remarks on majority rule apply very much to universities — many academics insist that everybody must recruit and manage his staff in a uniform manner.

The other attribute mentioned by Nietzsche is 'that claim to honour and recognition (which above all assumes recognizability); that sunshine of good reputation; that constant ratification of his worth and usefulness . . .', i.e. an inordinate desire for adulation. So long as the academic is content with recognition from specialists in his own field, no harm results. He may seek it in the public press, an innocent indication of insecurity. The attitude becomes more dangerous when, in conjunction with the other one, the academic seeks approval as a reasonable man from lay groups, sometimes political or religious, but especially governing bodies of universities. On such bodies, the 'reasonable academic' might present the requirements of colleagues as the whims of naughty children and attempt to hush up the deliberations: secrets are so impressive! Or something which deeply affects the work of colleagues must be done in such a hurry that the colleagues cannot be consulted. The most abysmal example of this kind of thing was the concurrence of the Professorial members of the Council of the University of Tasmania with the legalistic attitude that their then colleague, Orr, and hence themselves, were in a simple master-servant relationship to the Council. It is therefore essential that the individual in the academic community, in his perilous position of non-adherence to orthodoxy, should be safeguarded by properly drawn rules of due process for proof of disqualification. In addition he should be a member of the corporate body with all the community and legal obligations and privileges which result therefrom.

In conclusion: Our nation exists in an age when what is true and what is possible change from day to day. Our stability results from the institutions and callings devoted to the orthodox; our capacity for adaptation results from those devoted to the heterodox. Accountancy, the law and the church keep us stable; the entrepreneur, the politician and the academic keep us advancing. All require well organized support and protection of the freedoms necessary to their special functions. A free society can survive only if the practitioners in each group understand their own reasonable requirements and those of their companion groups. Each is a minority, and foolish ganging-up on the other can result only in reduction of the total freedom of our society.

If such ideals had been universally shared, *Meanjin*'s fortunes might have been very different. Political opposition within the university reached a climax in 1959–60. It was announced that the building *Meanjin* had been occupying was to be demolished, and for some time it seemed that no alternative accommodation would be offered. Christesen dug in his heels and refused to budge until the building was eventually knocked down around him. There were also renewed attempts to cut off university support, and the idea of a takeover was again mooted.

Nevertheless, it would be unwise to dismiss the opposition to the magazine as mere irrational prejudice. Perhaps the most convincing statement of the grounds of opposition came from Vincent Buckley, in a letter that he wrote in response to a verbal challenge from Christesen that he substantiate his description of *Meanjin* as 'pro-Communist'.

Vincent Buckley to C. B. Christesen

22 June 1959

I am sorry that this arrives on your desk so soon after the disorientation of your move (I hardly realised you were going before you were gone, and I sympathise with you very much); but I have been studying the files of *Meanjin* in order to check on my sense of its political sympathies, and since I have done the job I guaranteed to do, I may as well send it to you straight away. As I said in conversation with you, I don't expect my account to satisfy you that 'pro-Communist' is the appropriate word to use of some of *Meanjin*'s policies; I never expected to be able to do that. But the contributions and emphases which I point to are of precisely the sort which lead a lot of your readers (few McCarthyites among those of them I know) to suggest that 'pro-Communist' *is* an apt word. As for myself, the more closely I looked at the files, the more I was persuaded that it is the only appropriate word to describe the socio-political policies displayed by *Meanjin* over a number of years.

Even so, it is a term with a very loose popular usage. I don't share that usage, and I don't intend it to apply here. Later in these notes I shall define the sense in which I am using it, and in which a number of other intellectuals use it of *Meanjin*.

It may help to clarify my approach if I set down certain preliminary points to make clear why this comment is being written.

First, I write it not gratuitously but because I have spoken of *Meanjin*'s 'pro-Communist policies', and, when you objected strongly to this, I said it could be supported from an analysis of the files. I am putting the comment down in formal manner only because you have challenged me to do so.

Second, the statement that *Meanjin* has 'pro-Communist policies' is not, and was not, made as a 'charge' but as a relatively disinterested comment on what a number of people already agree to be the case.

Third, I am conscious that the view which I hold, and have held for several years, of *Meanjin*'s sympathies is not held only by myself but by a large number of other people including several who, while being anti-Communist, are quite happy to publish in *Meanjin* and are not interested in making 'charges'. This is substantially my own position: I am not interested in making 'charges', have no 'McCarthyist' interests or tendencies, and am happy to publish in *Meanjin*; on the other hand, like a number of other people, I am and always have been disturbed by some of its policies. Some of these other people, by the way, apparently see its position as pro-Communist in a fuller sense than I do.

Fourth, I am aware that your personal artistic interests, and large elements in your personal Weltanschauung are unsympathetic to Communist theory and practice.

Fifth, I don't suggest that such policies as a denunciation of McCarthyism, support of the Authors World Peace Appeal, and a concern for personal liberties, are necessarily in any way signs of a sympathy for Communism. God forbid! I am myself strongly opposed to McCarthyism and to denials of civil liberties, and would expect an intellectual journal to speak out at the relevant time against these things. As for the AWPA, I was one of its Australian signatories. But, given certain other conditions, these policies (which in themselves I support) can become or can be used as factors in enforcing sympathy for Communism. That is what I think *Meanjin* tended to do. So for honesty's sake I have included these things in my account, at the risk of increasing misunderstanding between us.

Of course, the comment about 'pro-Communist policies' is limited in two ways: in the extent to which these policies influence the editorial sense of what is relevant in literature and the other arts; and temporally, in that no-one would maintain that *Meanjin* had *always* had pro-Communist policies.

On the first point, I want to make clear that whatever other people may think I don't take *Meanjin* as an organ of the Communist Party in anything like the sense that the *Communist Review* is; nor do I take it as the organ of a cultural front dominated by Communists in anything like the sense that *Overland* is or was. Nor do I think that it has ever been consistently and deliberately pro-Communist in all its concerns. The greater part of *Meanjin*'s contents — most of its literary and artistic comment — has been politically neutral, and *Meanjin* has been to that extent an 'open' journal, having something of the quality of a forum. What I am pointing to is not a concern to support Communism or the Communist Party in everything (however subtly) but to a heavy recurrent bias in several important matters.

On the second point, I should say it is pretty clear that it is not the whole lifetime of *Meanjin* that is in question, but a sequence of crucial years. I would be inclined to say that the question of pro-Communist policies hardly arises in the period between *Meanjin*'s foundation and (say) 1949. The crucial years are from about 1949 to 1956; and it is these that I will chiefly be looking at. The years from 1956 to the present are also relevant, but in a somewhat different way.

From (say) 1949 to (say) 1956 *Meanjin* seems to me to have followed policies which were in certain clear respects objectively pro-Communist. In fact, in socio-political matters it had the air of a typical fellow-travelling journal. Whether or not this objective state of affairs corresponded with editorial *intentions* (which it may not have), the pro-Communist bias during those years seems to me to have been so strong, so recurrent, and in some ways so decisive, as to be quite unmistakable.

It is in 1949 that the Editorials begin talking of 'witch-hunting' and 'calumny'; and it is apparent that McCarthyism is to be one of the chief preoccupations. Not that this in itself means anything at all; but it does set up an emotional climate in which one can see the pro-Communist bias, or perhaps empathy emerging. In the following year the Editorial columns become 'The Uneasy Chair', and start to be a much more prominent component of the journal.

Between 1949 and 1956, the pro-Communist policies of the journal were expressed in various ways:

(A) *Direct Editorial Comment*: By this I mean the editorials delivered under the title of *Comment* or from The Uneasy Chair; the small quotations inserted as fill-ins in the body of the journal; and the choice of overseas News Notes by which to give readers an impressionistic account of what was going on in intellectual circles in other countries.

The Editorial Comment for several of these years was largely concerned to attack alleged assaults in America and Australia on freedom of thought and expression, to criticise in very general and emotive terms the state of American society, to advertise and press for the Authors World Peace Appeal and the activities of the World Peace Council. So constant is this comment that one could call it a campaign. It was waged not only by the direct editorials but also through the footnote fill-ins and through the choice of news notes. The picture presented of the world situation was of a world threatened by America and Americanism, a world in which the necessary and natural allies for the liberal intellectual were the supporters of the Peace Council and, ex hypothesi, the Communists. The editorial campaign may have been directed to criticising 'McCarthyist' tendencies (a laudable intention to which *Meanjin*, however, gave too exclusive an emphasis), but its effect was to endorse the local Communist Party line and Soviet foreign policy. This effect, of course, was only possible since during all these years *not one word* of criticism was editorially voiced of the Soviet bloc, of Communism, or of any Communist tactic, official, or writer. At least twice fill-ins spoke of the imprisonment of left-wing writers in Turkey and Greece; but there is no reference at all to the greater difficulties experienced by leading Soviet writers under the Stalin–Zhdanov policy. As well as this, the overseas News notes pretty openly showed right-wing and Christian writers in a shabby light and pretty consistently praised communists and certain others, like Sartre, who at that time were collaborating with them.

(B) *The Privileged position of certain Communist writers*:

For three or four of the relevant years, the degree of privilege accorded to Communist and fellow-travelling writers was quite extraordinary, when one considers the meagre contribution they were actually making to Australian intellectual life.

(i) During these years, only four guest writers occupied the Uneasy Chair: two of these were Communists; and of the other two, one

(I. R. Maxwell) was defending *Meanjin* against charges, made by F. T. Macartney, that it was pro-Communist.

(ii) One Communist writer, David Martin, appeared so often and in so many roles that he looked like a contributing editor: he published stories and poems, book reviews and even one editorial. On one occasion, you devoted part of an editorial to welcoming and praising him.

(iii) A high proportion of *Meanjin*'s stories were by Communist writers such as Martin, Waten, Lambert, Prichard.

(iv) Of the very few overseas poets printed, most were Communists or fellow-travellers. One, Thomas McGrath, had several poems printed which made no claim to be anything other than propagandist statements — a privilege which was accorded, I think, to no other poet, except Jack Lindsay, whose very long and openly propagandist poems were published on three or four occasions. Actually to import this sort of material seems excessive.

(v) The Australasian Book Society was probably the only publishing house all of whose productions (or very nearly all) were reviewed. Often the reviews of Communist books were inordinately long; and more than half the time the reviews themselves were written by other Communists or close sympathisers. Some of these, both writers and reviewers, were people whom, so you have mentioned in conversation, you considered pretty feeble. The books reviewed were often slight and ephemeral, but they still received substantial and favourable attention.
[*Marginal note*: I am not urging that any literary journal should discriminate against the *creative work* of these writers simply on the grounds of their politics. But some of them seem to me — and, if I may judge from what you have said in conversation, to you — creatively poor. And the space and attention given to their work and opinions seems, given the other facts I mention, significant and suggestive.]

(vi) The letters from overseas — London and Paris — were generally written by Dymphna Cusack.

(C) *Bias in Contributed Articles*: As I suggested above, the articles on literature and the arts were generally without political bias of any kind; and of course they comprised a relatively high proportion of the matter in the journal. *Meanjin*'s record with regard to them has been admirable. But these are, for most reasonable men, politically neutral subjects. The choice of sociological and political articles, however, leads to a different picture. There are a large number directed to endorsing the editorial policy of attacking McCarthyism and supporting the Peace Council. Others enforce the view of America as the authoritarian and war-mongering centre of a would-be-empire. Still others enforce the view of Russia and China as liberal and friendly countries, whose policies are much misunderstood. There is not one single article unequivocally analysing, or even accounting for, authoritarian tendencies in any country of the Communist bloc. On one occasion, when there is an article by Professor Copland, making some mild criticisms of Russian policies, it is flanked by another, longer article which is strongly and uncritically pro-Soviet. One article was an uncritical account of Hungarian Communist writers. I mention this one for a special reason, that it relates to *Hungary*. Several others, even more uncritical, gave substantial sponsorship to cultural activities in 'the New China', a country which came to have a particularly privileged position in *Meanjin*'s columns.

Another aspect of this bias was the undermining — amounting even to a discrediting — of writers who openly attacked Communism. For example, James McAuley's article 'Tradition, Society and the Arts' was accompanied *in the same issue* by an article criticising it. Similarly with the Australian Committee for Cultural Freedom: a symposium on this Committee consisted of one justification of it followed by three strong attacks on it (your editorial states that a second favourable review was commissioned but not forthcoming). But there was other material on the CCF, all strongly unfavourable. Both in an earlier and in a later issue the bias of the symposium was supported by articles, one of them reprinted from an American journal; and all editorial reference to the CCF was scornful. Possibly you have justification for dealing with the CCF in this way; but not for dealing with McAuley.

The *Forum* section was of course quite open to Communist as to other writers. But, if I may strike a personal note, my one attempt to enter it was less successful than those of most Communist writers apparently were. I may add that, on this occasion, I was replying to a review by a Communist, Elizabeth Vassilieff, who used a poem of mine as an occasion for a two-page attack on Cardinal Mindszenty and on my own creative integrity. I was told by yourself that my comment on this attack couldn't be included in the *Forum* section for three issues; whereupon I withdrew it. I mention this incident because it is one of which I have intimate knowledge. . . .

As I have said, several of these items, taken by themselves, are not necessarily pro-Communist: I mean such things as the Authors Peace Appeal, criticism of America, a concern for personal freedoms. They become so in the context which *Meanjin* supplies. For they are part of a pattern of policies, a pattern built both of silences and sponsorships; your editorial practice makes it very hard for the reader to take them by themselves. For when it all appears together, and with not one unequivocal word or gesture in criticism of Communist policies, tactics, or writers, we can't escape the conclusion that it shows strongly pro-Communist sympathies. In fact, in these years *almost all* the politically relevant material in *Meanjin* is from Communist or fellow-travelling sources.

The pattern lasts until about 1956. After that, *Meanjin* has for a year an acting-editor (A. G. Serle) and the pattern almost disappears. It is during his occupancy of the Editorial Chair that the one and only criticism of Communist policies is voiced: there is a brief but strong attack on the Russian suppression of the Hungarian rising. This has never been echoed in subsequent issues. There has been, for example, no editorial comment on the imprisoning of the former Communist writers, like Tibor Déry, whose work was reviewed in an article (already mentioned) in *Meanjin* in 1954.

Certainly, in the issues for 1958, the pro-Communist policies are much less obtrusive than before; but they do persist, as one can see by studying, for example, the contents of No. 1 for 1958. There is still a tendency to carp at America, and to be silent about the indignities visited by the Governments of the Soviet bloc on writers and artists. The only movement towards protest, in fact, comes in the discussion on *Dr. Zhivago* in No. 4 for 1958; and that is a pretty uncertain movement, leaving a pretty equivocal effect. The *literary* burden of that discussion is borne by Nina Christesen, who reveals no political prejudices; but the criticisms of the Soviet censorship, made on p. 451, are quickly overlaid with criticisms of 'the West' for being annoyed at the actions of that censorship. *Meanjin*'s policies seem to me now to be in a stage of transition from a kind of fellow-travelling to an uneasy and ambiguous emotional sympathy for its own past. If we take the issues for the last three years *by themselves*, without reference to that past, we can hardly urge that they show 'pro-Communist policies.' But of course it is impossible to take them in isolation; and certain silences are still obtrusive. But the book reviewing is now much more widely apportioned, and there is every chance that the transition stage itself will be soon ended. In the meantime, the large number of *Meanjin*'s readers who are conscious of the sympathies which it once openly held (and not so long ago, at that) are entitled to wonder to what extent it still remains fellow-travelling.

Well, I am sure you won't agree with my reading of all these facts; but I am also sure you will agree that it is not a wanton or irresponsible reading. I can assure you in all honesty and personal good-will, that it is also a fairly representative reading. You know where I stand on most important issues, that I am neither a blowhard nor a *provocateur*, that I can criticise severely without animus, and that I have friendly dispositions towards you. I know you will accept these notes as an honest execution of the job you have asked — challenged me to do. Even if you don't accept the term 'pro-Communist' as adequately descriptive, the analysis I have given will probably show you why I think it is.

Not all *Meanjin*'s critics were so open or so reasonable. Yet, as Lynne Strahan points out at length in *Just City and the Mirrors* (217–39), Buckley's assessment also rested on a number of simplifications. Many of the writers he referred to as 'Communists' had far more ambiguous relationships with the Party than he suggested, and very few of their contributions were overtly political in the narrow sense; furthermore, in assessing the texture of the magazine as a whole, Buckley had passed over many other writers who put forward countervailing views. His comments, which Christesen roundly rejected, are nevertheless indicative of the temper of intellectual opposition to the magazine.

Perhaps the clearest statement of intellectual support came from the art historian Bernard Smith. Smith earned Christesen's enduring gratitude when he spoke out strongly in the Melbourne University debate about *Meanjin*'s future.

NOTES BASED ON COMMENTS BY DR. BERNARD SMITH AT ARTS FACULTY MEETING ON AUGUST 4, 1960

Mr. Dean, I want to support the motion, and to question the opinion expressed at the last meeting on this matter, that *Meanjin* is not an academic journal. To my mind *Meanjin* is an academic journal and in the best sense. It is an academic journal first, because over the past twenty years it has maintained a standard of writing in both original literature and in literary criticism second to none in this country. It has published more good poems, and more good criticism, than any other Australian journal over the past twenty years. And it seems to me, Mr. Dean, that the maintenance of good writing and good literary standards is essentially an academic virtue. Secondly, *Meanjin* has to some extent been an academic journal in a more specialized sense. It has provided space for members of this and other universities to publish their, as we call it, research and investigations. Last night, Mr. Dean, I did a little homework, and I find that according to the Report on Research and Investigations which the University publishes annually, 27 articles are listed between 1951 and 1958, which were published in *Meanjin*. These articles were contributed largely from the Departments of English, French, German and Fine Arts, with an occasional article from History and Architecture. They are articles embodying research, wide reading and informed judgement. Admittedly, the existence or the emergence of more specialized journals such as *AUMLA* specializing in analytical and exegetical literary criticism has provided alternatives. Clearly we need learned journals which cater for the research needs of University Departments. But there is a very real danger in the Universities' becoming too much involved in the creation and financial support of learned journals which promote the research of an individual department at the expense of a journal like *Meanjin*, which does provide avenues of publication for several departments, and in addition is very much concerned with those wider but intensely important issues with which the Faculty of Arts and the Humanities as a whole have in common. If *Meanjin* does fold up at the end of the year, as well it could, those members of this faculty in the language departments who once contributed to *Meanjin* will no doubt find space in *AUMLA*. The historians will talk to one another in *Historical Studies* and in the *Journal of Politics and History*, those of us in Fine Arts will contribute to the *Annual Bulletin of the Gallery Society*, and so forth. But something vital will have been lost, because in *Meanjin* intellectuals of different disciplines and different persuasions met on common ground.

Mr. Dean, *Meanjin* to my mind is the greatest literary journal this country has produced. It has been active in: (1) The creation and maintenance of high literary standards. (2) Intelligent and informed communication between different disciplines of the arts. (3) Fruitful contact between the writers of original verse, short fiction, and criticism. (4) Deliberate involvement in controversial issues.

The thing I want to stress, Mr. Dean, is this: If *Meanjin* folds up at the end of the year it will be a victory for those tendencies in our society which are fragmenting the humanities into specialized compartments and making it increasingly impossible for us to talk in published writing to one another. Whatever you may think of *Meanjin*, it has provided for twenty years a place where the best writers of original prose and verse could publish, and were pleased to publish in the company of academic and at times, thank God, not so academic critics, and where representatives of the different academic disciplines of this Faculty might meet on common ground and discuss issues of more than departmental interest. A whole generation of Australian letters has grown up with *Meanjin* and in the closest possible contact with it.

In its range of interests, its sustained quality, and its continued concern with those issues which affect the Arts Faculty in common with the world of letters as a whole, *Meanjin* has without doubt been the most successful literary journal ever published in this country. And only the *Bulletin* during the first quarter of its existence has had a comparable effect upon Australian letters.

Smith's defence appears to have been decisive in defeating the move to cut off *Meanjin*'s financial support, and in the following years the hostile atmosphere gradually abated as the political polarization of the Cold War period eased and the magazine itself showed a mellower face. Though *Meanjin* hardly had a smooth passage through the 1960s, it was at least able to proceed without constantly guarding both flanks.

C. B. Christesen

Part Four
Beyond the Cultural Cringe

Number 4, 1950

The Cultural Cringe

Arthur Phillips

The Australian Broadcasting Commission has a Sunday programme, designed to cajole a mild Sabbatarian bestirment of the wits, called 'Incognito'. Paired musical performances are broadcast, one by an Australian, one by an overseas executant, but with the names and nationalities withheld until the end of the programme. The listener is supposed to guess which is the Australian and which the alien performer. The idea is that quite often he guesses wrong or gives it up because, strange to say, the local lad proves to be no worse than the foreigner. This unexpected discovery is intended to inspire a nice glow of patriotic satisfaction.

I am not jeering at the A.B.C. for its quaint idea. The programme's designer has rightly diagnosed a disease of the Australian mind and is applying a sensible curative treatment. The dismaying circumstance is that such a treatment should be necessary, or even possible; that in any nation, there should be an assumption that the domestic cultural product will be worse than the imported article.

The devil of it is that the assumption will often be correct. The numbers are against us, and an inevitable quantitative inferiority easily looks like a qualitative weakness, under the most favourable circumstances — and our circumstances are not favourable. We cannot shelter from invidious comparisons behind the barrier of a separate language; we have no long-established or interestingly different cultural tradition to give security and distinction to its interpreters; and the centrifugal pull of the great cultural metropolises works against us. Above our writers — and other artists — looms the intimidating mass of Anglo-Saxon culture. Such a situation almost inevitably produces the characteristic Australian Cultural Cringe — appearing either as the Cringe Direct, or as the Cringe Inverted, in the attitude of the Blatant Blatherskite, the God's-Own-Country and I'm-a-better-man-than-you-are Australian Bore.

The Cringe mainly appears in an inability to escape needless comparisons. The Australian reader, more or less consciously, hedges and hesitates, asking himself 'Yes, but what would a cultivated Englishman think of this?' No writer can communicate confidently to a reader with the 'Yes, but' habit; and this particular demand is curiously crippling to critical judgment. Confronted by Furphy, we grow uncertain. We fail to recognise the extraordinarily original structure of his novel because we are wondering whether perhaps an Englishman might not find it too complex and self-conscious. No one worries about the structural deficiencies of *Moby Dick*. We do not fully savour the meaty individualism of Furphy's style because we are wondering whether perhaps his egotistic verbosity is not too Australianly crude; but we accept the egotistic verbosity of Borrow as part of his quality.

But the dangers of the comparative approach go deeper than this. The Australian writer normally frames his communication for the Australian reader. He assumes a certain mutual preknowledge, a responsiveness to certain symbols, even the ability to hear the cadence of a phrase in the right way. Once the reader's mind begins to be nagged by the thought of how an Englishman might feel about this, he loses the fine edge of his Australian responsiveness. It is absurd to feel apologetic toward *Such is Life* or *Coonardoo* or *Melbourne Odes* because they would not seem quite right to an English reader; it is part of their distinctive virtue that no Englishman can fully understand them.

I once read a criticism which began from the question 'What would a French classicist think of *Macbeth*?' The analysis was discerningly conducted and had a certain paradoxical interest; but it could not escape an effect of comic irrelevance.

A second effect of the Cringe has been the estrangement of the Australian Intellectual. Australian life, let us agree, has an atmosphere of often dismaying crudity. I do not know if our cultural crust is proportionately any thinner than that of other Anglo-Saxon communities; but to the intellectual it seems thinner because, in a small community, there is not enough of it to provide for the individual a protective insulation. Hence, even more than most intellectuals, he feels a sense of exposure. This is made much worse by the intrusion of that deadly habit of English comparisons. There is a certain type of Australian intellectual who is forever sidling up to the cultivated Englishman, insinuating: '*I*, of course, am not like these other crude Australians; *I* understand how you must feel about them; *I* should be spiritually more at home in Oxford or Bloomsbury.'

It is not the critical attitude of the intellectual that is harmful; that could be a healthy, even creative, influence, if the criticism were felt to come from within, if the critic had a sense of identification with his subject, if his irritation came from a sense of shared shame rather than a disdainful separation. It is his refusal to participate, the arch of his indifferent eyebrows, which exerts the chilling and stultifying influence.

Thinking of this type of Australian Intellectual, I am a little uneasy about my phrase 'Cultural Cringe'; it is so much the kind of missile which he delights to toss at the Australian mob. I hope I have made it clear that my use of the phrase is not essentially unsympathetic, and that I regard the denaturalised Intellectual as the Cringe's unhappiest victim. If any of the breed use my phrase for his own contemptuous purposes, my curse be upon him. May crudely-Dinkum Aussies spit in his beer, and gremlins split his ever to be preciously agglutinated infinitives.

The Australian writer is affected by the Cringe because it mists the responsiveness of his audience, and because its influence on the intellectual deprives the writer of a sympathetically critical atmosphere. Nor can he entirely escape its direct impact. There is a significant phrase in Henry Handel Richardson's *Myself When Young*. When she found herself stuck in a passage of *Richard Mahony* which would not come right, she remarked to her husband, 'How did I ever dare to write *Maurice Guest* — a poor little colonial like me?' Our sympathies go out to her — pathetic victim of the Cringe. For observe that the Henry Handel Richardson who had written *Maurice Guest* was not the raw girl encompassed by the limitations of the Kilmore Post Office and a Philistine mother. She had already behind her the years in Munich and a day-to-day communion with a husband steeped in the European literary tradition. Her cultural experience was probably richer than that of such contemporary novelists as Wells or Bennett. It was primarily the simple damnation of being an Australian which made her feel limited. Justified, you may think, by the tone of Australian life, with its isolation and excessively material emphasis? Examine the evidence fairly and closely, and I think you will agree that Henry Handel Richardson's Australian background was a shade richer in cultural influence than the dingy shop-cum stuffy Housekeeper's Room-cum sordid Grammar School which incubated Wells, or than the Five Towns of the eighteen-eighties.

By both temperament and circumstance, Henry Handel Richardson was peculiarly susceptible to the influence of the Cringe; but no Australian writer, unless he is dangerously insensitive, can wholly escape it; he may fight it down or disguise it with a veneer of truculence, but it must weaken his confidence and nag at his integrity.

It is not so much our limitations of size, youth and isolation which create the problem as the derivativeness of our culture; and it takes more difficult forms than the Cringe. The writer is particularly affected by our colonial situation because of the nature of his medium. The painter is in some measure bound by the traditional evolution of his art, the musician must consider the particular combination of sound which the contemporary civilised ear can accept; but ultimately paint is always paint, a piano everywhere a piano. Language has no such ultimate physical existence; it is in its essence merely what generations of usage have made it. The three symbols m-a-n create the image of a male human being only because venerable English tradition has so decreed. The Australian writer cannot cease to be English even if he wants to. The nightingale does not sing under Australian skies; but he still sings in the literate Australian mind. It may thus became the symbol which runs naturally to the tip of the writer's pen; but he dare not use it because it has no organic relation with the Australian life he is interpreting.

The Jindyworobaks are entirely reasonable when they protest against the alien symbolism used by O'Dowd, Brennan or McCrae; but the difficulty is not simply solved. A Jindyworobak writer uses the image 'galah-breasted dawn'. The picture is both fresh and accurate, and has a sense of immediacy because it comes direct from the writer's environment; and yet somehow it doesn't quite come off. The trouble is that we — unhappy Cringers — are too aware of the processes in its creation. We can feel the writer thinking: 'No, I mustn't use one of the images which English language tradition is insinuating into my mind; I must have something Australian: ah, yes — ' What the phrase has gained in immediacy, it has lost in spontaneity. You have some measure of the complexity of the problem of a colonial culture when you reflect that the last sentence I have written is not so nonsensical as it sounds.

I should not, of course, suggest that the Australian image can never be spontaneously achieved; one need not go beyond Stewart's *Ned Kelly* to disprove such an assumption. On the other hand, the distracting influence of the English tradition is not restricted to merely linguistic difficulties. It confronts the least cringing Australian writer at half-a-dozen points.

What is the cure for our disease? There is no short-cut to the gradual processes of national growth — which are already beginning to have their effect. The most important development of the last twenty years in Australian writing has been the progress made in the art of being unselfconsciously ourselves. If I have thought this article worth writing, it is because I believe that progress will quicken when we articulately recognise two facts: that the Cringe is a worse enemy to our cultural development than our isolation, and that the opposite of the Cringe is not the Strut, but a relaxed erectness of carriage.

Some things are easier to say than to do. That 'relaxed erectness of carriage' was a phantom — a phrase that was bound to induce its own reflexive cringe in anyone who did not have the physique, the confidence or the connections to walk comfortably around Wesley College and its ilk. Yet in this brief essay Phillips coined a phrase that is still with us. It is one of *Meanjin*'s small legacies to vernacular Australian English. Such are the powers of alliteration, as Phillips himself later remarked.

Christesen did not especially like the essay, but agreed to publish it, and was impressed by the response. Certainly the timing was apposite. The question of developing an appropriate national posture was very much at the heart of intellectual debate, and was to remain so for much of the next twenty years. The long-standing urge to develop a sense of Australian tradition was sharpened by the changes that were occurring on the world stage as Britain's economic and cultural influence waned and the USA moved into the ascendancy, bringing with it what Christesen derisively termed the 'Koka-Kola culture'. These shifts confronted Australian writers and intellectuals with an acute problem: could the nascent Australian 'high' culture survive and establish a distinctive identity for itself without succumbing to a numbing isolationism?

This was an issue on which Christesen took a number of different but complementary tacks. At one level, he adopted an unashamedly propagandist line in favour of the local product. He kept up a barrage of commentary on the plight of Australian writers and artists, the inadequacy of government support for the arts, the parlous state of the local publishing industry, and the neglect of Australian literature in the universities, an issue on which Christesen initiated a major series of essays in 1954. One of the most cautious, but also most influential, contributions on the last matter came from A. D. Hope, by this time head of the English Department at Canberra University College.

Number 2, 1954

Australian Literature and the Universities

A. D. Hope

About five years ago the Fellowship of Australian Writers (Melbourne section) invited me to talk to them on this subject and in the discussion which followed there occurred some polite but trenchant criticism of the Australian universities for their neglect of our national literature. My talk had been a defence of the attitude of at least one of our universities but I was compelled to admit the force of what many of my critics had to urge.

It was pointed out that our literature is approaching its second century and, while it has produced few outstanding writers, it has already a respectable and growing body of writing to show. And yet of the eight teaching universities in the country not one has so far established a course in Australian Literature. While there are literatures which it is important for any university to study, it is the peculiar right and the duty of each country to establish and to foster the study of its own writers.

The second point was that the study of literature depends on a number of ancillary studies, historical, biographical and bibliographical, which can only be carried out by expert research workers and this sort of research it is the proper function of universities to maintain. They spoke of the material for these studies still uncollected and unassessed and of the scholars of the future who would deplore our neglect. As they talked I remembered how a year or two before, after a lecture on Charles Harpur, one of my students had told me that she was a descendant of the poet and that only a few months earlier her mother had put a whole trunk-full of Harpur's papers under the laundry copper thinking that there was no longer any interest in keeping them. I was compelled to admit that our universities were at fault.

Why then have they neglected Australian literature? I think it is not hard to see why. In the first place modern literature has only just come to have a recognized place in the English courses of universities. Until recently their attitude was that noted by Henry Handel Richardson of her schooldays:

> . . . We had learned a fair amount of Milton, Wordsworth, Gray, Cowper and so on; *but Tennyson was not yet accounted a classic*, and stray scraps were all I knew of him. [The italics are mine.]

Australian literature in fact shared this general feeling in the past that nineteenth and twentieth century literature were too modern for university studies, which ought to be reserved for the established classics. However this attitude has been out-moded for a good many years now, so that it will hardly account for the fact that Australian literature is still a neglected subject in university studies. Yet modern English literature has found a place there. A more important reason perhaps is a vague feeling that Australian literature is not good enough or that it is not well enough established as a separate branch of literature, or again, that there is not yet enough of it to justify its having a course to itself. And although it may be infuriating to some partisans of Australian literature, I believe that these feelings are substantial and just. To argue against them is I think the wrong sort of argument and the right sort of argument is to show that, even if these contentions are true, there are other good reasons for universities to establish such courses. The pass course in English in our universities is usually one of three years. Some universities have honours courses of four years. But the plain fact is that English literature can only be covered in this time with the greatest difficulty. To give a considerable part of this time to the study of Australian literature would mean that neither could be properly dealt with. On the other hand to establish separate and independent courses in Australian literature is a luxury that none of our universities, always desperately short of money, has so far been able to afford.

To see the reason why, in spite of its justice, this argument ought not to be accepted, I think we need to ask ourselves what sorts of justification there are for establishing a subject of study at a university. There are three sorts of answer: educational, intellectual and utilitarian.

In the first place certain university studies have the function of helping to maintain and promote a cultural tradition. Their aim is, in part at least, educative, and their method is to foster critical understanding and to civilise the imagination. For this the study of English literature is of prime importance. And if we have to choose what shall go into such a course, we are right to choose the best we can get. It would, I think, be hard to argue that Australian literature has anything comparable to offer. It is not a matter of arguing whether Goldsmith is inferior to Henry Handel Richardson, or Lovelace to Shaw Neilson. It is the more general argument that the great English writers cannot without loss be replaced by even the best of our Australian writers and that if we are to study great writers we ought to study them in their natural context of the lesser writers of their periods. To find a place for Australian literature within the present English courses is a disservice to both. And I am not sure that the present practice of most universities, the compromise by which, not Australian literature, but a few Australian books are included in the English course has anything to be said for it at all. It may be argued that the body of literature is one body and I think that this is so. But the man who graduated with B.A., honours, in English literature has had an opportunity of knowing that body in all its range and beauty: the man who graduates with B.A., honours (Aust. Lit.), would be like a doctor setting out to practise medicine after having dissected the left knee and the liver.

Yet even if we admit this, there is an argument for the study of Australian literature as a separate subject. In the maintenance of the cultural tradition the study of English literature may have claims immensely superior to those of Australian literature. But it would be foolish to ignore the fact that our native literature has something important to contribute in the very fact that it is *native*: that the civilisation, the way of life and the problems of this country are our own problems and that it is through literature that a civilisation expresses itself, through literature its values and its tendencies become conscious and its creative force becomes eloquent and evident.

Even if it were argued that the cultural tradition of Australia is not yet a very important one, it is still true that it is very important for Australians to consider it. However, I shall be prepared to maintain that the cultural tradition of Australia already has considerable importance and that quite apart from this there is a growing body of Australian writing which is well worth studying in itself. I would certainly not suggest that the only reason for studying Australian literature is for its historical interest and the light that it throws on local problems.

But universities exist for another purpose than the education of individuals. They exist primarily for the promotion of studies, for the advancement of knowledge in particular fields. As their name suggests, they exist in theory at least for the promotion of studies in *all* the fields of knowledge. No single university can do more than dream of this, but for each there will be subjects which have special claims not likely to be felt so strongly in other universities. And one of these claims is indisputable: the claim of the national literature to be a subject of study in the universities of the home country. It is not only the natural and obvious place for such studies but it is the natural and obvious duty of the home universities to initiate such studies so that they may take their due part in the idea of the *universitas*, the universal body of knowledge which nowadays can be covered not by any single university institution but by the general body of universities in the world. From this point of view it is not a question of whether Australian universities can afford to establish courses in the study of Australian literature but whether they can afford not to do so if they are to carry out their functions. If literature is recognized as one of their proper fields of study, the universities as a whole should study literature as a whole wherever it exists and Australian universities have the right and the duty to see that the literature of their own country does not form a gap in the general body of studies.

The third reason for the establishing of a university course is technical and practical: the provision of the community with experts in the arts and sciences. Even if the study of literature is not a means, it depends, as I have said, on certain technical and expert studies, bibliographical, historical and so on, without which it cannot do its work effectively. And this forms another reason for the establishment of courses in Australian literature. If you are to have the study of literature in itself, you must have these ancillary studies as well.

From these considerations I would draw certain conclusions. In the first place it is high time that we had courses in Australian literature in our universities, that universities themselves and the sources from which they draw their funds should be prepared to budget for this. In the second place these courses should not form a part of, or an addendum to, existing courses in English literature but should be independent and separate courses of study. In the third place, because our native literature is a minor one among the literatures of the world, because it is limited in range and has hardly any writers of first rank, and because it is a branch of English literature in general, its study should not be simply an alternative to the study of English literature. It should, I believe, be undertaken only by students who have already undergone or who are undergoing training in one of the major world literatures, preferably that of England. With such ideas in mind Canberra University College is at present experimenting in the establishment, for the first time in this country, of a complete course in Australian literature. The present course has been designed on historical lines and we hope that it will develop and in time help to encourage the establishment of studies in other places.

Hope's comments elicited responses from all over the country, mainly from other academics who were anxious to develop the study of Australian literature within the parameters of the existing English departments. Meanwhile Vance Palmer quietly noted that there was not much point in trying to establish university courses in Australian literature until publishers were prepared to keep Australian books in print.

Another string to the editor's bow was the vigorous promotion of high culture in all its forms against the burgeoning of mass culture. Confronted with the rapid commercialization of cultural life, *Meanjin*, its editor and contributors opted to stand against the tide. In retrospect it is remarkable how many pages of the magazine were devoted to the subject of comic books (which, Albert E. Kahn informed *Meanjin* readers, 'pour an unending torrent of filth and bestiality into the minds of American children'). On the question of censoring comic books the editorial line was significantly less liberal than it was with regard to 'works of literature'. And in the mid-1950s, with the introduction of television imminent, *Meanjin* published a flurry of articles for and against the new medium; the overwhelming impression was that the Australian intelligentsia was waiting with bated breath to see what would eventuate, and in the interim was being given a free choice of prejudices in a situation where it had little control over the outcome.

A more positive side of Clem Christesen's resistance to American mass culture was his determination to cultivate constructive, critical debate about Australian culture, and particularly to develop an understanding of the ambiguous relationship between European arts and letters and their Australian counterparts. Oddly enough, while Christesen's political opponents were complaining about the amount of political comment in the magazine, *Meanjin* was in fact devoting far more space to the visual arts. Each year Christesen published a comment on the main round of art prizes (the Archibald, Wynne and Sulman awards). He also found space for a swingeing review of Sidney Nolan by John Béchervaise, and for Robin Boyd's scathing comments on a photographic exhibition on Victorian architecture: 'Looking over the photographs, it did seem that there were, after all, quite a number of presentable buildings in Victoria. It is only necessary to look out the window to correct this impression.'

In its reviews and literary criticism, *Meanjin* trod the fine line between encouraging local writers and developing a strong critical tradition. It assiduously reviewed Australian books — not only poetry and novels, but also works of literary and art criticism, history and biography — many of which were published by small presses and received little attention elsewhere. But Christesen sensibly discouraged uncritical reviews; though at one point Vincent Buckley slyly referred to the 'literary double standard' that prescribed different values for the assessment of local and overseas work, praise was usually given only when it was due.

Apart from the book reviews, *Meanjin* also published many substantial critical essays surveying the work of major Australian writers — Vincent Buckley and F. T. Macartney on Kenneth Slessor, Bob Brissenden on Judith Wright, A. D. Hope on Henry Handel Richardson, Mary Gilmore on David Martin, and a full issue dedicated to the work of Vance and Nettie Palmer, to mention only a few. Among all these critical essays, one of Christesen's greatest scoops was to commission Marjorie Barnard to write an extended essay on Patrick White's work at a time when White's writing had received little public attention in Australia. There was a palpable sense of excitement; here, at last, was a writer whose work was powerful and original, modernist and distinctively Australian. And he had seemingly come from nowhere.

Number 2, 1956

The Four Novels of Patrick White

MARJORIE BARNARD

Of Patrick White, the man, I know little save by deduction. The Mitchell Library catalogue is biographically silent and *Who's Who in Australia* has nothing to say. A few details of his life will be found in Morris Miller's and F. T. Macartney's new edition of *Australian Literature* (p. 491). He now lives at Castle Hill, near Sydney, after an absence of many years abroad. There are, however, five books from his pen, beginning with *The Ploughman and Other Poems*, written overseas between 1932 and 1934, and culminating in the life-sized novel, *The Tree of Man*.

Consideration of his work, which is remarkably homogeneous over the twenty-years span of his writing life, falls naturally into two parts: 1) the content and technique of his books, and 2) their underlying philosophy. . . .

HAPPY VALLEY

In the fatal year 1939, White's first novel *Happy Valley* was published in England. It rose, like Artemis, complete from the troubled waters and it bears few of the marks of a first novel, its occasional angularity being a persistent feature of White's work. It is the most closely patterned, the most efficient of his books.

Ironically, *Happy Valley* is the name of a village in the southern snow country of New South Wales; small, remote, isolated:

> In Happy Valley the people existed in spite of each other . . . the country slept, inwardly intent on some secret war of passion or trying to separate the threads of old passions spent. This made the town seem very ephemeral. In summer when the slopes were a scurfy yellow and the body of the earth was very hot, lying there stretched out, the town with its cottages of red and brown weatherboard, reminded you of an ugly scab somewhere on the body of the earth. It was so ephemeral. Some day it would drop off, leaving a pink clean place underneath. (p. 28)

Australian literature offers many pictures of country towns: Norman Lindsay's Rabelaisian *Redheap*, where all is sordid in a lusty, cheerful way; Kylie Tennant's *Tiburon*, warm and full under its rough surface; Vance Palmer's delicately articulated reconstructions in *Daybreak* and *The Passage*; Leonard Mann's emotional, staccato *Mountain Flat* . . . *Happy Valley* is more ingrowing than any of them, at once more secret and more diagrammatic. It is a place seen from a distance, dwindled and interpenetrated by a highly personal viewpoint. It is curiously inorganic, shown in semi-petrified strata. There are the inhabitants, of whom the Everitts are the prototypes. There are the necessary intruders, the Belpers at the bank, the Moriartys at the school, the doctor and, though of earlier date, the Quongs, who brought enterprise to the town by which all profited, but who were never accepted. Beyond this close circle are the squatters, the Furlows, accepted but not belonging, as unlike the squires of England as they could be.

Into this tightly-drawn, static pattern are thrust two strangers — the new doctor, Oliver Halliday, and Furlow's new overseer, Clem Hagen. From the impact springs the narrative; and once begun by the accident of propinquity, it moves on to its resolution through the logic of character. The love of the frustrated doctor for Alys Browne, one of the inhabitants who does not run true to type, and the affair between Vic Moriarty and Clem Hagen, born of boredom, end on the same day — the day that Ernest Moriarty, maddened by his own impotence, kills his wife just after her lover has left her, and himself dies upon the road of a heart seizure. It is his body in their path that turns back the escaping lovers, Oliver and Alys. Halliday realizes that he is a doctor and a husband and can never be anything else. The field is possessed by the strong and the insensitive. While Alys loses both her chance of happiness and her money, through the irresponsible advice of the banker, Halliday must remain forever in the trap of his own nature; but Hagen is saved from possible implication in the murder by the sullen nineteen-year-old Sidney Furlow, who claims him as her lover and arranges what is virtually a shot-gun marriage. Only the ruthless survive. The story is ugly and pathetic. In its genre it belongs to the tough-and-tender school, but it has little to do with Hemingway or any other exponent. It is handled with sensitiveness rather than delicacy. The treatment is full of paradox. It is uneven, as though it reacted against itself in sudden turns and contradictions. The story itself is lucid; but it is in its handling that the writer appears at war with himself, as though he must redress tenderness with violence, and subtlety with starkness. He can delineate a mood, as when the young soldier, Oliver Halliday, listens to Bach in a church near the Luxembourg Gardens:

> The music came rushing out of the loft, unfurling banners of sound. You could touch it. You could feel it. You could feel a stillness and a music all at once. You were at once floating and stationary, in time, all time and space, without barrier, passing with a fresher knowledge of the tangible to a point where this dissolved, became the spiritual. (p. 20)

Or:

> There is nothing so calculated to make you feel forgotten as somebody else's leather chair in a fireless room. (p. 166)

Or the portrait of Margaret Quong, who learned so early that life would hold little for her because of her mixed blood.

The book is sensitive and then suddenly it is brutal; a stone is flung among the quivering, exposed nerves:

> I repeat there is not much crime [in Happy Valley]. Only the publican before the man they had at the moment once set fire to his wife and, on another occasion, a drover from the Murray side ran amok and crucified a road man on a dead tree. Old Harry Grogan found the body. It was like a scare-crow, he said, only it didn't scare. There was crows all over the place, sitting there and dipping their beaks into the buttonholes. (p. 10)

The action of the novel is slow; it inches along until it reaches its crisis and then it is suddenly bold and stark. It builds up quietly, the sensitive pen explores delicately but pitilessly the nerves of the characters, their hidden thoughts, their frustrations, their blind and painful inarticulateness. There is understanding but it is difficult to know if there is sympathy. The people are manipulated, but the reality is beyond their small lives in the whole.

The prose is fluid, sometimes arresting. Patrick White may be discursive; he introduces irrelevancies but always with a purpose — a pinch of this, a pinch of that, a dash of purple to throw up the colours. It is not the traditional Australian discursiveness, like a yarn told at the campfire. White is an artist who knows how to use his material and is sometimes too skilful for verisimilitude. He uses various styles to achieve his ends. Sometimes it is the stream-of-consciousness, admixing thought and speech, sometimes the trick of the broken sentence:

> There was a hard efficiency in the doctor's face, like the face of someone who does things well facing someone who. She turned over a page. (p. 99)

Sometimes he employs a Joycean idiom in which characters flow together in sleep:

> Slabbed in sleep their legs apart licked a stamp or went up the hill on the

> curve of the moon played Schumann it was chalk chalk in his bones or heartburn as he tossed the ticket took a train Rodney Rodney there on the map is Queensland yellow for Sun and she stretched out her arm that clove white a slice of the darkness she put up her face with pins drawn back into a roll and then crackled the arpeggio you could always tack down the hem and write and write and write to blot out another purpose if you write. (pp. 111–12)

At moments it is almost in the vein of Gertrude Stein:

> The wind is wind is water wind or water white in pockets of the eyes was once a sheep before time froze the plover call alew aloo atingle is the wire that white voice across the plain on thistle thorn the wind pricks face the licked fire the wind flame tossing out distance on a reel. (p. 185)

The prose never becomes incomprehensible. In their context the passages quoted are fully intelligible as they pick up familiar threads and re-weave them in a strange pattern. White uses devices only to highlight his meaning; he does not allow them to become monotonous.

He uses pattern in a similar manner. There are several recurring incidents and symbols that are never repeated too often: Oliver at sixteen reading poetry to Hilda in the Botanic Gardens; the music in the French church; Margaret's shell; Mrs. Everitt's dead geranium . . . These are like recurring themes in music and serve the same purpose.

THE LIVING AND THE DEAD

The second novel, *The Living and the Dead*, issued by a different publishing house in 1941, is in the same mould as *Happy Valley*; a little more intricate, a little less real in its setting. It is the only one of Patrick White's novels set in England and this may be the root of its unreality. Well as he may know England, he still moves more freely in the country of his youth. Of Australia he writes from within, though as an expatriate, seeing it always in the changing terms of memory. He brings to the English scene a different sort of awareness — which emanates from the book and can be felt but not pinned down. The descriptions are like colour prints:

> The fog shifted on the miles they walked, and spilt open like a paper bag, spilling a powdered field, a hillside with an oast house, the little feathery branches of a Japanese orchard. But near the sea the land continued sour, the salt marshes with a crust of ice that lifted sometimes round the roots of reeds, a lid of silver opened on the black mud. They came to a house, a thin, pale house, like the last slice of a house left standing in a field. The house was called Mon Repos. There was a Hovis sign and a plaster pixie in the parlour window. (p. 291)

The structure of the book is in the shape of a loop. Its end is its beginning. It begins on a note of departure and despair, just as *Happy Valley* began with a still birth; it ends where it began with Elyot Standish getting on a bus, going he knew not where. The story is mainly concerned with three people, Catherine Standish, her son Elyot and her daughter Eden. The two women are the dominants. Catherine, née Goose, begins diffidently, gains a false assurance from which she gradually slides to complete moral collapse. Eden begins as a determined and spirited child, grows to disillusioned womanhood and recaptures certainty in sacrifice. Elyot remains throughout a sort of emotional sounding board. He feels, he observes, he does not act:

> His work had evolved out of his innate diffidence, the withdrawing from a window at dusk, saying: I must do something, but what? Out of this bewilderment he had taken refuge behind what people told him was a scholarly mind. He hung on gratefully, after a month or two of uncertainty, to remarks made by tutors at Cambridge and the more wishful and hence more helpful remarks of his mother. So that he became before long, forgetting the process, a raker of dust, a rattler of bones.

In other words, he wrote scholarly books about obscure people. He could afford to as he had a private income.

His desiccated affair with Muriel Raphael came silently to its end on a flippant remark; the glamour his mother had cast over him crumbled into irritation; his relationship with his sister remained like a hard green apple. He resisted his pity for the love-sodden Connie Tiarks.

The word 'lumpy' followed Connie about like a classical epithet. She was as depressed and humble as Muriel was hard and brittle. Even her hat betrayed her:

> It was a kind of beige tam o'shanter hat with an apologetic drooping bow, put there it seemed by accident, the whole undeniably found in a sale. Connie's hat made him shudder. It was such an outspoken comment on her own life.

Elyot was much oppressed by his womenfolk — his mother with her meretricious glitter; his sister with her dark, closed fortitude; Muriel who was incapable of giving; Connie who wanted to give too much. It was a four-way stretch.

It is an unhappy book; all the characters are lost or frustrated or decadent so that it is difficult to know who are the living and who the dead. There is a nightmare light over the scene:

> There were threads from the so many threads of the mystery you had to accept and in the streets at night, with the interweaving of passionless faces, the passage of solid buses, the downward falling of a steady Neon rain, it was easy enough to accept. The whole business was either a mystery, or else meaningless, and of the two, the meaningless is the more difficult to take. (p. 4)

Practically all London was dead:

> under a spring sky the chimneys pointed at an illusion of their own solidity and greatness, gardeners pressed the earth round the roots of flowers, as if you could transform with so many heads of bloom what was a sour sick earth. Beyond the park were streets of houses. He preferred these to the decorated corpse, rather the closed, unseeing eyes of houses. There was a smell of cooking, of cabbage, of midday activity in the close streets. A huddle of identical houses. Like their tenants these

> chose the uniform in which to ignore discrepancy. The women ladling cabbage in their kitchens were almost interchangeable, behind the skin the identical wishes, the pale hopes, the thin desires spoke from the closed eyes of houses. (p. 325)

The book is drenched in the pathetic fallacy. It is an inside-out book. Every object — a plant, a glass box, a salt marsh, a bus — becomes a symbol of an inner life. The characters look out of windows and see their own desolation. The weather is never good.

Catherine Standish was in any case dead; she was a fake of a fake of a fake. Elyot was dead, though for him there was a gleam of hope:

> He still failed to grasp, but beyond the nothing and the death there was some suggestion of growth. He waited for this in a state of expectation. He waited for something that would happen to him, and would happen in time, there was no going to meet it. (p. 369)

Adelaide and Gerald were dead of their snobbery. Muriel Raphael was dead because she had chosen death in preference to Jewry. Julia Fallon was dead of her suppressed and denied motherhood. Wally Collins was dead because he was barely human; an appetite and very little else. Connie was dead because she could not find her way into life.

Only Eden and Joe Barnett (for Eden gave her love beneath her, as her mother married above herself) are left alive and they doubtfully:

> [Joe] believed in rightness, . . . [Eden] said, giving him this, she had given it to him with her own voice, he believed in the living as opposed to the dead. This was also what made him ache sometimes in the pit of the stomach. He read the newspapers and felt sick. The certainty of your own life, the day to day in Crick's workshop, the Saturdays with Eden, were no guarantee against the sick feeling in the pit of your stomach. This became the sad, sick, stinking world. He was responsible in a way. But his hands were helpless, could not cope. (p. 289)

And again:

> He stroked her throat. She could feel a kind of absent tenderness in the hand. He could feel her softer skin, that was like a lapse of conscience. I love Eden, he said, but what can this do for the world, the sick, stinking world that sits in the stomach like a conscience? He was helpless. He was always helpless, unless it was something he could do with his hands. He could love with his hands, he could shape things out of wood, but the wind slipped through his fingers, the dark disturbing wind of distant forces and ideas, the things you sensed and could not deal with. You sat and stared at your hands, that could give no answer but their own emptiness. (p. 297)

Joe eventually solved his difficulties by going to the Spanish War and there was killed. Eden accepted this with fortitude:

> Walking over dead grass she talked about right and wrong, glibly, as abstract concepts. But this was the expression of rightness, the southward face, the beginning in an end, rather than the end in a beginning. If you could accept the personal end. She had to, had to cultivate accept-

ance. There is no Eden Standish, just as there is no Joe Barnett, you said. There is more than this, there is the stock of positive acts and convictions that two people infuse into the dying body of the world, their more than blood. (p. 334)

Eden followed him to Spain:

> The arch enemies were the stultifying, the living dead. The living chose to oppose these, either in Eden's way, by the protest of self-destruction, or by what, by what if not an intenser form of living. (p. 379)

Insofar as the book is resolved, the Spanish War is its solution. It is the cause outside the individual and none the worse for being a lost one.

The Living and the Dead is a book of its times. It was written between 1939 and June 1940, published in 1941. It came into a troubled world and bears its imprint. There is a flavour of Sitwell's *Before the Bombardment* about it, and at moments White writes as Henry Moore paints; or so it seems to me:

> Sleep met him halfway, or the allegory of waking, it was the Greco she had seen, the centurion in Spain, he was walking in the field which was where he lost, beyond the white cocoon, when others asked a priest or went to Spain, there were many roads out of the field of sleep, the difficulty was to choose, there were many roads the feet took without faces, these were directionless, he was walking in a white sleep, there were the priests as white as aspirin, there was the saxophonist talking to the old ladies, the old clown, and the sleeping figures, your own, lay in the white cocoon, it was a personal Spain, it was a destruction of the superfluous, either the priest or the glass box, it could not write, write too fast, it could not write the papers black from white, this was sweat, the necessity, if I do not do this you said, if not the singing priest the no more love, the wilted brown nipples that were bitter on the mouth, and losing the face, it was the face of Joe, they had lopped the tree, it lay in blood, you could not touch because the eyes, your eyes, became the mirror that moved too clearly to, that saw too clearly right down to the heart, and the blood moving in a cone of glass, it was the clearness that revolted, that you didn't want to see, you put up a hand to hide your own bones and a transparent, fruitless egg. (p. 323)

Despite the general drear there are more flashes of humour in *The Living and the Dead* than in *Happy Valley*. The picture of Mrs. McCarthy, for instance: 'Her hand was a plump hot water bottle. She was a series of hot water bottles in plush. Tonight she was enjoying the luxury of neuralgia and the sympathy that nobody gave'. (p. 97) Or: 'When it suits us, Mrs. Standish tapped. When it suits us to martyrise ourselves in draughty halls. Then we go to bed with a cold, and feel we've contributed something towards a cause'. (p. 319) Or, the light touch: 'The two languid female voices soaped at space somewhere on a crossed line.'

In general the style is more lucid and conventional in *The Living and the Dead* than in *Happy Valley*, the pattern more fugitive, the individual characters more symbolic, dwarfed by a masked battery of abstracts.

THE AUNT'S STORY

The Aunt's Story shows a retreat from the abstract and a return to the individual theme. Where *Happy Valley* was the picture of a community and *The Living and the Dead* an intensive study of three people under the shadow of the looming war years, *The Aunt's Story* is an even more intensive delineation of the secret life of one woman, Theodora Goodman. Like *Happy Valley*, the novel begins with death, the death of old Mrs. Goodman; an event, desirable in itself, but which frees Theodora from the quasi-normal life forced on her by circumstances and sets her feet upon the path that only ends in the lunatic asylum of an obscure American town.

The book is in three parts: 1) Theodora's childhood and youth at Meröe, the family property, where the seeds of mortal frustration are sown; 2) the Jardin Exotique of the Hotel du Midi where Theodora's frustration finds a strange blooming amid people who are nearer to the figments of a disordered imagination than to flesh and blood; and 3) 'Holstius,' the consummation of a dream in insanity.

The story has its own painful logic, the prose is richer than in the earlier books, the imagery more striking and ingenious. This is the most imaginative and bizarre of Patrick White's novels. It has impetus and unity and is constructed with great skill. There is a terrible, warped logic about it.

Theodora was the unloved child who made contact only with her father, and he died. She found him dead in his library and she buried her face on his knees, just as she afterwards did on the knees of Holstius, the last creation of her unhappy imagination. When she had communed with her dead father:

> She walked out through the passages, through the sleep of other people. She was thin as grey light, as if she had just died. She would not wake the others. It was still too terrible to tell, too private an experience. As if she were to go into the room and say: 'Mother I am dead, I am dead, Meröe has crumbled.' So she went outside where the grey light was as thin as water and Meröe had in fact, dissolved. Cocks were crowing the legend of the day but only the legend. Meröe was grey water, grey ash. Then Theodora Goodman cried. (pp. 195–6)

She grew up to be plain and awkward and with a black moustache. She lost her first love to her pretty sister. She became nothing but an aunt, 'ugly as a stone, awkwardness in her empty hands'. (p. 133) To be an aunt was her only contact with reality.

The landscape of Meröe fitted her like a skin:

> The hills were burnt yellow. Thin yellow scurf lay on the black skin of the hills, which had worn into black pock marks where the eruptions had taken place. And now the trees were more than ever like white bones. Out of all this exhaustion formed the clear, expectant weather of autumn, smelling of chrysanthemums and first frost. (pp. 93–4)

Later, when she has changed her skies, the Hotel du Midi became an externalization of her changed mood:

> In the Hotel du Midi the night slowly solidified. From the brown

lounge Theodora listened to the doors closing, which was a quite definite closing, on other lives. She was left to her own devices, like a mouse in a piano picking the bones of a gavotte. Under the once-pink shade the light still burned, that somebody had forgotten, and the beads were still there to tell. On such occasions the soul will have faded a good deal. It jumps beneath its attempted composure. This was apparent to Theodora. She heard the exhausted springs of the arm-chairs. She saw the ash trays, which had brimmed almost over, with ash, and the exasperated gnawings of pale nails. (p. 228)

The sharp spikes and fleshy leaves of the Jardin Exotique are at once exotic and erotic. In the garden she finds for a time a make-believe resting place. It is Theodora's clumsy and ineffectual attempt to attain a full life, a story book life. The reader is never sure if the other guests at the hotel have existence outside Theodora's feverish imagination: General Alyosha Sergei Sokolnikov, who talks like a Russian novel and who spent his mornings with his young love, Varvara, and his afternoons with Ludmilla, his sister who is also his conscience and with whom he identifies Theodora; Mrs. Rapallo with her illusions of grandeur and her daughter the Principessa who is as illusory as Varvara and Ludmilla; the Demoiselles Bloch who count their possessions every night before they sleep; the curious lovers, Wetherby and Lieselotte, ('Love is undoubtedly an acrostic [thought Theodora] and that is why I have failed'); the young girl Katina Pavlou, who is Theodora as she might have been; and all the rest. In her nightmare Theodora is always practical and full of commonsense, enjoying the illusion of sanity, the heroine of a mad world.

But it cannot last. The nautilus shell, which is the grail of that strange world, is destroyed; the hotel is burned down and Theodora is forced onward in her journey toward nothingness. She had taken the first steps long before when she was a child:

> things floated out of reach. She put out her hand, they bobbed and were gone. She listened to the voices that murmured the other side of the wall. Or she followed the Syrian at darkness, and the Syrian's brown silence did not break, the sky just failed to flow through. (p. 39)

Now she must leave another world. She goes to America, where 'the desperate hum of telephone wires that tell of mortgages and pie, and phosphates and love, and movie contracts and indigestion and real estate and loneliness' is more alien to her than the Jardin Exotique:

> In the bland corn song, in the theme of days, Theodora Goodman was a discord. Those mouths which attempted her black note rejected it wryly. They glossed over something that had strayed out of some other piece, of slow fire. (p. 311)

She makes a last attempt to assume normality. Living in a derelict house, she embraces her last illusion, Holstius, who is in part her father, in part the Man who was given Dinner (the rejected), in part Moraïtis, the musician who had opened but not filled her heart. Holstius tells her what she already knows:

> You cannot reconcile joy and sorrow, or flesh and marble, or illusion and reality, or life and death. For this reason, Theodora Goodman, you must accept. And you have already found that one constantly deludes the other into taking fresh shapes, so that there is sometimes little to choose between the reality of illusion or the illusion of reality. Each of your several lives is evidence of this. (p. 334)

As long ago Theodora had destroyed the little hawk, whose beauty had enchanted her, because to destroy it was pain, so now she tears up her travel tickets, and soon gives up her name, the last link with home and her identity:

> But now her name was torn out by the roots, just as she had torn the tickets, rail and steamship, on the mountain road. This way, perhaps, she came a little closer to humility, to anonymity, to pureness of being.

The Aunt's Story is an allegory of pain, a shifting image of frustration. It is executed with great artistry and it is surprising that it is not more moving. It is bound together by a labyrinth of recurring images — the Syrian, the shot bird, the Man who was given Dinner, the nautilus shell and others — but this is always done so inconspicuously that the effect is achieved without hammering on the reader's attention.

THE TREE OF MAN

The three earlier books, complete in themselves, are a prelude to the fourth, the very large novel, *The Tree of Man*, published in the United States in 1955 and just available in Australia. It is more massive than its 500 pages, for its theme is man, man almost at his simplest, living a life with the minimum of external event. The title comes from A. E. Housman's *The Shropshire Lad*:

> There, like the wind through woods in riot,
> Through him the gale of life blew high;
> The tree of man was never quiet:
> Then 'twas the Roman, now 'tis I.
>
> The gale, it plies the saplings double,
> It blows so hard, 'twill soon be gone:
> To-day the Roman and his trouble
> Are ashes under Uricon.
>
> (XXXI)

The lines express the book's simplicity and universality. If *The Aunt's Story* was florid in treatment and overstuffed psychologically, *The Tree of Man* is at the other pole: it tells with infinite quietness the story of ordinary people. It is as stark as, but perhaps more subtle than, Knut Hamsun's Nobel Prize book *The Growth of the Soil*. In Stan Parker there is the same fortitude and integrity as in Isaac, and beneath him is the earth. The story begins in his young manhood when he takes up a selection, not far from Sydney; a pioneer in a small way, marries a wife as inarticulate as himself and founds a family. Neighbours spring up about them. Stan fights in the first World

War and comes home again. The Parkers attain a modest prosperity. Their son and daughter are lost to them, one in a life of petty crime, the other in a good but desiccated marriage. The encroaching city draws them into its suburbs, the farm is subdivided and Stan and Amy are alone in their old cottage half lost in Amy's triumphing garden, with one cow and a few rows of cabbages; and after all why had they planted the cabbages when there was no market for them any longer? Here Stan died in the moment of illumination for which he had blindly sought all his life, and his grandson accepts the same blind search as though he picked up the torch from the old man's calloused, lifeless hand.

In *The Tree of Man* Patrick White turns away from the strange, the curious, the accidental, the pressure of abstract ideas, to the elementals, and delving deeply into them he uncovers the whole of life. It is done with great patience, insight and art, and it is deeply moving. It cannot be said that *The Tree of Man* is better written or more skilfully constructed than *Happy Valley*, but it is more deeply felt, more warmly human. Virtuosity remains, as in the spectacular description of the fire at 'Glastonbury,' but it has passed over into the blood. The vanity of writing has passed away, which is a phrase every writer will understand.

Structurally *The Tree of Man* is discursive. It tells again the story of a community, it follows the natural patterns of life both in the community and in the characters, from youth to age, to extinction.

The book begins with a *tabula rasa*:

> A cart drove between the two big stringybarks and stopped. These were the dominant trees in that part of the bush, rising above the involved scrub with the simplicity of true grandeur. So the cart stopped, grazing the hairy side of a tree, and the horse, shaggy and stolid as the tree, sighed and took root.
>
> The man who sat in the cart got down. He rubbed his hands together, because already it was cold, a curdle of cold cloud in a pale sky, and copper in the west. On the air you could smell the frost. As the man rubbed his hands, the friction of cold skin intensified the coldness of the air and the solitude of that place. Birds looked from twigs, and the eyes of animals were drawn to what was happening. The man lifting a bundle from a cart. A dog lifting his leg on an anthill. The lip drooping on the sweaty horse.
>
> Then the man took an axe and struck at the side of a hairy tree, more to hear the sound than for any other reason. And the sound was cold and loud. The man struck the tree, and struck, till several white chips had fallen. He looked at the scar in the side of the tree. The silence was immense. It was the first time anything like this had happened in that part of the bush. (p. 3)

The Parkers were the first settlers. By the time Amy was a matron 'a comparatively young and robust woman, of some experience':

> the bush had opened up. There was a man tilling the chocolate soil in between his orange trees. Outside a grey shack an old man sat beside his hollyhock. Children spilled from the doors of bursting cottages. Wash-

ing blew. It was gay on this morning, as Amy Parker had not seen it along the two miles to O'Dowds'. Bright birds fell from the sky, and ascended. Voices could be heard where once the sound of the axe barely cut the silence, and your heart beat quicker for its company. (p. 139)

At last Durilgai becomes a suburb:

> During the last few years a number of other homes had been built down the road at Durilgai in which Parkers had always lived. There were the original few weatherboard homes, of which the landscape had taken possession, and which had been squeezed back from the road, it seemed, by other developments. The wooden homes stood, each in its smother of trees, like oases in a desert of progress. They were in process of being forgotten, of falling down, and would eventually be swept up with the bones of those who had lingered in them, and who were of no importance anyway, either no-hopers or old . . . The brick homes were in possession all right. Deep purple, clinker blue, ox blood, and public lavatory. (p. 408)

Only on Parker's diminished property the trees make a last stand:

> In the end there are the trees. These still stand in the gully behind the house, on a piece of poor land that nobody wants to use. There is the ugly mass of scrub, full of whips and open secrets. But there are the trees, quite a number of them that have survived the axe, smooth ones, a sculpture of trees. On still mornings after frost these stand streaming with light and moisture, the white, and the ashen and some the colour of flesh. (p. 498)

This is the background and the human lives follow the same curve — beginning, middle, end, resurrection. 'So that, in the end, there was no end.'

There is the most deep rooted, painfully angular triangle of the family, father, mother, children. Each is bound to the other in love or hatred or exasperation. It is something that cannot be undone and cannot be expressed. The children left the home inevitably. First the son:

> For he had gone, slipping from her as easily and naturally as the seed from the pod, to become lost in the long grass. If she suffered a great spasm at the moment of realization, with lesser ones recurring over many days, it was more perhaps for her vanity, though she did remember the little stubbly-headed boy in short trousers, and the baby gorging itself with placid confidence on her breast. So she cried at times, mostly at dusk, standing at a window, when shapes have grown tender, and she herself was disintegrating, and sucked onward, the years streaming behind her like skirts in the wind, or hair. It was frightening then. Her face abandoned the mealiness of personal sorrow and became a brooding skull, or essential face. (pp. 254–5)

Then the daughter, Thelma, left for the business college:

> The father did not struggle, because the situation was being taken out of his hands. For a long time, though, the mother put up a show of authority and advice, till it was time to bow her head, under the large

> dark hat. Then the children do take over, she was forced to admit. She received on her mouth with gratitude, even humility, the last kiss, wondering if it signified love; she would have liked to believe this. (p. 253)

Stan and Amy are both entrapped in inarticulateness. They cannot express their feelings, but their feelings are nonetheless intense. They fumble for the meaning of life; they thirst, in their parched, inadequate lives for the moments of ecstasy and illumination. Amy looks for them in her children but they are not there; then in her grandson, but the relationship is broken and transitory. She seeks fulfilment in infidelity, but that is worthless for her, and she knows it. She has her amulets, the silver nutmeg grater, which was a wedding present and something of mystical value though they never found a use for it, and in the white rose bush she planted outside her window. She touched another world when she saw the girl, Madeleine, ride by in her green habit on her black horse. She had her friend, Mrs. O'Dowd, but that was only through the necessity of neighbourliness; and her gossip, Mrs. Gage, the postmistress, whose husband, to the scandal and later enrichment of his wife, painted pictures. These pictures touched Amy's core and gave her one of the few, brief, fleeting experiences of release:

> Then she would go inside her house, rather a secret woman, into the brown house, inseparable from the garden, from the landscape in which it was. (p. 371)
>
> She would have liked to love. It was terrible to think she had never loved her son as a man. Sometimes her hands would wrestle together. They were supple, rather plump hands, broad, and not yet dry. But wrestling like this together, they were papery and dried up. Then she would force herself into some deliberate activity, or speak tenderly to her good husband, offering him things to eat and seeing to his clothes. She loved her husband. Even after the drudgery of love she could still love him. But sometimes she lay on her side and said, I have not loved him enough, not yet, he has not seen the evidence of love. It would have been simpler if she had been able to turn and point to the man their son, but she could not. (p. 285)

Stan, equally inarticulate, set his heart upon his strength with axe and crowbar and on the pattern of his work:

> In the beginning, as a young man, when he was clearing his land, he had hewn at trees with no exact plan in his head, but got them down, even at the expense of his hands, though these in time became hard, and there were boulders to be moved, that he strained against with his horse, till the soft bellies of man and horse grew hard and stony too, and the stone of will prevailed over rock . . . He was also an improvisor of honest objects in wood and iron, which, if crude in design, had survived to that day. His only guide in all of this had been his simplicity. (p. 275)

Simplicity was not enough. He took the blows of his wife's infidelity and his son's guilt and his simplicity was no shield. His strength failed him as he grew old. He looked for what he had never found in religion but the lips that took the sacrament were cold and dry. He had suffered his Gethsemane ignobly in a pub:

> After this he began to go outside, many coats and yellow, thin overcoats opening willingly for him to pass, until he was out, or his legs had carried him there. He was tittuping. He was opening and closing. He got round the corner to some side street, of which he could not read the name, while trying; it seemed so necessary to locate a degradation. And old banana skins. There was a paper sky, quite flat, and white, and Godless. He spat at the absent God then, mumbling till it ran down his chin. (p. 333)

Then at last, strangely, he found God in his own spittle after he had reached the final disillusionment. 'All things of importance are withheld or past.'

All the characters are fully drawn; there is room in such a book. There is room for humour and irony. Mrs. O'Dowd is the comic relief right down to her Rabelaisian death, but never a figure of fun. Even Thelma is pathetic and real in her gentility, even Ray has his validity. The neighbours, by old acquaintance, become your neighbours. They are human beings but also part of a pattern, just as Madeleine returns to complete Amy's disillusionment and Stan, in his darkest hour, meets again the Greek who once worked on the farm and who had had a special quality for them all.

The onomatopoeic scenery streams behind the characters. Brown is now the predominant colour on Patrick White's palette, as the white of snow was in *Happy Valley*, grey in *The Living and the Dead*, and mauve and amethyst in *The Aunt's Story*.

The balance of event is individual. Major events are often passed over in a few lines while some detail is pursued to its ultimate source. Irrelevant incidents are used as tuning forks:

> Stan Parker drove in his high, ridiculous car along those roads. Most of the flesh had left his face. He drove past Halloran's Corner and the turn off to Moberley. People who did not know what had happened were continuing to live their lives. An old woman in a big hat was cutting dahlias, convinced that this momentarily was the activity of mankind. She looked up, shading her eyes to see, but her sun had yellow petals. And Stan Parker drove on. Two children near Bangalay were looking at something in a tin, from which soon they would begin to tear the wings. Under their cold gaze the universe had shrunk to the size and shape of a doomed beetle. (p. 331)

The prose has the same cut-on-the-cross quality. Its effect is cumulative. It is chameleon. It has moments of flatness, that are intentional; short, stabbing sentences; long sentences slowly unwound; metaphors taken for granted and sharp emotional pictures:

> She did not express her disgust with more than one petal. Her camellia graces were not of the generous, blowing order, but tight and small, greenish white, and not for picking. (p. 247)
>
> 'What do you mean, happy?' he asked lumpishly. He did not like this

> kind of catechism. It bordered on air. It was like opening a door and finding that the floor had gone. (p. 249)

A night at the pictures is succinctly described. 'Horses' feet were beating on the face of boredom and the patent leather lips sucked them down.'

So much could be said about this novel that its commentary would be as long as its subject. It is woven of many threads; it has its great moments, its slow infiltrations, its images and echoes. It is a world but a world beneath the visible surface of the world. Perhaps all that should have been said about it was: 'Go, read it.'

In twenty years Patrick White has produced one book of poetry and four novels. He has not forced his talent, nor has he let it go by default. He has written enough to declare himself.

What is the kernel of his writing? Though he has wit, the deft wit of words and the ironic and sardonic wit of situation, all his books are sombre. He writes of the frustrated and the inarticulate, of the mad and the lost ones. There is always the burden of pain.

The quotation from Mahatma Gandhi which strikes the note for *Happy Valley* reads:

> It is impossible to do away with the law of suffering, which is one of the indispensible conditions of our being. Progress is to be measured by the amount of suffering undergone . . . The purer the suffering, the greater is the progress.

Patrick White is obsessed with pain and loneliness, the inability of human beings ever to know one another, which is the ultimate loneliness. Amy Parker, after a lifetime of marriage, realized that 'it was quite possible she would never succeed in opening her husband and looking inside, that he was being kept shut for other purposes'. (p. 432) Between Oliver Halliday and his wife there was no more than kindness and a long-dead romantic illusion. Between him and Alys Browne there was only a newer illusion borne on the wings of Schumann and it could not stand up to reality. Between Sidney Furlow and Clem Hagen there was only her domineering, unripe sensuality. Oliver Halliday was no nearer to his son than Amy and Stan to theirs. The child, Margaret Quong, early embraced her loneliness. There was no understanding between Elyot and Eden, nor did they attain any satisfying closeness in their loves. Mrs. Goodman and Fanny were strangers to Theodora. Never in any of the books is a satisfactory and satisfying human relationship portrayed. In Patrick White's philosophy of pain and loneliness it would seem that none were possible.

In *The Tree of Man* his philosophy seems to be resolved, the goal of man's long, inarticulate seeking is glimpsed. It is the ineffable moment. It has no substance, it is of the creative spirit, it comes and it goes; but that it should come, even once in a lifetime, is a positive gain, an apotheosis. It is the troubling of the waters at Bethesda. It does not touch the loneliness for it is a personal, private and detached revelation. Each man's life is a mystery between himself and God.

This solution is presaged in the earlier novels by the accent on music and poetry. Oliver Halliday is a poet manqué. It is music that he shares with Alys. Theodora is transported by music. In *The Tree of Man* the brittle Thelma is 'drenched by the violins.'

Poetry, music, religion are the paths that the soul, imprisoned in flesh, may take, 'the paths out of sleep.' Love is an illusion, pain a certainty but the capacity to feel pain is the mark of the human being. And pain is its own reward.

Patrick White to Marjorie Barnard

Castle Hill
15 June 1956

Dear Miss Barnard,

. . . Again I must say how impressed and gratified I am by your work. A great many people have become excited over *The Tree of Man*, but it is the first time anyone has shown that I have been working towards it over the last twenty years. Your phrase 'the vanity of writing has passed away' is a magnificent and telling one. Nor has any other critic, however sympathetic, put his finger so firmly on the point of *The Tree of Man* as you have in your: 'Each man's life is a mystery between himself and God.' I had begun to feel that perhaps I had not succeeded in making this clear, or perhaps it just is that people recoil from it. . . .

Christesen continued to give White's work prominence in the magazine, publishing an extract from *Voss*, two short stories and a large number of essays on White's fiction. White's work became something of a touchstone precisely because its modernism was in marked contrast to the dominant tenor of Australian fiction in the 1950s, which was very much within the social realist tradition: formally conservative, well-crafted, and often bearing a political and social message.

Number 1, 1951

Read Politics, Son

J. L. Waten

I was born in a country town, a railway junction where my parents had settled soon after they came to Australia. For as long as I can remember I could speak the language of the new land although it was not spoken in our house. When I was a small boy neither of my parents knew much English but father was better than mother. He worked around the district and was in touch with many people. But his dealings with them were solely confined to buying and selling so that his vocabulary was limited. Neither he nor my mother could read or write more than a word of the new language.

Because they were tongue-bound and because strangers were then viewed with a certain amount of distrust my parents had no friends in the town and lived entirely to themselves. For news from the big world they depended on letters from relatives and friends, visits to the house from other foreigners who lived in the city and stories father heard on his journeys and only half understood.

When I was nearly five father would often say:

— Why don't you grow up quickly? Then you could read the papers to me and I would know what was going on in this great world of ours.

A strong desire to be able to read took hold of me and I told our neighbour, the widow Mrs. McIntyre, of my longing. For once her stern face wrinkled into a smile and she patted me on the head. There was no finer ambition than to want to learn for the sake of one's parents. If I wanted to I could come to her house every evening and she would teach me and her boy Harry the alphabet. If we were good pupils we might even learn to read before we went to school.

So the next day as soon as tea was over in the McIntyre cottage and Harry had helped his mother to wash the dishes and sweep out the kitchen, we sat down at the table while Mrs. McIntyre picked up Blackie's first reader and dourly took us through the alphabet. A, B, C to X, Y, Z, over and over again until we knew every letter; cat, mat, hat and so on until we graduated to the pencil and exercise book stage.

Harry and I were attentive pupils and we soon mastered the first reader. We read simple sentences and Mrs. McIntyre gazed at us with pride.

— There is no better thing than to be a good scholar, she said.

Turning to me she went on:

— Mr. McIntyre was a very good scholar. He was a school teacher in Scotland before we came to this country.

Then she asked me:

— Would you like to see his books?

Her unusual friendly manner bewildered me but I nodded my head and for the first time I went into the front room with her and Harry. The blinds were drawn and the air was heavy and musty. On a table in the middle of the room there was a bowl of freshly cut lilies and above the small organ hung a black framed enlargement of the late Mr. McIntyre. His books lined the dark shelves and here and there stood smaller photographs of Harry's father in army uniform and one of a cross above a grave somewhere in France.

Suddenly I felt as I did in synagogue on the special holy days. My mouth was dry and words could hardly make their way from my throat as Mrs. McIntyre pointed to the books that had been her husband's dearest possessions. She removed them from the shelves, lovingly blew specks of dust from the covers as she talked of Carlyle, Scott and Burns. Then she took from a glass-enclosed bookshelf a sacred book, the family Bible, that had been in the possession of the McIntyres for ever so long. Tears appeared in her eyes and without another word she ushered us out of the room.

I was so awestricken that I hurriedly left Harry and went home where father sat at the kitchen table blankly looking at the morning newspaper. I was glad to see him and I felt there was nothing I wanted to do more than to please him. He suddenly looked up and gazed at me with humorous eyes.

— Still taking lessons? he asked.

— Yes, I said. I can read a bit now.

— Is that so, he said. Well let's see what you can do.

As he thrust the paper into my hand I eagerly spread the paper over the table. Kneeling on the chair I surveyed the print with the eye of an expert. But I couldn't make out most of the words and to hide my sudden embarrassment and shame I began to turn over the pages.

— What's wrong, father said. Haven't you found anything interesting?

In my humiliation my eyes found refuge in the cricket scores. I knew the names of cricketers by heart and the first letter or so was enough for me to reel off the name. I read: Armstrong hit 50, Collins 40, MacCartney 100, Gregory bowled out 3, Mailey 4 and so on.

— What are you talking about? father asked in astonishment. What's the 50 and 40 and bowled out 4?

— Cricket, Dad, I said.

Father looked at mother in amazement and shrugged his shoulders. Cricket, he said to himself.

Then he fixed half serious eyes on me.

— Read politics, son, he commanded.

I went back to the front page. With difficulty I made out the name of William Morris Hughes but not enough words came after to make any sense. We soon gave up.

— You'll need a lot more lessons before you'll be a professor, father said.

My first attempt had been a failure but night after night father brought home the paper and stubbornly I continued to stammer through the pages. As I was now at school my reading got better and better until I could read the politics and make sense for father. Thus unwittingly I became as familiar with the names of Lenin, Lloyd George, Wilson and Hughes as I was with the cricketing giants of the day.

I shared my knowledge with Harry McIntyre and after two years at school he and I knew more about political affairs than all the other boys and girls. But neither of us as yet had formed any attachment for a party or person. We were neutral, enjoying our knowledge in the same way as we found pleasure in gathering facts about the cricket and football heroes of the past and the performances of runners and swimmers.

About that time there was an election in our state and Harry and I spent every evening listening to the speakers of the various parties. Once after school while we were playing with cigarette cards in a paddock close to our home Harry said:

— I bet you can't make a speech.

— I bet I can, I said.

We found a kerosene tin and I stood on it and began to speak to my audience of one. Harry heckled me just as we had seen at the meetings. Both of us talked in gibberish, in our own made up words mixed with words and phrases we had heard from the politicians.

While we were entertaining ourselves three older boys who were walking through the paddock came over to us and heard some of our talk. They jeered at us. I got off the tin and with Harry made for home, turning and shouting back at them. They broke into a run and chased us and we could hear their leathery feet padding behind and their voices shouting,

Ikey Moses King of the Jews
Sold his wife for a pair of shoes.

Just as we were nearing home they caught up with us. Harry managed to get through the gate after reeling from a cuff over the ear but I was grabbed around the neck by a wiry arm and pulled to the ground. Two boys held my arms crucifix fashion on the ground while another boy sat on my chest.

— You won't give us any lip any more, will you, the boy said and slapped me on the face.

I shouted for mother.

— Cry baby, the boys jeered and I received another slap on the face.

The boys quickly rose to their feet as mother and Mrs. McIntyre ran out of the lane that separated our cottages. The boys edged back as Mrs. McIntyre advanced towards them.

— You bullies, you larrikins, she said.

— He's only a Jew boy, Missus, one of them said.

— If you touch him again I'll have the police on to you, she said.

Mother who had helped me off the ground stared with a strained, bloodless expression at the boys who had poked out their tongues to Mrs. McIntyre, turned on their heels and run shouting down the street.

— Hooligans, mother muttered to the widow. Black hundreds in the making, she added.

When we went into the house I asked mother what she had meant by the black hundreds.

— At home before the revolution there was a party called the black hundreds who killed and tormented the Jews, she said.

A party that killed and tormented Jews: that was beyond my imagination and outside my experience of parties. I pestered mother with questions about the black hundreds. What did they stand for? To this day I can't remember what mother said they stood for but she did tell me what they didn't stand for.

— They were against the workers as well as the Jews, she said. They killed many workingmen.

Her words made a deep impression on me so that when I went to the meetings I began really to listen to the speeches and to sympathise with those speakers who seemed to stand for the cause of the workers. In some childish way I identified myself with this cause and soon I could think of nothing but the elections. It was as though I were taking a part in fighting the black hundreds.

On the eve of election day Harry and I went to the final rally of the candidate against whom we had ranged ourselves. For a while we stood in the dim light on the outskirts of the large crowd and laughed loudly at all the humorous quips made by a number of hecklers. Then we ourselves began to shout but our childish voices were lost in the deep growls around us. Then a new speaker took the platform, none other than our sloyd master. We pushed through the crowd and stopped right in front of the platform. We looked up into our master's florid, excited face and his large open mouth. This was our opportunity to settle some old scores. We got hold of his party's election leaflets and tore them up demonstratively, applauded by a group of men who had just come from the hotel across the road.

Then we screeched at the speaker,

— You don't know what you're talking about!

There was laughter from our new friends but an elderly gentleman said it was disgraceful for young boys to behave as we were doing. We were shouting again when a policeman strode over to us and caught us by the elbows.

— Now then, he said, it's past your bed time. Hop it, both of you.

We turned on our heels and ran all the way home, never once looking behind us. We made no mention of the incident to our parents but next day at school we were called to the head-master's study. Mr. Grogan's fierce moustache quivered with indignation as he questioned us about our conduct at the meeting. We were nothing but larrikins and would end up badly. But he would give us something to remember for our behaviour. He reached for his long cane on top of a cupboard. He ordered us to put out our hands and brought the cane down heavily six times on my right palm and six times on Harry's.

By the end of the day we had recovered from the shock of the punishment and the blow to our pride, but when we reached home we met our parents deeply engrossed in discussing our crimes, in the lane near our side gates. Mrs. McIntyre was the first to speak. Turning to Harry she said,

— Mr. Grogan has sent me a note about your conduct. If Mr. Grogan hadn't punished you today I would have done so myself.

— He had no right to give us the cane for something we did outside school, I said.

— Harry, Mrs. McIntyre said decisively, you were punished justly.

She ordered him into the house and as she followed I heard her say,

— You've both been neglecting your studies and that always leads to trouble.

I was obliged to tell father everything, even what Mrs. McIntyre had said and he stared at me wrathfully.

— I ought to give you the hiding of your life, he shouted. What have you got to do with politics? You whippersnapper, you're hardly out of napkins. Stick to arithmetic.

Mother smiled quizzically at father's terrible rage and went inside the house.

— Don't you ever again bring shame on your father's name, he said. Policemen, hidings at school, what next? Leave politics alone unless you want to stand at meals for a week.

With a threatening swipe of his fist he turned his back on me and walked away with stiff-backed dignity.

When I came into the house father was turning the pages of his newspaper, staring briefly at the pictures of politicians, brides and horses. I sat down quietly at the table and began to read my school reader. A few minutes passed and he coughed loudly, once, twice and blew his nose noisily. But I kept my eyes on my book. Then his everyday voice floated over to me.

— Would it greatly interfere with your school work if you read this paper to me for a little while? he said.

— No, Dad, I said. I didn't think you wanted me to read tonight.

— Of course I do, he said in the friendliest of voices.

Mischievously I began to read about the cricket and then about a ball that had taken place in Government House the night before. Stolidly I read the names of the guests and the descriptions of the dresses worn by the ladies.

— That's not important, he interrupted me. Read politics, son!

Number 3, 1952

Lena

JOHN MORRISON

Half-past three, and the usual note of irritation has crept into Lena's voice.

— Tins, Joe!

Without getting from my knees, I reach backwards, seize a couple of buckets, and push them through under the drooping leaves of the vines. Before I can release them they are grabbed and pulled violently away from me. Between the top leaves, and only fifteen inches away, I get a glimpse of a freckled little face, keen eyes leaping from bunch to bunch of the clustering grapes, always a split second in front of the darting fingers and slashing knife. I hear the thump of tumbling fruit, and get up wearily. No use trying to feed her with tins as we go — she's too quick, too experienced, too enthusiastic. Or is it just that I'm too old and too slow?

Empty tins are thrown only into alternate rows, leaving the other rows clear for the passing of the tractor that takes away the gathered fruit. Right from the start of picking it has fallen to me, no doubt a gentleman's privilege, to work that side of the vines where the empties are. As Lena and I made equal division of the day's earnings, I try to keep up with her, but every now and then forget to keep her supplied with tins.

— You should let me know before you cut right out, Lena, I say gently as I push the first ones through just ahead of her.

She doesn't answer, which means that she's lost patience with me. I, too, am irritated, irritated by this tally-anxiety that seizes her every day about this time. But I remind myself that at tea to-night, with the day's work over, she will forget everything, wait on me as though a devoted daughter, chatter brightly about the circus we're all going to in Redcliffs, ask me if I have anything for the wash to-morrow. So I go about twenty yards down the row, pushing through a couple of tins every few feet, and say nothing until I get back.

It is a relief to bend my aching legs again, to press my knees into the warm red earth, to get my head out of the sun and stare into the cool recesses of the vine leaves. Of the first bunch of grapes I pull a handful, stuff them into my mouth, swallow the juice, and spit out the residue. While I was away Lena has conscientiously picked right through to my side, leaving only one or two clusters she can't reach, so that in only a few minutes I'm up with her again. I can't see her, but the violence with which she is banging the buckets tells me that she is still sulking.

— Angry with me? I ask.

No answer. I wait a few seconds, then bang a bucket myself just to let her see that I, too, can be provoked.

— You never have much to say this time of day, do you? I venture.

— You can't talk and work.

— You can in the mornings. You were telling me all about your dad before lunch.

That's why we're behind. We only got two hundred and ten buckets this morning.

— Only? Isn't that good?

— We should have got two hundred and fifty. We'll be going flat out to get four hundred and fifty to-day.

— Do we *have* to get four hundred and fifty?

— Yes, she says very emphatically.

To that I give no reply. Everything I could say has already been said, more than once. I can, at the moment, think of no new lead in an argument which has become wearisome. To Lena, piecework is the road to riches — 'harder you work, the more you get.' She's too young to know anything of the days when armies of unemployed converged on the irrigation belt to struggle for a chance to pick grapes at 5s. a hundred tins. We're due for a visit from a union organiser; I keep wondering what she'll do when he asks her to take a ticket.

I'm working on, not saying a word, but she takes my silence as a sign of weakness, and presses the attack herself:

— It's all right for you. I need the money.

— We all need money, Lena.

— You'll get plenty when you get back to the wharves. And get it easier, too, I bet.

— Sometimes. It depends on what the cargo is. But we never get paid by the ton!

— Wharfies wouldn't work, anyway.

Hitting below the belt. She must be quite upset to say a thing like that. I let it go, though, because it would be a preposterous thing to fall out with her. We're both Australians, but in a way that has nothing to do with geography I know that we come from different countries. She's a big loveable child, inherently forthright and generous, and usually quite merry, but her philosophy is a bit frightening to a man brought up on the waterfront of a great city. She comes from a poor little grazing property deep in the mallee scrub over the New South Wales border. One of a family of eleven. Forty-six weeks in the year she works sheep, helps to bring up nine younger brothers and sisters. The six weeks' grape-picking is the annual light of her drab little life: money of her own, appetizing food, the companionship of other people's sons and daughters; above all the fabulous Saturday morning shopping excursions into Mildura. After the picture of home that she painted for me this morning I can understand all this, but I'd give something to open her innocent young eyes to the world I know. Her conception of fighting for one's rights extends no further than keeping a wary eye on the number of filled tins.

'You've got to watch these Blockies,' she tells me knowingly every day. It would never occur to her that there are robbers higher up, that hard-working Bill McSeveney may also not be getting what he deserves. That is why at night-time here, looking out through the fly-wired window of the men's hut, I'm conscious of a darkness deeper than the heavy shadows that lie between the long drying-racks and over the garden of the sleeping house.

And it seems to me that this obsession of Lena with piecework is where the darkness begins. There was the twilight of it just a minute ago when she passed that unpleasant remark about wharfies.

We pick on in silence for perhaps fifteen minutes.

I'd always imagined there was a fair amount of noise associated with grape-picking. Perhaps there is on some blocks. On this one it is always quiet. The rows are unusually long, and between the visits of the tractor to replenish the supply of empty tins and take away the full ones, we hear nothing except the occasional voices of the two boys picking several rows away, and the carolling of magpies in the belars along the road. The sun is beginning to go down at last, but it's been a particularly hot day — 110 degrees in the shade at noon — and I'll be glad when five o'clock comes, whatever the tally. That is always the best part of the day, when we trudge up to the house and throw ourselves on to the cool thick buffalo grass under the jacarandas, and Bill the boss cuts up a big sugar-melon and passes around pink juicy slices that we can hardly span with our jaws. It would be better still, though, if they would talk of something else then besides the day's work. Smoky, the house cat, usually joins us, and I can never contemplate his great lazy blue hide without reflecting:

'Oh, you wise old brute! Even as I went out to work this morning you were lying in the coolest spot under the water-tank, and every hour of the day you've followed the shifting shadows. While I . . .'

— Here they come. How many have we got?

— If you were a good union man you'd be counting them yourself.

True, no doubt, but coming from Lena it's quite meaningless. She just doesn't know what a trade union is. Instinctively I cast a glance up the row to see if our long-expected visitor, the Rep., is coming.

— Aren't you going to tell me the tally?

— All I know is we're behind. We only had three hundred and thirty at smokoh, and this is the shortest run.

— That patch of mildew kept us back early in the afternoon.

— It wasn't that.

— Was it through my not keeping you up in buckets?

She doesn't answer that. Whether she knows it or not, she's angry with me not for what I do or don't do, but for the things I say. I work hard, but I've said some harsh things about piecework, ridiculed her persistent argument that 'the only way to get money is to work for it.' It would be a good world indeed if that were true. She knows I don't approve of competing with the boys for big tallies, but she can't see that nevertheless, out of principle, I must try to keep up with her because I get half of our combined earnings.

The tractor pulls up, and I crawl through to Lena's side and go for the water-bag hanging from the canopy. The grimy faces of Bill the boss, and Peter the rackman, smile down at me. They call me 'Sponge-guts' because of the vast amount of water I drink without getting pains.

— How's your mate, Joe? asks Peter.

— She's got the sulks again. She thinks I'm sitting up on her.

Bill, in the driving-seat, gives Lena a friendly wink. Naturally . . . they're his grapes. He's a good employer, even as employers go these days, but I'd be interested to see his form if pickers were easier to get. He and his wife think the world of Lena. She's an expert picker, but she's also a nice change in the home of a couple who've raised three sons and no daughters.

He's eyeing her now with all the detached benevolence of a bachelor uncle.

— Get your five hundred today, Kid?

She steals a cautious sidelong glance at me, pouts, and shakes her head. She makes a charming picture of bush youth, standing stiff and straight in the narrow space between the tractor wheel and the vines. She wears old canvas shoes, a pair of jodhpurs several sizes too big for her, a man's work-shirt with the sleeves cut off, and a limp-brimmed sun-bonnet that throws a shadow over half of her cherubic face. The fingers of the hand nearest me fidget ceaselessly with the keen knife. Usually she's full of talk, particularly with Bill, but at the moment she only wants to work. And she can't even kneel down with the tractor standing where it is. Her restless eyes leap from me to Peter, and from Peter to Bill.

— Come on, she says, load up. We've got over a hundred buckets to pick yet.

— All right, boss! Bill engages the clutch, and as the tractor moves on I swing the first bucketful up to Peter.

Slowly we move along the row. Sixty full buckets, about 20 lb. of fruit to the bucket — 'fill 'em up to water-level!' They get heavy towards the end;

one has to work fast to keep up with even the snail-crawl of the tractor. I come back to Lena sweating afresh, and blowing a bit.

She hears me, and without stopping, or looking at me, demands peremptorily:

— How many?

— Sixty on the load, and twenty-five left.

— That makes three hundred and ninety. We've got fifty minutes to get sixty more.

— Who says so?

— I do.

— Suppose we don't get them?

— We've got to get them.

It's on again, but before the usual evening dispute can get properly started a man I haven't seen before ducks through from the next row and confronts me. I give him good-day. Lena takes a long curious look at him, then goes on working. Middle-aged, and wearing a blue suit with an open-necked sports-shirt, he carries a couple of small books in one hand, and in the other a handkerchief with which he wipes his moist forehead. He'd have made a better first impression if he'd kept those books in his pocket a few minutes longer.

— Sorry I've been so long getting around, he says affably. I'm the Union Rep., A.W.U.

— I'm glad to see you.

We've been picking for four weeks here, and the A.W.U. is the wealthiest union in Australia. Something of what I'm thinking must show in my face, for his manner becomes a trifle apologetic.

— I've been flat out like a lizard since eight o'clock this morning. My God, it's hot, ain't it? How're you for tickets here?

He just can't get to the point soon enough.

— I've seen the boys through there; they're all right.

— I've been waiting for you, I tell him, bringing out a ten shilling note.

He opens one of the little books, takes a pencil from his breast pocket.

— Good on you, mate! How about the girl?

— I'm one of the family, replies Lena, with a promptness that shows not only that she has been listening, but that she has been well schooled. Bill has no time for trade unions.

The organiser gives me a conspiratorial smile, which I don't return.

— You could still join if you wanted to girlie.

Lena doesn't answer that. She hasn't stopped picking for an instant. She's already a few feet away along the row, slashing and bucket-banging in a way that tells both of us not to be too long about it.

I watch him write in the date.

— I wish they'd all come in as quick as you, he says in a lowered voice. You've got no idea the song some of the bastards make about it. I can give you a full ticket if you like. Cost you thirty bob.

My gorge rises. What does he think he's selling? This great Union wasn't built by men like him.

— No thanks — just a season ticket. I'm already in a union. You don't cover me in my usual job.

— Okay. What are you in?

He begins to write. Just making conversation, he doesn't really care.

— Waterside Workers' Federation.

And for the life of me I can't keep a note of superiority out of my voice. I get the very devil of a kick out of it.

He goes on writing, without looking at me, but I can fairly see the guard coming up.

— That's a pretty good union. You'd make better money on the wharf than up here, wouldn't you?

— Yes. We're well organised.

A deliberate challenge, but he pretends not to see it.

— Up here for a bit of a change?

— I was crook. I had to get out of Melbourne for a few weeks. A man has to keep working, though.

I wouldn't tell him even that much, only I don't want him to think I came here for the 'big money.' 17s. 6d. a hundred tins! — and fill 'em up to water level . . .

I'm tempted to ask him if he's been to the next block, where the pickers are working all hours and living like animals, but he's too easy to read. He isn't an organiser; he's a collector. If he were doing his job he would talk to Lena as I've talked to her. I watch him tramp away through the dust quite pleased with himself — he's got my ten shillings. He didn't ask me if I am getting the prescribed wages, where I sleep at night, what hours I work, or what the food is like here.

It's a relief to get back to Lena. At least she's honest. She'd fight all right if she thought anybody was trying to put something over her. She just doesn't understand, that's all.

For minutes after I catch up with her we work without speaking. She's picking furiously, savagely, and by and by I find that I, too, am clapping on the pace. I've seen it elsewhere, the instinct to do one's bit, to keep up with one's mate. Piecework isn't an incentive; its a device. But there's something else fermenting in me. A longing to please her, to win her respect, to get her to listen to me, to chase out of her eager young head some of the lies and nonsense that have been stuffed into it. Only last night I put in a hectic hour at the dining-table trying to explain to her — and others — that it isn't wharfies and railwaymen who gum up the works of the man on the land. Not wharfies and railwaymen . . .

The falling bunches go plump-plump into the buckets. I know that she, too, is thinking. She wants to say something. Every time I catch sight of her bobbing head through the leaves I observe that she is peeping, as though trying to gauge what kind of humour I'm in.

By and by it comes, a non-committal uncompromising little voice that nevertheless sends a thrill through me:

— Joe.

— Hullo there.

— What *is* a trade union, anyway?
Lena, Lena, where am I to begin . . . ?

Number 4, 1960

The Last Australian

XAVIER HERBERT

Old Josie, dressed in faded blue, with a sacking apron about her bulging middle, a battered stockman's wideawake on her white head, a heavy rifle in her large freckled hands, stood at the big barred gate before her homestead, shrieking at the traffic rolling along the highway:

— Go for your lives, you dingoes. Call yourselves Australians . . . this's the day of Australia's shame. Go for your dingo lives!

None of the grim-faced passers-by could have heard her above the din of their going. Indeed, few even saw her, intent as they were either on the road ahead or on what could still be glimpsed of what they fled from. They were all headed the same way — South!

It was a strange procession: vehicles of all sorts and sizes, half-military, half-civilian, government trucks and private cars, even a couple of road-graders and several big-wheeled tractors, and the entire sanitary outfit of the municipal council, rubbish-trucks and night-carts, all so packed that men rode on roof-tops, running-boards and fenders.

There were few women, because most had already gone South as the threat of invasion from Asia loomed. Old Josie had been urged by security officers to go along with the rest when they had come to take her blacks away. The authorities had commandeered her few remaining head of stock.

Josie had said that she was not leaving the home that she and her old man, Watty, had given their years to building out of the wilderness — this place called Twenty Mile Lagoons. Here she had borne Watty's children, and buried some. The others had gone their way. Here she had buried Watty, in the little grave-yard over in the home-paddock, beneath the clump of milk-wood trees.

Josie had said: 'Watty left the place for me to carry on, in case one of our boys comes back. I'm not going to leave it even when I die. If the Japs come, they'll take it over my dead body. Ain't we been waiting fifty years for the Japs to come? Then what's the idea of evacuating? This is my home and this is my country and I'm staying to fight for it if necessary. I can look after myself. I've got Watty's buffalo rifle.'

Brave talk, and easy enough to deliver while yet that ancient barrier between Australia and Asia, the Timor Sea, lay between us and the Asian hordes. But it was not vain talk. For there on this fateful day, when with one fell swoop of his bombers the Asian surmounted the barrier and now was ravaging the sacred soil, old Josie stood in arms before her white-washed homestead, shouting contempt for those who fled:

— Call yourselves Australians! Call yourselves men . . . tchah, I spit on you!

Some who saw her waved.

What they fled from could be seen from this distance only as a cloud, black-billowing and flame-flecked, rolling upward, higher, higher, into the northern sky, cloud of the storm of war, the first ever to darken these southern skies, the detonations no more to the ear at Twenty Mile Lagoons than the muttering of far thunder.

What Josie knew of events away up there in the town she had learned when she had gone out onto the road and halted the procession to inquire the meaning of it. While those who were held up behind brayed their horns and shouted for the right of way, and in some cases sought to escape the delay by taking to the shimmering crimson sand beside the road to go roaring on their way, she had heard that the town was in ruins. The dead were lying in the streets, the harbor was a sea of blazing oil in which a score of crippled ships and a thousand men sank or drifted to their doom. She had heard that the enemy was expected to land his troops the moment the bombing ceased.

When she had asked her informants why they had not stayed to deal with the enemy, the reply was that there was no proper equipment for the purpose, no proper command, so it was every man for himself. When she had expressed her contempt for them, rejecting their offer of a lift, they had sworn at her for an old bitch and gone roaring South.

She stood now at the gate with Watty's rifle, wearing Watty's old hat, her comrades two cattle dogs, an old goat, a ginger cat.

The first frantic scramble of traffic was soon past, and the procession tailing out. Then there came along a small convoy of military vehicles, led by a utility truck in which rode a couple of officers and several n.c.o.'s.

Josie let the utility have a particularly powerful blast of abuse. The occupants heard her, eyed her as they passed. Then the truck drew up, and with it the vehicles behind. The utility swung off the road and came wheeling back toward the gate.

A dark, lantern-jawed young captain leaned out of the cab.

— I say, what are you doing here?

Josie's voice was torn with her screeching:

— Not what you're doing, anyway!

— Eh?

— I'm not running away like the rest of you dingoes.

The captain scowled.

— You're not supposed to be here. Come on, get in.

— I'm all right here.

— I'm not asking you, madam, I'm ordering you.

— I take no orders from anyone while I'm standing on my own property, and least of all from bloody cowards running away from the enemy invading their country.

The captain flung open the door, leapt out, to stand a gangling figure in faded khaki and bleached webbing harness. He roared:

— Madam, you're under arrest!
— You go to bloody hell!
He turned to his n.c.o.'s:
— Put her in the truck, men!
As the men tumbled out, Josie presented the rifle at them, shrilling:
— Anybody comes near me I'll shoot!
The dogs raised their voices. The men stopped in their tracks. The captain shouted:
— Drop that rifle!
She swung the rifle on him.
He snatched out his pistol:
— Drop it, I say!
— I'll drop you!
He stood glaring, with pistol hanging in his grasp.
Sudden uproar in the halted convoy on the road snatched away the attention of the group. Men on the trucks were pointing north-westward where, flashing silver in the sun, a flight of aircraft was sweeping low over violet hills some ten miles distant. Men were yelling:
— Here they come!
The captain turned back to Josie.
— Come on, old woman, I can't risk the lives of my men hanging about here arguing with you . . . get in the truck!
— I tell you I'm staying to fight for my country, if I have to fight you cowards to start with!
His lean jaw worked as he snarled:
— I'll have you know that I've been fighting for my country for the past two years . . . and there's my service stripes to prove it! I've only just got back from the Middle East . . .
Josie whooped:
— Middle East . . . fighting for the Pommies, you mean! Tchah . . . you'll fight anywhere the Pommies send you — Gallipoli, France, Middle East, anywhere — but now the day's come to fight for your own country, you're boltin' like bandicoots before a bush-fire . . .
The captain raised his pistol, and his voice rose to a scream:
— Damn you, you old bitch . . .
Boom . . . Boom . . . Boom!
The dull thunder of bombs not so far away roused the convoy again to uproar. The lieutenant laid a hand on his superior's upraised arm. The captain turned to him. The lieutenant pointed northward. Three pillars of black smoke rose above the violet hills.
As he stared, the captain lowered his pistol and muttered:
— Better get cracking.
He turned back to the utility. As he got in, he shouted at Josie:
— I'll report you to rear H.Q. for what you're doing. I'll tell 'em I had to leave you behind because you threatened the lives of my men and I didn't want to have to shoot an old woman.
Josie screeched:

— Tell 'em the truth . . . that you left an old woman behind to fight for you . . . tell 'em that I'm the last Australian left!

As they drove off she bared her yellow teeth at them. They stared back stony-eyed.

The utility swung back to the road. The convoy was on the move again. Soon it was gone, out of sight, out of sound. And now the road was empty.

In the quiet, Josie looked northward across the familiar scene. Beyond the homestead with its weedy garden, its fowl-run, its goat-yard, lay the home-paddock, bright with wet-season's verdure, the grass so high for want of stock to keep it down that only the tips of the red anthills could be seen. There was the clump of milk-woods, with the graves beneath. There was the high-railed stock-yard, the elevated water-tanks, the windmill beside the first lagoon. So thick were the lilies on the lagoon that the shimmering air above it seemed to glow with heliotrope. White ibis were perched in the paper-barks, preening, and a couple of old horses dozed, swishing their tails, in the shade. The bullock-paddock stretched from the line of lagoons, a vivid green carpet, to timbered ridges shimmering blue and silver in mirage. The beloved landscape, Terra Australis, to which, incredibly, the backdrop was now the rolling smoke and dust of war!

Now the drone of the hunting aircraft was louder. Shading her old eyes, Josie searched the enamel-bright sky for the source of it. As if sensing her need of comradeship, her animals drew closer, dogs and goat vying for the hand she extended to them absently, the cat leaping to the top rail of the gate to smooth against her shoulder.

Suddenly the droning was a roar . . . and there, sweeping down from northward, over the timbered ridge beyond the paddocks, flying so low that it seemed to leap the ridge, came one of the harrying hawks of war.

Josie snatched her hand from the dogs to raise the rifle to the ready. The dogs burst into furious barking at the intruder.

In a moment the plane was over the lagoon. The birds scattered in frantic flight and the horses bolted.

Flame flickered from the wide-spread wings of the hunter, and smoke came streaking ahead of him, and the sails of the windmill crumpled on the instant like a broken flower, and the grassy earth tossed and billowed like a stormy sea . . . and the detonation of the guns smote the ear like the cracking of mighty timber — *CRA-A-A-A-A-A-A-A-A-A-CK!*

Great jets of silver burst from the crumpling water-tanks. The milk-woods were shorn of leaves as by a hurricane. Timber of the rails of graves and stockyard was hurled in splinters in the air.

CRA-A-A-A-A-A-A-A-A-A-CK!

The white roof of the homestead buckled and smoked under the leaden hail, and fowls and fowl-house disintegrated in a whirl of dust and feathers, and the red earth boiled as the storm ripped through the garden toward the gate, flattening the very earth with the roar of its going — *WHAAAAHNG!* — with the swiftness of lightning cutting down those by the gate into whose gaping faces the red disks on the wings glared like devil's eyes — *WHAAAAHNG!*

It was gone . . . and Josie sat sagged on mangled legs, her back to the splintered gate, shrieking in chorus with her mangled animals rolling in death-agony about her.

It was coming back, the silver devil-bird with the unwinking red eyes, high now, banking steeply in the turn to survey the handiwork of wrecking in a flash what had taken a lifetime of love to build . . . the god-man within, the mongoloid superman, squatting like a bronze Buddha in his perspex.

Josie found the rifle in the rags and bloody pulp that had been her lap, and raised it, and her screaming became articulate:

— Watty . . . Watty . . . send the slant-eyed bastard down to me!

There he was within shot even as her prayer was uttered ——— *WHAAAANG!* Only the leap of the rifle in her bloody hands told that the shot was fired.

Past in a flash and climbing again, away up over the home-paddock. Josie watched, grey-faced and fighting for her breath, the sweat of death upon her, the crimson sand beneath her deeper crimsoned with her ebbing life.

Up, up, up the destroyer rode his sky-steed, as if returning to his very god the sun. Then suddenly he yawed, dropped a wing, came spinning back to earth, the earth that waited on him to avenge his defilement of it ——— *BOOM!*

He struck near the broken windmill, vanished in a golden ball of fire that became an inky pall.

Josie saw it. The light of life blazed for an instant in her eyes.

— Watty . . . Watty . . . she gasped and slid sideways onto the torn belly of the goat.

A dispute over payment for 'The Last Australian' occasioned a serious breach between Christesen and Herbert.

C. B. Christesen to Xavier Herbert

20 September 1960

Dear Xavier,

I've now had time to cool down since receiving your letter of September 9. Although I'm still bloody angry, I'll make this letter as moderate as possible.

I find that I've paid you £65 since January. [marginal note: + £10] You have been paid at higher rates than any other *Meanjin* contributor and at higher rates than by any other Australian journal to my knowledge. I paid you those rates not because you are so much better than any other Australian writer but to help you a little over a difficult spot and to give you a bit of genuine encouragement and appreciation. I would have liked to feel that you would have done the same for me if I were ever in a similar situation, and I'm not making a song and dance about it. I simply asked in a normal friendly way if the fiver completed payment for the story. Payment has been slow but the bloody thing hasn't even been published yet. I should have checked on the payments before I wrote but I didn't. You give me no credit for paying you in advance — again in an endeavour to help you. Now you imply that I might welsh on you — and that makes me hopping mad. You might be incapable of understanding this, but I do keep to my agreements, no matter what the inconvenience to me personally.

Seemingly you don't keep to yours. You offered me an article to accompany the story and I accepted the offer and promised to send you a tenner. You now write, 'You can't pay for my work. But others can' — and mention some other bloody quarterly. (And all that psychopathic crap about my 'decrying' your work, whereas in fact I've done the exact opposite.)

I tell you what, mate — you can get stuffed. I've gone to quite extraordinary pains — and a hell of a lot of expense — to publish a pen-and-ink sketch, a story, a full-dress essay, an article, and an extract from an unpublished work, all for the bloody glorification of bloody Herbert. I did this thinking the material would come out to coincide with publication of *Soldiers' Women*, as I had been told by A & R, and thus would give the novel a flying start and place you right back in the forefront. And you now have the arse to talk about 'hypothetical' tenners, 'raising the ante' and so on.

I've long ceased to expect a spot of gratitude from writers, but I'm damned if I expected to receive an example of that kind of abject insensitivity.

I also delayed this reply because I had hoped you might have 'second thoughts'; but no other letter has arrived.

I can understand something of how you feel — for Christ sake I've been through it myself for long enough — and for the most part I'm prepared to make allowances; but I'm buggered if I'll accept innuendos of that kind from you or anyone else.

I'm enclosing a tenner which completes payment *in advance of publication* for 'The Last Australian'. If you keep to your promise and send me the article you'll get another tenner — again in advance of publication. I'd want it by mid-October. If not, you are all washed up so far as I'm concerned.

The poetic climate in Australia in the 1950s was predominantly one of formal restraint. The lively conflicts of the 1940s simmered down, leaving the anti-traditionalists out of the cultural mainstream. In retrospect, the 1950s have been seen as a time of muted poetic voices and careful handling of traditional forms. If the voices of A. D. Hope, Judith Wright and Rosemary Dobson dominated in the 1940s, the most noticeable development of the late 1950s was the emergence of Gwen Harwood, whose poetry was an important continuation of the formal, enlightenment traditions established in the 1940s. But the 1950s weren't all cool formalism; they were years of overlappings and cross-currents, many of which were represented in *Meanjin*'s pages.

Number 2, 1951

Tapu

W. HART-SMITH

Buried beneath the hearthstone
the stone tools finished and unfinished;
the final act before departure: in my name
this place is sacred, and the buried stones.

There would be the return, sometimes alone,
the hearthstone lifted when the place was known,
new growth accounted for in grass and tree,
and grass and tree more tangled grown, more green.

Beneath the stone, the deeply buried stones,
the stone tools finished and unfinished,
lifted one by one from under the stone . . .

Ten inches down in loam
by the measuring stick. It's logic I lack:
you say there must have been one day
when he would never come back.

Number 3, 1954

The Tomb of Heracles

JAMES MCAULEY

A dry tree with an empty honeycomb
Stands as a broken column by the tomb:
The classic anguish of a rigid fate,
The loveless will, superb and desolate.

This is the end of stoic pride and state:
Blind light, dry rock, a tree that does not bear.

Look, cranes still know their path through empty air;
For them their world is neither soon nor late;
But ours is eaten hollow with despair.

Number 4, 1956

Montebellos

RANDOLPH STOW

No trace was ever found of Australia's first colonists, the 97 Englishmen left on the Montebello Islands when the Tryal *wrecked there in 1622.*

In radio-active islands laid to sleep
We have long ceased to wonder at the world,
Knowing the causes must be grave and deep
That bring on us these Armageddons, hurled
Out of the heavens on our uncounted bones.
Death having neither interests nor fears,
Let nations, if they see a need, pull down
A thousand skies and islands round their ears,
We care not. Yet we muse, grown sage in ease,
King James was not so wise a fool as these.

Number 1, 1955

Apocalypse in Springtime

LEX BANNING

So I was in the city on this day:
and suddenly a darkness
came upon the city like night,
and it was night;
and all around me, and on either hand,
both above and below me,
there was — so it seemed — a dissolving
and a passing away.

And I listened with my ears, and heard
a great rushing
as the winds of the world left the earth,
and then there was silence,
and no sound, neither the roar of the city,
nor the voices of people,
nor the singing of birds, nor the crying
of any animal;
for the world that was audible had vanished
and passed away.

And I stretched forth both my hands,
but could touch nothing,
neither the buildings, nor the passers-by,
neither could I feel
the pavement underneath my feet,
nor the parts of my body;
for the world that was tangible had vanished
and passed away.

And I looked around and about me,
and could see nothing,
neither the heavens, nor the sea, nor the earth,
nor the waters under it;
for the world that was visible had vanished
and passed away.

In my nostrils there was a fleeting
fume of corruption,
and on my tongue a dying taste
of putrefaction,
and then these departed, and there was nothing;
for the world that was scent,
and the world that was savour had vanished
and passed away.

And all around me, and on either hand,
both above and below me,
there was nothing, and before me and behind;
for all of the fivefold
worlds of the world had vanished
and passed away.

And all my possessions of pride
had been taken from me,
and the wealth of my esteem stricken,
and the crown of my kingdom,
and all my human glory,
and I had nothing, and I was nothing;
for all things sensible had vanished
and passed away.

And I was alone in nothing,
and stood at the bar
of nothing, was accused by nothing,
and defended by nothing,
and nothing deliberated judgment
against me.

And the arbitrament of the judgment
was revealed to me.

Then the nothing faded into nothing,
and that into nothing,
and I was alone in a darkness like night,
but it was not night;
then the darkness faded into darkness,
and that into darkness,
and there was no light — but only
emptiness,
and a voice in the void lamenting
and dying away.

A Postcard

(To Antony Riddell)

Gwen Harwood

Snow crusts the boughs' austere entanglement.
Bare spines once fleshed in summer's green delights
pattern an ice-green sky. Three huntsmen go
vested for the ritual of the hunt
with lean, anonymous dogs for acolytes.
Shadowless, luminous, their world of snow
superlative in paint: so we assume
on snowlit air mortality's faint plume.

Often in the museum I would stand
before this picture, while my father bent
to teach me its perfections. It became
part of the love that leapt from hand to hand
in a live current; a mind-made continent —
familiar as my shadow or my name
were the near, sprawling arabesque of thorns,
the looping skaters, and the towering horns

the Moses-mountain lifted, gripping its stone
covenant between cold and solitude.
My foursquare world! Homesickness, sit in tears
turning the mind's old scrapbook, the long known
pastiche of yesterdays, believing good
and incorruptible the uneasy years
of childhood learning treachery in its slow
budding of cells, and heartsblood on the snow

that day my dolls did not return my kiss.
In their blank eyes all flashing evidence
sank to lacklustre glass; about me spilled
the shrouding light of a new genesis.
No hand lay palm to mine in innocence.
A blind, beaked hunger, crying to be filled,
nestled and gaped, was fed, and whipped again
its bird-clear syllables of mortal pain

through a rare kingdom crumbling into paint.
A father's magus mantle sleeved no longer
an old man's trembling gestures towards his gift
sealed in with myrrh; and sovereign youth grew faint
hearing that crystal voice cry still the hunger
tented in flesh: 'Time's herod-blade is swift.
Hunt me down love, the snow-white unicorn,
I'll drink in safety from its twisted horn

Your childhood's relic poison, and lie quiet.'
Now I am old. The fabulous beast, grown tame,
dreams in heraldic stillness of the chase;
the sick heart, chafed by memory's salt-rough diet,
craves for lost childish sweetness, cannot name
its old heroic themes. My early face
withered to bone, fretted by wintry change,
flowering blood-bright cheek and lip grows strange:

my children's children, with my father's eyes
stare with me at this postcard, seeing only
a sharp and simple winter, while they wear
the hard sun like a skin. And my love lies
imprisoned in stiff gestures, hearing the lonely
voice call: 'I hunger' through the snowbright air.
Spilling the days no memory will restore
time's fountain climbs its own perpetual core.

Last Look

A. D. Hope

His mind, as he was going out of it,
Looked emptier, shabbier than it used to be:
A secret look to which he had no key,
Something misplaced, something that did not fit.

Windows without their curtains seemed to stare
Inward — but surely once they had looked out.
Someone had moved the furniture about
And changed the photographs: the frames were there,

But idiot faces never seen before
Leered back at him. He knew there should have been
A carpet on the boards, not these obscene
Clusters of toadstools sprouting through the floor.

Yet Arabella's portrait on the wall
Followed him just as usual with its eyes.
Was it reproach or pleading, or surprise,
Or love perhaps, or something of them all?

Watching her lips, he saw them part; could just
Catch the thin sibilance of her concern:
'O Richard, Richard why would you not learn
I was the only soul that you could trust?'

Carefully, carefully, seeming not to know,
He added this remembrance to his store.
Conscience, in uniform beside the door,
Coughed and remarked that it was time to go.

High time indeed! He heard their tramping feet.
To have stayed even so long, he knew, was rash.
The mob was in the house. He heard the crash
Of furniture hurled down into the street.

'This way!' The warder said: 'You must be quick.
You will be safe with us . . .' He turned to go
And saw too late the gaping void below.
Someone behind him laughed. A brutal kick

Caught him below the shoulders and he fell
Quite slowly, clutching at the passing air,
And plunged towards the source of his despair
Down the smooth funnel of that endless well.

Number 3, 1960

Bog and Candle

ROBERT D. FITZGERALD

1

At the end of life paralysis or those creeping teeth,
the crab at lung or liver or the rat in the brain,
and flesh become limp rag, and sense tap of a cane —
if you would pray, brother, pray for a clean death.

For when the work you chip from age-hard earth must pause,
faced with the dark, unfinished, where day gave love and jest,
day and that earth in you shall pit you to their test
of struggle in old bog against the tug of claws.

2

What need had such a one for light at the night's rim?
Yet in the air of evening till the medley of sound —
children and birds and traffic — settled in the profound
meditation of earth, it was the blind man's whim

to set at his wide window the warm gift of flame
and put a match to wick for sight not like his own —
for his blank eyes could pierce that darkness all have known,
the thought: 'What use the light, or to play out the game?'

and could disperse also the fog of that queer code
which exalts pain as evidence of some aim or end
finer than strength it tortures, so sees pain as friend —
good in itself and guiding to great ultimate good!

Then he would touch the walls of the cold place where he sat
but know the world as wider, since here, beside his hand,
this flame could reach out, out, did touch but understand . . .
Life in a man's body perhaps rayed out like that.

So it is body's business and its inborn doom
past will, past hope, past reason and all courage of heart,
still to resist among the roof-beams ripped apart
the putting-out of the candle in the blind man's room.

Number 4, 1960

Arrows

MARY GILMORE

I

Why gibe
That woman is a woman?
As man
She, too, is human;
So human
That, since time began,
She gives her son
What makes him man.

II

Since from the boundless
To the limited life came,
Prayer is the cry of man
For oneness with the Infinite
Again.

III

Save that by memory
Man's reason lives,
For all we see or do,
Lives are but sieves.
If memory went
What would remain?
Only the scattered chaff
Without the grain.

IV

Not life but memory makes man.
Life leaves no mark on time;
But memory has given us words.
Words are the steps by which we climb.

The Last Romantics

(To C. E. Mulford)

BRUCE DAWE

Across the badlands of their lives
Littered now with whitening bones
They ride like thunder, at their side
Butch Cassidy, Tom Mix, Buck Jones.

On yucca flats they spur along
Each rowelling his sweaty roan,
While cacti's thorny arms extend
A benediction of their own,

And cotton-mouth and Gila mark
Their passage with unblinking eyes,
The desert's bitter children, they
View all but death with mild surprise;

For who knows what dim canyons hold,
What ambush there may well be planned,
Where dry-gulch gentry from the rocks
Throw down on them from every hand?

No ranny knows this much is sure
Such transitory fear must pass:
With triggered hearts they urge their mounts
Towards the sunlit sea of grass

Which lies beyond the canyon's mouth
(Incredible and far country!)
Where owl-hoot trails all peter out,
And rangeland's cheap and water free,

And weary saddle-tramps light down
From heaving broncs and set awhiles,
Oiling their hardware in the sun,
Remembering, with easy smiles . . .

A Case

GWEN HARWOOD

Uprights undid her: spires and trees.
One night she lived a vital dream.
By water and by land she came
delayed by manifold stupidities
into a wicked, feasting town.
Her Samson mind cracked pillars down
and left no trees, no upright towers.
By righteousness endowed with powers

extravagant beyond belief
she resurrected from the gutter
the President of Dogs, whose utter
gratitude made words of barks: 'O Chief
Lover of Cleanliness, no more,
I swear, shall dogs befoul your door
or copulate in public places.'
She resurrected girls whose faces

purified of alizarin shame
were safely quarantined from sex;
charms against men hung from their necks
to the division she would never name.
All sweet, all clean this level town.
A phallus rose, she whipped it down.
Day broke.

Erect, the bawdy spires
poked in red clouds' immodest fires.

She bathed. She munched her food chopped raw.
Blackstrap molasses charged her power.
'Shadowy Redeemer, come this hour!
Help me enforce thy horizontal law,
and scourge the crude obscenities
of dogs and girls and posturing trees.'

She met him in a crowded street,
Tore off her clothes, and kissed his feet.

Number 4, 1961

At My Grandmother's

DAVID MALOUF

An afternoon, late summer, in a room
Shuttered against the bright, envenomed leaves;
An under-water world, where time, like water,
Was held in the wide arms of a gilded clock,
And my grandmother, turning in the still sargasso
Of memory, wound out her griefs and held
A small boy prisoner to weeds and corals,
While summer leaked its daylight through his head.

I feared that room, the parrot screeching soundless
In its dome of glass, the faded butterflies
Like jewels pinned against a sable cloak,
And my grandmother winding out the skeins I held
Like trickling time, between my outstretched arms;

Feared most of all the stiff, bejewelled fingers
Pinned at her throat, or moving on grey wings
From word to word; and feared her voice that called
Down from their gilded frames the ghosts of children
Who played at hoop and ball, whose spindrift faces
(The drowned might wear such smiles) looked out across
The wreck and debris of the years, to where
A small boy sat, as they once sat, and held
In the wide ache of his arms, all time, like water,
And watched the old grey hands wind out his blood.

The Literary Heritage

H. P. HESELTINE

'So much horror in the clear Australian sunlight!'
Douglas Stewart: *Ned Kelly*

That Australians have a literary heritage is a proposition which, I imagine, few critics of our culture would seriously deny. The general function of that heritage, too, would probably be a matter of common agreement. It is the continuing definition of ourselves to ourselves through the forms of literature; it is the monuments of the used and usable past which can still enforce their relevance upon us; it is that element in our most accomplished literary works which makes known their Australianness. But the specific forces which have controlled the development of our literature, the special attitudes which reveal the Australianness of Australian writing — these are matters on which finality has by no means been reached. It must be said, indeed, that some of the prevailing interpretations of our literary heritage are not adequate either to its particular exhibits or to its accumulated quality.

The view of our literature which has acquired perhaps the widest authority is that which sees it as a contest between an exclusive and an inclusive culture, in which the latter has consistently marshalled the superior forces; it is the democratic theme which is at the heart of our literature. This very plausible view has been argued powerfully and frequently, nowhere with more critical tact than in A. A. Phillips's *The Australian Tradition*. 'The Currency Lad,' he writes in the essay on 'The Democratic Theme', 'could be defined, almost, as the man who did not touch his hat'. (p. 35) And the Currency Lad stands as the most compelling image of man presented in our writing. Nobody could deny the enormous force of the drive towards egalitarian democracy in Australian writing, or ignore some of the concomitant attitudes it has established in our literature — the suspicion of heroes, for instance, or the tendency towards left-wing political commitments.

Belief in the primacy of the democratic theme, with all its attendant consequences for personal and public action, naturally enough places Henry Lawson fairly and squarely at the centre of our literary heritage. It is no accident that Phillips's book is distinguished by sympathetic and sensitive essays on Lawson and Furphy. The democratic theme clearly does occupy — and occupy significantly — the minds of many of our earlier writers. I do not question its importance or value; I do wonder if it is at the very centre of the Australian imagination. Is it the grain of sand which irritates the oyster into protective action? Or is it the pearl which makes the grain of sand bearable and (incidentally for the oyster) beautiful? If, in the past, the democratic theme has been the secret stimulant to our artistic creation, then certain quite real difficulties are posed for us. In an article, 'Winds of

Change in the Australian Novel', Norman Bartlett has stated quite flatly that 'The national billy tea literary tradition — the gum leaves make all the difference — no longer satisfies us'. (*Australian Quarterly*, 4/1960, p. 75) And again: 'Those who still march under that once grand old banner, "Temper democratic, bias Australian," are merely marching in circles'. (80) With these words Bartlett voices an attitude that is increasingly felt abroad among writers and critics. If all that Lawson and his tribe can offer is outback mateship and proletarian protest, they must regretfully, even painfully, be relegated to the past — historical monuments from which the life of relevance has departed. I do not happen to believe that we need so completely to turn our backs on Lawson: yet the difficulty remains. If our literary heritage offers us nothing but the simple virtues appropriate to a simple frontier society, what can we do but reject it? We are left with a heritage which is an empty inheritance.

The cultural historian will not for long be left at a loss by Lawson's qualities and by Bartlett's rejection of them. He will soon go to work, fitting them into a larger pattern which will comprehend them both. The sub-title of Phillips's book is 'Studies in a Colonial Culture'. And it requires no great flexibility of the imagination to understand both Lawson and Bartlett as representing inevitable stages in the passage of what was once a colonial culture to national independence and maturity. The American scholars have long since marked out the pattern of the progress of their own civilization and literature; and in its general outlines the pattern seems to be a necessary one in any situation where a European culture has been grafted onto — through colonization and conquest — some less advanced society. First of all there is likely to be a period of imitation of the models provided by the parent civilization; this is likely to be followed by a period of intense and sometimes acrimonious debate between the forces of nationalism and those which continue to pay homage to the imperial source; for a time nationalism will appear to be triumphant; but as pre-condition of full maturity, nationalism must suffer rejection and be replaced by a sense of nationhood which is assured and un-selfconscious.

It is easy enough to translate this pattern to Australian literature. Harpur, Kendall and Gordon, the imitators, are followed by the nationalists of the 'nineties and the turn of the century — nationalists who did not have things so much their own way as we sometimes think, who had to contest their right to assert their Australianness. The force of nationalism carries it with some abatement through the first World War and into the 'twenties; in the 'thirties it experiences a revival of enthusiasm and vigour through the Jindyworobak movement. More balanced views, evident from the beginning of the century, are progressively given more and more weight; though, that the issue is by no means settled yet is suggested by the curious ambivalence of Ray Lawler's second play, *The Piccadilly Bushman*, and by the even more ambivalent reception it was accorded.

Australian's literary heritage as the record of her gradual liberation from the restraints of a colonial culture: the interpretation has as much validity as the democratic theme, and leaves us with the same uneasy sense of incompleteness. An interpretation which can be so widely applied — to the United States, to Canada, to South Africa, as well as to our own country — has its very considerable uses. It equally has its limitations. It holds out the seductive possibility of viewing the entire literature of the United States, Canada, South Africa and Australia as one single and inseparable mass — or mess. Which they aren't, if for no other reason than that the settlers of each land had to face and overcome enormously different physical environments. So, it might be argued, the finding of a true relation to the land, the very earth, has been the particular concern of every Australian poet from Charles Harpur to David Campbell. Not the bush workers, or the bush virtues, but the bush itself has been their one true subject. The peculiar ancient harshness of the Australian bush has demanded from our writers the exercise of all their most vital energies. The only way Harpur could live with it was to image it forth as the backdrop to the heroic achievements of the pioneers. Lawson accepted its harshness in bitter surrender to its power to hold him. Brennan, so far as he could and as an act of the will, chose to ignore it. Bernard O'Dowd hymned it as the spirit of Australia. The Jindyworobaks gloried in its primeval indifference to the condition of man. Now our younger poets are able to select from among its many features, and treat them for what they are.

Clearly we must include landscape as a component in our literary heritage. But when we have said landscape, have we said all? And if so, is that enough? Is it enough? This seems to be the question students of Australian culture are driven to again and again. Is our tradition, after all, to be summed up in this or that single word — Mateship? Landscape? Nationalism? Is what we have received from our literary past so *thin* that the simple labels do, in fact, suffice? Most of us would find it difficult to believe that the literature of any nation could be reduced to such direct and formulary clarity; most of us would not like to believe that our own literature could be so reduced. Using the same materials which have always been available, is it possible to construct a version of our literary heritage which will do justice to whatever discoverable complexity and force are latent in it, and at the same time will not disavow its Australianness?

The means of carrying out such an enterprise are, I believe, at hand. They can be usefully indicated by resorting to another formulation, but a formulation richer in overtones and implications than any thus far invoked. In an article entitled 'The Background of Romantic Thought' (*Quadrant*, II, no. 1), Herbert Piper asserts that 'there are still many Romantic elements in Australian culture, often unrecognised and unquestioned and yet serving to mark Australian literature off from the modern European literature which rejected Romanticism at least a generation ago'. (p. 49) Professor Piper is here, I think, half right and half wrong. He is right in stressing the importance of the Romantic sensibility in Australian literature; he is wrong in those aspects of the Romantic sensibility which he selects as particularly important in our culture; and he is wrong in suggesting a kind of backwardness in our Australian engagement with the Romantic response to life. What I wish to propose as a fundamental element in Australia's literary heritage may be stated something like this. Australian literature is historically a Romantic and post-Romantic phenomenon. Due to certain circumstances of history and geography, it came much *earlier* than European literature to deal with a number of key themes of late Romantic awareness. Although these dealings were very much disguised by colonial necessities, Australian literature, in fact, early took as its central subject what is *still* one of the inescapable concerns of all modern literature. Such a proposition may well seem to be gratuitously grotesque; it certainly requires the kind of defence afforded only by the display of many items of evidence. Some such items, from within the mainstream of Australian writing, I will provide here; many more could readily be assembled. But first I must isolate that peculiarly modern element in modern literature which, it is my contention, Australian literature so early laid hold on.

I can most conveniently do so by referring to an article by an American critic, Lionel Trilling — 'On The Modern Element in Modern Literature' (*Partisan Review*, XXVIII, no. 1). Towards the end of his article Trilling is driven to speaking of 'the subversive tendency of modern literature'. (p. 31) It subverts not through this or that political action, not through its Leftism or its Fascism, but in its alienation from any kind of politics, men organized into rational communities. Behind much modern literature, Trilling argues, lies the German Nietzsche. And 'Nietzsche's theory of the social order dismisses all ethical impulse from its origins — the basis of society is to be found in the rationalization of cruelty: as simple as that'. (p. 28) A rationalized cruelty is perhaps not likely to recommend itself to the creative artist as an object worthy of his sustained attention. So he becomes an outsider. He becomes Diderot's Nephew of Rameau; or, like Dostoevsky, he sends back Notes from the Underground, brutally destroying all our humanist pieties. The writer, then, is likely to reject society because it is founded on cruelty and sustained by petty rationalistic rules: also, because there are kinds of experience which are positively much more interesting to him. Trilling comments: 'Nothing is more characteristic of modern literature than its discovery and canonization of the primal non-ethical energies [p. 25] . . . I venture to say that the idea of losing oneself up to the point of self-destruction, of surrendering oneself to experience without regard to self-interest or conventional morality, of escaping wholly from the social bonds is an "element" somewhere in the mind of every modern person who dares to think of what Arnold in his unaffected Victorian way called "the fullness of spiritual perfection"' (p. 35). In exploring the primal energies, the artist is likely to discover that they can command horror as well as delight, yet he will continue his exploration with unabated fascination. 'Is this not the essence of the modern belief about the nature of the artist,' asks Trilling, 'the man who goes down into that hell which is the historical beginning of the human soul, a beginning not outgrown but established in humanity as we know it now, preferring the reality of this hell to the bland lies of the civilization that has overlaid it?' (p. 26)

It is my contention that Australian literature is signalized by its early recognition of the nature of the social contract and by its long-standing awareness of the primal energies of mankind, an awareness which has known little of the sweetening and freshness of early Romantic optimism. Australia's literary heritage is based on a unique combination of glances into the pit and the erection of safety fences to prevent any toppling in.

'Australian literature,' writes Norman Bartlett in the article previously cited, 'so far as I have read it, utterly fails to grapple with the life of politics'. (p. 82) To be sure, we have not yet produced a C. P. Snow. Yet is it surprising that the creative minds in a country founded in convictism should have early learned to mistrust the political life? What better illustration than the first half century of British occupation of Australia of Nietzsche's notion that the basis of society is the rationalization of cruelty? When our authors turned to the convict system as viable material for their imaginations, its all-pervading sadism is what struck them most forcibly. The dreadfully enforced rules of the Ring, the absolute viciousness of characters like John Price: this is what we carry away most vividly from Price Warung's *Convict Days*. Marcus Clarke's *For the Term of His Natural Life* is crowded with incident, and saturated with pain, which affects all members and both sides of the system. It is small wonder that our literature has little to tell us about the life of politics — except its cruelty. Even comparatively recent novels like Dal Stivens's *Jimmy Brockett* and Frank Hardy's *Power without Glory* are centred in individuals who perceive the essential nature of political power and who achieve it by the imposition of their own cruel will on the lives of others.

Yet Australian literature is not without its genial elements. Indeed, *Such Is Life*, one of the great monuments of our fiction, is not only a major social document; it is downright sociable. Tom Collins, the narrator, is 'a government official, of the ninth class,' and therefore something of an outcast; but the basis of the book rests in talk — talk for its own sake, talk round the campfire, talk on the track. Yet all the time shaping and controlling the talk, the meandering meditations, is an ironic intelligence, powerfully aware of the importance of artistic form. Arthur Phillips's essay in *The Australian Tradition* is a first-rate demonstration of the carefully designed structure of *Such Is Life*. Yet this brilliant exposition of Furphy's craftsmanship is curiously deficient. The only use to which Phillips can see that craftsmanship being put is 'to present a complete and significant picture of Riverina life' (p. 19): *Such Is Life* as an especially well-organized and thorough historical document. In fairness, is should be said that Phillips goes on to add that below the aim of giving a complete account of the Riverina 'lay another layer of purpose: an impulsion to give the sense of Life, *the feel of how things happen*'. (p. 22) But here Phillips stops — he has little or nothing to say on what was Furphy's sense of Life, how he felt things happening to him. In spite of his sure grasp on the conduct of the narrative, Phillips overlooks the important hint offered by the title — *Such Is Life*. Legend has it that these were the last words of Ned Kelly before he swung — a nihilistic summation of the meaning of his existence. And it is worth refreshing our memories as to the last words of Tom Collins' long recollections:

> Now I had to enact the Cynic philosopher to Moriarty and Butler, and the aristocratic man with a 'past' to Mrs. Beaudesart; with the satisfaction of knowing that each of these was acting a part to me. Such is life, my fellow-mummers —just like a poor player, that bluffs and feints his hour upon the stage, and then cheapens down to mere nonentity. But let me not hear any small witticism to the further effect that its story is a tale told by a vulgarian, full of slang and blanky, signifying — nothing.

Such Is Life is, in effect, concerned with the discrepancy between what we are and what we appear to be, and with the futility of human endeavour. Nosey Alf appears to be a boundary rider, and proves in fact to be Warrigal Alf's forsaken love. Tom Collins pretends to a certain cynicism; he is, in truth, overflowing with a kindness (a kindness which can have tragic consequences). Mrs. Beaudesart, insisting on her well-bred airs, is for all that a decayed and snobbish gentlewoman. All the characters of the novel are preparing faces for the faces that they meet, and are continually thwarted in the purposes of their lives. And this is the point of the sociability of *Such Is Life*: it enables its characters to escape from the unbearable reality of being themselves. Society is an act, a decent bluff, which makes bearable the final emptiness, the nothingness of the honestly experienced inner life.

'Nothing' is the last word of one of the central classics of our literary heritage; and it is a word which echoes and re-echoes throughout our literature. In the nineteenth century a persistent and single-minded investigation of the horror of primal experience simply could not be tolerated. The first duty of a frontier society is physical survival; hence evolved that most famous of all Australian survival techniques, the concept of mateship. In our literature, mateship is especially the property of Henry Lawson. And one does not have to go far in his *Prose Works* (Angus & Robertson, 1948) to understand its value for him. It was a necessary defence against the kind of experience which most powerfully laid hold on his imagination. If mateship bulks so large in the canon of Lawson's writing (as indeed it does), it was because behind and beneath it was an even more compelling awareness of horror, of panic and emptiness. Here, for instance, is a passage from one of Lawson's best known tales, 'The Union Buries Its Dead', often cited as an example of Lawson's left-wing solidarity. That it may be; it is something else as well. This is Lawson's description of the actual burial of the unidentified corpse:

> The grave looked very narrow under the coffin, and I drew a breath of relief when the box slid easily down. I saw a coffin get stuck once, at Rookwood, and it had to be yanked out with difficulty, and laid on the sods at the feet of the heartbroken relations, who howled dismally while the grave-diggers widened the hole. But they don't cut contracts so fine in the West. Our grave-digger was not altogether bowelless, and, out of respect for that human quality described as 'feelin's', he scraped up some light and dusty soil and threw it down to deaden the fall of the clay lumps on the coffin. He also tried to steer the first few shovelfuls gently down against the end of the grave with the back of the shovel turned outwards, but the hard dry Darling River clods rebounded and knocked

> all the same. It didn't matter much — nothing does. The fall of the lumps of clay on a stranger's coffin doesn't sound any different from the fall of the same thing on an ordinary wooden box — at least I didn't notice anything awesome or unusual in the sound; but, perhaps, one of us — the most sensitive — might have been impressed by being reminded of a burial long ago, when the thump of every sod jolted his heart. (p. 47)

'It didn't matter much — nothing does.' The assertion is shocking in its finality, but it is the (sometimes unacknowledged) burden of much of Lawson's best writing. If some of Lawson's stories seem rather thin, it is not because they were without content. Rather, they could not afford to face up to their true subject — nothing. They had to take refuge in sociability, they had to create some kind of face or personality which would make shift in the world; in short, they had to opt for mateship.

But mateship has its corollary in Lawson's work — madness. His stories do take cognizance of those who choose to live for and into themselves. The typical fate of such characters is suggested in a story called 'Rats'. Some itinerant shearers come across what they take to be two men struggling in the road. It proves to be a mad traveller wrestling with his swag:

> they reached the scene of the trouble, and there stood a little withered old man by the track, with his arms folded close up under his chin; he was dressed mostly in calico patches; and half a dozen corks, suspended on bits of string from the brim of his hat, dangled from his bleared optics to scare away the flies. He was scowling malignantly at a stout, dumpy swag which lay in the middle of the track. (p. 112)

At the end of the story the old man is still there, but he has taken to fishing in the dust. Though a lonely old figure, he is not alone in Lawson's bush. Indeed, it is peopled by a remarkably high percentage of hatters, of eccentrics, of people who are plain out of their mind.

They have been driven mad partly by their election out of human society, partly by the nature of the Australian outback. It may be, as Phillips maintains in 'The Democratic Theme', that one of the early exaltations experienced by the Australian Common Man was 'the knowledge that life and victory over a harsh nature could be won only by the strength of the individual's quality as a man'. (p. 48) But for the Australian Uncommon Man, for the artist, the bush seems to have served from a quite early date a somewhat different function. For many Australian writers there has been an intimate connection between the nature of the Australian landscape and the quality of the inner life which they actually knew or which they embodied in their writing. Kenneth Slessor, in the first section of *Five Visions of Captain Cook*, has a moment of superb insight when he dates this connection from the beginnings of our history; he ascribes the very discovery of Australia and its subsequent cultural development to an act of madness:

> How many mariners had made that choice
> Paused on the brink of mystery! 'Choose now!'
> The winds roared, blowing home, blowing home,

Over the Coral Sea. 'Choose now!' the trades
Cried once to Tasman, throwing him for choice
Their teeth or shoulders, and the Dutchman chose
The wind's way, turning north. 'Choose, Bougainville!'
The wind cried once, and Bougainville had heard
The voice of God, calling him prudently
Out of the dead lee shore, and chose the north,
The wind's way. So, too, Cook made choice,
Over the brink, into the devil's mouth
With four months' food, and sailors wild with dreams
Of English beer, the smoking barns of home.
So Cook made choice, so Cook sailed westabout,
So men write poems in Australia.

(*Poems*, pp. 57–8)

Cook sailed over the brink to a continent which, for our nineteenth century writers, was literally capable of driving its inhabitants insane. Lawson and the other writers of the 'nineties were aware of the bush as a physical fact, inescapable present to their immediate lives. For them the insane horror of bush life was perhaps most powerfully projected into one of their recurring themes — the child lost in the bush; not the child lost and found dead, but the child lost, simply swallowed up in all that emptiness. With the possibility of such a fate constantly close to them, it is little wonder that our nineteenth century writers skirted round what they instinctively guessed to be their true subject, the individual human being confronting the primal energies at the centre of his being on the stage of the Australian continent. Instead, they took refuge in the defence of sociable yarning with a group of mates. When they did confront the primeval heart of the matter, it was usually in the form of an attempt to physically subdue the bush and so control its power to subvert the mind.

The first Australian poet directly to confront the heart of his own existence without the mediation of landscape was Christopher Brennan. The disintegration of Brennan's personal life is legendary in the Australian literary consciousness. He is our supreme myth figure of the Romantic artist. It is equally important to realize that in his verse he encountered and recorded just as much horror as in his living. More than any other Australian artist, Brennan suffered the paradox of the late-Romantic experience of love. By love possessed, the poet is driven to ever-increasing intensity of passion at the same time as he comes to ever-increasing knowledge of its final emptiness and capacity to destroy. Foreseeing the end, he yet will not, cannot, forsake his loving until it has accomplished its bitter fulfilment. In Brennan's work, this pattern is rendered with all the ambiguous fascination of its darkness. To be sure, Brennan writes with rare felicity of the brief Paradisal happiness at the beginning of love. But his perception soon shifts to the monstrousness of Lilith and her relation to Adam. In the Lilith sequence from 'The Forest of Night', Lilith, the legendary other wife of Adam, representative of dark and powerful sexuality, addresses her final line to Adam with shuddering and characteristic completeness; 'Go forth: be great, O nothing, I have said' (*The Verse of Christopher Brennan*, ed. Chisholm and Quinn, p. 140).

The first Australian novel to deal in depth with the relation between a man and a woman was published at much the same time as Brennan was writing some of his best and most characteristic verse — Henry Handel Richardson's *Maurice Guest* (1908). This fine book might almost serve as a text to Professor Trilling's account of 'The Modern Element in Modern Literature'. There is, for instance, Krafft's impassioned defence of the artist as the man who seeks his realities beneath the bland lies of civilisation, who gains his wisdom through personal suffering. More important and at the centre of the story is Maurice Guest's obsessed and self-destroying love of Louise Dufrayer. At one level, the novel is a splendidly objective and detailed account of the torments of sexual jealousy; at another, it is a fictional rendering of the Romantic myth of destructive passion. Maurice's life ends in suicide, and it is with these words that Richardson brings to a close her account of his existence:

> Then, as suddenly as the flame of a candle is puffed out by the wind, his life went from him. His right hand twitched, made as if to open, closed again, and stiffened round the iron of the handle. His jaw fell, and, like an inner lid, a glazed film rose over his eyes, which for hours afterwards continued to stare, with an expression of horror and amaze, at the naked branches of the tree.

Throughout the course of our literary history, then, Australian writers have had deeply located in their imagination (either consciously or unconsciously) a sense of the horror of sheer existence. In the nineteenth century, writers sought to protect themselves through direct assaults on their physical environment and by erecting a structure of sociability appropriate to the conditions of their time and place. At about the turn of the century, two major writers emerged who were prepared to confront the secret source of their inspiration directly and without flinching. Among our contemporary writers the strength of the basic stimulus remains unabated, but the honest virtues of the Lawson tradition no longer seem entirely adequate for containing its affronts to their civilized integrity. Have our modern writers developed any techniques to make bearable the nihilism of their deepest experience? It seems to me that they have, and that the most important of them have been generated within that range of activity which I have postulated as Australia's literary heritage.

A. D. Hope, for instance, seeks his salvation in valuing for its own sake the intensity of the experience which brings him to his knowledge of emptiness. Hope's love poetry has been described as puritanic in the bitter disgust which is often implied in the very moment of recording love's sensuous splendour. I would not absolutely repudiate such a view, but I would further suggest that the fury of his love poetry also derives from his need to grasp all that love can offer in order to make bearable the horror and disillusion that follow. In 'The Dinner', thus, he imagines love as a cannibalistic feast, whose savage delights are rendered the more savage and delightful because it is themselves the natives consume. This is how the poem ends:

Talking in deep, soft, grumbling undertones
They gnaw and crack and suck the marrowy bones.
The tit-bits and choice meats they puck and press
Each on the other, with grave tenderness,
And touch and laugh; their strange, fierce features move
With the delight and confidence of love.
I watch their loves, I see their human feast
With the doomed comprehension of the beast;
I feel the sweat creep through my bristling hair;
Hollow with rage and fear, I crouch and stare,
And hear their great jaws strip and crunch and chew,
And know the flesh they rend and tear is you.

(*Poems*, p. 74)

Poetry of this order is among the most intense being written in Australia today. It seeks to cope with the historic dilemma of the Australian writer by insisting on its personalness. But there are other writers who have kept their eyes turned outwards and have developed a means of using the Australian landscape which, while derived from the earlier writers, has taken on a new sophistication. A feature of a good deal of recent Australian writing has been its willingness to use an exploration of the bush as an analogy for the exploration of the individual soul. The bush becomes a metaphor for the self. Just as at the heart of the continent is a burning, insane emptiness, so too at the heart of a man is the horror of his pre-history. James McAuley's poem, 'Terra Australis', for instance, makes quite explicit the analogical uses to which the Australian land can be put:

Voyage within you, on the fabled ocean,
And you will find that Southern Continent,
Quiros' vision — his hidalgo heart
And mythical Australia, where reside
All things in their imagined counterpart.

It is your land of similes: the wattle
Scatters its pollen on the doubting heart;
The flowers are wide-awake; the air gives ease.
There you come home; the magpies call you Jack
And whistle like larrikins at you from the trees.

There too the angophora preaches on the hillsides
With the gestures of Moses; and the white cockatoo,
Perched on his limbs, screams with demoniac pain;
And who shall say on what errand the insolent emu
Walks between morning and night on the edge of the plain?

But northward in valleys of the fiery Goat
Where the sun like a centaur vertically shoots
His raging arrows with unerring aim,
Stand the ecstatic solitary pyres
Of unknown lovers, featureless with flame.

(*Under Aldebaran*, p. 51)

Fiction, however, offers more extended opportunities for the landscape to be used in this manner. A novel which accepts such opportunities is Randolph Stow's *To the Islands*. Set in the north-west of Western Australia, it tells of an ageing missionary, Heriot, who abjures his faith, commits what he believes to be murder, and deliberately loses himself in the land in order to find himself. He strikes out 'to the islands', the phrase by which the local natives mean death. In this literal metaphorical journey of self-discovery the word which recurs more than all others is 'nothing'. In a violent scene, before he flees from the mission, Heriot deliberately breaks a crucifix, symbolically shattering his old faith. 'I believe in nothing', he says, 'I can pull down the world'. (p. 75) And his thoughts are on nothingness until the ending of the book, when, with death approaching, his journey to the islands almost completed, he whispers to himself, 'My soul is a strange country'. (p. 204) In the strange emptiness of the land and of his being, Heriot has found a kind of strength.

One of the most celebrated of recent Australian novels uses, like *To the Islands*, the exploration of the continent as an extended metaphor for the exploration of the soul. The richness of *Voss* can be accounted for, in part, by the fact that it fuses almost all those aspects of Australia's literary heritage which define both its modernity and its Australianness. The genuinely subversive drift of White's thinking is brilliantly indicated in his earlier work, *The Aunt's Story*. The nature of this record of the progress of Theodora Goodman into insanity is set down with shattering clarity in the epigraphs which White appended to Sections II and III of his novel. Section II, 'Jardin Exotique', is preceded by a quotation from the American, Henry Miller, which concludes with the enlightening phrase, 'the great fragmentation of maturity'. Section III, 'Holstius', which chronicles the final and complete collapse of Theodora's reason, is headed by a single sentence from Olive Schreiner: 'When your life is most real, to me you are mad.' It might well stand as a text for many of the greatest achievements of Australian writing.

At the centre of *Voss* is the disturbing figure of the German explorer. White himself has indicated that his character was influenced by Hitler, 'the arch-megalomaniac of the day'. And Voss imposes his will on the small community he leads by exactly that process which Nietzsche diagnosed as the foundation of political life — the rationalization of cruelty. The distance between Patrick White and Price Warung may not be as great as we at first supposed. Voss lurches off into the fearful heart of Australia with his ill-assorted band of followers — lurches off first into contact with the land itself, ultimately with the continent's native race, those living representatives of humanity's pre-history. In the end, Voss is quite literally destroyed by the primal energies which he is obsessed to understand: the native boy Jacky severs his head from his body. With Voss, 'losing oneself to the point of self-destruction' becomes more than an idea, it is an actually achieved destiny. Before he reaches the end of his own life, he is responsible for the death of all his party save Judd, the tough commonsensical ex-convict who returns to civilization with his distorted account of the realities he has encountered beneath its bland surface. Palfreyman, the professional sufferer, perishes by the spears of the blacks; Le Mesurier, who has had faith both kindled and extinguished by Voss, slits his own throat — a curious descendant of Maurice Guest.

So Voss's mad determination to subdue the continent leads him to destruction at its unrelenting heart. He, too, finally comes to nothing. But his journey has not been in vain. As with Heriot in *To the Islands*, the very recognition of his nothingness becomes a means of salvation. It purges him of his burning pride and cruelty. At the moment of Voss's death, Laura Trevelyan, suffering in spiritual sympathy back in Sydney, rises up in her bed and cries:

> How important it is to understand the three stages. Of God into Man. Man. And Man returning into God . . . When man is truly humbled, when he has learnt that he is not God, then he is nearest to becoming so. In the end, he may ascend. (p. 411)

Voss's journey from pride to the final void has taken him through suffering, humility, and love. It has educated him into humanity. It has not been in vain.

If the alien figure of Voss can fuse so many of the deeper forces which have gone to the making of our literature, one might expect that our native myth hero, Ned Kelly, would elicit from Australian writers some of their most profoundly representative work. In Douglas Stewart's treatment of the outlaw, for instance, it is easy to point to many characteristic Australian traits — the hatred of authority, the masculine vigour and toughness, the outback independence, the refusal to admit defeat. Phillips, in his essay in *The Australian Tradition*, has gone beyond these obvious symptoms of nationality. 'Australian Romanticism and Stewart's *Ned Kelly*' (pp. 96–112) represents the play as a contest between the forces of Vitality and Respectability, or, as Phillips symbolizes the struggle, between Ulysses and Telemachus. This is a reading which clearly has much to recommend it; but also embodied in the very essence of the drama are some of those darker elements of Romanticism which, I suggest, have been so consistently present to the Australian literary imagination.

Ned, Joe Byrne, and the rest of the gang may possess the vitality of Ulysses, the willingness to 'give-it-a-go' we traditionally expect of the Australian. But in the end the energies which dominate Ned in particular are not so much vital as mortal. He strives towards death rather than life; and in this enterprise he is closely attended by the self-destructive irony of Joe Byrne. Their path to death leads through the madness of the Australian bush. For all Ned's talk of outback freedom, what emerges most strongly from the play is a sense of hatters baying at the moon, of the subversion that the bush works on those who commit themselves to its primitive keeping. Ned's vision, a distortion of our rational Australian values, becomes the nightmare of madness.

The dreams of freedom and power which bring Ned to death are not presented as a purely personal affair. Throughout the play, the verse works to make him not so much the representative Australian as the representative of Australia. He incarnates the spirit of the land. And in this incarnation he does not stand in direct opposition to the Respectable (the Livings, the Tarletons, and the rest). It is not simply Ulysses *versus* Telemachus. The Kelly gang and the men they rob are complementary, needing each other to complete a single image of the Australian spirit. Ned and his mates are betrayed by those they have loved (Aaron Sherritt) or those who profess to love them (Curnow); they are destroyed by the men to whom they are tied by the indestructible bonds of hate. 'What happens is the people's doing,' says Byrne; 'and if they hang him, / They hang themselves'. (*Four Plays*, p. 213) In the wild shouts of the troopers who close in on Ned in the last scene there is the fierce joy of those who are destroying part of themselves. It is the final paradox of *Ned Kelly* that Ned's expansive dreams can be realized only in death; that those who, in self-protection, destroy him extinguish in so doing their own most vital spirit.

And in that paradox lies the clue to our literary tradition. The canon of our writing presents a façade of mateship, egalitarian democracy, landscape, nationalism, realistic toughness. But always behind the façade looms the fundamental concern of the Australian literary imagination. That concern, marked out by our national origins and given direction by geographic necessity, is to acknowledge the terror at the basis of being, to explore its uses, and to build defences against its dangers. It is that concern which gives Australia's literary heritage its special force and distinction, which guarantees its continuing modernity.

Part Five

The Temperament of Generations

The tenor of *Meanjin* in the early and mid-sixties was decidedly pessimistic. There was a strong sense that writers and intellectuals in Australia were at odds with the wider community. Parodied as ivory-tower dwellers and 'pseudo-intellectuals', their aesthetic tastes far removed from the mass market, they were left drifting. Indeed, many drifted away entirely; expatriatism reached epidemic proportions. The flavour of the time was captured by Jack Lindsay, himself an expatriate, in an essay on intellectual alienation that was written in response to some adverse comments about Australia in the *London Magazine*.

C. B. Christesen to Jack Lindsay

20 September 1962

Dear Jack,
Have you read the September issue of *London Magazine*? If so, I'm wondering whether you are as disgusted as I am. Much of what is said about Australia is undoubtedly true, and should be said, but the tone of some of the disaffected contributors — Osborne, Mathew, possibly Seymour — is thoroughly odious. In my view this public peeing on their native country has done a great disservice to Australian literature.

Anyway, arising out of this exhibition of spleen and meanness of spirit, I'd like to have a full-dress examination of the problem of alienation — and I'm wondering whether you could let me have an essay of c.4000 words for publication in the Autumn issue. The Australian writer and the problem of alienation — the love-hate relationship of so many of our writers to their own country and people, and the root-causes. For all I know you might side fully with the contributors to *London Magazine* — what I want to do is to open up the subject for discussion at some depth. If you can agree to take on this assignment, could you let me have copy by the end of January? I could offer you a fee of £25. Let's have your decision one day soon.

Number 1, 1963

The Alienated Australian Intellectual

JACK LINDSAY

LONDON

In recent years the term *alienation* has become ever more fashionable, and is continually used by persons who have little or no knowledge of what it means. The reason for the vogue of the term is the discovery of Marx's 1844 Paris MSS, which were first published in Moscow in 1932, became known to a few intellectuals in the following decade, but only reached a wide audience in the postwar period. These writings opened a new dimension in Marx's thought, or rather they made this dimension for the first time clear and accessible. Lukács, for instance, in a book of 1923, had already realized that Marx's work was built up on the concept of alienation; he did so because of his profound knowledge of Hegel, which enabled him to divine how Marx had taken over and transformed, as the foundation of his thinking, the Hegelian scheme in which alienation plays a key-part. Hegel saw alienation as simply a necessary phase of the spirit's process of objectifying and realizing itself: the moment of separation and division when the spirit confronts the objective world as otherness, before it proceeds to overcome the antagonism by grasping the essential unity of the opposites and thus discovers the alien thing as an aspect of itself. Feuerbach adopted the term to describe the way in which religion robs earthly life of its significance, its essence, by an alienated version of man as God and of earth as otherworld; then Moses Hess took the decisive turn, seeing money as the alienating force that cuts man off from his own reality and turns all relations upside down in his mind. On the basis of the work of Hegel, Feuerbach and Hess, Marx developed his own highly complex ideas of estrangement and of alienation, which the Paris MSS set out. It is sufficient here to point out that he saw the division of labour (above all the division of mental and physical labour) and the concomitant systems of exploitation as playing a central rôle in the alienation of man from himself, from his fellows, and from nature, and that he laid stress on the consequent separation of the intellectual and sensuous elements in man, with particular degradation of the latter. The aim of all significant struggle he saw as the quest for wholeness. (His term *estrangement* I take to apply primarily to the unresolved conflict of man confronting a largely unknown and overwhelming nature.)

What Marx was attempting to deal with had close affinities with what T. S. Eliot has called dissociation of sensibility, a breakdown of sensuous wholeness that becomes especially apparent from the 17th century on; what Ruskin passionately realized as the fragmentation of man in a mechanized world; what Morris saw as the withering-out of all joy from the human personality through the ending of labour as a creative process concerned with the making of whole things; what modern social and psychological analysts of all sorts have described as a worsening world-condition of anxiety, frustration, and rootlessness; what others have seen in the fields of science as a trend of extreme specializations that threaten to destroy all possibility of any effective general knowledge; and so on.

I have made these preliminary remarks so that we may have some idea of what we are discussing when we turn to the Australian intellectual and his alienations. We have to understand that we are not dealing with some isolated phenomenon, but are looking at a particular example of a universal problem; and we must be able to distinguish what is here particular and what is general. My stimulus in setting out on this search is the September, 1962, issue of *London Magazine*. For there we find several Australian writers jeering at the Australian scene as though they have no more responsibility to it or for it than if they were superior visitors from Mars making their derisive report. Here we have persons alienated in the simple sense that they feel quite outside the thing they describe; they are cut-off and view the idiot scene from the other side of the asylum-wall.

Now, if an intellectual is worth tuppence he clearly must respond to the alienating pressures around him. If he is not aware of those forces, and aware of them with passion and anger, he is aware of nothing and deserves no attention; he is floating on the surface of things without spiritual or artistic penetration. In thinking the *London Magazine* sort of diatribe to be wrongheaded, one is not then protesting against an awareness of what the alienating forces do to men; one is raising the question of what that awareness implies, what artistic and moral problems it precipitates, and what are the various directions in which it can look and move.

A crucial point about Australian culture is that in the pioneering last-century, when production was at a comparatively crude level and the division-of-labour correspondingly simple, there existed among the common folk a definite sort of popular culture, with its key-emotion in 'mateship'. Because of the situation, this popular culture was something quite different from anything in Europe or even in the United States; it had its valuable elements despite its harsh limitations. However, by the turn of the century its validity was waning and the need to break through into new regions and levels of culture was growing ever more apparent. The need for a critical attitude to the culture of mateship had arrived as a national necessity, and we see it starting in such work as Barbara Baynton's. The conflict thus opened up is still in various degrees unresolved.

On the one hand we meet an effort to overvalue the pioneering phase and its expressions because of their simple sense of human solidarity, or rather of the solidarity of the commonfolk against the obvious large scale exploiters, whether the State or the squatters, the banks or the British investors. And because of this overvaluation there is the effort to carry on straight from the old forms in situations where they are increasingly inadequate or even phoney. On the other hand we meet the wholesale rejection of the pioneering phase and its expressions as a mere vulgarism that is best forgotten, or a depressing conviction that, while the rest of the world has continued to grow, the mass of Australians still remain hopelessly tethered to the superficial and sentimental coarseness of the past, which is now seen as philistinely false. Thus in his *London Magazine* piece Ray Mathew writes:

> This convention in politics, sex, and religion has not changed because Australia has not changed. Nothing has happened to force Australians to reconsider themselves and their values. *The War* and *The Depression* — the shibboleths of my generation's childhood — merely emphasised the protective possibilities of union, against the foe or against authority, the way mates help or lie if one is hungry or AWL. Despite the achievements of some writers and some painters, most of us are still sheltering under the nineties image of ourselves. Discontent with society is expressed usually by a renewed nostalgia for the world the nineties writers reconstructed.

There is a tincture of truth in that statement; but only a tincture. I hope to show in my following comments that it is the kind of truth which one discovers as the only truth when one awakens to something of the nature of alienation and its omnipresence, and when one halts at that first blink of separation-out, with a sense of total alienation from the social scene that has begotten one. It implicitly denies that the awakener is himself a part of the scene; for if he were a part he would have to explain what there is in the scene so different from what he describes as to bring about his own consciousness of disillusion and opposition. His consciousness appears as something quite outside the situation of which it is in fact a product; we can then describe it as alienated, but unaware of alienation except in a passive way. . . .

It is absolutely right, let me stress again, that the intellectual should wish to expose and attack the alienations of which the mass of the people are unaware, however much they may suffer from them; and in this urge his impulses are inevitably ambivalent, contradictory, and complex. His problem is not, and cannot be, one of simply separating-out the lords of the system and attacking them — though if he is to be effectively clear-sighted, he will have to grasp to some extent the mechanisms of oppression, exploitation, and power-domination which play a key-part in perpetuating and deepening alienation. His artistic problem must be incomparably wider than the political task of isolating and pillorying the persons or groups who supremely profit by the systems of alienation. He may, and should, feel pity for the victims of the system, but he is forced at the same time to recognize the complicity of the victim in his own murder. For if the victims were to face their own nature, the whole system would end overnight. Compassion and anger must then go hand in hand, and will certainly become inextricably entangled in the artist's images, his definitions. There is nothing wrong about that so long as his sense of values remains unaffected, so long as he sees the link-up between the individual distortion and the general structure and movement of alienation.

From one angle then he must fight against the pressures that tend to overwhelm him with a sense of the hopeless and pervasive alienations at work in people. In this mood he cannot but echo the words of the Russian poet Yesenin-Volpin, which, as I write, are being denounced in the Soviet Union:

> I know not why I live,
> Nor what I want from the animals who populate this evil Moscow.

That is, if the poet, as I take him, is using his words in a sense that implies the possible substitution of London, New York, Sydney, etc., for Moscow in his lines. A sense of horror before the vast unconsciousness of the alienating forces that mould and condition people is inevitable and, in its place, necessary and salutary. Yesenin-Volpin's terms might be defended as precisely correct from a Marxist viewpoint, since Marx stressed that alienation cuts man off from his own senses, which then become dehumanized, animal, degraded; and insofar as alienation exists in a socialist country, this process of dehumanization is present, even if not in the same way and in the same complex of relationships as in a class-world.

But if this anguished discovery of alienation is the root of all wisdom today, it does not mean that we can halt at it. For the process that has made us aware of alienation cannot but carry at its heart a system of values that condemns alienation root and branch. The horror is meaningless unless it implies an outlook that denies alienation and opposes it. The notion that one can expound the doctrine of alienation from some superior or neutral point of vantage is thus the first and worst falsification that one can make of one's realizations; and it is inescapably present if one resorts merely to denunciations, whether in direct rhetoric or in the indirect form of art-images. Such a notion seems to me present in fulminations like those of Ray Mathew.

A second falsification seems to me to come about if one uses one's vision of the alienated nature of one's people in their way of life in order to excoriate them as nationally peculiar in their distortions and backwardnesses. Each people, it is true, has its national tradition of the philistine and the insensitive, and its intellectuals need to know and understand this tradition. But they should see it as one aspect of a wider problem, in a perspective of world-philistinism. To stigmatize the Australians as specially and peculiarly backward and empty — with the implication that the English whom one is addressing are a superior cultured race, lacking in all such stupidities and aberrations — is to confuse the issue at the outset and to reduce the serious problem of attacking alienation to a game of bear-baiting and cock-pelting. Indeed it is to show oneself afflicted with the barren and arrogant sense of unsubstantiated superiority that one is castigating in the herd.

As I have said, all this is not a new problem for Australia, though since 1945 its extent and its intensity have probably kept on fast increasing. It began importantly when Chris Brennan, Norman Lindsay, Hugh McCrae and others launched their onslaughts, their attempts at kinds of art that had little or no connection with the pioneering phases. And yet, for all their bitter sense of separation, they had also their own brands of union with the people, the nation. Brennan, with his vision of wholeness symbolized in the Eden that

lives by strife
of loving powers that all may reach
the plenitude of beauty and life,

expresses in *The Burden of Tyre*, written against imperialist war at the height of his powers, both his anger and his feeling of unity with 'the Folk'.

Another day is dead and they
have lived it not: such price they pay
daily, to fend the hunger-dread,
that death may find them in safe bed.

Pale wretches! yet this hour at least
they spend, when yon dark hive releas'd,
in dreams that soar beyond the night
and cheer the heart to front the light:

for lo! each steadfast window fire;
would you not say, tho' stars may tire
and the heavens age, man yet maintains
his watchfires o'er the homeless plains;

close worlds of love and hope, that glow
more golden-soft for that they know
how one undying fire in all
burns, and the march harks to one call . . .

Lines that may be relevantly cited here; for they bring out powerfully the way that a great artist cannot but feel a twofold impulse in regarding the city of alienation, a scorn and a love. Brennan here recognizes in the dream of the exploited and deprived the counterpart of his own vision of Eden. In a different way, Norman Lindsay, while violently repudiating the pioneering phases, yet hoped to help in bringing about a great renaissance in Australia, in which all vital past forms would be taken over and revalued. In despising nationalism, he paradoxically uttered his faith in a national rebirth that was to be brought about by the arts.

Such conflicts had their vital aspect; and we find them again in the 1920's, begetting such poets as Slessor and FitzGerald, while Vance Palmer in his own way, as K. S. Prichard in hers, drew on the pioneering world, but with a critical focus that purged the earlier tradition of elements liable to turn into falsity and sentimentality if applied to a more developed Australian society. At the same time various weaknesses or insufficiencies in the Australian situation tended to make writers look to England and visit there. On the one hand there was the poverty of the critical tradition and the consequent feeling that a merely Australian reputation was of little value; and on the other hand the primitiveness of the book-producing trade system, which made it impossible for an author to live on his work unless he were ready to do a crushing amount of hackwork as well. But though Lawson, Prichard, Palmer, McCrae and many others felt impelled to try their hand in England for a while, they were never dominated by English values and soon returned home. Whatever emotions of national inferiority they had to struggle with, they overcame them; they found a fruitful relation to the Australian scene, however numerous may have been their criticisms of it or their angers at its frustrating aspects. It is only in the last decade that the exodus of intellectuals has become large-scale and significant.

I am told that now some 20,000 Australians visit England yearly by sea, and some 12,000 by plane, and that about half are persons who plan to stay in England. A large proportion of these are members of the arts or professions; and it is certainly unfortunate for Australia — at any time, but particularly at the present phase of its expansion as an industrialized country — that it should lose these intellectuals. What is of interest in relation to our argument is that this exodus should come about just as it is becoming possible for the previous Australian weaknesses to be overcome and as the situation in England is weakening and worsening all along the line.

There is thus no comparison with the movement of the American exiles in the 1920's; for those intellectuals clustered in Paris, which was then a centre of important intellectual advance and artistic experiment, and despite the inevitable casualties, many of them were able in time to return with important gains to the United States. England in the 1950's and 1960's, a decayed imperialism (as the U.S.A. is rudely rubbing in at the moment), has had no outstanding new talents, no vanguard movements of any wide significance — unlike England of the 1920's and 1930's when important things were culturally happening. I pointed this out to an intelligent young Australian in London, and she was staggered. She considered England still the cultural pace-setter and, when pressed, cited the theatre, which is certainly the brightest spot in the intellectual sphere though hardly vital enough to justify London as a centre of pilgrimage. She added: 'And anyway it's impossible yet to get a real reputation in Australia. Look at Nolan. He's achieved fame of a serious and stable kind only by coming here.' No doubt there is truth in the latter statement, which brings out some of the elements of cultural immaturity yet holding back Australian developments. But I cannot think the solution lies either in mass-exodus to England or in the acceptance of English judgments as constituting the sole way for an Australian to gain a widely accepted status in the arts. We see in such attitudes a survival of the old inferiority-complex, which once had understandable roots in the comparative backwardness of many national fields, the lingering tradition of colonial dependence, and all the rest of it — an inferiority-complex which had as its complement an aggressive affirmation of bumptious superiority that still persists. As a friend recently said to me: 'You need only look in at the pub near Australia House where they sell Australian beer to have any doubts settled as to who is the master-race.'

Certainly then we find many of the worst elements from the old Australian tradition still alive in the new situation, and growing yet more unpleasant in the process: the earlier forgivable crudities and narrow outlooks corrupted into suburban stereotypes. And here is a field crying out for the satirist. But the satire cannot be artistically or socially effective if its wielder is in any way himself the dupe of the situation. I have tried above to suggest the pitfalls lying all around for the intellectual who begins to awaken to the realities of postwar Australia — and the postwar world in general. And I think we can exemplify them at length from the work of Patrick White, who is certainly the most talented writer coming up in postwar Australia and who appears with an excellently characteristic story in the complained-of issue of *London Magazine*. White is sharply and continuously aware of existing in a society of alienation, and this is what gives the sustained force and passion to his work. He is therefore a portent in Australian letters and can be truly said to mark a radically new phase. But at the same time he shows the blind spots to which I earlier drew attention as the dangers besetting the intellectual who grasps with any fullness the forces of dehumanization and inner division let loose by a matured capitalism. All his weaknesses stem from an unconsciousness of his own relation to the world he condemns, and for this reason he is unable to define relationships within that world itself. His people can collide, but not really impact; they are in the last resort dummies of isolated force, of totally inturned and alienated essence.

Because the world Patrick White describes is one of pure alienation, it is not Australia any more than it is England or the U.S.A. The wholly isolated individual cannot belong to any group or nation; he is abstracted and abstract, a cipher of anguish and loss. This quality in White's work puzzled me at first. While on the one hand he was obviously writing about Australia, in effect there was not the least fraction of a tone, colour, characteristic, etc., which had the faintest Australian note about it; in reading *The Tree of Man* I kept thinking I was reading about the American Middle West, since the text had more literary affinities with the United States than with anywhere else, and had actual affinities (in its essential material) with no nameable country whatever. This sheer anonymity gives the book its undeniable and massive unity of effect, but also begets tedium, since nothing new is said, or can be said, after the first section.

In *Riders in the Chariot* White tries to overcome the rather crushing monotony of a vision of mere alienation by adding as sympathetic characters the few who by totally and voluntarily contracting out of a corrupted world achieve the vision of wholeness, of union with universal life. He comes closer here to communicating a genuine horror and to defining the existence of pure wells of feeling amid the socially-demented scene; but the inability to deal with more than the hopelessly-isolated individual deadens the impact. For this reason I cannot accept Mathew's evaluation: 'In such a world, White's *Riders in the Chariot* is a rabbit-killer, a blow so foul it can be forgotten only in the sensual orgy of the Agricultural Show which each capital stages annually; there — sight, sound, smell, and touch — all combine to remind us of our world of once-upon-a-time.' If White's novel was merely a debunker of the Australian once-upon-a-time, it would be small beer. The enemy is not the sentimental carrier-on of the past, as White himself well knows; the enemy is the entire world of dehumanizing forces, in which, for Australia, the falsification of the national character in terms of outdated attitudes is only a minor factor, a mask for the deeper distortions. And the trouble is that the novel is not a rabbit-killer, much as I would like to hail it as such. White's inability to conceive any answer, any defiance of alienation, beyond the spontaneous harmonies of the crushed but unresentful soul, makes him unable to oppose effectively the thing that he so sincerely and fiercely hates. In the last resort it unites him with the hated thing, since no real alternative to the latter exists. There is thus an unresolved contradiction between his act of writing, the whole motive force of the act, and the picture he presents.

To discuss White has not been irrelevant to my thesis. Though he is 'sticking things out' in Australia and is doing his best to attack the enemy there, his inability to come to any terms with his own allies, with the elements in the people and the culture that also fundamentally repudiate the evil forces, marks him out as in the last resort manipulated by those forces. He is unconscious of the way in which his revolt has been generated; he flattens and narrows the complex social and spiritual pattern and thus shuts himself out of the universe of his own perception and creation. And what we see powerfully expressed in his work is what we see expressed in more trivial and superficial ways in the other alienated intellectual trends I have discussed. Further, it is clear after reading his early novel, *The Living and the Dead*, that many of his anomalous characteristics, such as the lack of any organic Australian qualities in the midmost of his grappling with Australian essences, derive from the fact that his roots lie in English culture and society. *The Living and the Dead*, though lacking the remarkably sustained force of his Australian novels, shows him at home in the environment of genteel English middle-class decay; here we recognize from last to first an authentic note, a concreteness, in the description of people, their social setting, their interrelations. What he has done in the Australian novels is to take external Australian conditions and details, and to infuse into them abstractions born from his English experience. If only he could come down to earth in Australia, the abstractions would become concrete, and his profound sense of what is truly evil in our world would at last find its effective outlet. But to do this he would have to realize what is alienated in himself as well as what is alienated in the world.

It seems to me that to the half-truth of Yesenin-Volpin's lines, we must add the other half-truth:

> I know why I live
> and what I want from the people who inhabit this human city.

Then we attain the balanced relation which is implicit in the lines I cited from Brennan. But despite what seem to me the limitations of Patrick White's work, he has set Australian culture problems that cannot be ignored; he has permanently changed the perspective. What else can be brought forward as truly deep-going expressions of urban Australia, of what is done to people by the maturing industrial and capitalist formations? There is a handful of poems by Brennan that precociously grasp what is happening and going to happen; and there is Frank Hardy's *Power without Glory*. It may come as something of a shock to find Hardy's book linked in any way with White's; but in fact Hardy's novel is the only one that goes deeply and extensively into an Australian exploration of the Evil City. The overt stress on the political purpose, and the violent struggles waged round the publication of the book, have prevented critics from recognizing that Hardy has in fact a complex attitude toward his material. He is fascinated by the corruption he denounces, he sets out to expose West, and does so, but at the same time he makes West both a symbol of corrupter and corrupted, of socially-explained dereliction and of impalpable and ubiquitous evil. A rich interplay of hate and love goes to the unfolding of his character; what the book gives us in the end is a whole darkening phase in the development of a people, not an exposure of dirty work in some segments of the Labour Party. Hardy in writing the book lacked the many skills of White in handling his material; but he came closer to the full creative problem, to the revelation of what alienation is, in a human world, in a world struggling to be human or at least to preserve a criterion of what human wholeness is.

The prevailing sense of gloom is also evident in Christesen's correspondence from the period. As new magazines, including *Quadrant*, received funding from the CLF, *Meanjin*'s allocation was more and more thinly spread.

T. Inglis Moore to C. B. Christesen

22 May 1963

. . . today I had to cancel my flight tomorrow to Adelaide to attend the C.L.F. meeting there on Friday. Roughed out hurriedly a long screed which I took to Jim McCusker this afternoon for duplicating and circulating to Board members at Adelaide, giving my views on a few items on the agenda but mostly devoted to *Meanjin*. I put in a resolution recommending that our grant be raised to £1500 p.a. for the next five years, and listed ten arguments as grounds for the rise. This is the best I cd do under the circs. I also rang Kylie in Sydney and Chis in Melbourne tonight to whip up support for my resolution. Kylie is in bed with flu, and I only spoke to Roddy to pass my plea on for her to give *M* a burl. The exchange cdn't raise Chis, so I'll try again in the morning. I want him to second my motion. . . .

I'm terribly afraid that I'm in a minority, and feel that my arguments will fall blunted against a pretty general sentiment that further aid will only mean your getting deeper into debt with more extravagance in an inflated set-up. Your cry of 'Wolf at the door' has been cried so often that people are inured to it — or impatient. There is criticism of expenditure items, e.g. £300 for Books, Papers and Subscriptions and £204 for Entertainment — as against only £296 for Contributors, much less than the sum paid by other magazines who don't spend anything like £504 for the above two items. Nor can some people see why *M* shd be so large, especially when you can't afford it. Here, of course, you can't use the argument that you have a lot of material in stock accepted you can't use, since the obvious comment comes that it is rotten editing to accept stuff you can't use, and unfair to the writers, who cd otherwise use material frozen in your bulging frig. There is certainly a feeling that some £10,000 — your income for 1962 — shd be enough for you to do a decent magazine on. They look at the income of other magazines, running from approx. £1400 to under £5,000 for total costs, and wonder why you want more and why you can never keep within your budget, always run at a loss, always spend more than you can afford, and pile up an accumulated deficit of almost £2,000.

There are other criticisms, of course, such as that your material is too highbrow, that it doesn't have enough general appeal, or it devotes too much space to overseas material, French issue, etc. These are minor, however, compared to the main ones cited in the last par.

Of course, I know by heart your answers to the criticisms, and generally speaking I feel you put up a good case. [marginal note: except in taking material you can't use.] My own main argument is that you have produced a really first-class high quality literary and cultural magazine, a remarkable achievement under all the circs, and hence deserve support for the job done. Also that its reputation is high abroad, thus constituting an international asset we shd try to preserve at present level.

But I find little understanding or real appreciation of your problems, coupled with a really strong sympathy. In fact, I shd say that I only know one person who has both — Alec Hope. [in margin: And Chis, or course.] I think you may add myself. There may be others in Melbourne, of course, with whom I've not had a chance to discuss *Meanjin*, such as Arthur Phillips perhaps.

I might add that *M* is doing a specially valuable job in publishing full-length critical articles, but I can't find many who share my enthusiasm. It is one of the principal reasons why it wd be tragic if *M* had to be cut down drastically.

I might add that you are mistaken when you say 'For many years the argument has been put forward that if only the University wd increase its grant to £1500 wd do likewise' etc. The C.L.F. has never officially taken this view — only Chis and I have tried to put it forward. I saw Paton some years ago personally and suggested to him that he increase his grant to £1500 and ask the CLF to do the same, and he spoke favorably towards the suggestion, but didn't act on it. Certainly the Board has never accepted this as a commitment. . . .

Sorry, Clem, if I seem pessimistic, but I'm trying to be realistic on the evidence. I only hope I'm wrong, and that screed may find stronger support than seems likely. I won't be able to write to you about any decision in Adelaide under the new ruling — which I think unnecessarily stuffy and bureaucratic — that Board members may not communicate anything to anybody about decisions until the Secretary has given official advice to the person concerned.

Here's hoping for the best.

C. B. Christesen to T. Inglis Moore

31 May 1963

Dear Tom,
I have sent a copy of my editorial script to Alec, together with a slightly revised copy of his 'Open Letter'! I haven't spare copies, so will you please go through my script and let me have your frank comments? It was written before I saw Alec's, and will now require some modification in galley-proof form.

There doesn't seem to be any point in replying here to the list of criticisms of *Meanjin* by some Board members. My script covers some of the points of criticism; and as you say, you are already familiar with my 'answers'. If anything were needed to convince me that the Board (yourself and perhaps Chis excluded) didn't have a clue as to what *Meanjin* was all about, your account of their criticism provided it. It's really a shocking indictment.

However, if you think my script is still not convincing enough for them, for Pete's sake let me know immediately. I want to make a 'bird' of it this time, once and for all. Do please be a good chap and do this for me.

For instance, the allegations about crying 'wolf', the pileup of manuscripts, the expenditure on books, entertainment, etc.; about my 'rotten editing', not keeping within a budget, piling up a deficit, and so on. All these points must now be discussed, brought right out into the open, and explained. Otherwise we'll make no real progress at all, be more or less back where we were before. There must be no misunderstanding, no shadow of doubt remaining among Board members; each point of criticism must be fully explained. Don't you agree? I wish I'd received your letter before I'd written my script.

It seems I'm (in part) wrong about the 'CLF agreement regarding the £1500'. But this argument was in fact used — by Chis — and taken up by Maxwell and my Committee, and finally accepted by Paton (seemingly with your help).

I wish I knew what was the outcome of the Adelaide discussions . . . I wouldn't mind the bureaucratic ruling about 'Silence', providing Jim did in fact tell me, directly or indirectly, what in God's name did happen from time to time. But I'm kept very much in the dark.

I read Kylie's utterances in Adelaide. Absolute crap.

By the way, here is something which no one else knows about, — and you might keep this to yourself. I obtain from A.& R., Cheshires and other Australian publishers, copies of their 'acceptance of manuscripts' sheets and printing schedules about a year ahead of publication. I therefore have a pretty fair idea of what books are coming along, and of publication dates. As a result I've been able to select reviewers and line-up reviews well before the books appear. Very often I am also able to send galley-proofs or page-proofs or advance copies to reviewers, again well ahead of publication. On very many occasions *Meanjin* has been the first to publish a review — not easy for a quarterly magazine. For instance, apart from individual books, that's how I got in ahead for the Poetry, Fiction and Short Story Chronicles. Even the authors hadn't received copies when *Meanjin* published reviews of the books.

But I've been hoist by my own industry! Now there is one hell of a pile-up of reviews because issues of the magazine were not large enough. Still, our coverage last year was far ahead of any other literary periodical here.

I thought I'd tell you this, for it does go towards explaining the pile-up of scripts. The rest of the 'explanation' you can hear if you wish.

A great pity I had to hold over the Indonesian material. Would have been topical, and of course tremendous value to Australian–Indonesian relations.

A point which seems to have been ignored is that most, perhaps all, of the other magazines would not *want* to be as large, to have such a large structure, as does *Meanjin*. Who among the editors could even remotely *afford* to devote so much time and energy to a *Meanjin*-type journal? They certainly need increased financial aid; but to edit, produce and manage a substantial literary quarterly requires full-time attention and very much larger grants. No comparable literary magazine in the world is published on a part-time basis. Of this I have proof.

Think about these points; they might be very useful. It's only by a series of 'accidents' that I'm (allegedly) in a position to handle a *Meanjin*-size magazine.

Alas, whatever the outcome, it's now too late to 'save' *Meanjin* this year. Perhaps next year we'll again be able to get cracking.

The sense of disorientation reached a peak in the mid-1960s, particularly in the 'Godzone' series of essays in 1966 and 1967. The dominant tone of the series as a whole was very much that of a middle generation of intellectuals looking with some trepidation at Australian popular culture, and particularly the youth culture that was making its presence felt as the postwar 'baby boomers' began to approach adulthood.

Number 2, 1966

The Retreat From Reason

IAN TURNER

> And even when they became discontented, as they sometimes did, their discontent led nowhere, because, being without general ideas, they could only focus on their specific grievances.
>
> George Orwell: *1984*

Once, the great barn in West Melbourne had been simply 'the Stadium'. Hungry-eyed men had packed it on Saturday nights, seeking escape and release and perhaps a new identity. The roar as the boxers entered the ring and slugged their way desperately through the bouts came from men who were as much participants as partisans. But the money went out of the fight game. The old Stadium, refurbished and regraded, became Festival Hall. The same tough-faced attendants watched suspiciously as eager customers slipped through half-open doors. But the cavernous bleachers now stretched open to swallow affluent young worshippers in the temple of Pop. For most of the old crowd, Saturday night at the Stadium was a corner carved out of life. For many of the young crowd Festival Hall is life itself.

This night it was not some new pop star, accoucheured by the Brodziak–Wren combine. It was Yevgeny Yevtushenko, declaiming and posturing his way through the poems that were, in his own country, making history — in the non-metaphorical sense of the expression. After the recital came the argument — it seemed to me the same argument, repeated over and over. The poems, it was said, were prosaic, moralistic, naive, over-simplified; at the end the point was driven home with a pile-driver:

> so that on earth all men will have the right
> to say to themselves: 'We are not slaves!'

It was not possible to combine the personal vision and integrity of the poet with accessibility to audiences of thousands. They claimed the day of public poetry was done . . .

In a sense it was an argument between generations — between those, the older, who were not yet prepared to throw the last spadeful of clay onto the coffin of ideology, and those for whom grass had already covered its grave.

Politics determines our living; it may decide our dying. Once it seemed that ordinary people might mould politics to their will. But the political process has slipped beyond our grasp; and losing a grip on politics, we lose control over our lives and deaths.

To many of the post-war generation the Bomb has represented the final, impersonal threat, our inexorable destiny. But the Bomb is not self-acting; it is subject to politics. It is not the Bomb but the men who control the Bomb who are beyond our rational argument and control.

Start from the top. Parliament, long held the pinnacle of British democratic achievement, is no longer an arena for rational debate. The effective decisions are made not in Parliament but in Cabinet, sometimes even by individual Ministers. Cabinet determines what shall be discussed, and when, and for how long. Cabinet controls caucus; back-sliders from Cabinet decisions lose not only preferment but preselection. Within the party rooms critics may protest and propose, but Cabinet prevails. Of what use is it for the individual member on the government side, or for the whole of the opposition, to think, to work? The Whips ensure that what they say might just as well have gone unsaid. Individual cases may be raised, individual interests pressed. Here and there a concession may be made. The conscientious politician, believing in a fair day's work for a fair day's pay, spends more and more of his time on the needs of his constituency and the woes of his constituents. For there can be no effective debate of the great issues, because these are pre-determined.

Pre-determined by popular vote, perhaps? Hardly. The great issues are barely raised, let alone decided by the electoral process. Reality is hidden by the cliché, the smear, the half-truth, the lie. Each of the two parties, one eye on the swinging vote, seems determined not to look too different from the other. The parties huddle together for comfort, holding out hesitating hands with a little more of this and a little less of that. 'Anything you can do, I can do better' is the theme; there is no suggestion of 'I wouldn't be seen dead wearing one of your policies.' Only when the great issues are wedged between the parties from without do they tend to fly apart; otherwise the issues are left to rest in peace. And meanwhile, shying away from fundamentals, the party directors hot-foot to the agencies to discuss the image.

Whatever images may be, they are certainly not rational. The Australian agencies, filling the prescriptions of the American old masters, probe for warmth, security, adventure, envy, the hidden fear, the collective unconscious, the outer reaches of the Id. Harold a-go-go . . . Arthur might be everybody's mum. Warning: voting is compulsory. You pays your taxes and you takes your choice — but whoever you vote for, a public relations man always gets in.

Is there then no difference? There is, of course, but it is more sociological than political. Most workers still vote Labor; most non-workers don't. And because Labor was built on the workers' votes, its structure is different from that of its opponents. In principle it is a mass movement which determines its basic policies by democratic process, and delegates its parliamentary representatives to carry them out. In principle its opponent is a group of like-minded parliamentarians underpinned by a mass of more or less enthusiastic supporters. And there is some reality in this distinction: the 'faceless men' of the Labor Party are in fact elected, and therefore not faceless at all; the 'faceless men' of the Liberal Party are self-appointed, and so self-effacing that they do not seem even to exist.

Given the difference of structure and social base, my preference is Labor. The working-class base ensures that Labor will be more egalitarian, more conscious of mass welfare, than its opponents — at least in purpose. The democratic structure offers hope that policies and rational discussion can be initiated from below. But between hope and fulfilment is the party machine.

Labor's decisions are made at the top, and the top is three removes of indirect election from below. Only thirty-six men get there, and they are all men who have devoted the best part of their lives to this end. A long apprenticeship in the innumerable and interminable committees of the movement is demanded of those who would reach the heights where policy is made.

Perhaps this is a characteristic intellectual grievance. Yet it is not an objection to hewing the movement's wood and drawing its water — even when the wood is brittle and the water stale. Most intellectuals who are involved in the Labor movement are happy to speak or to write for it, to knock on uninterested doors, to push leaflets into unresponsive letter-boxes and how-to-vote cards into the hands of unwilling voters. Most would like to use their minds for the movement. But they are unwilling to accept the unremitting demand of the committees on their time. And so the only political machine which holds out hope to those who believe that reason is the proper foundation of politics is left to those for whom the machine is *sui generis*.

What does it mean to say that reason is the proper foundation of politics? Let the petrol bowser stand symbol for the ultimate irrationality, the psychosis of a whole society. The visitor from space who, landing at Albury at 3.30 a.m., approached the disciplined ranks of bowsers with the demand, 'Take me to your leader,' had misread the situation. The bowsers were already in collective inanimate control. Who dares challenge the bowsers? Who is there to say that all petrol, disguised though it may be with additives and balloons and party hats, is still benzine? That we do not need a gasolinatorium on every corner of every cross-road? That all internal combustion engines are an abomination and the time has come to Save Our Lungs? That any man who is found with a tiger in his tank should get six months? No-one will say it, because it means demanding a state-distributed one-brand petrol; it means challenging the automobile companies with a state-made Stanley Steamer; it means making urban travel by private automobile so expensive that commuters will accept a re-planned public transport; it means denying the right of car-owners to pollute the atmosphere and slaughter their fellow-citizens; it means denying the right of the developer to pervert the land for his personal profit. To blow up the bowsers means to reconstruct society. Who will save us from the bowsers? That is what I mean by reason in politics.

This is the great intellectual heresy — the demand that reason has the right to push criticism and the statement of alternatives as far as evidence and logic will allow. This is a politics not of compromise but of conflict, not of 'a little more of this and a little less of that' but of fundamental change, the change from an irrational, disordered, out-of-control society to a society in which men are subjects and not merely objects. And this is a politics that most politicians fear and hate.

When governments, and even oppositions, are challenged to reconsider the assumptions underlying their positions — whether on the proliferation of petrol bowsers, or literary censorship, or the desirability of sending conscripts to Vietnam — they characteristically respond with the magical incantation, 'pseudo-intellectual'. A 'pseudo-intellectual' is someone who investigates and challenges assumptions. But if there are 'pseudo-intellectuals', somewhere there must be real intellectuals, and where are they? My guess is that, in the minds of many politicians, they are to be found in the advertising agencies, preparing pre-packed images. Or, perhaps, dancing around the margins of the consensus in celebration of the end of ideology.

The 'pseudo-intellectual' is damned because he disturbs the even tenor of pragmatic politics. (The expletive is only used, I should point out, by those who have some pretence to intellectuality themselves; for those who don't, 'intellectual' by itself is sufficient to condemn.) The pragmatist takes refuge in an arcane expertise. The 'pseudo-intellectual' knows either too little — or too much. He sees too far ahead — or not far enough. He forgets a mass of detail that would invalidate his argument — or drags in side issues that are irrelevant. But the real objection to the 'pseudo-intellectual' is that he thinks.

This is no new phenomenon. Pragmatic politicians have always been opposed to thought which leads towards far-reaching change. But that is where thought must lead. To analyse any phenomenon, to define it, is to state the alternative conditions which might exist. To analyse a whole society is a profoundly revolutionary act.

That is why so many intellectuals made revolutionary politics their own. Pragmatic politics is not based on reason, except in the very limited sense of horse-trading for votes. Only that kind of politics which traces inhumanity and injustice back to its social roots, and then attacks those roots, is fully rational. It was not some apocalyptic death-wish which drove intellectuals towards revolutionary solutions, nor even some ingrained and half-comprehended guilt. It was rather a life-wish, the wish for a life regulated and ordered by reason. And it was a social force outside the framework of pragmatic politics — the working class and other dispossessed groups — whose action would restore the rule of reason.

But revolutionary politics, once it had established itself, proved just as pragmatic as the rest. Again those who propounded new critiques and total solutions were condemned as 'pseudo-intellectuals'. The real intellectuals were advised that they were 'engineers of the human soul' — operating on blueprints drawn by the architects of communist man.

Pragmatic politics denied the claims of reason; revolutionary politics betrayed them. Politics, which controls our lives and deaths, has slipped beyond the control of reason. The rule of the political machines has come.

In simpler times, solutions were possible. Within the framework of family and local community, it seemed that men could make their own decisions, control their own lives. In mass industrial society this can no longer be done. The 'machinofacture' of politics is complemented by, indeed based upon, the mechanisation of production.

The central social facts of modern industrial technology are the displacement of men by machines, and the division of labour. Man as producer is fragmented and denied. The Australian labour force draws nearer the American model. Unskilled labouring and process work is vanishing. Technologists and social servicemen increase. Man returns to his pastoral beginning — except that, instead of shepherding unthinking animals, he shepherds machines which calculate. Increasingly, no man can know or control the whole process of production; only the machines can do that. The area of choice and effective decision declines. Man is liberated from nature and enslaved by the machines.

Not only is material production fragmented, but intellectual production too. The state's education system prepares its lambs for, and reconciles them to, the industrial slaughter. The universities, which once claimed to provide universal knowledge for universal man, are reduced to making impotent gestures towards 'the cross-fertilisation of disciplines'. But no-one now can comprehend the whole of life. The machines demand servitors, and the universities provide them.

Once, ideology meant an explanatory model of the human condition, at the same time an analysis of man's nature, his culture and society, and a prescription for change. Ideology presupposed that men made their own history, that there existed the possibility of choice, of moulding society and culture to the human will. But the very technological revolution which liberated man from nature and seemed to deliver his destiny into his own hands externalised society and culture and made of them vast bureaucratic apparatuses beyond control. And ideology was buried. To proclaim the end of ideology is to concede the victory of Fritz Lang's *Metropolis* and to abandon the possibility of choice.

The political and productive machines stand apart from and inimical to man. Reason, which created the machines, has lost control. With the defeat of reason on the central battlefields there begins the retreat from reason on all the peripheries of human endeavour.

The time is long past when Australian workingmen proclaimed that their condition was the consequence of the middle-class monopoly of knowledge, and set out, through unions and societies and mechanics' institutes, to acquire that knowledge which was power. The knowledge they did acquire gave them some understanding of their condition, but not of how to liberate themselves from it, for the social relations created by the new technology changed faster than did their understanding; and knowledge, instead of being a revolutionary means of reconstructing society, became a means of self-advancement within it. The rational comprehension of society as a whole gave way to a technical understanding of one small cog in the machine.

But the retreat from reason has proceeded much further than this. Let us consider some isolated cultural phenomena, to determine whether there are any underlying themes.

Twenty years ago the music at student parties was traditional jazz and blues. Today it is the Beatles and the Rolling Stones and whatever other groups are currently heading the charts. Superficially there is some resemblance. Both have the insistent rhythm and the urgent expression that offer immediate kicks. The Beatles and their epigones use an attenuated version of the musical language of jazz, and some of them do it with considerable technical skill. But there the resemblance ends. Jazz required attention and thought. Louis, Jelly Roll, Bix, Mezz — each was a unique creative artist with a history that demanded to be known. The blues were a philosophy ('Doncha leave me here, doncha leave me here; But, sweet papa, if you *must* go, leave a dime for beer . . .') and a way of life ('Stood on the corner with her feets just soakin' wet . . . Beggin' each and every man she met . . . If you can't give a dollar, give me a lousy dime . . . I wanna feed that hungry man of mine . . .'). The techniques of scholarship were brought to bear on jazz history, sociology, discography — but who but Brian Epstein would want a discography of the Beatles? And at the most elementary physical level, the gut-tearing sexuality of Bessie Smith ('Bought me a coffee-grinder, got the best one I could find, So he could grind my coffee, 'cause he has a brand new grind') is streets of experience removed from the immature and mindless lyrics of the Beatles. The reach towards the heights and depths of emotion, the search for perfection, and the need to know how and why all this was happening, give way to self-immolation in the pre-adult, asexual dream world of 'I love you, I love you, I love you'. The walking transistor is only one short technological step removed from Ray Bradbury's fifteen-year-old nightmare (in *Fahrenheit 451*) of the transistorised receiver small enough to fit into the ear, but large enough to block out the rest of the world. . . .

The elevation of sensation above reason and emotion has even invaded literature, traditionally the home ground of these qualities. This is not just a matter of the word-painting indulged in by poets, the endeavour to re-create in words (without analysing or illuminating the nature of the experience) a sensory response. It goes much closer to the heart of modern writing than that — what is at issue is the cult of the orgasm, whose high priests are Miller and Mailer and William Reich.

The point becomes obvious when one contrasts, say, *Another Country* with the *Tropic* books. Orgasm is obviously tremendously important to Baldwin; he writes of it with great passion. But it is only one part — a central part, certainly, but not the whole — of the terrible complexity of the relation between man and woman or man and man. The sexual relation symbolises the whole relation; orgasm is seen in an emotional and rational context. For Miller, a kick is a kick is a kick.

The isolation of the sensory aspect of sex finds a theoretical base in the writings of Reich, the text-books of the libertarian onslaught on traditional moralism. In the hands of the Sydney Libertarians this becomes the basis for a profound and reasoned attack on conventional mores. But for many, all that remains is the sensation.

The same sort of point can be made about the other great cult among young intellectuals — the drug kick. (This is a touchy subject, and perhaps I should make it clear that I have no personal knowledge of the use of drugs. Nor do I believe that they are widely used among young intellectuals in Australia — but pub talk with students suggests that there is a certain fascination with marihuana and LSD.) Drugs are of two kinds. On one side are alcohol and the various pep pills (the amphetamines which circulate under the name of dexedrine, purple hearts, and so on); on the other are marihuana, mescalin and LSD. The former are stimulants; they encourage sociability and the interchange of ideas which, even if they may seem more lucid at the time than they do in retrospect, at least aspire to rationality. The latter turn the users in on themselves — into a world of enhanced sensation. It may be that student fascination with the idea of reefers and LSD is no more than the normal and desirable youthful interest in self-enlargement through new experience. Or it may be that this, too, is linked — although the links are not articulated — with the elevation of sensation over reason. . . .

This is, I agree, a one-sided picture. I have not attempted to describe the whole of Australian society, or of its culture; I have tried only to delineate one trend. What I am saying is that the Enlightenment principles, the belief in the power of reason, which have shaped our thinking for two centuries or more confront their moment of truth. Reason is denied by absurdism, subverted by the elevation of sensation as an end in itself.

The retreat from reason does not derive from fashion, or intellectual perversity; it is a response to a social situation — a situation in which men confront the possibility of their involuntary participation in the mega-death race, in which they seem no longer able to control the productive and political machines they have made. Those who think of their condition rationalise it in the form of determinism or absurdism; those who do not, relax and enjoy their fate. The retreat from reason is the end-product of human alienation; denying the mind, man is left with only his senses which become himself.

This is not counsel of despair. I believe in Reason, as some men believe in God, for the acceptance of reason is finally an act of faith. There are countervailing tendencies — notably the response of the young to particular situations which they believe to be inhuman or unjust. But this is as yet an immediate, almost an instinctive response; the protestors are like Orwell's proles who cannot yet generalise from their specific grievances. There are alternatives to the retreat from reason, and they can be stated in relatively simple terms: the rehumanisation of politics and the restoration of ideology.

The essential revolutionary demand is for the revolt of people against the machines, both political and productive, which are at present external to them and dominate their lives. But revolutionary action requires consciousness, or ideology — both a comprehensive understanding of the nature of the present impasse, and the conviction that choice is meaningful and can be made effective. Education must be directed towards the twin ends of developing this understanding and conviction, and asserting the claims of reason and emotion over the accumulation of sensation. Whether enough people think this possible, or worthwhile, is of course another matter.

It was another night at the Stadium/Festival Hall. This time it was not the poet who had become a voice of his generation of young Russians, but the singer who spoke just as surely for young Americans and Australians.

Bob Dylan's hazy images and half-articulated thoughts had brought to the surface the instinctive responses, the fears and hopes of the young millions for whom he sang. Now the figure on the stage seemed too slight to support this burden; the glaze over his movements hinted at automation; the pallor suggested doubt and withdrawal. Dylan's agonised drawl demanded

> You know that something's happening
> But you don't know what it is
> Do you, Mr Jones?

It was Everyman's question to Everyman, and the answer awaits.

There were, however, signs of hope, particularly in the world of poetry. After the formal, restrained climate of the 1950s, a new generation of poets began to shoulder their way forward.

Number 1, 1964

A Man's Got His Pride to Consider

JUDITH BARBOUR

(From the French of Laforgue)

She'd say, with that affectation which is her native air,
'You are my sole desire.' Oh yeah? A likely tale.
Like Aesthetic Distance. Higher Things. No sale
Rung up for the Pure and Fair.

What's more, she'd fib. 'Behold, an innocent rose!'
Eyes wide and candid as a blessed moon-girl.
Sure, just for the fun of the thing you've taken a whirl.
Played for chips, I suppose.

But say that, one fine day, pushing her luck too hard,
She dies. Yeah. Well. Food for thought.

But you'll be up and about soon! The grave's just caught
You on a three day transit card.

At least you'll be immanent in our burgeoning bailiwicks,
And on you'll traipse with the usual train of males,
Hot on the trail of the Feminine, hocking their grails.
I might come along for kicks.

Number 1, 1967

The Burial

DOROTHY HEWETT

He couldn't have expected to die on holiday,
Beneath that mountain, within close call of the sea.
Yet he came here every year, he must have known
It would have to be here or there, asleep or awake,
Between the fall of a sparrow or flight of a bee.

After the platitudes in the Methodist pews,
Abide with Me and the vulgar veneered coffin
(We asked for jarrah), and the blustery wind outside
Blowing the ladies' church hats into the harbour,
It was a relief to stand at the clayey grave
And listen to the parson clanging his dust and ashes.
You can't do much to pretty up that ceremony.

'He was a man who achieved much honour,' the parson said,
'A man who reaped his reward and died content.'
How bitter the grin wreathing those iron jaws,
Locked in the paltry coffin with the hymns in his ears.
Come home to his own, my father, rich in nothing
But the money that lay like pennies over his eyes.

His mother, that immigrant woman, once sang, long ago,
In her rich contralto in this same grey church on the Harbour,
Till the parson asked her to stay and lead the choir.
Well, *he's* staying here now, but I was the only singer,
His atheist daughter to whom he had nothing to leave.

We buried him in the dark scrub, the gulls flashed out at sea.
An old man teetered at the hole, read Rupert Brooke
And 'They shall not grow old': this was the final irony;
They were all so old, telling tales about French girls and gyppos
It was hard to imagine any of them had been young.

Yet that ragged boy chasing cows through the Gippsland fern,
Scaring the crows off the clover, had died a rich man.

He was honoured with medals, sprinkled with red cloth poppies,
The King of the Belgians had kissed him on both his cheeks,
But couldn't warm them; there was some canker he carried
Into the earth with him. I don't think he'll grow good flowers,
Or sleep in peace, he had insomnia badly these last few years;
It was that Methodist conscience giving him hell.

Remember him, leaping off the troop ship, laughing
Into the harbour, deserting the smell of death, the lice
And the dried blood in a ridge under his collar:
Deserting Dan McGee with his head in the mouth of a cannon,
Crying, 'Goodbye boys, I've had a gutful of it,' the hand
Shaking on the Lewis gun with the blood between his fingers.

'He was wild, that boy,' the old man jabbed at my ribs.
'We were in Egypt together, the things he did!'
And I think of his wildness under that weight of earth,
My father, sardonic mouthed, whom life had ground like a pestle,
Hidden behind some General's memoirs: my mother said,
'He read such deep books. I couldn't follow them.'

There was nothing to think, nothing, except to be sorry
It had all turned out so badly, and let the old men
Unpin their RSL badges and go off home for a sleep.

'Take him,' sang the sea. 'Take him and let him sleep.'
Six feet of scrubby earth for the boy with the curly hair,
And the old man pottering lost in the shell-grit garden,
With the shadow of the mountain settling on his face.

Number 1, 1967

Whip-Bird

ROLAND ROBINSON

The page blurs
in the lamp's
nimbus. Warm,
I loosen, sink
into the storm.

A shape stoops,
grasps the shack,
timbers strain.
Crack of whip-
bird wakes me

to mountains in
rain, a thong
echoing beyond
an age to come,
the ages gone.

Number 1, 1967

Shadow of War

THOMAS W. SHAPCOTT

We had never seen black cockatoos, though in the park
at home sometimes we'd begged our mother along
to the safe wire to stare at the white cousins
for a taunt of trained vowel and diphthong;
but here, up in the country where our father had sent us
(evacuees from a real and newspaper terror),
one morning we were shown on the dead tree near the kitchen
black cockatoos gathering, over and over,

crowded in warfare of black wings, black feathers,
quarrelling for a few stiff branches in their thick dozens.
'Look at them!' we cried to the farmer, our taciturn host,
as they covered the charred tree with acrid blossoms,
jagged and torn by red shadows, red crests.
He stood in the dry yard where we shouted and pranced.
'I see them' he said, then, 'It's the corn they're after.
A gun would shift them.' But he only walked away, and cursed;

while we crowded and shrieked to see the birds keep the tree,
not like the sleek crows, sly and silently,
but angrily, arrogantly, with black and red noise,
forcing their own terms triumphantly.
We were too young to price the waste of a crop,
or the shrug of that grim man — whose son was newly dead
in a battle out of reach. On the dead verandah
we played at soldiers, khaki and black and red,
and our cries were birds on fire overhead.

The 'battle out of reach' to which Shapcott referred was the Second World War, but in the Australia of 1967 his words conjured up the shadow of a more immediate conflict: the Vietnam war. It was that war, more than anything else, that began to change the temper of Australian politics in the late 1960s. The protests during the visit of US President Lyndon Baines Johnson in October 1966 were a foretaste of the anti-war

and anti-conscription movements that were to dominate the Australian political stage until the election of the Whitlam Labor government in December 1972.

Meanjin responded to the changing political mood. Polemical essays became more numerous, shorter, less 'academic'. In 1967 Christesen published commentaries on the LBJ visit (including a satirical poem by Dorothy Green and a witty prose piece by Dennis Pryor), but the trickle of political essays became a flood after 1968. It was the student revolts in Paris that marked the turning of the tide; and *Meanjin* readers were given a first-hand account that was imbued with a strong sense that destiny was in the making.

Number 3, 1968

'Rendez-vous with the End of an Age'

CATHERINE DUNCAN

> Nous avions rendez-vous avec la fin d'un âge. Et nous voici les lèvres closes, parmi vous. Et le Vent est avec nous — ivre d'un principe amer et fort comme le vin de lierre;
> Non pas appel en conciliation, mais irritable et qui nous chante: j'irriterai la moelle dans vos os . . .
>
> Saint Jean Perse, '*Vents*'

They fought all night under my windows, and I stood shivering in the cold May darkness of the balcony watching the battle sway up and down the street.

On the opposite footpath I could see the CRS, booted and helmeted, with shields to protect them from the missiles, and the sinister grenades of tear-gas hanging from their belts. At the lower end of the street the students made forays, individually or in small groups, hurling paving stones and insults.

'*Salauds!*' '*Assassins!*' And the supreme charge: '*Charonne!*' This the name of the Métro station, doubly accusing in its assonance and its associations, where five people were killed by the police during a demonstration against the Algerian war.

The students looked terribly young and vulnerable under the street lights, but the police were wary, hugging the doorways, or crouching behind cars which had been slewed sideways across the road to form barricades.

Suddenly the shutters of one of the windows opposite opened, hands shot out dumping some heavy object in the middle of the police, the shutters closed again in the same movement.

A CRS ducked. 'Look out for your heads!'

I reviewed my flower-pots, but my youthful prowess as a baseball player suggested I'd be more likely to lay out one of my side than hit a policeman. And as if suspecting my intentions, one of the CRS raised his rifle and fired a tear-gas grenade in the direction of the balconies.

The air became unbreathable and I began to cry, the involuntary, stinging tears that seem to leave a bad taste in the lungs.

Momentary retreat to close the windows and listen to Europe I, the commercial radio station which had mobilized all its forces to cover the street fighting.

In the Rue Gay-Lussac and at the corner of the Rue St Jacques there were pitched battles. The students had raised barricades and were systematically tearing up paving stones with picks and pneumatic drills. The police charged with truncheons after sending over a massive barrage of grenades — not only tear-gas, but more lethal varieties developed by the Americans as weapons against the Viet Cong and for which no known antidote was available. If a military doctor had not risked court-martial by releasing the secret formula, there would have been no remedy for the effects of the gas. Several hundred were wounded, some of them seriously. The barricades had gone up in flames.

I could see the columns of smoke rising all around the Quartier Latin and hear the explosions of grenades. It looked as though a fire had started on the Place de la Contrescarpe at the top of the street. The pam-pom-pam-pom of a fire-engine picked its way through the debris and police reinforcements arrived in three long black cars which blocked the street. The students made the most of this diversion to stretch a trip-wire across the road between two cars. The next police charge was a glorious moment of pure farce which could have been a scene from the Keystone Cops. A little old woman with white hair and in a white nightdress danced up and down on her balcony, clapping her hands and throwing chocolates to the students.

But such moments were rare that night. Europe I was broadcasting appeals from professors to allow the wounded to be evacuated. A girl of twenty had almost certainly been permanently blinded and the police refused to let the ambulance through. Teams of taxis which had volunteered to transport the wounded to hospital waited helplessly on the fringe of the battle areas. A doctor came to the microphone, just released by the police after questioning. While trying to help one of the wounded he had been truncheoned from behind, arrested and taken to the Commissariat where other wounded were lying on the floor. The only treatment they received was to be *passés à tabac* — the popular term for police bashings.

Accusations. Official denials. Refutations. Statements from the Prefect of Police. Reports from the thick of the battle — Europe I served as a headquarters for information and instructions, a field map in sound which covered the whole of Paris from the Elysée, where de Gaulle received three of his Ministers before 7 a.m., to isolated telephone calls offering help or asking for ambulances. At only one point did the musical punctuation seem hysterically funny: 'I'm in the mood for love, dear.'

The moods of love nevertheless changed that night from a certain impatience with these unruly students and rebellious schoolchildren to an almost unanimous sympathy. Doors of private apartments opened to receive the hunted. An old maid of seventy summers unfolded the lavender-scented sheets of a far-off trousseau and spread them over dirty tennis shoes and blood-stained sweaters. Other boys found themselves in an elegant Louis XV salon where a gentleman in dressing-gown reviewed them with military brusqueness.

'Nobody seriously damaged? Fine. Then, to work!' and led them onto the balcony where they were astonished to find a positive armoury of missiles arrayed. 'Start throwing!' ordered the gentleman.

A colonel's wife risked arrest and her husband's reputation by hiding sixty students outside the service entrance while police ransacked her apartment.

When the sick grey dawn came, the Students' Unions gave the order to disperse, and one by one the exhausted, hungry students went home.

The Boulevard St Germain from the Deux Magots to the Place St Michel was closed to traffic. For days afterwards workmen would be repaving the road in the Rue Gay-Lussac. There was blood on the stones of the Rue St Jacques.

One hundred and eighty cars — those status symbols of a materialist society — had been burnt down to their metal skeletons, and nothing so clearly expressed a whole generation's grand Refusal of the degraded values of that society. In a grocer's shop next morning I heard a man, shaking with rage, say, 'If they'd done that to my car, I'd have killed them!'

But on Saturday morning there were few Parisians or provincials who were ready to defend the values of violence with a clear conscience.

By some miracle it seemed that nobody had been killed. Partly perhaps because the students were the sons of the bourgeoisie and the police had received orders to pull their punches. At Charonne the dead had been workers.

At 10 a.m. a special edition of *L'Humanité* was on the streets. The Party had weighed in late on the side of the students. On Thursday afternoon I had been at the meeting where Aragon spoke. The whole of the Boul'Mich from the Rue des Ecoles to the Luxembourg had been taken over by students. The side streets and the Place de la Sorbonne were blocked off by police cars and lines of what looked like gorillas in battle-dress. The students squatted all over the middle of the road listening to their principal spokesman, Daniel Cohn-Bendit. When Aragon took over the megaphone there was a roar.

'I am with you!' Aragon shouted. 'I am with you!'

'Prove it!' they demanded. 'Publish an apology for all the lies about us printed in *L'Humanité* — if you can't do that, give us a page in *Les Lettres Françaises*, since you're the editor!' And a single voice of contempt: 'Surrealist!'

It was not the first time a leading Communist had been rejected by the students — 'the Chinese of Nanterre' as *L'Huma* described them bitterly. The old lion had lost its teeth. The revolutionary vanguard had shifted, leaving a dangerous gap between the official parties, the trade union leadership and the youth. More dangerous still, if the students refused to be absorbed by any party, they appealed directly to the workers for solidarity. By Saturday there were signs that the mass of workers was ready to respond to the revolutionary lead of the young intellectuals. Unless the parties and trade unions were to be completely discredited they had to close the gap, try to wrest back the initiative and canalize the movement. The reluctant support of the Communist Party and the call for a general strike and a mass demonstration on the Monday by the two major trade unions, the C.G.T. and the C.F.D.T., were attempts in this direction. The F.O. climbed hastily on the bandwagon at the last moment when it saw how things were going.

For five and a half hours on Monday nearly a million workers, students, teachers and parents cut through the heart of Paris from the Gare de l'Est to the Place Denfert-Rochereau. For the first time the black flag of the anarchists marched beside the red flag and the banners of the trade unions. Africans, Vietnamese, Spaniards, Portuguese — a shiver of recognition ran through the older members of the crowd who remembered the Popular Front of '36. But this was the celebration of another event, the tenth anniversary of de Gaulle's presidency. Ironic, the banderoles and the slogans:

'Bon anniversaire, mon Général.'
'Dix années, c'est assez.'
'De Gaulle aux archives.'

And thousands of handkerchiefs waving a long adieu.

The hostility toward the CRS was even more menacing: 'CRS SS. CRS SS.' And a sweet, almost caressing little hunting song (adapted):

'Salauds. Salauds.
CRS répondit l'echo.'

Not a policeman in sight. The reinforcements had been hastily bundled back to their holes in Marseille, Toulouse, Orleans. Pompidou, returned from his official visit to Iran, had made the grand gesture of liberating the arrested students, promising a review of those in prison and a general reform of the university. It was a little late.

The bells of the Sorbonne rang a tumultuous carillon of victory when the students reinvested their faculties. From then on the university was to be permanent headquarters for the Committees of Action. In the inner courtyard Anarchists, Trotskyists, Maoists, Communists set up stalls of literature side by side. Photographs of Marx, Mao, Trotsky and Che placarded the walls, with scrawled slogans, notices announcing discussions in various amphitheatres, quotations from poets and revolutionaries. Hundreds of leaflets poured from the roneotype machines. Newspapers were published. A pianist played on the chapel steps, and the entrance hall trembled under an avalanche of psychedelic jazz. Students parked their babies in the nursery and joined the groups that milled and eddied around impromptu speakers.

In spite of the warning placard, 'The Sorbonne is not a tourist site. Get political', the curious turned up in droves, vaguely alarmed or exhilarated by their visit to what seemed like another world, where the word 'democracy' had been given a new meaning.

'It is forbidden to forbid.' And above a NO SMOKING sign somebody had scrawled: 'You have the right to do NO SMOKING.'

A democracy without interdictions, without apparent organization, where an Open Tribune of students, workers, and public held permanent session night and day in the Grand Amphitheatre; where students and professors — including six Nobel Prize winners — discussed the future of the university as equals.

Not so many months ago Jean-Luc Godard's film *La Chinoise* had introduced us to 'the handful of extremists' centred round the faculties of Nanterre where the movement of the 22 March was born. For the first time in a highly industrialized capitalist society in full development the dream of primitive communism was revived, an alliance of workers and intellectuals in soviets of autogestion. Tenuous at first, it had required only a few days of violence in May for their rage of negation to gain the whole student body and the majority of the teaching staff. Even the lycées went on strike, and schoolchildren of fifteen and eighteen were organizing sit-ins on the war in Vietnam and the programmes of public instruction and examination.

'But what do they *want?*' those of pure conscience and unburnt cars demanded, honestly bewildered by the dissatisfaction of these golden boys and girls.

On Monday night, 20 May, in the Grand Amphitheatre of the Sorbonne, crammed with thousands of students clinging to the galleries and sitting on the knees of the august statues half-way up the wall, Jean-Paul Sartre suggested an answer to this question:

> The first day a young worker takes over a semi-automated machine in a factory, or a student enters a class-room, they both know pretty well what life has in store for them. They know that once they enter this society and accept what it offers, they're caught like rats in a trap. It's for this reason that the bourgeoisie has broken in half. You, its sons and daughters, have decided to join forces with the young workers to refuse this society and radically to change it.

But the problem remains of how those who have been submitted to an effective and successful domination by society, who tacitly support this domination by the acceptance of its largesse in the form of a high standard of living, can themselves create the conditions of a real liberty.

'Contest' is the key word of action, and Herbert Marcuse, rebellious philosopher of *One-Dimensional Man* and adopted as theorist by the students, has at least elucidated the direction of the struggle: against a society which is a productive combination of consumer goods and war; against a society which allows the 'free' election of masters, but which implies the continuing existence of masters and slaves.

Marcuse demands a refusal of all complicity with a society riveted in immobility between more cars, the wasteful and destructive methods of production and the 'clean bomb', a technology which turns out condensed classics and Bach in the bedroom; a context of received ideas which excludes the logical processes of thought. And because thought, the conquest of a private space where man can reintegrate his life and be himself, is the only hope of replacing false needs by the real needs of liberty, the intellectuals have taken the lead in the new revolution.

Can they succeed? Not alone, certainly. Nor was this ever their objective. From the first they made every effort to integrate their movement into that of the working class and to overcome the traditional suspicion of workers for the intellectual. If they have been prevented from doing so it is not their fault, and one is entitled to question the accusations levelled against them to justify the 'cordon sanitaire'. Are the students really an 'irresponsible element', or are the attempts of the government and trade union leadership to isolate them based on the fear of contagion?

For the students the only valid aims in a highly developed industrialized society go far beyond claims concerning salaries, conditions of work and social insurance, and set out to attack and transform basic structures. During the weeks when strikes paralysed the whole of the economy and red flags fluttered over France the fear of such changes became very real for the conservative petit-bourgeois with his 'sou in the sock' mentality. The exploitation of this fear during the elections ensured the return of de Gaulle and a government committed to preserving the status quo, even if the cost were high in rising prices and the suppression of liberty.

But whatever the immediate outcome, there can be no doubt that the May revolution demonstrated the fragility of present structures, and that the means exist for young workers and thinkers to control their future and to fashion the kind of society in which they choose to live. For this reason the bloody nights of May will go down in history as a rendez-vous with the end of an age.

The events of May 1968 galvanized Christesen into organizing a series of essays under the heading 'The Temperament of Generations'; by contrast with the earlier 'Godzone' series, this new series included contributions from a number of younger writers associated with the new movements. This was in line with a wider shift in editorial policy. Christesen began to speak openly about developing *Meanjin* more as a journal of comment, moving it away from the scholarly orientation that had been enforced on it during the Cold War. He aggressively sought out younger writers and thinkers, though in his correspondence with them there was a sense that the veteran editor, who was now approaching the age of sixty, was uneasy about some aspects of the new political culture that was emerging.

Number 3, 1968

Protest and Anaesthesia

DOUGLAS KIRSNER

Herbert Marcuse has described modern man and his society as 'one-dimensional'. Establishment mores are all-pervasive. It is difficult now to differentiate individual from social needs, what the individual actually wants from what society wants him to want. True, these 'needs' are not imposed on him by force. Ideology, having extended itself everywhere, becomes even more insidious because its presence so often goes unnoticed. Values are thought of as facts to be known, rather than as preferences to be decided.

Those who disagree with the basic functioning and structure of society are regarded as neurotic, irrational, in need of adjustment and understanding. Society no longer locks up its critics; it renders them ineffectual by more subtle means. There is an accepted arena of rational discussion and action, and anything outside this is deemed irrational — or at least unalterable. Thus the foundations of society cannot seriously be questioned since they are assumed to be rational.

By being translated into more ameliorable terms genuine problems about society are gutted of real content. Work problems are solved by higher wages, Vietnam by more or fewer troops, boredom by more television. Problems about the quality of life are redirected on to quantitative and thereby more manageable grounds.

Society is paternalistic. The people are passive recipients of goods and governments. Apathy is regarded as good, a sign of stability. Intensity of experience eludes modern man. When it occurs it is regarded as unusual or neurotic; it is institutionalized so that others will not be infected. Creativity and spontaneity are packaged together with artists and ardent lovers. The happiness of ordinary people is equated with a 'high standard of living'; freedom with a choice between fundamentally similar automobiles or political parties. 'He has no cause to be unhappy — a family, a good position, house, car, education. What more could a man ask for?'

We seldom realize just how far we are the objects of manipulation and management. By giving the illusion of free, individual choice, democratic capitalist society provides one of the most effective forms of domination yet devised. Freedom has hitherto performed a critical function, but now it is formalized, it is empty, itself enhancing man's alienation. But the 'otherness' of society is still felt. Whatever it is, it is not *ours* in any but a formal sense. Man's alienation is becoming increasingly objective. There are enormous areas of society over which we have no control. Democracy is always defined as 'political', which means that we are allowed to have a say in certain *political* decisions. But what about industrial democracy? What control has the worker over his product or the way it is produced? Or economic democracy? The major investment decisions are taken by the large companies and corporations. Huge profits go to a numerically insignificant section of the population. The consumer is not sovereign since his 'needs' are manufactured for him by the corporations and their advertising agents. Or social democracy?

Even within the strictly limited ambit of political democracy how much power has the electorate? Irrational factors such as chauvinism and the 'downward thrust' of communism can win elections. The elected government often does not put its platform, if it has one, into effect.

More lies are told to this generation than to any previous. The Vietnam war has made this clear. Many governments have been so exposed on this issue that there is now an accepted 'credibility gap' on a great number of other matters. Youth everywhere — from Tokyo to Paris — are rebelling, and even where the aims of the rebellions are not precisely enunciated, a feeling of abhorrence for what is happening in society can be sensed. Never has the Establishment been in a better position to mould the individual to its wants from birth. With the aid of the mass media the government can deceive the people most effectively on a large number of matters. The Gesture has become very important. Demonstrations, if not always of any immediate perceptible effect, are a means of searching for the truth denied the young demonstrators by a society whose watchword is 'deceit'.

Youth are faced with a reprehensible, deceitful society which does not seem capable of fundamental change through the accepted methods of transformation (such as political parties seeking parliamentary power). Many withdraw and go about the life-work of raising a family, others seek change through public and unconventional methods. Students certainly seem to receive a press coverage and influence vastly incommensurate with their numbers. The riots in France and civil disobedience in Australian capital cities imply strong beliefs among the protesters about the inherent dignity of man which is being stifled by society.

The overt and direct physical 'violence' of some of the students is a reaction against the more sophisticated 'violence' of the Establishment which injures or destroys its subjects in one way or another. Rationales for protest such as the 'Situationist ethic' do not lead to anarchism or chaos. They look at society in a fundamentally *social* way and view the present set-up as so immoral that it has to be changed so men can really live their own lives in their own ways. Many protesters cite the Nuremburg charter as evidence that it is the moral duty of man to protest against an immoral state of affairs.

Those who criticize students for breaking the traditional patterns of behaviour should ask themselves: if they were faced with situations which they regarded as morally iniquitous and not the subject of change by traditional means, which have turned out to be useless by themselves, and they felt very strongly about the evil being done, what would they do? If they did nothing, would they not be morally responsible for the persistence of the evil state of affairs? The revolt of youth is a moral one.

The inevitability of violence is accepted in our society. Television screens tell us what is happening or has happened. Although the bomb dropped over Vietnam explodes also in our room, we know we are safe. But we also know we are powerless to prevent it. Instantaneous communication may only increase man's sense of impotence.

Although accustomed to vicarious physical violence, the young generation has not known war. We may know somebody who was conscripted to Vietnam, and we glance through the latest casualty lists. In Australia at least, the war has changed our lives very little.

The nature and type of war have changed. Weapons have become far more sophisticated, with the result that soldiers rarely see the 'enemy'.

Since World War II the oppressed have not been on 'our' side and we have not been able to identify with them. The wars have largely been anti-colonialist, or wars of national liberation. We cannot identify with the Vietnamese because they are either on 'our' side fighting against the North Vietnamese, or they are slant-eyed Viet Cong. What has not struck home is that the people 'we' are fighting are on 'our' side.

There are many more radicals among the young today than there were during the 'thirties. The enormous rise in the size of universities has brought many of them together. Despite its numerous faults, mass education has put people in a better position to think about issues. The modern radicals generally read more than their predecessors. The massive growth in communications and travel has made the radicals more aware of an international responsibility. The hydrogen bomb, which has brought about the imminent possibility of almost total destruction, has made the concepts of internationalism and humanism more real. Compared with the radicals of the 'thirties, those of today are very wary of organizations and dogmas and often do not present positive alternatives to the present society.

Nevertheless modern radicals feel transformation of society in a socialist and democratic direction to be essential. But they are faced with no acceptable model. Although certainly not on the same basis as the U.S.A., the U.S.S.R. is undemocratic and bureaucratic and in many ways as remote from democracy (meaning the individual's control of his own destiny) as is America. Some young radicals seek inspiration from the national liberation movements of the Third World. Che Guevara, Ho Chi Minh, and Chairman Mao are seen as the charismatic symbols of the new world. Change from within existing western society is seen as almost impossible.

But that does not mean that radicals subscribe to the 'end of ideology' — that belonged to the 'silent Fifties'. Unrest, rebellion, dissatisfaction with the Affluent Society have reached new peaks. The New Left is gaining greater influence. The emergence of (say) Dr J. F. Cairns, Senator Eugene McCarthy (U.S.A.) and Prime Minister Trudeau (Canada) symbolizes a turn to a more *moral* view of society. People are becoming sick of the mundane, useless, often immoral machinations of the old politicians and are beginning to seek something new.

The need to transcend the present is now accepted by many of the young. They cannot do this by using the system's own methods — by its own self-seeking definition of 'rational action' — but rather by entirely new modes of action, more akin to poetry than to prose, existentialist rather than linguistic, 'utopian' rather than 'realistic'. Some live a type of transcendence by the 'turn on, tune in, drop out' formula; others by participating in movements to change society. If they have not articulated a complete programme to replace the existing system, they at least know that the system must be changed. It is this 'moral' thing that fires radicals. They are incensed with the Napalm State. They do not want to be the subject of a total (albeit 'pluralistic') administration. They attack liberals not because they disbelieve in liberal ideals, but because these ideals have been and can only be vacuous within the present society. They do not believe that alienation is an unalterable fact about man and his relations with his society and his world. They believe that the individual's potentialities are stifled in our society, and that the general monochrome level of apathetic existence can be replaced with a society of free persons in which the individual's capacities can be fulfilled. They believe in an intense, multi-dimensional existence. They are utopian only in the sense that their demands cannot be satisfied within the present framework. The radicals want to have real control over the decisions of the community upon which they are dependent.

That's what the New Left is all about.

Over the following years, *Meanjin* once again became home to a wide range of critical voices — from Alan Healy's scathing denunciations of Australian colonial policy in New Guinea, to Humphrey McQueen's critique of Australian racism, to Craig McGregor's exploration of the dark side of rock culture.

Number 2, 1971

'The revolution will not be televised'

CRAIG MCGREGOR

You will not be able to stay home, brother.
You will not be able to plug in, turn on and cop out.
You will not be able to lose yourself on scag
and skip out for beer during commercials.
The revolution will not be televised . . .

Gil Scot-Heron
New York

Nothing's simple, of course, and even though *Gimme Shelter*, the Maysles Brothers' *cinéma vérité* account of the Rolling Stones' disastrous tour of America, is indeed a ritualistic tragedy over which Professor Albert Goldman, at New York's Columbia University, can rub gleeful hands ('They blew it!') and Michael Goodwin, in the underground magazine *Rolling Stone*, can achieve the self-propelled orgiastic martyrdom which *Easy Rider* has made fashionable ('We blew it!' says Goodwin-*né*-Fonda), it was sort of nice to find the cinema so grass-filled the other night that you could get a contact high and to rediscover that, even second time round, when Jagger blasts off at Madison Square Garden with *Jumpin' Jack Flash*, the fantastic, exhilarating power of hard rock slams you back in your seat yet again and your body lifts blood lifts and reels and even though you know how it all ended, like those Greek audiences in their stone Madison Squares, yet you still vouchsafe the music its life-dynamic and are forced to confront, once again, the paradox at the heart of what is still optimistically called the Revolution: that even within this particular sub-culture, there still exists all the terror, egotism, peacefulness, extremism, beauty and delusion — in a word, *plurality* — which makes the human situation human, and that in America today these contradictions are magnified a millionfold by their incarceration within the most violent and bloody-minded Empire State since Rome. Which was the message, beaten in with billiard cues and diffused on 300,000 bad vibes ('It's scary, really weird, man, really weird': Jefferson Airplane even before the Jagger debacle) understood at last at Altamont.

Please people please stop hurting each other.

The voice is Grace Slick's and she is trying to cool it at Altamont. But people have been hurting each other for a long time, they have been hurting each other ever since Cain slew Abel with a Stanley Kubrick jawbone and it is perhaps only this generation of young Americans who have been able to foster the self-delusion that if you turn your back on violence, which Rap Brown thinks is as American as cherry pie, it will like the bogeyman simply disappear in a whiff of good vibes and grass smoke. 'If we're all one let's fucking well show we're all one,' Jagger complains petulantly into the mike, his Superhype cloak drooping from his shoulders.

All one? That's another of the myths which the mainstream counter-culture has been assiduously propagating these last few years, what with George Harrison going on a treat about Within You Without You and the Maharishi preaching a sort of transcendental Oneness with the Unity or whatever other bloody Oneness we are supposed to be at One with — while in front of Jagger a black guy, a college student, is just a few seconds away from being stabbed and stomped to death and Hells Angels are leaping out into the crowd like killer whales, battering and smashing people's heads open with pool cues, blood everywhere, kids flashing pathetic V signs or scrambling for their lives and bearded guys like Hashidic rabbis trying to get between the Angels and their victims and next to the stage two guys who look like students are looking up at Jagger with pain in their eyes shaking their heads NO NO NO NO ('Twerpy hippies . . . demanding punishment,' sneers Goldman) and next to them there's a girl with an utterly immobile face and tears streaming down on to her neck and later there is this hysterical girl standing next to the stretcher (Meredith's girlfriend?) screaming 'I don't want him to die, he isn't going to die' but Meredith Hunter already has a blanket over his face and blood has soaked right through his hip green jacket and the chopper is waiting and he is dead.

We are not One, we never have been One, there is conflict Within Us and Without Us, and the lesson the counter-culture(s), hopefully, will carry away from Altamont is that deluding ourselves we are One is a surrogate for working out how to deal with the fact we are not. 'I ain't no peace creep,' snarls Hells Angel Barger afterwards — 'they got got'. 'That was insane,' says drummer Charlie Watts, looking at the re-run of Angels gunning their hogs through 300,000 peace creeps. 'The Angels . . . seem more like heroes than villains,' says Michael Goodwin of *Rolling Stone*.

Don't follow leaders
Watch the parkin' meters
Bob Dylan

In its desperate search for heroes the rock culture some time ago seized on, of all people, Mick Jagger . . . Jagger! Ole Mr Mephistopheles himself, the showbiz Lucifer who dabbles (Whist! dare we mention it?) in black magic and phony Satanism (*Their Satanic Majesties*), him of the Mandrake costume and liver-lipped *fin de siècle* decadence of Performance Occult, him of the painted face and Regency kisscurls who opens his set at Altamont *opens* it for Chrissake with kids being chopped unconscious in front of him and people screaming and running and falling and that terrifying roar you get at football crowds and fight crowds when the blood shows yes *opens* it with *Sympathy for the Devil* and who when the song finally stumbles to a halt with Angels his own mock-Satanic hirelings stalking the stage and the rest of the Stones transfixed over their guitars at the mayhem at their feet can only blurt out 'Something very funny happens whenever we start that number' (giggle). And a few minutes later Meredith is dead for Chrissake Jagger DEAD you bloody fool — how does that fit with your phony devilry? Meredith who is one of the few black guys in that colosseum of 300,000 roaring onlookers who made the mistake of taking a gun to a love-in given by the love generation and made the further mistake of pulling it to ward off The Wild Ones and ended with a knife in his head and a mouthful of blood likewise of years and then — nothing. 'Love is coming, love is coming to us all,' sing Crosby, Stills, Nash & Young. It is an elegy. There has always been murder in the Garden. '*Because your Adversary the Devil walketh about as a Roaring Lion, seeking whom he may Devour.*' At least Meredith picked up the gun. And in a single terrible act confronted the dilemma which haunts the 'counter-culture': when face to face at last with the death-dealers, whether at Altamont or in the White House, what do you do?

The revolution will not be televised.
There will be no pictures of pigs shooting down
brothers on the instant replay. . .

What the hell were the Angels doing there? We all know the answer to that: they were hired, in a bizarre showbiz stunt, as bodyguards for the Stones. But it isn't just Jagger's fault, or the Stones'. Altamont wasn't an accident. The rock culture's long-standing flirtation with the Angels is just another facet of the we-are-one myth, the secular monism which preaches that everyone who is outside straight culture is the same. If *Gimme Shelter* demonstrates anything it is that at Altamont there were two different and explosively opposed cultures — a fact which is dramatized in those climactic sequences in which Jagger, the ass-wiggling unisexual hero of new-found liberation, prances around the stage with his little tailfeathers quivering in cockerel-invitation ('I think Mick's a joke, with all that fag dancing, I always did': John Lennon) while a few inches away Hells Angels in insignia-splattered leather jackets and Herakles lionskins stare at him with disgust and contempt. The Angels are outsiders, sure, but their alienation is the only thing they have in common with the 'peace creeps' who trod on their precious bikes ('Something which is your *whole life*,' says Sonny Barger) or with the brave new wave of sexual freedmen who Flash Mick represents. Jagger's right to do his thing: every gain in liberty, personal or social, is precious. But the Angels belong to a more brutal and repressive culture, one which has yet to be liberated, in which violence is the central motif: it is the only thing which gives their lives (working class 'proles', no future, a worse past, the discarded offal of the technocratic society) any meaning. Violence and hogs provide the power which a merciless System has stripped from them: and in their brutal reaction they enact, vicariously, the violent rebellion which the Woodstock Nation has so resolutely turned its back against. And so the Angels, like Jagger, become yet another surrogate. . .

> The theme song will not be written by Jim Webb or
> Francis Scott Key nor sung by Glen Campbell,
> Tom Jones, Johnny Cash or Engelbert Humperdinck.
> The revolution will not be televised . . .

There is no counter-culture: there are many. There is no Hero: everyone must be his own. There is no One: there are only ones, and it is only our differences which make the command 'come together' meaningful. We must beware of surrogates. We must beware of surrogate heroes like Jagger, whom we idolize because we have more sense than to idolize ourselves and not enough guts to make ourselves worthy of idolatry; we must beware of surrogate violence, because then those whom we vest it in will turn it, Angelically, against ourselves; we must beware of surrogate prophets and doomsayers, who lose heart and blow it secondhand to fulfil their own Jeremiads. Above all, we must beware of surrogate Revolutions, the portable apocalypse of the rock festival and the mass freak-out — because what America, and the world, needs right now is the real thing.

> The revolution will not go better with Coke.
> The revolution will not fight germs that may cause bad breath.
> The revolution will put you in the driver's seat.
> The revolution will not be televised.
> The revolution will be no re-run.
> The revolution will be live.

In his pursuit of literary contributions, too, Christesen actively set out to develop new contacts in the late 1960s and early 1970s. He established a vigorous correspondence with Kris Hemensley, one of the young Turks of the poetry world at the time.

Kris Hemensley to C. B. Christesen

Southampton, U K,
7 March 1970

dear Clem Christenson —
. . . literature — & here let us speak of literary magazines — the quarterly offerings of wit & turn of tongue on any number of subjects from a history of union ballads to the fauna of the eastern seaboard in any manner of mediums from poetry to belles lettres — well — *that* is gone — is irrelevant to the modern world — & if 'world' is too big a vista then it aint good enuf for Australia. Do ya hear me Clem! Mike Dugan once told me that in conversation with you you had said that it wasn't true that you wd not publish the new writing but that you were not receiving any of quality. (please excuse me if i am incorrect here — maybe it was Murray-Smith who sd that to Dugan.) The fact of the matter is that there exists feeling ranging from reluctance to outright hatred of established literature in which category Meanjin so easily falls. The necessity to write *is* strong with the new writers but just as important is *where* they publish & *why*. There is no status gained by publishing with a magazine which is not functioning as a compound of statement/fact/lyric/& vision — ie. as the strongest compound of energies available. . . .

C. B. Christesen to Kris Hemensley

23 April 1970

Dear Kris,
. . . I wish I had time to comment at length on points made in your long letter. I told Dugan I didn't receive much 'new verse' of *quality*, and that's godsgospel. The truth is bloody little new verse of quality is in fact being produced here, or elsewhere for that matter: most of it is windy rhetoric lacking substance; it's spurious. (What do I mean by 'quality', you ask? We could go into that later.)

As for a battered old bugger like me who's been trying to produce a literary magazine for just on thirty years, I'm now lumped with the Establishment drongos by the wall-eyed younger blokes. Ya can't win. But I've *always* sought, and been receptive to, experiment, new formulations, innovations, in whatever art form — as the 120 issues of *Meanjin* amply prove. All I insist on is *quality* — in verse, fiction, criticism or whatever; the best available at any given time. What I can't do is conjure up material out of a bloody hat. The *forum* has always been there, for the past thirty years. The local snake-pit being what it is, it's pretty tough blaming me if the forum is not used. And I very closely follow developments in other countries, from France and Germany to Brazil and the USA. You should see my files, library, and the stuff that pours into this office every week from all over. But I'm not meaning to attempt a defence: I'm only too well aware of the journal's defects. . . .

It's a terrible business here trying to introduce new ideas, new formulations, to lead/change local opinions, etc. Most Australians slouch along under a dun-coloured banner. But I've said all that before, and at length. (*Do you in point of fact know that?*)

I'm confessing that I as editor need help, from you and others like you. I'm confessing too that I can't seem to get much help from my immediate associates. It's not simply a 'generation gap' problem — they range from their early twenties to late sixties. It's more a matter of lack of interest, responsiveness, awareness — and stimulus.

We probably clash on many matters; but as you had enough wit to see, our interests may well be the same. For my part they are, fundamentally.

Number 4, 1968

Nursery Guernica

LEON SLADE

The castanet click-clack from the nursery
is the sound of Young Pablo's building blocks
making a memorial to the building block cities
he has created every day and then destroyed.

Build them up and knock them down,
'I am a napalm bomb,' he says
and the legless teddy droops in the corner
and the rocking-horse with peeling spots rolls his eyes and neighs.

Number 1, 1970

Epiderm

MICHAEL DRANSFIELD

Canopy of nerve ends
marvellous tent
airship skying in crowds and blankets
pillowslip of serialized flesh
it wraps us rather neatly in our senses
but will not insulate against externals
does nothing to protect
merely notifies the brain
of conversation with a stimulus
I like to touch your skin
to feel your body against mine
two islets in an atoll of each other
spending all night in new discovery
of what the winds of passion have washed up
and what a jaded tide will find for us
to play with when this game begins to pall.

Number 2, 1970

King Tide

PETER STEELE

An hour ago the light could glaze alive
a dozen crumbling peaks to the green sand,
and fuse your mind with water into dream.
Later tonight, omnivorous, lurching inland,
a salient nightmare breeding darkness in darkness,
the tide will pulse its own anabasis,
fretting at pasture, a savage timed by the moon.
But now, the rough grown smooth enough to place,
the flow is neither, washing the river's mouth,
not poise or throb, the brazen or bestial serpent,
but only most of the world shifting a little,
unobliging, unobliged, vulgar and fecund,
fuming gods and death. Hock-deep in sand
I plough the wind, my mouth pebbled with prayers,
waiting for king-tide, slurring over and over
the lone unlikely epithets of God.

Number 4, 1970

Clearing Away

ANDREW TAYLOR

Today I chopped back irises
spear-sharp
layers of leaves
long as our memories —
Vietnam, savage green
in the March decline;
paler, lank low leaves
almost brittle — Korea —
then a tangle of grey —
dusty, forgotten rubbish
the last war, second World War —
crumbling to the blade.
Beneath —
the red-backed spider
angry at being disturbed.

Sturt and the Vultures

Francis Webb

Mincing, mincing we go. And it follows, follows,
This hot nor'-easter: sometimes even a little testy at us
So that these poor horses sprocketed to its whirring coils
Slew away, working at the bit. Browne may be dying.
Little hot tantrums of wind and tiny pebbles
Desiccate and annul the few words I toss to him.
My thoughts skip among the stones. And it follows, follows,
This hot nor'-easter.
                    Back at the Depot
Our old Grandsire, misunderstood, is moping with Poole.
I gave Him his text at five sharp.
Feel for Him there, old bearded Predestinator
Trying to look kind . . . it's the plan He's tied to:
The elect and the — the — *wind, stones, pebbles.*
Browne may be dying.
                    Remember, my father's fireplace,
That lithograph beside the clock (Him there, as if the good Calvin
Had set Him there with St. Michael and a sword):
Yes, once at tea when prankful vermilion spat
And wriggled up out of the grate
I was solidly in the army — *Browne may be dying* —
There were cannonballs and bolting horses
And heathen by the barrel converted (I was about fourteen),
A girl, and benighted beachheads named after me
(*Hullo, Mr Browne*) and always the Search for something,
An opal, a prisoner . . .
                    Yes, I saw that prankful vermilion
Frisk up almost to His face. At the Search it was.
— *Wind, stones* — for an instant the Old'un looked hopeful
And about my own age.
                    Every morning now, the same:
I give Him His text early and wander off from Him
Leaving Him sob over the dear sacred scheme of His dotage
Dispositioning the just and the damned. *Stones, stones, stones.*
. . . Picture His poor tired old hands working away at the bellows
To keep up this hot nor'-easter. How it follows, follows.
Mincing we come, we go. Sand, pebbles all frills and furbelows.
Browne may be dying. *Water back at the Depot.*
— If only to rest His poor old hands a little . . . . How it follows
This hot nor'-easter . . . the Void, the sand, the pebbles,
Little tattered pockets of the Void . . .

Browne is calling,
I was dreaming.
— The birds, the birds! Crying like children,
Closer, wheeling, wheeling, descending, closer!
They come in ecstatic flight, rapturous as the Paraclete,
Tongues of fire — it's a well of voices. Crying like children.
My horse props, makes to rear, shivers, and cannot move.
They come at us, begging, menacing, at eye-level, above.
I lash at them with my hands, filled with terror and love.

Fire a shot, Mr Browne. And, poets, you wheel away.
You are lost, gone. Where do you come from? (Feel the caressing nor'- easter
Following, following, chanting.) Are you from the Void?
Poets of dry upper nothingness, you are hunger, we are hunger,
You are thirst, we are thirst.
We go mincing along followed by the hot nor'-easter
— But sometimes we stray towards Sacrament, creek-bed, Virgin —You
stray, poets. But you ride neither high Heaven
Nor the earth of statuesque stones. Something lures you down,
Quartz, slate, limestone, an eyeball, an opal, a prisoner,
Till hunger and thirst wheel into madness within you,
Your immaculate Words, cryings (O hear the sweet nor'-easter)
Piping to us, see the lovely Madonna-faces in the gilt
Frameways of pure sand and pebbles!
But neutralities or wrath
Of man — or is it of God! — expel you again from earth
Driving you out of sight and mind like exhausted breath,
The wing-whimper, the talon. Only something far beneath
Cowers away when you come.
And its name is Death.

Number 3, 1971

Emily Dickinson Judges The Bread Division at the Amherst Cattle Show, 1858

Fay Zwicky

I *Volume*

Here is bread:
not more nor less than what you see,
It asks for mercy — I am God to give —
Stands as I stand (armoured, gleaming white
Behind my muslin smile, grand upon
The sweetness of this fearful day),
Waits on my step, my virgin adversary,

Life unflinching whole, upon a weathered bench
Pleading a tiny pellet of justice.
Of *me!*
    Reaper or victim, so far the act is fine;
Pastor Jenkins' nose approves my draped humility
But cannot smell my pride — I shine
Upon his coat behind a smile.
Yes, there is Bread:
    and I am where I am,
Winged, decorous, stony-hearted captive judge;
Nobody dare befriend me.

II *Texture*

Moonscape sways, the crested craters yawn
Under my knife, propitiating sabbath stroke:
        My father's economic vestal,
He would eat no bread but mine,
Contractor for my crumb, his own communicant
Forever wrapped about a stone.
Votaries rebuffed resume, their crown awry,
The silvered lacey cells; and God
Marks time, awaits the silken even grain.
        Today
Your starving eaglet breaks pitted bread
With sparrows — no question of friendship.
        But is't for this
I'll go, strangling in smiles, to heaven?
Mourn the eagle, mourn the sparrow,
Pastor can you? Test the crater's rim for me,
Shelter my responsibility beneath
Your tight black coat — here,
Here is the knife!
A healthy crust but I suspect
Surfeit of saleratus.

III *Aroma*

        I cut, cut, cut,
My culprit dies in my wrath.
Wafted by bells on his winged collar
Rises, buoyed by sweet wraiths
Into fine new air.
        Strutting
In yeasty quicksands I send him at last,
About my neck the acid victor's wreath,
My smile stuck fast.
        Amherst's pigeons
Ponder the sourness in the air.

IV *Colour*

White is the colour of tribulation
White is the antimacassar of my cell
White is the inexorable collar
White is the dealer's hand
White the entrenched priestess.
Full marks.

Number 1, 1972

Midnight

Anne Elder

At night, late,
I put out the dog
and the bottles for milk.
There in the dark elm at the gate
a strange fruit. It is the moon
hung ripe for me to eat.

I think then
of my father, his life done,
an old dead tired man
who had not looked at the moon
for twenty years.
I put out my hand for that excellent fruit
to nourish and steady him.
But he cannot eat.

I think long
under the dark elm
of what the night prepares
for those gone from home;
of all who sleep or cannot
behind their myriad walls,
known or unknown.

I see through the walls
to the best known, the one
who sleeps light, who is near,
I will put my chilled hand
to his side, he will moan
and turn away to fitful dreams.
For close to thirty years
we have lain there
under the moon.

I put out my hand
to my young female child
over the city in a room
locked in her twenty years;
and to the firstborn, a man
across the city in a room
his dark head down on his desk
like a child perhaps. Their lamps
and their dark eyes
burn late and quiver my heart
as the close and far of the moon.

At night, late,
the moon is a whole fruit
I have wanted for fifty years.
It does not fall
to a stare. Complete,
so lovely, it drips
a cold nectar
for me only.

Number 4, 1973

Backing Out

JUDITH RODRIGUEZ

Upside-down greyness: the scrubby gums
worry and backtrack in water moving across
that still goes on spreading. Such watery morning
cloud in sunlight, such ruffled willow-lined levels
among their hummocky shores, but will not quite shimmer;

this is the stretch where the heron rambles on clay
and over tussocks; the bushes have him considering.
For a whole short age of lagoon-time we can't pick him
till his cry grates, he's up, and his emblemed wings foldingly
lift and spurn and lift from the line of flight.

Out from behind the car-door where bending and peering
they followed his finicky stroll, the children run
for his rising away; and are stopped in the gluepot mud
of the unmade road bulldozed for human going
he touched on, just printing. The shoes will take hours to clean.

Number 4, 1974

Inspectors of Mines: Major's Creek

David Campbell

A township the size of Bath or Queanbeyan. Where
Thirty six pubs fired twenty thousand, one
Drunkard in George Street lights his way to beer
At the Elrington (late Major). Not a good town
For drunkards homing through blackberry that sprawls
Over the pitted diggings. An Inspector of Mines,
Charles Harpur, turned from newchums sinking holes
In the land he loved (At dusk the woods — his lines —
'Hang like mighty pictures of themselves')
To raise his glass (like Kendall at Araluen
Clinking to bellbirds — and now on the same shelves);
But alcohol soured like friendship and mockers moved in
As sly as saplings. Again the woods look down
At dusk from mullock on the one-pub town.

Christesen also continued his policy of publishing Australian writing alongside a careful — but by no means unadventurous — selection of work from other countries. The names of the writers of international repute whose work appeared in *Meanjin* could form a kind of litany: Alexander Solzhenitsyn, Eugene Ionesco, D. M. Thomas (both in his own right and as translator of Anna Akhmatova), Philippe Jaccottet, Raymond Roussel, Norman Mailer; more surprisingly, perhaps, R. K. Narayan, Chinua Achebe, Ngugi wa Thiong'o, Pramudya Ananta Tur . . . The litany, however, is less important than the cumulative effect of Christesen's insistence on maintaining an open cultural posture at a time when Australia generally was in the throes of xenophobia.

The wide range of fiction published in *Meanjin* included the work of Christina Stead, Alan Marshall, Hal Porter, Patrick White, Thomas Keneally, Finola Moorhead, Peter Mathers and Peter Carey, and the elegant humour of expatriate Martin Boyd.

Number 2, 1969

Expatriates Dine

Martin Boyd

The chambermaid awakened me half-an-hour before the usual time, and said: 'Telefono'. I struggled into a dressing-gown and went to answer it. After a few bewildered misapprehensions I realized that Nada Mushkin was asking me to dine that evening.

'Oh-er-yes, I think I can,' I said. 'Yes, I'd love to. Yes, of course I can. What time?'

'Half-past-eight,' she answered. 'Ring up Daisy. She'll give you a lift.'

Nada was a Russian baroness who had been lady-in-waiting to the murdered Czarina. She was the same age as myself, as she informed me when we first met, adding: 'There's no difference between rotten apples.' Although she suffered from spasmodic bouts of penury, she had very grand friends. Daisy was one, and not only had a huge private fortune, but her husband was a former ambassador and also a peer.

Still dazed by my premature awakening, I did not realize that a woman of this consequence would hardly be pleased to be disturbed equally early by someone asking for a lift. The domestic who answered sounded dubious, but I was connected with, presumably, her bedside telephone. I heard a drowsy voice say: 'Hullo. What? Who? Nada Mushkin? Who? What?'

I was disconcerted to find that Nada had not forewarned her, and that my request was a bolt from the blue. However she said: 'All right. Shall I call for you, or will you come here?' I said that I would go there, as I was unwilling to put any more crumpled rose-leaves into her gold bed.

At half-past-seven I set out, standing squashed and suffocated in a bus that moved with the traffic of the Corso like a pebble in a glacier, and at about the same rate. When I arrived, a little late, at Daisy's palazzo, she said: 'Billy Shelley will take us, so I've let my driver go home.'

Billy Shelley was an ex-guardee bachelor, also very rich, and rather a pet of people like Daisy. On the few occasions when I had met him, he had bowed with courteous reserve, and I was a little diffident about intruding uninvited into his luxurious motor-car. This, equally with my smelly bus, had been caught in the glacier of the Corso, and he was half-an-hour late. With him was Princess Belladramini, perhaps the grandest lady in Rome, being descended from Augustus Caesar. Even physically she was among the most massive, so that Daisy had to take a back seat with me.

We arrived at Nada's apartment on the Aventine after nine o'clock, but she did not notice our unpunctuality. We walked down a long room lined with gilt chairs, which for her may have echoed that imperial palace whence she came. At the end was a terrace with magnificent views, from S. John Lateran to the dome of S. Peter's.

'How nice!' said the princess, the only one who was Roman born.

Here the table was laid and the other guests were waiting — they were an attaché from a transatlantic embassy and his wife, and a Russian prince, so small and bent and ancient that he seemed to have turned to ash: one felt that if he were touched he would fall to pieces. He kissed the hands of the princess and Daisy, and said something in such a faint, squeaky voice that it was as if a mouse had spoken.

Nada, with powder-white hair, pink cheeks, pink chiffon and pearls, was less frail, but stiff with rheumatism; so Daisy, in yellow taffeta and diamonds, had to go into the kitchen and carry in the food, as there was no servant except a daily woman who came in the morning. The food was delicious, but did not seem to be served in the right sequence.

Soon after we were seated Nada dropped a two-litre flask of chianti on the tiled floor, and we sat throughout dinner with our feet in red wine, which was not disagreeable, as the night was warm. However, the prince kept a grey felt hat on his lap, which occasionally he put on his head. The conversation was in English, Italian and French, and very melodious, though the attaché and his wife sounded rather like transistors against flutes.

There were many glasses on the table, but perhaps owing to the collapse of the chianti, or more likely to Nada's vague memory, we were only given vodka.

That afternoon there had been a demonstration against the Vietnam war, and the attaché spoke contemptuously of 'hysterical riff-raff'.

'But it is horrible what they are doing there!' exclaimed Nada, suddenly and surprisingly passionate.

'We have to contain Communism,' said the attaché, a little disconcerted, but with an aggressive jaw.

'If you contain one bad thing with another, you only increase it,' said Nada.

'You don't understand Communism,' retorted the attaché. A barely perceptible gasp went round the table, as Nada's closest friends had been shot by Bolsheviks, and herself had only escaped by a miracle. The attaché ignored this tremor and went on: 'We don't want it in our country and we haven't got it.'

'How nice!' said the princess, and asked for more caviar.

Later we moved into the room with the gilt chairs. Shelley lifted one of then over a low table on which there was a tray of glasses. The seat fell out onto the tray. Nada was unperturbed and no one made any comment.

I found myself sitting near Princess Belladramini. She mentioned a friend of hers, another grandee, whom I had met in the previous summer while paying a visit north of the Alps. This lady's son had since been the victim of a gruesome tragedy, of which I had heard but did not know the circumstances. The princess now gave them in detail, describing how a young man of the bourgeoisie had brutally killed him, when he found him paying attention to a girl on whom he himself had designs.

'It was in all the European papers,' she said. 'And what made it so dreadful for his mother was that the murderer was not poor Josef's equal in rank.' She emphasized this point, mentioning it three times in the course of her narrative.

Billy Shelley's manner towards me now became less reserved: I knew a duchess, even if her son had been murdered beneath his station in life.

The attaché and his wife, in spite of their profession, had not been coached in the rules of precedence and they stood up to leave before the princess. She, however, with her practised skill in dealing with such occasions, and in spite of her large bulk, managed to take Nada's hand and to thank her for a delightful evening before the attaché's wife could do so. She did this not from self-importance but from sheer kindness, as she thought how terrible it would be for them if later they discovered their blunder. However, they managed to reach the lift first.

I was the last to say goodbye, and when I saw Nada looking like a Boucher portrait, but with wine-stained feet and standing among the broken glass and general disorder of her apartment, I felt a sudden *attendrisement* for her, and I murmured to Daisy: 'I'll stay and help her wash up.'

'No. Don't,' said Daisy. 'The woman will do it in the morning.'

On the landing the fragile prince again kissed hands and squeaked some mousey compliments. He then put on his felt hat and tottered to a small apartment he had on the same floor. Daisy said he was Nada's boy-friend.

'How nice!' said the princess.

The lift was small and only intended for three. As the princess occupied the space, and was also the weight of two people, there was only room left for Daisy; so Shelley and I went down the stairs, first noticing that the lift seemed to descend with unusual speed. When we reached the ground floor there was no sign of it, but we heard Daisy hallooing from the sub-basement, which was the coal cellar.

Shelley ran down, and returned to say that they had pressed the wrong button and had not a ten lire piece to put in the slot to make the lift work. Neither had I, so he ran up about six flights to Nada's apartment, and obtained her last ten lire. He was then able to retrieve Daisy and the princess from the coal cellar.

Driving back, the princess said that if she had known Nada had no servants she would have brought her cook and her footman, who was a most intelligent young man. She also said this three times.

When Shelley had decanted Daisy at her *palazzo*, I asked him if he were going in my direction, and if so would he take me a little further. As we drove on the princess pointed out historic monuments connected with her family.

Outside my modest *pensione* she said goodbye most graciously; and looking up approvingly at the flaking ochre façade of the building, said, 'How nice!'

As I turned the key in the door it occurred to me that in personnel this must be one of the grandest dinner parties I had ever attended, even though it was rather comic, yet basically sad, like a dwarf at a mediaeval court. Then I saw on the lift a square of cardboard, torn seemingly from a boot-box, on which was scrawled 'Guasto' — out of order. After the poltergeist atmosphere of Nada's flat, this struck me as sinister, and my reaction was not only one of annoyance.

It may have been due to the unaccustomed vodka, but the party now seemed no longer to have been comic, but faintly macabre, and to have had some sociological or even ethnological significance. I had met these displaced grandees occasionally at tea parties, but had not hitherto been conscious of their singularity.

Was my awareness due to the presence of the transatlantic attaché? Would I have accepted as normal the ethos of these relics of European history if he had not been there? Would I have been conscious of the murdered Romanoffs in Nada's background; or of the oddity of her nonagenarian lover, so discreetly occupying a separate apartment but only ten yards away on the same floor? And what had induced the princess to give those gruesome details of the death of her friend's son, and then to end up in the coal cellar?

The vodka sent my mind wandering in fantastic regions of cause and effect, until I reached the conclusion that these people, and Europe itself, would still appear normal if the torpedo had missed the *Lusitania*.

The next morning, when the fumes of the vodka had evaporated, they left as residue in my mind the belief that it would.

For Christesen and other Cold War survivors, the victory of the Labor Party under Whitlam in the federal elections of December 1972 marked the end of a long drought — or, as Christesen put it, the 'end of the Ice Age'. To mark the occasion, he commissioned essays from Whitlam himself, and from Manning Clark (who labelled the long period of conservative rule 'the years of unleavened bread'); but the prevailing sense of relief was best captured by historian Russel Ward.

Number 1, 1973

From: The End of the Ice Age

RUSSEL WARD

. . . After a long hibernation and the final low farce of the McMahon government's term of office, almost any change could only have been for the better. We had all come more or less to expect nothing but ill from political action. Nevertheless the Whitlam government, so far, has done a great deal more than tinker cautiously with what needs to be done. Many of its supporters have been equally astonished and delighted, and its enemies seemingly bemused by the confidence, the authority and the speed with which it has set about making up for wasted time. I know of no precedent in the history of British governments anywhere for the promptitude with which it has implemented so many of its campaign promises. Within a month of the election, the new government had ended the lottery of conscription for military service and released gaoled draft-resisters, negotiated an exchange of ambassadors with China, abolished race as a criterion of our immigration policy, set about the reform of our archaic health service, revalued the Australian dollar upwards, moved to support equal pay for women, begun reform of the divorce law, increased unemployment aid to the states, banned from our soil racially-selected sports teams, banned the slaughter of the nearly extinct Australian crocodile, abolished British titles (as the Canadians did a generation ago), put the contraceptive pill on the medical benefits list and abolished the 'entertainment tax' on it, abolished the excise on unfortified Australian wine, and increased subsidies to the arts. The list is by no means exhaustive: but who ever heard of a democratic government actually doing so much of what it promised and doing it immediately? No wonder the opposition seems disconcerted. Homing travellers, whether of radical or conservative bent, report that for the first time in the memory of thirty-year-olds Australia appears frequently and favourably in the overseas press. Our image abroad glows somewhat. At home the age of fear lasted so long that even those who struggled incessantly against the tide can hardly believe it has turned at last, that we no longer have a government about which we had become inured to feeling ashamed, embarrassed or apologetic.

There will be compromises and troubles soon enough, of course, and shoddy deals and salutary criticism, not to mention loads of abuse. This article, I expect, will attract a modest share of the last two commodities. No doubt it does resemble more the fanfare of a fundamentalist trumpeter announcing the Saviour's second coming than a properly impartial and coolly judicious academic exercise. It does so deliberately because, as I have tried to show, more is at stake than a game of ins and outs or left versus right. Australian history this century shows that, in general, Labor quite naturally puts Australian interests, ideas and policies first, while the parties of resistance equally naturally are guided mainly by what they believe at a given moment to be the wishes of their leading overseas patron. On present trends, incidentally, and before very long, our great and powerful friend will be Japan.

Take for example the scandal of foreign capital buying control of more and more Australian assets — stations, farms, land, mines and industries. Though Labor is supposed to be hell-bent on the destruction of capitalism, in fact it acts much more readily than do the parties of 'private enterprise' to protect Australian capitalists from foreign takeovers. It is really committed to our own control of our own destiny, including that of the capitalists among 'us'. It is interesting that Gorton, in this respect, was more of a Labor man than a Liberal. Just before his election to the party leadership, consciously contrasting himself with Menzies, he said on a nation-wide TV programme, 'You might say that I am Australian to my boot-heels'. And indeed he was. At least he *talked* more boldly (if hardly more coherently) than any other Liberal leader about the need for curbing foreign capital investment: but look at the result. Though obviously the most popular vote-getter the Liberals had, 'Jolly John' was drummed out of the leadership in favour, Lord have mercy upon us, of McMahon. The parties of resistance preferred even that to a leader who showed such dangerously independent tendencies. He seemed to be thinking sometimes of formulating Australian policies without first finding out what the United States had decided they ought to be.

In the past century a policy of total and unconditional dependence on Britain made some sense. At least it was probably the only realistic one open to us. Such a policy makes sense no longer, whether the United States, or Japan, or China, or farthest Iceland be conceived of as the semi-divine parental figure who will always cherish her colonial child. This policy for twenty-three years has done little for our prosperity, nothing for our social progress, and untold damage to our reputation and long-term security.

Australia now has after all the strongest, best-balanced and most advanced economy in the southern hemisphere. As long as the ingrained colonial cringe remains basic to the anti-Labor parties' instincts and policies, they must govern by reference to long-dead myths and dreams rather than to the actual world around us. On 2 December 1972 Australians decided, not before time, to step forward into reality. An exhilarating thaw is breaking up the ice in which we have been frozen for a generation. Let us hope that it heralds not merely a brief interglacial period but a new era in our national life.

The new era, however, was not one from which Christesen could draw any great comfort.

C. B. Christesen to Dr Jim Cairns

28 November 1973

. . . The trouble is, Jim, that you chaps were in Opposition far too long! Now that you are in office, scarcely any of the younger members of administrative staff know me. I feel today even more on the outer than when the Liberals were in office. And apart from yourself, Gordon Bryant, Bill Hayden and (recently) Al Grassby, I don't have any personal contact with Cabinet Ministers, or even for that matter with back-benchers. I'm not known, the journal is not really known — certainly it's not widely read by ALP supporters — the struggle to 'hold the fort' during those twenty-five years of 'unleavened bread' is largely forgotten. So it's time I retired before I begin to feel too bloody bitter. And I wish I could persuade Nina to pull out, also; for she has received scant recognition for all the years of dedicated service she has given to this University and to Russian studies in Australia generally.

But I think I can say this with some assurance: If *Meanjin* should cease publication next year — if the Summer issue should prove to be the last — the whole Labor movement will be the poorer. I mightn't have achieved so very much over the thirty-three years, but I *did* manage to place on record some immensely important material which no other journal here could have published. And I didn't allow *Meanjin* to become a right-wing *Quadrant* type of magazine.

The Labor movement should be doing everything in its power to strengthen the cultural/intellectual side of our national life. There have been remarkably valuable gains in providing writers and artists with better material reward, but that only touches the fringe of the problem. I'm not aware of any effort at all being made by the ALP or THC to get the creative artists and the working-class movement together. And until worker and intellectual join in close association, no restructuring of Australian society can be possible.

With warm regards, and to dear Gwen. Al Grassby has invited Nina and myself to have dinner with him soon. If we can make it before the House rises, I'll let you know.

But the last word here must go to Nina Christesen. Both the title and the subject of this essay are significant, not merely because they give the lie to the narrow-minded Cold Warriors who had accused Nina Christesen of Communist sympathies, but also because they at least give an inkling of the commitment, erudition and humanity that had kept her going through those long, hard years. Here, one believer in the power of unarmed truth writes about the work of another.

Number 1, 1974

The Power of Unarmed Truth
Solzhenitsyn's Plea for Human Values

NINA CHRISTESEN

Arkhipelag Gulag 1918–1956. By Alexander Solzhenitsyn. Parts 1 & 2 (YMCA-Press, Paris, 1973); pp. 606.

This book, so far untranslated into English, constitutes two parts of a projected seven-part history of the Russian Revolution. It is described by the author as 'an essay in literary research'. There are no fictional characters or invented happenings in it and wherever possible men and places are named. The work is dedicated to 'all who did not live long enough to tell the tale', and the author begs them to forgive him 'for not having seen all, recalled all, or divined all'.

The story is based on personal recollections, on interviews, memoirs and letters collected by Solzhenitsyn from 227 informants; on facts and statistics obtained from published records by such public prosecutors as Lacis, Vyshinsky, Krylenko and Auerbach; and finally on the work of thirty-six Soviet writers headed by Maxim Gorky, 'who were the first in Russian literature to write in praise of slave labour!'

Arkhipelag Gulag is a piece of research in so far as Solzhenitsyn's main objective is to find and record the truth about the terror and the labour camps in the years 1918–1956; and it is a piece of literature — 'one of the most delicate and sensitive tools man possesses' — in so far as he tries to understand and present facts imaginatively, communicating through art his insights and emotions. The shattering and horrifying facts are arranged in certain patterns and consist of rhythmic tensions. Like ocean waves, these tensions build up, break, reform, build up again and keep pounding at our consciousness. The facts are presented against a vision of a better world, for 'the writer has the gift of sensing more acutely than others the harmony of the world and beauty and ugliness of man's contribution to it,' — as Solzhenitsyn had put it in his Nobel Prize lecture translated into English by Nicholas Bethell and published by Stenvalley Press, London.

In his *Island of Sakhalin* Anton Chekhov gave a similar sober documentary description of a Czarist penal colony, occupying *one* real island in the Far East. Like Chekhov, Solzhenitsyn is strictly factual, so far as facts are available to him, but he speaks with less detachment; he speaks with passion and irony, scorn, sarcasm and indignation and tells his story in the form of one protracted metaphor. He visualizes the U.S.S.R. as an archipelago of forced labour camps — or as one vast waterway with an archipelago of thousands of islands, large and small, sometimes close to each other, sometimes far apart, extending from the Bering Strait to the Bosphorus. This allegorical archipelago exists side by side with the cities and villages of ordinary men and women who are frequently not even properly aware of its existence.

Solzhenitsyn attempts not only to describe the Archipelago but to understand how it was possible for it to come into being and last so long. He does not claim to be writing history — lacking, as he does, access to sufficient historical documentation, evidence, counterchecks — but he tells the story diachronically, searching for prime causes that would satisfy the artist in him. (Much as Tolstoy who, setting out to write the story of the Decembrist rebels upon their return to Russia from exile in 1856, ended by writing the story of the year 1805, which in turn developed into *War and Peace*.)

The imagery of the Archipelago is complicated by the metaphor of a sewerage system and of the great Russian river system. Drop by drop currents of water polluted with the blood, sweat, and urine of the unhappy millions grow into springs and streams and mighty rivers. The 'flood' of prisoners sent to the Archipelago in 1929–30 carried some fifteen million 'kulak' peasants to the *taiga* and the *tundra*, and is compared in volume to the River Ob; the Stalin Terror flood of 1937 is compared to the Volga; the millions of deportations in the year 1945–1946 are compared with the River Yenisei; this time the flood included 'whole nations', together with whole armies of Russian soldiers returning from German captivity in order to be reincarcerated in their own country.

In addition to these three major torrents there were many other 'streams' of the condemned — the various 'bourgeois elements', landowners, business proprietors, monks, priests and nuns, those who resisted the appropriation of church treasures by the State, those 'who failed to report their bourgeois origins', those who failed to pimp on others, members of various Socialist groupings other than the Bolsheviks, Tolstoyans, Tolstoy's youngest daughter, Alexandra, members of various religious sects, those who became cannibals during the terrible siege of Leningrad, ethnic minorities after their revolts, those who practised Esperanto as their form of communication, those suspected of espionage — as for instance Russian émigrés who returned to the Soviet Union out of sheer nostalgia for their native land — ordinary criminals, some genuine enemies of the Soviet Union, people who happened to be related to those already sent to the labour camps, certain scientists obstinately refusing to recognize the imposter Lysenko as a true scholar, old Bolsheviks, those who praised American technological successes or American democracy, or who generally 'worshipped the West' . . .

What made it possible to fill this vast Archipelago with millions upon millions of wretched inhabitants during all those years between 1918 and 1956? In trying to understand, to reach to the very essence of this gargantuan human tragedy, Solzhenitsyn has exposed himself to a charge of treason against the Soviet Union.

There is much more open criticism and discussion of the state of affairs within the Soviet Union today than is generally recognized in the West — and this criticism is carried out with impunity, provided it is 'placed in a certain historical perspective' and provided the sanctity of the Party and of Lenin are not impugned. Solzhenitsyn began by questioning Stalin's authority from the position of an efficient officer who sees his soldiers 'betrayed' by the stupidity, unpreparedness and incompetence of the Supreme Commander. The search for first causes, like Tolstoy's before him, eventually led Solzhenitsyn to question the very fundamentals of Soviet society. *Arkhipelag Gulag* throws much light on the steps by which the writer had arrived at this position. A conforming, successful young officer, ready with pat answers, indifferent to religion, he closely missed becoming 'an executioner': 'had I chanced to be sent to the NKVD school under Yezhov — perhaps I should have graduated just in time for Beria?' he asks in one of his many self-searching questions, not hesitating to disclose some acts of his own moral cowardice and disclaiming the rôle of a political fighter. Taking the stance of Boris Pasternak in the matter of politics and life, i.e. that life is infinitely more delicate and complex than is remotely envisaged by those who would 'remake' it, he exclaims:

> If only things were so simple! If there simply existed somewhere some bad men who are responsible for all the wickedness around us, so that all we had to do was to single them out and destroy them! But the line dividing good from evil runs across each man's heart. And who would destroy a fraction of his own heart?

The second great 'act of treason' ascribed to Solzhenitsyn is his alleged 'Vlasovism'. He is accused of being a 'literary Vlasov' and of sympathizing with the Germans in the epic struggle of the Russian people against their Nazi invaders. On what is this accusation based? Describing his first encounter with the Vlasov traitors, Solzhenitsyn comments on the desperate way in which they fought the Red Army:

> . . . they could not fight in any other way . . . If being purely and simply captured was already regarded as an unpardonable betrayal of their motherland, what of those men who took up the enemy's arms? Our crude propaganda machine ascribed their behaviour 1) to treason (was it biological? was treachery in their blood?) and 2) to cowardice. It was certainly not cowardice. A coward seeks an easy way out . . . But only the last extremity, only boundless despair, only insatiable hatred of the Soviet régime, only contempt for their own personal safety, could lead them to enlist in the Vlasov regiments of the Wehrmacht. For they knew they could expect no mercy. Once captured by the Russians they were shot on the spot the minute they uttered a single distinguishable Russian word. Russians fared worst of all when captured by the Russians, even as they did when captured by the Germans. Altogether this war revealed to us that the worst thing on earth is to be a Russian.

Elsewhere Solzhenitsyn describes how ambivalent the Vlasov followers were, how bitterly they came to hate their German masters, and how they 'saved Prague' by unexpectedly turning against them.

In comparing the treatment meted out to the Russian prisoners of war with that of all the other prisoners he says: 'The Russians are bearing the brunt of the war — why is this [i.e. the worst possible treatment] their particular lot? Why?' And he blames it partly on the refusal of U.S.S.R. to participate in The Hague Convention and on the Soviet failure to recognize the International Red Cross.

Solzhenitsyn finds it natural that the Vlasov followers are tried for treason (though he would have the trials tempered with mercy and with understanding of the total situation in which they found themselves before surrendering to the Germans), but he revolts against placing millions of innocent people into the category of traitors. In the long military history of the nation the Russian soldier was not known to be prone to treachery. Why then, 'under the fairest, the most just of all régimes', in a 'war that is the most justified of all wars', should there suddenly come into being millions of traitors from among the ranks? How is one to understand it? How to explain it? Soldiers who had the misfortune to be encircled by the enemy were, at the victorious end of a war fought on the vastest possible scale, arrested and condemned to spend years in labour camps and exile in their own country 'so that they would not talk about Europe among their fellow villagers'. (Or were all these labour camps a simple matter of economic calculation? Who would have voluntarily gone to open up the virgin soil in Siberia, Vorkuta, Kolyma? How else was the Plan to be fulfilled? Were the *numbers* of those to be condemned to labour camps determined not by their guilt or innocence but by socio-economic considerations?)

Much of *Arkhipelag Gulag* is taken up with discussions of legal codes and illegal practices. The author's quarrel is not with the Soviet law and the Constitution but with the failure of their implementation. Just as he traces the Stalin terror to an edict by Lenin, so step by step he reveals the procedures that degenerated into closed courts, into trials without proper defence, into arrest and exile without trials, 'preventive' arrest and 'preventive' execution.

Solzhenitsyn says he is not a political man. Like Tolstoy's and Pasternak's, his concerns are 'above the barricades', or as he himself put it at the meeting of the Union of Soviet Writers secretariat in September 1967:

> It is not the task of the writer to defend or criticize one or another form of government organization. The task of the writer is to select more universal and eternal questions, such as the secrets of the human heart and conscience, the confrontation between life and death, the triumph over spiritual sorrow, the laws in the history of mankind that were born in the depths of time immemorial and that will cease to exist only when the sun ceases to shine.

But such moral and philosophical considerations lead him into making statements that infuriate those who are incapable of intellectual speculation. In *Arkhipelag Gulag*, for instance:

> The simple truth is — and one must learn this through suffering — that it is not the victories that are blessed in war, but defeats! Victories are necessary for governments, defeats — for the people. Victories breed a desire for more victories; after a defeat a man wants freedom — and usually achieves it. Defeats are necessary for peoples, just as suffering and misfortunes are necessary for individuals.

He illustrates this argument by claiming that the victory over the Swedes at Poltava was a misfortune for the Russians since it led to two centuries of tension, impoverishment of the people, unfreedom and new wars, while it was a blessing for the Swedes who became the freest and most prosperous and peaceful people in Europe. Similarly, the victory over Napoleon deferred the liberation of the serfs by some fifty years and had so much strengthened the monarchy that it had no difficulty in smashing the Decembrist Revolt — while defeats in the Crimean war, the Russo–Japanese war, and World War I brought certain freedoms and the revolutions in their wake. Is this reasoning defeatism? Can such statements be interpreted, as they have been, as contempt for his own people? Or is it a new blend of seemingly incompatible precepts by Tolstoy and Dostoevsky?

It is not impossible that there are factual inaccuracies and even grave errors in the book: indeed it would be short of miraculous were it not so in a work of such dimensions and if one remembers the conditions under which the author had gathered his material together. The important thing is whether or not the book has its own inner consistency and truth. To quote again from Solzhenitsyn's Nobel Prize lecture: 'a work of art carries in itself its own checking system. Strained, invented concepts do not withstand the image test.'

The reader of *Arkhipelag Gulag* is carried away by the convincing eloquence, the passionate concern for the humiliated and the injured. It reads as though it has 'drawn upon the truth' and it is presented to us 'in live concentrated form'. The piling up of argument upon argument, one horrifying example upon another, of emphasis and hyperbole, is closely knit with the passionately experienced content. The rhythm of exhortation, indignation and argument is now and again interrupted by lyrical digressions. For example, here is a young 'traitor's' inner monologue: 'Motherland? The cursed, the unjust and yet such a dear Motherland. Pardon? So that one could go back to his family? And walk along the Kamennoostrovsky bridge? Well, why not, after all we are Russians! Forgive us, let us return and we shall be so good, so good!' The 'traitor' gives himself up upon a promise of pardon, but he receives no mercy and is sent to a labour camp, and Solzhenitsyn comments: 'Thus irrevocably a man yields to the temptation of a "wisp of smoke" from his native land. Like an aching tooth that remains sensitive until the nerve is taken out, so we never fail to respond to our country's call until we swallow arsenic.'

The words 'wisp of smoke' are redolent of literary associations. Every literate Russian knows the Griboedov line which means that the Russians so love their native land that they find sweetness and delight even in the smoke of its chimneys. Turgenev extended the metaphor in one of his major novels and a Soviet novelist used the same device. Solzhenitsyn time and again refers to this stubborn love toward the unkind Motherland; as for instance in his exquisite prose poem about the ants returning to their death on a burning log. He defines his own attitude to Russia by identifying himself with Lieutenant Shmit's lines from Pasternak's fine poem: 'For thirty years I had carried love for my country in my heart . . .' He shows this love indirectly by his censure of Russian émigré writers — the Nobel prize-winner Bunin, Nabokov, Aldanov, Amphiteatrov: 'How could they have frittered away their priceless liberty! Writing about a woman's body, passionate embraces, sunsets, beautiful dainty heads of young maidens, dusty anecdotes — how could they have done anything but devote their energies to writing about their unfortunate native land?'

The impact of *Arkhipelag Gulag* upon Western readers will depend largely on the translators. The relentless catalogue of iniquities will provide ample material for the enemies of the Soviet Union. But the book was written for Russians. Its greatest literary asset and its greatest strength and conviction lie in its language: clear, direct, rich in literary associations, enriched by concentration-camp jargon, combining the vocabulary of a contemporary urban community with that of the toilers of the 'virgin soil'; the constitution, the Bible, the technicalities of the law courts, prison slang, and philosophical speculation. It is the language of a man who has achieved inner freedom and whose speech comes freely and from the heart.

The sections that will naturally appeal most are those few in which the author speaks directly of his own experiences — how he was arrested, how his brave commander shook his hand at the risk to his own safety, how he failed to call for help when led by guards through the streets of Moscow, why he 'loved' his first prison cell, his first speech with a young Soviet man who believed in God, and so on. But whether speaking personally or on behalf of millions, Solzhenitsyn speaks directly and insistently to the reader. With Tolstoyan relentlessness he penetrates layers of misunderstandings, excuses, rationalizations, lies; he reveals, accuses, appeals to conscience, to good sense, driving home the lesson of universal responsibility. His book is a voice speaking to humanity. And the message might well prove to be epoch-making for the entire world.

Chekhov's heroes were fond of speculating on what would happen to their native land in twenty/forty years' time; could they have possibly believed that thirty-one varieties of torture would be introduced within forty years, taking their society back into the Dark Ages? The shattering revelations of *Arkhipelag Gulag* are not new to the West; but there remained among 'the faithful' a lingering hope that conditions were being grossly exaggerated by the Western press, that it was all part of Cold War propaganda; and there was the revulsion against association with professional anti-Communists who took positive joy in Soviet failures and who hated the Russian people as well as its government. Solzhenitsyn speaks with sympathy of the generation of Russian migrants who grew up in the West, accepting their life's values from the Russian classics. These people loved their native land, idealized conditions in the Soviet Union and were prepared to die for it, despite the precepts and experiences of their own fathers. For them especially this book makes infinitely sad reading.

On 12 February 1974, while waiting for his arrest, Alexander Solzhenitsyn released a letter to his compatriots through *samizdat* (the 'underground' press), showing that there *is* a way.

Solzhenitsyn is *not* advocating the forceful overthrow of the Soviet régime, not even an introduction of 'democracy' for fear that that would merely lead to a 'melancholy repetition of 1917'. He advocates the implementation of the existing law and constitution and the original practice of the Soviets. He asks the government to have the courage to give certain freedoms to the artist and the ordinary man and he asks this ordinary Soviet citizen to have enough courage not to take part, any longer, in any lies.

> Let each one decide that from this day on he will not write or assign or print any remarks, not one phrase that in his opinion distorts the truth. Not a phrase — neither in private conversation, nor in public. Let him not lie in his own words nor according to printed instruction, neither in his rôle as an agitator, a teacher, an educator, nor an actor. Neither in painting nor sculpture, in photography, through technical media, through music — let him not portray or echo or relay any false ideas, any distortion of truth that he recognizes himself. Let him not quote either orally or in writing anything in order to please, to ensure his own safety or the success of his work, if he does not fully share the ideas he quotes or if they are not strictly relevant. Let him not force himself to take part in any demonstration or meeting if they go against his own wish or will. Let him not raise his hand to vote for something he does not sincerely sympathize with. Let him not vote either openly or in secret for a person he considers unworthy or about whom he has doubts. Let him not allow himself to be forced to come to a meeting where it is expected that the discussion will be compulsory and distorted. Let him leave a meeting, a lecture, a theatrical performance, a film the moment he hears the speakers lie or utter ideological nonsense or shameless propaganda. Let him not subscribe to or buy an issue of a newspaper or a journal which gives distorted information and hides essential facts.

Alexander Solzhenitsyn believes almost literally in the old Russian proverb: 'One word of truth shall outweigh all the rest of the world'; and he illustrates in his own life and work how 'irresistible is the power of unarmed truth and the attraction of its example'.

Jim Davidson

Judith Brett

Jenny Lee

Part Six
The New Brigade

By the second half of 1973 Clem Christesen was in poor health and thoroughly worn out by the constant strain of producing issue after issue of the magazine. He began to look around for a potential successor, and raised the question of establishing some kind of company or trust, with university support, to take over the ownership of the magazine. He eventually invited Jim Davidson, a promising young history postgraduate studying in England, to succeed him as editor.

The changeover occurred under difficult circumstances. Economic times were hard, with the first international oil crisis producing a surge in inflation and unemployment. The political climate, too, was deteriorating. After coming to power with such fanfare, the Whitlam government barely survived the elections of May 1974. The forces of reform seemed to be back on the defensive, and much too soon. The sense of disappointment and disorientation on the liberal left was palpable. And, in spite of all Christesen's efforts to develop a new constituency for *Meanjin* among the generation of '68, the magazine was struggling to survive. Financially it was incurring regular losses. Within the literary world, its longevity had become a liability; by virtue of its sheer survival, *Meanjin* was instantly identified as part of the 'establishment'. The review pages of the major newspapers tended to treat the magazine as an obscure variety of academic esoterica, if they took notice of it at all.

Christesen envisaged that Jim Davidson would serve an apprenticeship on the production side, working as a kind of associate editor for several months. This was probably a mistake. It was never going to be easy for the old hand to pass his life's work over to anyone else, and there were no clear guidelines specifying just how far the new editor would be responsible for determining the content of the magazine in the interim. Day-to-day contact exacerbated the differences between the two. Eventually the situation erupted in an open conflict that involved virtually everyone associated with *Meanjin*, leaving the magazine's hereditary enemies to chortle on the sidelines.

But Jim Davidson's editorship soon transcended its inauspicious beginnings. Like his predecessor, he had a nose for a good story. He quickly showed that he was no fly-by-night opportunist, but a talented editor who was prepared to put all his energies into the magazine. His principal work, and the hardest task of all, was to establish a new constituency without losing the old.

Making *Meanjin* Survive

JIM DAVIDSON

(Interview by Jenny Lee, 12 June 1990)

JL: What ideas did you have for *Meanjin* when you got there?
JD: I suppose I was aware that the journal to some degree had lost its position. A lot of that was inevitable. It had identified and promoted that

great wave which came to prominence during the forties: A. D. Hope, Judith Wright, James McAuley. On that basis it had been able to be totally open to people like Vin Buckley and others who emerged during the fifties, and to survive both the onslaught of the Petrov Commission and the emergence of *Quadrant*. But once we got to the Vietnam period and immediately after, it couldn't respond to the new circumstances quickly enough.

A lot of things in Australia changed decisively in the mid-sixties. I'm old enough to remember that, when I went to university, intelligent young men — and women too, probably — were basically determined to be as old as they could as soon as they could: they were identifying with their elders. All that changed in the mid-sixties. You had a youth culture that was not only new, but hostile. And this was the first significant new wave for almost a full generation. *Meanjin* had to be redefined or possibly go under, because it was losing touch with this whole wave of energy which was not only cultural, but also political and Whitlamite.

Another thing I was conscious of was that Australia was still, to use a term I coined at the time, being de-dominionized. It was a former British dominion which had never created a confident high-cultural structure for itself. We were not yet, in any real sense, culturally self-sustaining. It seemed to me that it would be useful to have a journal which would discuss ideas across a broad spectrum, with a view to trying to create a sense of the culture exploring itself, but also constantly adapting things from overseas. Australia might possibly become its own metropolis, or at least have a firm geocentric grip on the world.

It was still a wee bit too early for multiculturalism; feminism then was much smaller than it is now. But all those things, including the Aborigines a bit later, were part of a new Australian ethos that would eventually go beyond de-dominionization, and throw off the shackles created by a culture which was still partly marking off from Britain. But in the early seventies you could say that it still was a national problem. Part of the success of the last twenty years is that to speak of things in terms of 'Australian' this and 'Australian' that is not very fruitful any more; indeed, sometimes it seems that the world is flat and ends fifty miles north of Darwin.

In the early seventies it was different. There were still so many things appearing in Australia for the first time — or levels of expertise being reached and significant contributions being made, even in international fields, also for the first time. These were the kind of things I was conscious of. It seems to me that every editor has to refashion *Meanjin* a bit, but then there really was a lot of refashioning that had to be done.

JL: What sort of individuals are you thinking of there? Who did you have to set out to get back into the magazine?

JD: The first thing I had to do was get the writers back on side — people like Frank Moorhouse, who was crucial and really quite open-minded. In May 1974 I went along to a festival at the University of Melbourne where he attacked *Meanjin* — not realizing I was in the audience, because he didn't know me from Adam. I went up to him afterwards and said 'Psst, hey, mister, want a dirty magazine?' He looked at me, and I said, 'I've reason to believe I might be the next editor of *Meanjin*.'

JL: What about the journal's relationship with popular and mass culture?

JD: When I hear the words 'popular culture', I reach for my pop gun. I think the misfortune of Australia, in many ways, is that we did not succeed in fully indigenizing a high culture before the present emphasis on mass culture really got under way. I would have liked there to have been two generations of Whitlamism, to establish some sense of structures and traditions, which might then be assailed and overturned. But we never really had them in place. It's as though we never quite succeeded in de-Anglicizing enough of our high culture, and much of the rest just collapsed. It's a pity that we didn't start doing it earlier. If we had got as far in the fifties as we did in the early seventies, that would have been fine. The Whitlam period was the only time when there was any sense of government and intelligent opinion putting their shoulders behind an Australian high culture. And it was very short.

The combination of popular culture and multiculturalism, while in the end it may be fruitful, in the short run is culturally confusing. The present mood, to some degree from necessity, is so deconstructionist that it's very hard to see exactly what the next step will be. There have to be some givens for a creative cultural climate.

In France and England there was a confident high culture to deconstruct: here there was very little. So little that the children of migrants from the Peloponnese are conscious of being Greek, often aware of a Periclean heritage, and see Australian culture as a nullity, a thing of football, meat pies and *Crocodile Dundee*. Not of Patrick White (who writes insightfully of their homeland) or a glorious line of opera singers (which they don't have).

JL: You put together some interesting special issues. The Aboriginal issue in particular was breaking a lot of new ground, and then there were also the New Guinea and women's issues.

JD: Yes, that was an interesting example of how the women's movement was still low-key in a way, because although it was International Women's Year, it didn't cross anybody's mind to criticize me, as a male, for editing the issue on the women's movement. Today that would be totally impossible, and undesirable. Although the women's movement was quite up-front, it was still very much a sectional interest — it's too vast to be called that now. And a lot of women were very glad that *Meanjin* was doing it; certainly it was the only literary magazine that did.

The New Guinea issue arose out of something else. I had been interested in New Guinea ever since my father had taken me up there as a kid. It struck me that the place would not have the resources to put out an issue like that itself. For Australia's premier literary magazine to put out an issue which would come out on the day of Independence would be a nice symbolic act: a copy was handed to Michael Somare on the day. Not only was it current for 1975 when it appeared, but it also had the value of being a kind of time capsule: this is what New Guinea looked like at the moment Australia withdrew.

JL: How conscious were you of the subscribers?
JD: Certainly a thing like the Papua-New Guinea issue really did presume on the subscribers' goodwill. Fortunately they all knew why it was there, because Australia's biggest colony was becoming independent. But I was terrified of losing the old subscribers before gaining new ones. It was obvious to everybody that *Meanjin* was going to change. Things had to be done slowly. It took me nearly three years to be able to get to the new format, and that was the point at which the revolution was more or less complete.

One of the things that you become aware of is that, once you start to make changes, then others become possible. It becomes like contour ploughing. Certain things you never dreamt you'd change get called into question, and go.
JL: What led you to do your issue on Sydney versus Melbourne?
JD: It's a non-problem now, thank goodness: partly a result of the Cain Government's real push in the arts, and the advent of Greiner and the astronomical cost of housing in Sydney, so that some Sydneysiders are now coming here. But in 1979–80 there was a real morale problem in this town. It was absurd, a city of three million having so little confidence in itself. People were going to Sydney, much as they had gone to London twenty years before. It wasn't just David Williamson; there was a general sense that Melbourne was dull and dated, and had really lost its way. It suddenly occurred to me that, since *Meanjin* had a fortieth anniversary, it would be a terrific idea to have a conference — which *Meanjin* could do because it could call on people right across the spectrum — to discuss the ways in which Sydney and Melbourne were different, and also address the question of the undertow. So that was the beginning of the 'St Petersburg or Tinsel Town?' conference, which got a lot of publicity and eventually ended up as a book.
JL: Did you work on one issue at a time, or did you work forward to any notable extent?
JD: Generally not much more than an issue or two at a time. I'm probably not as efficient as you, but I had also been out of the country for six of the previous seven years. At the beginning I felt that I could be caught out. I hadn't any sense of where the movements were, the long-term shifts, and where the sources of energy were located. When I walked into a performance of *Brumby Innes* at the Pram Factory, it was a complete mystery to me as to how that production had come about. So there were a lot of things I had to learn, and rather smartly. I had to make *Meanjin* survive. I didn't want it to disappear into the English Department; I didn't want it to be too identified with the Pram Factory or with Carlton. I wanted it to re-emerge in its own right. So that meant that I had to extend a presence, go to a lot of conferences, theatre, and just generally be seen about.
JL: How far did you see it as being a Victorian presence, and how far a national one?
JD: I always saw it as being a national one. The two great allies I had were Frank Moorhouse and Humphrey McQueen. I had quite a high profile in Sydney, where Moorhouse was very important. He was in some ways the

most professional writer there: involved with the Australian Society of Authors, with copyright, with film and television, and he was much closer to the newspaper world then — so he was a very good ally to have. By 1977–78, when I went to Sydney I would not only go to English Departments, but also to the ABC, where I was very friendly with Allan Ashbolt, and talk to producers and so on. I would also spend some time with young people who were redrafting their first article. I went to Sydney at least three times a year; trying to create a sense of people not being terribly surprised if I suddenly turned up somewhere.

I used that strategy with the Literature Board, too. I would turn up with sufficient frequency so that people knew me, while also trading on my out-of-town-ness. All of that was very necessary, because in 1976 there was still quite a bit of opposition to *Meanjin*. A person who will remain nameless took a measuring stick to it and decided that it didn't have enough short stories and poetry, and I was summoned to an interview with the Board. Actually, the police got in first. A few days before, I was picked up off the street as a suspicious-looking character: my greatest fear during this bizarre experience was that I'd be stuck with a false murder charge, while poor old *Meanjin* was slaughtered in Sydney.

There was constant pressure and a lot of people, particularly in Sydney, were sceptical about whether *Meanjin* could be saved. It was an overwhelmingly Sydnitic Board, and it was very hostile. I had a mock-up of the new format, and I took that along, and that seemed to win them over. I think they just wanted to be sure that *Meanjin* was going to change.

JL: What was your sequence of poetry editors?

JD: The poetry editor when I walked in was Paul Fahey, and I asked him to stay. In 1975 I appointed Kris Hemensley, and I did that partly as a sign to the people of '68 that things were changing and that *Meanjin* was open to all sorts of influences. Kris was good for *Meanjin* at that time. But I did make a mistake in that I didn't appoint him for a fixed term, as I did his successors.

The poetry editorship *should* change. I came to the view very quickly that poets are basically Balkan chieftains, constantly fighting one another, and that each one believes that the others are the biggest rogues in the entire universe. There's nothing you can do about it, except seal off the whole area as a kind of national park, and in the meantime play the sorcerer's apprentice when the mail comes in — for there's no end to bad poetry. You must shove your head over the fence from time to time to see what they're up to, and make sure that the knives aren't going in too deeply between the shoulder-blades. Because you do bear ultimate responsibility, and you will find that *Meanjin* is discussed in poetry circles and poetry magazines as if it only existed to print poetry. The poets have this delusion that they are the Union Jack in the corner of the flag.

Since it was basically going to be a mess no matter what you did, the important thing was to get a known poet who had their own reputation at stake, and make them park ranger for three years. And that's basically the system that's been adopted since. It's not a bad one, because it has its own in-built corrective. After Kris Hemensley, the poetry editor was Judith

Rodriguez. She would come up with twelve pages and, when we got together, I would choose ten. She worked at it very diligently.
JL: What were your arrangements with the fiction?
JD: Peter Pierce and Arthur Phillips read it, and I would choose the pieces for publication. But I actually read all the stories, partly because I liked to, and because I felt the need to keep an eye on what was being said. *Meanjin* rejection slips have always provided comments to would-be contributors.
JL: What was your relationship with the university?
JD: The university basically exists as a cultural manufactory, to use a wonderful eighteenth-century term. Or, to be more contemporary, Accaland is the intellectual Safeways. It doesn't like culture too much in the raw. While Lynne Strahan was employed classifying the *Meanjin* archives, she was paid a salary considerably larger than mine. So I drew the only logical inference: the University of Melbourne believed that the only good *Meanjin* was a dead *Meanjin*. But if we had not had the support of university people like Ray Marginson, John Poynter and Geoff Serle, there's no doubt *Meanjin* would have been closed ages ago. It was basically their personal enthusiasm which resulted in money being found to supplement the Lockie Grant's portion of the editorial salary, which dwindled further every year. But it is nevertheless a fact that right up until the late seventies it was still the result of an annual vote. I had security of tenure 'subject to financial viability'. So there was not really security of tenure as academics understand the word at all.
JL: Was there ever an active push within the university to shut the journal down?
JD: I was told on one occasion that I would be the last editor of *Meanjin*, and I thought, not bloody likely. Can you imagine a bigger albatross hanging around your neck than that? One of the greatest anxieties of any editor of *Meanjin* is about passing the torch on, because any closure would be seen as basically your fault.

When the time came, I worded up people at the *Age* that I was going to resign and that the University might try to close it down. But by then things had changed a bit, and Serle took the very proper line that it wasn't the University's prerogative, but a matter for the Meanjin Company to determine. After due consultation the job was advertised, and that was that.
JL: How did the shift in government affect *Meanjin*?
JD: By the end of '77 Fraserism had got into its stride, and a lot of academics were very depressed. The kind of free-wheeling intellectual inquiry which had been going on in the Whitlam years to some degree ceased. Partly it had been replaced by greater professionalism, but I think part of that was also that people were abandoning public issues for the pursuit of their own careers.

Another thing that has to be said is that during the Whitlam era the newspapers were much better. The *Age* now is a disgrace. Gorbachev can be meeting Bush, but day after day parochial issues hog the headlines. Having a good newspaper is terribly important, because if it is a centre of intellectual activity in the sense of being serious-minded and having a nice sense of curiosity and a certain freshness, it can prompt *Meanjin* articles, and perhaps five years later they in turn might lead to a book. But once you have a paper as bland as the *Age* has now become, then the whole system has been dealt a mortal blow.

JL: I have a nuts-and-bolts question. I'm interested in the craft of editing, and I think one of the really interesting things about *Meanjin* over the years is that there is a strong tradition of interventionist editing. At times you were a very interventionist editor — which is exactly what you accuse me of being!

JD: I used to think that there was one article an issue which involved log-rolling. In other words, there was often a subject that you wanted an article on, but the prospective author may not have had much experience at writing, certainly not at *Meanjin* standard. But if you wanted somebody to write on community arts or women's theatre, and it was important that they be in there, then you were prepared to put in any amount of work to make it possible. There came a point, though, after they'd had a couple of goes, when you had to say: 'Right. This is now under President's rule. Give it here, and I'll do it, and show it to you, and get your approval.' So they're the ones where I'm conscious of having been extremely interventionist, but it wasn't as if those articles came fully fledged. They were by people who were not writers. I still think that this was a useful thing to do, even if both parties ended up feeling like the Assyrian lioness in the British Museum, dragging its carcass along with all those arrows in its bum.

In most issues there would have been one or two articles where I didn't change a word. I always felt that it was better to slightly under-edit. There should always be an element of giving the author the benefit of the doubt. After all, there was a sense of the journal being a contest of voices; there was no house style.

JL: One of the great allegations made about *Meanjin* is that it's just a postbox — that all you are doing is sorting the mail and putting one half into a pile to be sent to be published, and the other into a pile to be rejected.

JD: Well, that's not true. It's always had a very strong entrepreneurial side. I was constantly trying to find people who could write articles.

JL: What percentage of the journal would the entrepreneurial articles have taken up?

JD: It would have varied, but I think that overall at least fifty per cent would have been articles that I had directly commissioned. In addition, I used to say that if I got the sack, then in my last issue I'd put all my editorial emendations in red: it would have been a nice little demonstration of how much invisible mending had gone on. Because, needless to say, one of the big shocks you get when you go to *Meanjin*, or are involved in any editorial job, is the sudden horrendous discovery of just how badly most writers write. While you don't seriously indulge the fantasy that because you are a re-writer you must be twice as good, there are times when you could be forgiven for thinking so. In fact, editing is a different kind of mind-set. Certain people can be brilliant editors, yet not write very well — or at least not with much originality.

JL: The other thing that you introduced was the interviews, which were quite an innovation for *Meanjin*.
JD: Although there had been the *Makar* series a little earlier, I think I can say that most literary interviews in Australia really relate back to that series. Certain things have now become impossible. *Australian Literary Studies* was then publishing interviews that were two years old: nobody would dream of doing that now. The whole business of exchanging drafts with the author, putting the date on it, based on the *Paris Review* model, did help to raise the standard of interviewing generally.

I did them for another reason, too, in that it seemed to be a good way of having an editorial presence without writing editorials. At that stage it still took about four weeks for the magazine to appear from the date when copy closed. Having felt initially that I had missed out on so much recent Australian experience, I didn't feel very happy about prognosticating. Besides, any writing for *Meanjin* should be of the highest possible standard. So I thought that this was one way of giving people a sense of who was presiding over this journal, through having a conversation with other people. Later I did write one or two long articles, for which I was criticised. But I think that it is good for people to have a sense of what you are capable of. It's a false and limited idea of integrity to presume that you shouldn't publish your own stuff.

Particularly when they came out as a book, those interviews were often criticized for the fact that the interviewer was very present in them. But that was actually the intention: I suppose I should have called them conversations. And I think they worked that way, helping to give some kind of cohesion to those issues from the second issue of '77 onwards, even if only for me.
JL: How did you view your editorial responsibility?
JD: The feeling I had was one of tremendous responsibility. *Meanjin* is a job without cruising speed. It may have changed a bit, but I doubt it. You never knew if you were going to be ignored, relegated to the margins of everybody's existence. It was possible to put out a whole issue and have nobody give you any response at all. That happened once or twice — and they weren't the worst issues, either. Or you could open up the paper and learn that Manning Clark had been attacked in Parliament, and so 'Are we a nation of bastards?' from the last issue of '75 ended up being written into Hansard. A novel form of distribution, but one from which *Meanjin* received very little benefit. As Anthony Trollope said when confronting President Brand of the Orange Free State, 'He has an exact appreciation of both the highness and the lowness of the position he has been called upon to occupy.' Well, a *Meanjin* editor doesn't have that sense at all. You are really just a cork bobbing up and down on the ocean, or the custodian of an adventure playground about which everybody has fantasies. That can be a bit tiresome.

Number 4, 1975

The Mexico International Women's Year Conference

LAURIE BEBBINGTON

. . . The International Year of the Woman was celebrated with ritual and solemnity in the humidity and debilitating altitude of a Mexican June. The definitive symbol of womanhood — a mother and child supported by the wings of a United Nations eagle — towered above the celebrants; thus, utilising woman's greatest strength as her greatest weakness, feminist vision was frustrated and limited as delegates to the World Conference and Tribune were kept firmly within the realms of patriarchal possibility. For there were, in fact, two gatherings convened simultaneously by the United Nations in Mexico. The World Conference was attended by Government delegations from most member nations, together with observers from non-government organisations affiliated with the UN. The International Women's Year Tribune, however, was attended by non-Government organisations and interested individuals.

The World Conference was held at Tlateloco, the site of the 1968 massacre of hundreds of students, intellectuals and workers by the army in the last public protest against poverty and political repression in Mexico. Repression is still severe: kidnapping by police, interrogation, torture and death are regularly meted out to alleged dissidents. However, the Mexican Government is greatly concerned with maintaining a world image as a progressive and enlightened regime, so formulates advanced policies though it lacks the financial means to carry them out. In keeping with IWY, the Government created a number of Mexican Women's Movements to give the impression that the Mexican woman's status is really changing — and also to keep the eyes of the world away from scrutinising Mexican politics and the enormous problems facing most Mexican women. In a city where 1,600,000 abortions are performed each year, and 50 per cent of the female workers are domestic servants working under a Federal Labour Law which allows 'enough time to rest in order to take their meals and sleep during the night', an expensive and elaborate façade is indeed necessary.

The Mexican Government was not alone, however, in its deception concerning the status of its women. Listening to delegates from the many members of the United Nations present at the World Conference left one sincerely wondering why a year to improve the status of women was necessary at all. It appeared that women had enjoyed equality with men in most eastern bloc nations since 1945, while the USA had pioneered both the Equal Rights Amendment and legal abortion. Neither these nor other nations could imagine what else women might require, except to join with men in the struggle against 'imperialism, colonialism, neo-colonialism, foreign occupation, alien domination, racism and apartheid'. Equality, Development and Peace could not be far off!

Fortunately for women, the prevailing air of comfortable self-congratulation was shattered by the forthright feminism of the Australian delegation. The only delegation with a brief from its government which allowed complete honesty, Australia's performance was regarded as outstanding by delegates at both the Conference and Tribune — a fact the Australian Press managed to entirely overlook.

Prompted by anger and frustration, Elizabeth Reid, in her speech to the Conference, called for an honest discussion of the problems facing women throughout the world and the right of women themselves to discuss these problems and find solutions. She analysed the problems facing women in terms of 'sexism' — 'the artificial ascription of roles, behaviour and even personalities to people on the basis of their sex *alone*'. She charged that in our patriarchal society, women are colonised by mute consent. The subtlety of this colonialisation demands a reworking of old solutions to oppression in order that they include women.

Reviewing the three goals of International Women's Year — Equality, Development and Peace — Elizabeth Reid asked for a redefinition of each before they would mean any real change in the lives of women. In discussing Development, she pointed out that traditional Western concepts were unacceptable as future goals because they were often dehumanising and oppressive. In many developed countries the personal has been made a female province, and yet 'women have been deprived of the economic and political power necessary to destroy the dichotomy between the personal and the political, the home and the work place'. True development could only be achieved if the experiences of women, as well as of men, were listened to and used as a basis for decision. In discussing the next goal, Peace, Elizabeth Reid drew a distinction between violence among the nations and violence within societies. Discussions of peace usually focus on the former; it is the latter which probably affects most women more closely. Much to the delight of the assembled female delegates, she went on to list types of physical violence against women — rape, immolation, forced sterilisation, indecent assault, infibulation, unwanted pregnancy, clitorectomy, unnecessary surgery, wife beating and shackling. Mental violence, such as 'the labelling and treating as deviant any women who in any way does not act out accepted roles', the lack of recognition of women's work in the home, and the abuses of psychiatrists who resort to shock treatment and brain surgery against women were all condemned. Finally, Elizabeth Reid questioned the value of 'Equality':

> Equality is a limited and possibly harmful goal. Associated with the struggle for equality have been some needed and just reforms . . . But we can no longer delude ourselves with the hope that formal equality, once achieved, will eradicate sexist oppression — it could well merely legitimise it.

In spite of the efforts of the Australian delegation and the general assent to Elizabeth Reid's speech, the World Conference was incapable of becoming a feminist conference of true benefit to women. This is best illustrated by glancing briefly at the Conference's major document, the World Plan of

Action. Based upon the principles of Equality, Development and Peace, the Plan provides guidelines and principles for international, regional, and national action to ensure equality and full integration of women in development over the next decade. Its purpose is to stimulate action which will 'solve the problems of underdevelopment and socio-economic structure which place women in an inferior position'. But as a programme setting out to improve the conditions of women's lives, the World Plan of Action fails dismally. It is a paternalistic and jargonistic document which foists a compulsory parenthood on all women, who are continually seen as reproductive animals and as part of a family rather than as individuals. This is its greatest flaw. For in accepting without question the present female role as homemaker/child-rearer for *all* women, the Plan seeks to improve existing conditions, while failing totally to envisage the changes away from this role which many women are already making. . . .

A large section of the World Conference spent many days agonising over this, the major instrument of the Conference and the United Nations in its 'great leap forward' in policy-making on women. Many delegates to the Tribune also considered the document important: important enough, that is, to occupy a major part of the energy of the Feminist Caucus, who set themselves the task of rewriting the Plan in the hope of rendering it more realistic and useful for bringing about change for women. The Feminist Caucus's twenty-eight pages of amendments to the Plan were presented to, and ratified by, 2000 women at a special session of the Tribune. It is not surprising that the women at the Tribune, from all parts of the world, felt they had something to say to the World Conference which had relevance to its deliberations; however, the delegation sent by the Tribune was not permitted to address the Conference. The World Plan of Action remained as it was — untouched by ordinary, non-governmental female hand.

While the official delegations were experiencing difficulty producing a plan of which the main feature was a confused conservatism, the non-aligned developing countries published a remarkable document entitled the Declaration of Mexico, 1975. This document could well serve as a model for the World Plan of Action, as it contains the sort of progressive, feminist statements the United Nations seemed incapable of making.

The Declaration of Mexico, 1975, recognised that all women, regardless of their differences, share the painful experience of oppression, and that this determines the revolutionary potential of women as a group. The Declaration assumed that the problems of women are the problems of society as a whole. Thus, changes in their present economic, political and social situation must become an integral part of efforts to transform the structures and attitudes which hinder the genuine satisfaction of their needs. The Declaration also proclaimed a number of basic principles among which certain are outstanding, given the cultural background of the non-aligned developing nations. These include the assertion that women and men have equal rights and responsibilities within the family, and thus men must play a greater role in family life. Other principles included the right of women to choose whether or not to marry, and whether to bear children.

The Declaration emphasised that the issue of inequality was closely linked to the economic structures of nations and of the 'profoundly unjust world economic system'. It proposed the New Economic Order, a world-view of the economic situation supported by the developing countries, as a replacement for the present individualistic, capitalist approaches which benefit only developed nations. The New Economic Order emphasises a strong but non-aggressive nationalism in the form of strict adherence to the principle of the sovereign rights of states. It seeks an economic equality between all nations, through full and permanent sovereign control of natural resources; an international division of labour according to the specific abilities of each nation; income-sharing between nations in order that poorer nations could attain certain basic standards, while the wealthier ones restrained their own enrichment and sacrificed certain profits; and finally, control of international corporations. In this way the developing countries believe that the problems of oppressed peoples in general could be solved, and even those of women in particular.

It was the Latin American women at the Tribune who re-emphasised the need to look at women's problems as stemming partly from economic exploitation. They pointed out that the present Latin American economic, social, political and cultural structures were dependent and alienating. At the moment, solutions being presented to women were sexist and oppressive. For instance, population control was imposed on certain nations and races, compulsory sterilisation taking place without the knowledge or consent of the women concerned. Latin American women demanded the right to make decisions concerning their own lives; it was apparent that Western 'sisterhood' would have to be far less culturally dominating and more concrete in its understanding of the basic necessities of life before it could be relevant to Third World women. Even so, the Latin American Women's Caucus was already very 'feminist' in the Western sense. They did not regard their liberation purely as an economic question. But their analysis reflects a sophistication born of an economic and cultural reality of foreign domination which few of the Western women's movements have had to face.

Perhaps what is most interesting are the implications for the Australian Left of the level of analysis evident among Third World women. The Left in Australia, up till now, has been able to point to the insular and bourgeois nature of the Australian Women's Movement as a justification for rejecting the feminist analysis of society. But its attempt to invalidate the Women's Movement has in turn deprived the Left of a major energy source, in the form of the majority of its female support. More than that, the discounting of the feminist critique has blinded it from considering the psycho-social as well as the economic aspects of oppression. Men in the Left have often refused to tackle their own sexism and the intrinsically patriarchal and sexist nature of their organisations, their excuse being the nature of the 'revolutionary struggles of the Third World'. In the light of the critiques that emerged at Mexico, such protestations have a ludicrous solemnity about them: Australian Left groups which are more able to fight the problems of the Third World than our own are suffering from a misplaced identity. And there is no longer respite, not even in the mists of some far-off revolution, from angry women demanding personal as well as political change. . . .

By means of the International Women's Year World Conference and Tribune, the Mexican Government was able to maintain its progressive image and the collective conscience of the United Nations was assuaged. The World Plan of Action will join other UN instruments as a much-quoted but ineffective document. It stands for equality without liberation for the world's women, 'a limited and possibly harmful goal', commented Elizabeth Reid, 'merely legitimising sexist oppression'. All nations can honestly support the United Nations' policy on change for women, because of the limitations of this change; much of it would have occurred anyway, in the natural course of trends toward 'development'. The basic assumptions concerning the role and potential of women remain unchallenged.

Meanwhile the International Year of the Woman is drawing to a close. Marked by the continual frustration of petty promises broken, along with grandiose statements accrediting politicians with the discovery of women's 'inferior' status, it would better have been baptised the Year of the Whimper. Now that world Governments have discovered what women have known for some time, the depth of their unwillingness to deal effectively with the issues raised is a measure of the degree to which the liberation of women threatens existing power structures.

Jim Davidson to Harry Heseltine

15 October 1976

The mantle of Clem may now be said to have well and truly fallen upon me — Maurice Dunlevy has fanged *Meanjin* in the *Canberra Times* and the Libs have had a go at it in Parliament. But there's one respect in which it hasn't — I'm a lousy correspondent.

I feel rather guilty about that as far as we're concerned, for you were kind at the time of transition, and on those rare occasions I've seen you since. (Xavier's Farewell was certainly a 'rare' occasion!) Somehow I don't seem to have been able to get up to Sydney nearly as much as I would have liked. And living at the centre of the universe as you do, we never see you here.

The IAC has moved on to fresh fields and conquests new with its Publishing Inquiry, which sits in Syd. next week. I'm interested to see which wins out in the report, its crude nationalism or even cruder economics: time alone will tell. I must say I found the hearing quite terrifying, and was totally unprepared for a courtroom situation. My few flippancies went down like those of Dr Goebbels at Nuremberg. . . .

Otherwise *Meanjin* survives, and perhaps moderately prospers. There's even a vague prospect of something coming from P. White; and of a new look (oops, we've had one of those already) a new format in the New Year — smaller, *Paris Review* style. (Did some unkind person whisper *Southerly*?) Apart from being easier to handle and looking more like a book — and *M* after all sells in *book*shops — it is apparently a lot cheaper to print that way, in that size. So fingers crossed. Hope all goes well with you and yours.

Number 1, 1977

After Many a Summer: The 'Doll' Trilogy

JACK HIBBERD

Saturday, February the 12th, was one of those epic Australian days. Bushfires, ignited by an infernal heat, leapt through the grazing districts of Western Victoria, plundering towns and barbecuing sheep. Floods inundated Northern Queensland. At Sandown, a champion filly, Surround, sprinted to her ninth victory in succession, whereupon the jockey and other grown men were seen to weep. Similarly, at the conclusion of *The Doll* Trilogy in Melbourne that evening, the audience rose rapturously to their feet and applauded another champion piece of Australiana.

Since 1956 *Summer of the Seventeenth Doll* has held a unique and precious place in Australia's cultural mythology. Like Nellie Melba, the *Doll* intrepidly set off overseas and conquered, forcing the world to recognise that at least once we could mix it with the best of them in the theatre. More than Errol Flynn, Bernborough or Betty Cuthbert, this made us feel culturally enfranchised, a nation at last instead of a colony in the Artistic Atlas.

On that Saturday we were re-living, re-savouring the genesis of that experience in an expanded form — Lawler, stimulated by the Melbourne Theatre Company's John Sumner, has now added two plays anterior to the *Doll*. We were also creating history by participating all day in a three-play saga of almost Wagnerian proportions. In making history, I had the feeling that we were simultaneously closing a parenthesis, nostalgically celebrating the end of a period. Individually, the three plays will continue to be performed and to give pleasure, but will never again exert quite the same charismatic power. The *Doll* itself will always be capable of recall in this country, for theatrical reasons alone, though such performances will be rather like the rendering of a well-loved and plangent antipodean hymn. Sitting through *Kid Stakes* and *Other Times* I was struck by the remarkable way in which Lawler had managed to faithfully reproduce the modes and style of the *Doll* — that homely four-square craftsmanship of twenty years ago. Like a skilled neo-classicist he'd been able to lovingly resurrect old forms and instil in them, with great accuracy, the character and idiosyncrasies of different historical epochs. Dramaturgical considerations aside, these plays will stand up as important records of our past, a past evoked in a fashion beyond the capacities of any historian.

Thoughts of realist Ibsen, of Tennessee Williams and Arthur Miller tumbled through my head as I watched the three plays — Ibsen without the examination of a specific moral and social theme, without the black primordial undercurrents, Williams without that luxuriant melodrama, Miller minus the earnestness and tendentiousness. The trilogy's dramaturgy is of course rooted in common territory, and adorned with familiar naturalistic techniques: off-stage sounds and activities to extend the geography of illusion, mundane domestic rituals and rhythms, the rituals of expectation and the endless flow of visitors, the bas-relief of supplementary characters, the verbalisation of sometimes trivial, sometimes crucial outside events, the rigidly located world of objects, persons and time, the denial of the stage as a stage, and one capable of populating the universe.

Paradoxically, the *Doll* achieved its popularity around the period of Brecht's death and the birth of *Waiting for Godot*, whilst Pinter and Arden were at the point of incubation. These dramatists variously abandoned the notion of theatre as a mirror or lens of life, and charged their works with unabashed theatricality or expressive individuality.

For all its archaic conventions, the *Doll* still vividly documents, among other things, a special kind of Australian heterosexual sterility, a discrepancy between the sexes — the competitive pseudo-independent male with his myths of mateship and virility; the patient passive waiting world of the female who fantasises half her life away. The *Doll* religiously reflects a lack of natural eroticism in relationships — its sexuality is all above stage (in the flies actually) and smacks of dentures in glasses of water and vaginal douches. As in the Fifties, sex is strictly taboo. Less coy perhaps in the Seventies, Lawler at least lets us know explicitly in *Kid Stakes* and *Other Times* that the couples are actually slumbering together.

The *Doll* also demonstrates that these male myths are ephemeral and destructive, that the dream worlds of the women are hollow yet awfully addictive, that Australia will only grow up when their untenability is recognised. Nancy (in the first two plays) is more practical and acute than Olive, and probably intuits this when she relinquishes Barney for wedlock with another, though what style of marriage that turns out to be we are left to imagine.

Instead of cane-cutting feats we now have GT chargers and occupational status, instead of Kewpie dolls we have dream homes and the latest deciduous mod-cons. *Summer of the Seventeenth Doll* bears witness to the decline of the Outback Legend and the burgeoning urbanisation of Australia, the replacement of the Coolgardie safe by the fridge, the drover by the commuting executive. It presages an Australia with a new face and a new set of clothes, yet one whose physiology is principally and depressingly the same.

The play also depicts our tragic lack of cultural preparation for senescence, how a narrow range of interests outside work and home appurtenances can stultify Australian lives. Roo, Olive and Barney, who have all conformed to certain limited codes of conduct, end up isolated and bereft of any supportive emotional apparatus.

That all these themes exist is in itself no mean sociological achievement.

Their very existence, however, depends on dramatic artifice — anecdotal information about Roo's diminishing powers as a mob leader and Barney's decline as a Romeo. We need to experience these processes for them to be authentically and organically precipitating. The appearance of Johnnie Dowd (Roo's rival in Queensland) later on is not enough. Lawler is trapped by his naturalistic space and time unity — the one-set exigency, the convention of a neat span of time. As a result, Roo's jealousy is theatrically unsubstantiated and rather ersatz; the fight with Barney teeters on melodrama. The last scene, a powerful piece of writing within its own terms, is nevertheless coloured by the previous manipulations and logically cannot escape overtones of bathos. . . .

For Lawler to write *Kid Stakes* and *Other Times* in the Seventies is a curious and retrograde act in relation to the contemporary development of our drama. Nevertheless, he frequently displays a generosity of feeling and a natural flair for detail that still sets a standard for our new figurative playwrights. At his best, Lawler's psychology is naturally rooted in the action and is never uncomfortably procrustean or textbook. At his worst, he can be merely domestic and mundane, even platitudinous — the accidental discovery of a letter, the token alcoholism of Nancy, the stereotyped Jewish German, and artificial after-the-event revelations such as Roo's self-sacrificing refusal to take promotion in the army, or Nancy's punishing announcement that she'd previously had an abortion, unknown to the sire Barney, and that Josef Hultz had been particularly sensitive and supportive about it all.

As a dramatist, the *Doll* has never affected me one iota. So I was quite bemused when Katharine Brisbane said to me at a break between plays that she thought a lot of the recent playwrights (whom she regularly publishes) had received too much acclaim too quickly, that on a day like this they should pay respect to their elders! I felt an upstart and whippersnapper, then reflected that she was talking from a context of venerables and the youth that should sit at their feet, rather than from a real analysis of what had happened in Australian theatre over the last ten years and its extremely tenuous connection with the Fifties.

It could feasibly be argued that Ray Lawler had been destroyed by success, a success somewhat out of proportion to substantial achievement, that he had been induced to remain outside his own society and community, an exile uniquely perilous to the naturalistic playwright. The *Piccadilly Bushman* and *The Man Who Shot the Albatross* hardly inspire respect. Respect can only be awarded to those figures and works that profoundly affect the way you think and feel about the theatre. The *Doll* Trilogy, for all its attributes, could hardly justify that status.

The immediate future of Ray Lawler almost certainly lies in the past. As a representational playwright it is going to take him some time to readjust focus on the different topography of Australia in the Seventies, if he is at all interested in such an approach. He might well be content to continue his scrutinies of those other times he knows so intimately. Deep dramaturgical advance into this century, however, would require his relinquishing many old habits and subsequently making fresh discoveries — a monumental task, though not entirely impossible when one thinks of a Jean Rhys, or even Verdi's feats after sixteen years of silence.

Number 2, 1977

Brown Paper Bag

Carolyn van Langenberg

1

Children milled in the house, laughing at me, a strange and pregnant woman lying in a dishevelled bed in the upstairs of a quivering summer-house, afraid of the violent weather, the blackened sky, the wind, the sea, its spray visible on the windows — sea pounding into my reasoned belief that the village was at least four centuries old and had never been awash in a frothing tide.

But she opened the door. She let the wind hiss through the house and around the chairs and tables and under my bed, rocking it. The wind forcing open the doors and windows. She leant over her great belly to pat a child on the head, smiled at another. So ridiculous, that great belly. She grabbed her coat and hat, and I saw her elevate and ride with the wind behind some houses in the direction of the *Huis Ter Duin*.

I struggled out of bed. The children, these centuries old children, clustered round me, their wizened faces hard-pressed against my pregnant body. They were ugly. Small and gnarled. Foetal ugliness.

I forced them back. Forced them away from me. I wanted my coat and hat. I had to follow her.

The children clung to me. Their hot breathing wetted my dress. The wind swept through the house and strengthened in gusts that sent the children reeling against the walls and furniture. Their ugly faces wrinkled with pain. The wind freed me of them.

But, as I began to walk to the esplanade, the wind tugged at me. Pulled at my legs. Tangled my clothes. Sand and ice pitted my face. I began to panic. The wind was too strong. I would lose her if I could not follow her. Then the baby inside me kicked savagely and locked across my abdomen, stopping me with pain. I held the rail of the steps to the esplanade and waited for the pain to pass, for the baby to move again. The wind was too strong, and I would have to turn back.

2

The children had left the house, and the doors and windows were shut, the furniture in place. The bed upstairs was unmade and empty. Its familiarity calmed me.

3

I fixed myself some bread and cheese, ate an apple and a pear, and drank a glass of milk. I wrote a letter home about the storm. The house was warm and, outside, disregarding the strong wind and the sleet, children were walking and cycling home from school. A neighbour's cat pushed against a window pane, curled round twice and leapt to the ground, glowering over its shoulder at the unrelenting window as it slunk across the yard. A woman across the road took her two poodles out for a walk on long leashes. A man strolled past with his glossy Great Dane . . . Framed by the curtainless glass doors of my house . . . A moving picture of suburban forms, windswept . . . I reread my letter's description of the storm, drew fresh paper towards me and wrote as follows:

4

The *Huis Ter Duin* stands above the sea which belts into the dunes under it, eats out its foundations, rages round the ballroom built over the beach for romantic European aristocrats of an era remarkable for its indifference and elegant repose. As I approach, I feel the lack of pink chiffon and a corsage of irises.

The wind drops. I walk quickly towards the house. The enormous pleasure house straddling the dunes, obvious on the height of the dunes, obvious by its blackness on the dunes. Horribly black. Stark. Its doors and windows small against the magnificence of its size.

Inside there is rubble and dampness. The sea echoes, pounds, belts, crashes under the house, frighteningly loud, shaking the structure and each step I take.

I find her there. She stands enraptured.

She knows I can see her. I see her pout and roll her eyes, coquettish and ludicrous above her belly, her fingers feathering the air. She reaches across her belly to touch the hand of a black man, a beautiful black dancing man. He throws back his head, mocking her with a silent laugh, and dances from the room.

A white man comes in. He circles the room and watches the sea from a window before he sits in a corner, at his ease, as if he were waiting for someone, or something. He does not appear to see either of us.

She has seen me. Though she has not acknowledged my presence she knows I am here. She likes to berate me with her insolence. Her free-spiritedness. And I wish I were able to blend my earthness with her gaiety. I want her to be me, an earth spirit, earth-bound, with no relief from my earth's clichéd expectations. I want her to know the small globe of madness that explodes into cruel splinters of disbelief, the pain exceeding even a body's suffering.

I hear her groan and see her face twist. She lies down on the rubble, rubbing her belly and pushing, sweat dripping from her face and through her hair. The white man sits beside her, smiles encouragement and rubs the contours of her belly. Tender. Gentle. He watches and smiles and rubs her belly, and she pushes and heaves and sweats. And when the baby crowns he begins to ease it out, carefully, without tearing her skin.

She nuzzles the baby to her breast and, after some minutes, he cuts the cord. She puts it in a brown paper bag. Then, hand in hand, they step outside the *Huis Ter Duin*. They send kisses to each other which run along the wind's currents, into the wind's force. Children gather round them, chattering loud incoherencies.

I watch them walk away over the dunes until they disappear. Behind a wall of sea, it seems. And I think I see a brown paper bag tumble on the wind. I stretch my hands across my belly and feel the baby rolling and kicking there. The weight of my body crushes my feet.

I am impatient to be her.

5

I pushed my writing aside and drank some tea. I felt a stickiness in my pants and a tightness gripping my belly. I began to feel the force of contracting muscles .

Fear of inevitable pain wracked my body terribly. Trembling with no control, unable to stop my body's fear, I called a neighbour who understood enough of my English and my terror. Her children and her dogs tripped her feet. She rang my husband and a doctor who came through the storm to the house. He sat beside me. I could see the broken vessels that coloured the white skin of his cheeks red. He sat beside me, waiting, easing the contractural pains with advice and gentleness, fatherly towards my husband when he came home from the Institute with an American companion, a tall black dancing man who slanted a smile at me before he walked through to the other room.

The baby crowned and the doctor delivered it and the neighbour washed it. They handed me a prune coloured thing rapidly changing to red, and wrapped in white. I fed it, giving myself over to a delicious primitivity, until I grasped that the voices above me were discussing the sea flooding the fields between our village by the dunes and the village below us.

Number 4, 1977

The New White Colonialism

BOBBI SYKES

I move:

That the Senate accepts the fact that the indigenous people of Australia, now known as Aborigines and Torres Strait Islanders, were in possession of this entire nation prior to the 1788 First Fleet landing at Botany Bay, urges the Australian Government to admit prior ownerships by the said indigenous people, and introduce legislation to compensate the people now known as Aborigines and Torres Strait Islanders for dispossession of their land.

Senator N. Bonner

Senator Bonner, encouraged by the Black community, proposed the above motion in the Senate hopefully as the beginning of a *real* course of action designed to bring the long-awaited 'justice' to the Black community. The motion was framed so as to spearhead an educational campaign which would, given sufficient media coverage and incorporation in school texts, etc., have effected widespread attitudinal changes in the white community.

Consider the current situation where successive Governments and also some international aid organisations, aware of the physical plight of Black Australians, allocate funds — and often quite large sums are involved — for the alleviation of this suffering. Whenever mention of this funding is made in the press, the next two words to appear in any public forum will be 'white back-lash'. So severe and well-organised have some of the back-lash movements been that they have been able to force dramatic changes to be made in funding allocations at times. Certainly it is obvious that when Budgets are discussed, 'white back-lash' is a major factor, and is considered a potential risk for whoever proposes expenditure. The result is that sufficient money has never been made available to actually alter even the physical manifestation of the oppression of Blacks.

On the other hand, it is also true that money alone cannot alter the situation. Indeed, money can be a destructive force when it is used only to gild the cage. It is, for instance, possible to erect beautiful houses, provide free and plentiful food — and then wonder why the problems have not been solved but have merely altered in form.

What is required is a very complex program, designed and implemented by Blacks, and supported, where necessary, by white expertise.

In this light, consider Senator Bonner's motion, and the support which it has in the Black community. The motion was passed unanimously in the Senate. However, because the follow-up which this spearhead motion required for it to become widely accepted didn't eventuate (the motion, now three years old, has not yet been debated in the House, for instance), it would have been more honest if the motion had been defeated unanimously.

While this is only one incident, it is not atypical. In fact, it is an extremely good example of how Black effort in this country is trivialised. Ideas proposed by Blacks are now often verbally supported — but negated by total inactivity along the proposed lines.

'Self-determination' continues to be the Australian Government password — but it is fast becoming the most common expression of Government derision in the Black community!

The Government continues to decide funding levels, and on which projects these funds will be spent. The funds remain totally inadequate, and successive Governments raise or lower the Budget figure, depending on votes, white reaction, inflation, media coverage, Petty's cartoons — in fact, anything except Black community needs. Which organisations receive funds, and what the level of funding — and therefore activity — will be, remains completely in the hands of the white powers. Blacks feel, correctly, powerless in this situation. They are aware that generally they lack the sophistication to compete with white Government departments and white-heavy organisations for the limited funds, and are therefore reduced to viewing the competition as effectively limited to other Black organisations.

Meanwhile, the situation of Blacks grows, if anything, even more dismal. Housing density, in many areas of N.S.W., ranges between 12 and 14 per two bedroom house, which does not necessarily even have running water — hot or cold. Most children have not had the experience of sleeping alone in a bed, but 'camp' four and five on any mattress available. The housing situation can only deteriorate, since funding for Aboriginal Housing co-operatives has been cut by 50%, and the population is expected to double by the end of this century.

In health, the position is similarly appalling. The National Trachoma and Eye Health team, led by Professor F. Hollows, Professor of Ophthalmology at the University of New South Wales hospital, Prince of Wales, has reported that Blacks, while constituting 1% of the population in this country, account for more than 20% of the blind population. Surveys conducted in N.S.W. reveal that in at least one country town, 100% of Black schoolchildren suffered from active trachoma, while no white child in the same town was afflicted. Ear disease occasioning a degree of deafness serious enough to constitute a handicap was also present in school children in alarming proportions.

However, by far the most horrific statistics to be brought to light this year were produced by the Aboriginal Medical Service, Redfern, a Black-controlled community operation. Their report, based on the medical reports of about 6,000 children seen at the Clinic, states that 25% of the children under five are so severely undernourished that they will suffer permanent brain damage. 80% of this group are under 3 years old, 64% are anaemic, 60% have a parasitic bowel infection, and 32% have at least one perforated ear-drum.

The current method of Government funding allocation means that all these factors, and more, are competing on an either/or basis for funds. Black organisations and Black community analysts, aware that all these problems are intrinsically interwoven, are despairing as they see time and lives wasted while the Government continues with its destructive funding policies.

United effort to try to force the Government to make more funds available has proven dismally unproductive. The Government, instead of being galvanised into action when confronted by united Black direction, becomes initially paralysed and then fearful. Instead of supporting and putting their strength behind this obvious Black thrust — which is actually 'self-determination' in action — they retire to backrooms and plot how to destroy the unity. Last year, for instance, they threw out a few more dollars to appease the Blacks who had united in the face of the savage Budget cuts, and encouraged the Black organisations to resume competition, knowing full well that the additional funds would not, in fact, reach the communities. $13 million was actually returned to Treasury because it had not been allocated or spent by the Department of Aboriginal Affairs.

Simultaneously, in a very paranoid manner, the Government has attempted to 'rein in' those Black organisations which remain outside of Government control because they do not request Government funding. The Aboriginal Embassy was the first nationally supported non-Government funded action by Blacks, and it is well-known what happened in that instance. Since then, there has been the Organisation of Aboriginal Unity (O.A.U.), and the Black Defence Group, both of which have suffered harassment. The Aboriginal Councils and Associations Bill, which requires that all Aboriginal organisations register themselves and list their members with the Federal Government, besides being an infringement on personal liberty and racist in that it is directed at one segment of the population, is considered by Blacks to be a serious attempt by the Government to exert some degree of control over these 'renegade' organisations and even casual meetings. . . .

It is, though, in the area of Land Rights and Land Rights Compensation that the most serious miscarriages of justice are taking place.

In the final recommendations of Justice Woodward, who chaired the Woodward Commission into Land Rights in the Northern Territory, he wrote:

> There should be no new mining on Aboriginal land for over two years and then only if the owners of the land and other Aboriginal people want it or if the Government says it is very important for Australia.

Following the adoption of the Woodward Commission's Report by the Federal Government, the Ranger Uranium Environment Inquiry, chaired by Mr. Justice Fox, advised the Government in regard to the then-proposed uranium mining venture in the Alligator Rivers area. In its Second Report, under the heading Conclusions, it stated:

> The arrival of large numbers of white people in the region will potentially be very damaging to the welfare and interests of the Aboriginal people there . . . the rapid development of a European community within, or adjacent to, an Aboriginal traditional society has in the past always caused the breakdown of the traditional culture and the generation of intense social and psychological stresses within the Aboriginals. There is no evidence which convincingly demonstrates that the result in the Region will be different . . .

Altogether the Ranger Inquiry Report shows that very little good will come from uranium mining so far as Aboriginals in the area are concerned. Instead the Report points out that there are very serious dangers for the people if uranium mining goes ahead.

Mr Silas Roberts, Chairman of the Northern Lands Council, also spoke against uranium mining on behalf of himself and other Aboriginals concerned.

Yet — on 25 August 1977, Mr Fraser announced that uranium mining in the Alligator Rivers area should go ahead! In so doing, Mr Fraser disregarded not only national Aboriginal opinion, and the wishes of the people directly affected by the decision, but also the recommendations of the country's best advisers given over the past four years. In the statement announcing the decision, the Prime Minister said:

> The Government will adopt special measures designed to advance the wellbeing of Aborigines and Aboriginal interests in the Region. Special efforts will be made to train them to be rangers in the National Park so that they may care for their land — the land of their ancestors and so be responsible for the protection of their sacred sites.

As the people themselves point out, as well as the Government's advisers, the only thing the people can look forward to is their destruction. The Government is not advancing their well-being, it is advancing their Doomsday!

Also, there are at least 800 people who will be directly affected by the mining operations — are they all to be trained as Park rangers?

Furthermore, for the Prime Minister to talk of the people being able to care for and protect their sacred sites is despicable double talk. Queensland Mines at Nabarlek have already desecrated the sacred site of the Green Ant Dreaming, Gabo-Djang. Ranger Uranium have crept closer and closer — dangerously close — to Mt Brockman, another sacred site, despite repeated representations to them from the people there expressing their concern about this intrusion.

It should be noted that there has been a great deal of talk about the royalties which the people will get from the uranium mining. Ostensibly such royalties may be regarded as 'just compensation' to the people for the mining of their land which they are opposed to. It should be pointed out that there can *never* be just compensation for the destruction of a people.

It is obvious that powerful interests are working against the Black community, interests that are able to cause the Government to destroy people, to ignore their own advisers, and to advance the profiteering of these same interests.

In the face of such opposition, the Black community, with very little in the way of resources, without representation at a Federal or even world level, would appear to have very little going for it.

Yet, from my position, this is far from the truth. Blacks have not, by any means, tried all the avenues that are open to them. To date we have largely attempted to work through white institutions, made representations to Governments, taken legal action through white courts. Our success rate is abysmally low. Eventually, of course, we are bound to exhaust all these possibilities, and by that time, our frustration level will be extremely high. This may even take until the end of this century — that is if uranium has not contributed to a sudden demise of the world — and by that time, as stated earlier, we will even have doubled our numbers, despite all attempts being made to curtail this prediction.

I wouldn't be so foolish as to speculate here as to what Blacks might do in the future if the present rate of increase of injustice and inhumanity continues. But I do know that, at this very time, political, social, and emotional frustration is being vented within the Black community itself, and that, like Harlem or Watts, it is bound to explode outwards — some time, some place.

Senator Neville Bonner, who for so long has been considered the voice of the well-mannered Black, is perhaps a reliable gauge of where even Black conservatives are these days. Speaking to his Motion for Compensation, he says in part:

> I do not deny that the present Government, in many areas of Aboriginal and Torres Island affairs, has instigated superbly beneficial schemes to improve my fellow Aborigines' and Torres Strait Islanders' way of life within our broader Australian community. But it is truly to no avail, dignitywise, when it is but an allocation of money for a disadvantaged people because it is but a form of charity. We, the indigenous people, for far too long have been the recipients of charity — the charity of the government of the day; charity, with its modern day connotation implying a handout mentality.
>
> What I am seeking is true and due entitlement for dispossession.

Warming to the subject, Senator Bonner then goes on to say in the same speech:

> As I said earlier, I do not decry the amounts that have been set aside but, again as I have already stated, this charity from one government sets one amount aside and the next government tries to better or perhaps to lessen the amount, depending entirely on the feelings of the people sitting within this chamber and the other place. When this is done, what is the cry? What in fact is the cry throughout Australia today? I suggest that it is the wail of the so-called white backlash. Why is this? It is because charity is being given to the Aborigines or to the Islanders or, as some people term it, to the boongs, the Abos or the blacks; but my God, forgetting that these very same boongs, Abos and blacks inherited this vast nation. Our forefathers indeed owned it.

Number 1, 1978

Heaven and a Hills Hoist: Australian Critics on Suburbia

TIM ROWSE

'It is never a waste of time to study the history of a word', Lucien Febvre tells us. Many images of Australia's social history have been garnered from a study of the colloquialisms that are Australia's and nobody else's. At first sight 'suburbia' does not seem to be one of those words, since it is manifestly part of a wider intellectual culture common to Britain and North America. Among social critics of these countries, 'suburbia', 'suburban' and 'suburb' have been used to describe a certain form of social life which emerged in the metropolises of Europe at the beginning of the era of

Imperialist and monopoly capitalism. With the expansion of the middle strata occupations of modern financial and commercial capitalism, and with the gradual improvement in the economic security of the industrial working class, the suburb became the typical mode of domestic living for the majority of people in these countries. As early as 1883, the suburban life style was sought and fostered by the British government in order to reduce the social tensions of the overcrowded inner areas of London. That year saw the passage of the Cheap Trains Act, which compelled the private railways to offer low commuting fares for workmen who chose to live away from the inner city. Since then, according to most observers, the suburban way of life has indeed been a peaceful domicile. A recent overview of studies in the USA and Britain listed the following as being the qualities most frequently attributed to suburbia: a preoccupation with family life; an active social life; a homogeneous population; a 'middle class' style of life; and political conservatism.[1]

Australian writers on suburbia are clearly part of this tradition of observation: they have been commenting on a nation which has been suburban since the 1870s and 1880s. Birch and Macmillan indicate the following changes in the distribution of Sydney's population:[2]

YEAR	CITY	SUBURBS
1871	74566	63210
1881	100152	124787
1891	107652	275631

In Melbourne, the suburbs expanded in the same decades with the extension of the railways. It is commonplace now to remark on the urban nature of Australian society, to which many commentators have added 'suburban'. In 1964 Donald Horne evoked Australia's typicality:

> Australia may have been the first *suburban* nation: for several generations most of its men have been catching the 8.2, and messing about with their houses and gardens at the weekends. Australians have been getting used to the conformities of living in suburban streets longer than most people: mass secular education arrived in Australia before most other countries, Australia was one of the first nations to find part of the meaning of life in the purchase of consumer goods; the whole business of large-scale organised distribution of human beings in a modern suburban society is not new to Australians.[3]

It is precisely because Australian intellectuals have made this equation between suburbia and Australia's 'civilisation' that the word's uses are so rewarding to study. For the history of its uses condenses a number of themes in the history of our ideologies: in particular the question of an Australian experience as evident in the rural-urban conflict, and the fate of working class radicalism. There is no doubt that Australia *is* a profoundly conservative country, a stable place for capital investment where the basic political institutions are respected. Accordingly there is something undeniably authentic in any observation of Australia as suburbia; it probably is the most suburban nation in a strictly demographic sense. However, relying on 'suburbia' as a summary image and in part as an explanation of Australia has entailed the unquestioning acceptance of a certain ideology of society. The ideology I am referring to will be illustrated extensively below, but it can be summarised in abstract form as consisting of three related themes. Firstly, the focus on and amplification of 'suburbia' suggests a homogeneity in Australian society. Preoccupied by a search for the 'average' Australian home and its life-style, commentators ignore important ethnic and class differences that are recreated daily in the context of work and reinforced by government policies. Secondly, commentators have tended to see Australia as an ensemble of discrete individual house-holders, ignoring the less visible but more important relationships which connect individuals (in ways of which they may not be aware), relationships that make up social classes and political forces. For 'suburbia' is a society without history or politics. Thirdly, though commentators have disagreed on whether suburbia constitutes a good or bad civilisation, they have all tended to pose the question of the good life in terms of what goes on inside the 'spirit', or at least within one's suburban plot; hence apathy and isolation from politics have been idealised by some writers. In short, there has been a tendency to idealise people's apparent ability to escape the nemeses of the world 'outside' suburbia: the world of work, industrial conflict, politics and collective action.

The distance between the rather abstract language of these last few sentences and the concrete and even colloquial discussion of everyday life and character that we find in our social critics is both a yardstick and a cause of the success, or the 'convincingness' of the 'suburbia' ideology.

Three periods can be discerned in its development. In the first period suburbia is portrayed as the antithesis of the fine place that a particular writer hopes Australia will be. In the second, the memory of this antithesis persists in an ironical *acceptance* of Australia's unquestionably suburban fate. In the third, the suburban home is reborn as a crucible of a more humane civilisation.

'The Suburban Home is a Horror'

In 1945 Nettie Palmer wrote to her daughter of some mutual friends:

> She was answering one I wrote her some time ago asking her to tell me at her leisure why and how she found the life here unreal and unsatisfying . . . I felt the subject was really interesting and even important. She has answered carefully: but I think part of the explanation is unexpressed — it is latent but clear that here at home she mixes mostly with people who are suburban, and satisfied to be so; I don't mean merely that they live out of town, but they have the suburban outlook. In London — didn't live in the mental suburbs — there and in the US she lived among intellectuals and cosmopolitans. There are such here, perhaps not so easy to find: or perhaps the suburbans are too easy to find.[4]

The antithesis between the cosmopolitan and the suburban was not one that existed between nations, say Britain and Australia: the struggle between them took place in every country. It was a contest between two attitudes to life: one whose intellectual horizons were broad, and which liked to look ahead and aspire to adventurous schemes of individual and social progress; and one that was narrow, self-satisfied, materialistic and parochial. This assured dichotomy was the property of a certain generation of Australian intellectuals which included the Palmers and their friends.

Louis Esson (1879-1943), a friend of Nettie and Vance Palmer, wrote into his play *The Time is Not Yet Ripe* (1912) a visionary protagonist and *alter ego*, Mr. Sydney Barrett. Barrett is a socialist, standing for the electorate of Wombat, whose socialism is not so much a scheme of social reconstruction but rather a provocative anti-morality, a precocious creed of nonconformist rebellion against the timid Philistines who formed the Establishment. His political failure is inevitable, for he is espousing a concept of revolution which is so much a matter for the individual spirit that it leaves the politics of mass persuasion behind. The text of the play is followed by a small essay, 'Our Institutions', which elaborates some of Barrett's aphorisms.

> The suburban home must be destroyed. It stands for all that is dull and cowardly and depressing in modern life. It endeavours to eliminate the element of danger in human affairs. But without dangers there can be no joy, no ecstasy, no spiritual adventures. The suburban home is a blasphemy. It denies life. Young men it would save from wine, and young women from love. But love and wine are eternal verities. They are moral. The suburban home is deplorably immoral.[5]

Esson's friend Vance Palmer shared similar hopes for an immanent Australian Socialism — a flowering of the best ethos of the Bush. By 1921, when it was clear that no such utopia was going to eventuate, Palmer ruminated sadly on 'Australia's Transformation'. Whereas in fact this transformation hinged largely on the defeat of working class militancy, Palmer portrayed it as a becalming of the national spirit in a Sargasso Sea of 'economic struggle'.

> Today villadom and proletaria combine to fix the national life or cross swords in the struggle for economic power. *The Man From Snowy River* is deposed to make room for a sentimental 'bloke' from the slums, and the life of the continent is held up by a quarrel between two classes of people on the seaboard.[6]

The contrast between the Bloke and Paterson's 'Man' is conducted at a number of levels. The 'Man' was bold and fine, riding forth on a metric scheme as wide as New South Wales; the Bloke's poetic gait and personal wants were simple and conventional. The 'Man's' domain was the Bush whereas Dennis sentimentalised the City. Palmer went on in this article to use the phrase 'the dominance of villadom', and denounced modern productive life as being nothing more than the 'supply of boots and chocolates to the suburbs'. It is true, as David Walker has recently pointed out, that the socialist ferment of the decade 1910-20 is important in reaching an understanding of Vance Palmer;[7] but it must also be pointed out that Palmer never realistically related his socialist vision to the actual contemporary struggles of the working class: instead he saw them as tainted by their obsession with the material and indifferent to the 'spiritual dimension'. Suburbia and 'villadom' for him evoked the pettiness of all parties to that 'quarrel on the seaboard'.

Hancock, an avowed admirer of the 'Palmer standard' of cultural criticism, repeats this trivialisation of the urban working class's defence of its economic rights. In *Australia* (1930), written in the midst of a serious crisis in the Australian economy, he expressed concern that the ruling ethos in political life had permitted a soulless prosperity to grow up in the cities at the expense of primary producers' industries. The visitor to Australia has expected to see some evidence of the rigours and heroisms of pioneering, and such a stolid mass of commonplace urban prosperity heaped around the doors of an empty continent will appear to him unnatural, unseemly.[8]

In the late 1920s this familiar dichotomy had a new, urgent and conservative pertinence to the struggle between and within classes. In 1928 Hancock had written on 'The Australian City' in the *New Statesman*. Starting with some sardonic cameos of the aesthetic innocence of the typical Australian home and the suburban wife's alleged hunger for social status, Hancock goes on to place these piquant vulgarities in the context of the political and spiritual dominance of the City over the Country. 'Suburbia' in this article functions as a metonym in an argument (then emanating from the Country Party and representatives of British economic interests in Australia) for the scaling down of New Protection on the grounds that it gave the urban populace a standard of living which primary exporters could not afford to subsidise.[9]

But Hancock had a sense of the political ambiguity of the suburban spirit. 'Conservatives may console themselves that, even in a so-called socialist community like Australia, this vast suburban mass is inevitably opposed to subversive change. There is no fear of its pulling down the comfortable house which it inhabits.'[10] Frederic Eggleston drew the same comforting conclusion in his *State Socialism* (1932). The final chapter attempts to explain sociologically the intractable materialism that he saw as the leading trait of an electorate which voted for 'state socialism' — an affluence underpinned by economically 'unsound' government policies. The political success of Labor had integrated the proletariat into capitalism; but their self-interested materialism was a dead weight in the process of economic adjustment. The masses lacked the civic virtue to renounce material wants for the sake of threatened profit margins. Eggleston sketched a portrait of this stubborn 'self-contained man'.

> The home of the 'self-contained man' is in the suburbs, and in the highly developed suburbs of an Australian city, with good accommodation, a nice garden, a back yard, vegetables in his plot and fowls in the shed, a fence against intrusion, he has probably reached a higher pitch of development than anywhere else.[11]

Vance and Nettie Palmer, Esson, Hancock and Eggleston all equated 'suburbia' with a stifling materialism of outlook. But whereas the first three intellectuals saw only the obliteration of their hopes of a spiritually finer Australia, the latter two also adopted a more pragmatic and political perspective. That spiritual banality stood as a bulwark against Bolshevism. The question of just how an individual suburbanite affirmed or denied 'civilisation' had started to become more complex.

No Flies on the Nature Strip

The generation of intellectuals who came to maturity just before, during or just after the First World War inaugurated a use of the term 'suburbia' in an overwhelmingly pejorative sense that is still sometimes heard. But the seeds of a different evaluation, found in Eggleston and Hancock, have germinated since World War Two in a more ironical appreciation of its strengths, particularly in the writing of a younger generation of intellectuals who had never known at first hand the earlier optimism about Australia's potential as a 'socialist' Promised Land. By the early 1950s, when the Keynesian welfare state seemed to have set mass material contentment on a firmer economic footing than in the interwar years, suburbia came to be seen in a more positive light — as an innocent utopia. This seems to be the viewpoint controlling Robin Boyd's classic evocation of suburbia in *Australia's Home* (1952). His point was that while 'factory, shop, office, theatre and restaurant were not radically different the world over . . .. in the suburb was experienced that essentially Australian part of town life which lay between work and home'. [12] Moreover, suburbia was coming to be seen not so much as an aberration of the Australian spirit, but as its abiding manifestation. The blurb on the Pelican edition of *The Australian Ugliness* stated the relevance of Boyd's concerns: 'Looking at the face of Australia, Robin Boyd goes deeper, to analyse the character that gave it the expression it wears.' As 'suburbia' became accepted as an authentic image of the way ordinary Australians lived, the critical connotations of the term began to lose their force, giving way to a gentle irony and even to an aloof benediction. No-one did more to facilitate this shift than Barry Humphries.

At the time when the humorous Australian archetypes Dad and Dave, Ginger Mick and the Sentimental Bloke were losing their appeal, undercut by demographic changes and the political failure of Labor's 'common Man' stereotype of the 1940s, Barry Humphries constructed new characters, notably Edna Everage and Sandy Stone. Neither inner urban larrikins nor bucolic yokels, they are truly 'suburban'. Everage apes but violates the conventions of taste, status and worldliness; Stone's life is a pathetic shell of would-be gentility and conformity. But the sense of their authenticity and familiarity has, over the years, come to undercut the critical edge of Humphries' satire: there has grown up an undeniable element of sentimental patriotism in the appreciation of Humphries' work. Edna and Sandy, understood as something indigenous, allow a cock-eyed pride in the uniqueness of Australian mores. That innocence was seen to be somehow admirable.

For many intellectuals in Australia, pride in its way of life and culture had always been a temptation to be resisted. The choice they faced until the Fifties was usually seen as between a sentimental and parochial defensiveness (as embodied in the Jindyworobak aesthetic or in Australian social realism) or a disdainful cosmopolitanism. In presenting suburbia as a satirical object, the dilemma of these alternatives was partly resolved by irony. Humphries made it possible to savour an authentic Australianness, without having to make a strong emotional commitment to it; irony afforded intellectuals a saving distance. Satire was the most appropriate mode for living with the ambivalence of needing to identify with a national ethos which did not completely measure up to one's standards. [13] This was the ironical 'populism' which grew up in the Sixties as a counter to the Left Australianism which saw in the Australian character an immanent socialism. Thus the celebration of the social peace of the Menzies era tended to reproduce and develop the complex and ambivalent estimate of suburbia that we have already seen in Eggleston and Hancock. Donald Horne and Craig McGregor represent this complex 'structure of feeling' well.

In *The Lucky Country* Horne adamantly rejected the interwar snobbery about suburbia: it effectively dismissed the whole nation. Instead, he defended the vitality of the suburban lifestyle. 'The profusion of life doesn't wither because people live in small brick houses with red tile roofs'. [14] Moreover, it was *the* national lifestyle, a classless ethos: 'The genteel have been vulgarised, the vulgar made more gentle. People now enjoy themselves more in the same kind of ways.' [15]

But this commitment to suburbia is not sustained by Horne elsewhere. In a 1962 essay he defended Australian businessmen from their negative stereotype which he described as: '. . . uneducated, provincially ignorant, suburban-minded, vulgar, anti-intellectual, reactionary, materialistic . . . more Babbitt than Babbitt'. [16] More recently, in *The Australian People* (1972), the section called 'The First Suburban Nation' is part of Chapter Fourteen: 'The End of Improvement: 1919-39' which traces, in the interwar period, the extinction of Australia's vital, progressive, nationalistic impulse. He pictures a period of philistine self-satisfaction in which life was privatised and domestic rather than open and communal, and in which 'women developed the rituals of afternoon tea (dainty sandwiches and many varieties of spongecake) into a complex art.' [17] Horne's critique of this period relies on the Palmeresque image of suburbia. But overall his work is clearly ambivalent: suburbia's domesticity is on the one hand in the spirit of Boccaccio ('the entire range of human comedy and tragedy') and on the other, a species of Babbittry. Horne's ambivalence towards suburbia is the inevitable result of an attempt to identify rhetorically with 'the people', who are sound and happy but who deserve better government, and substantively with an emergent body of technocrats — those confident they could govern more effectively than the Coalition governments of the Sixties.

Craig McGregor, presented by one publisher as a representative social critic of the young iconoclastic postwar generation, was more critical of Australian life than Horne was. But, like Horne, he also celebrated its vitality.

> There is a zestfulness about much of suburban life which is apparent in a thousand particulars from the sense of bustle and good humour in the thriving suburban shopping centres to the discotheques, sportscars, surfboards and juke boxes which help enliven the life of the younger suburbanites . . . Fairfield, probably Sydney's dullest suburb, also has the highest juvenile delinquency rate. Behind that facade, *something* is always happening.[18]

McGregor became a champion of 'Alf' — the archetypal suburban householder. Yet in a subtle way this populist affirmation undercut his critique of Australia. He was more interested in evoking a 'way of life' than in describing the structural features of Australian society which caused inequality and alienation in the first place. When he wrote approvingly that 'for most people life begins at five o'clock on Friday arvo',[19] he was spelling out a theoretical emphasis, an implicit sociology. The Australia he described existed outside the workplace: the relations of home and hearth were held to be the locus of the 'real' Australia, not the worlds of work and politics. He thus helped to support the apologetic image of Australia as an undifferentiated suburbia, composed of individual households standing free of class relations. McGregor was alert enough to see the dilemma raised by this perspective: if Australia was to change from being unequal and alienating, then each of its individual citizens would have to step away from the comfortable social anonymity of suburbia and become involved on one side or the other. Could McGregor endorse such involvement without shattering the image of suburban utopia?

> The man who becomes absorbed in his home is much less likely to become involved in public issues such as conscription or Vietnam or free enterprise, in the whole fabric of democratic activity. I think this is probably true but once again it has to be kept in perspective. There are some advantages in such a disengagement: the man who lives in a bung in Padstow is much *freer*, much less oppressed by community pressures and conformism, than Dublin terrace-dwellers or Naples proletarians; it is much easier for him to opt out of the church . . . mass prejudice and social authority and to choose his own allegiances. The Australian suburbanite is probably freer of the stifling pressure of social authoritarianism than any other city dweller in history.[20]

In this crucial passage, McGregor continues the ambivalent estimate of suburbia: Alf was apathetic about the Vietnam question and about poverty but at least he was happy and free and able to escape the pressures of the world. McGregor offers to suburbanites the prospect of continuing to opt out of history, as it were — a choice less happily acknowledged by Eggleston in the Thirties. Thus McGregor's Alf is the son of Eggleston's self-contained man.

Green Thumbs Up

During the 1960s the Australian Labor Party developed a theory of reform which was quite coherent with McGregor's and Horne's emphasis on suburbia as the locus of Australian civilisation. ALP ideologues saw reform as the task of equalising different regions' access to community amenities. More equality between suburbs was to be achieved by siphoning off a greater proportion of the nation's wealth and spending it on better health services, housing, transport, sewerage. Suburbs of the major cities which had been denied these services by years of Coalition neglect were to benefit. Labor's perspective was that it represented not the aspirations of a working class constituted by its subordinate place in production, but the needs of disadvantaged householders concentrated in regions. Just as the liberal-democratic notion of suffrage fragments social classes, by treating society as an ensemble of individual voters, so Labor's view fragmented the nation into privileged or disadvantaged households and neighbourhoods. As in Horne and McGregor, its emphasis was on the social world outside the workplace, where the mobilisation of interests was much less saliently that of a class. After all, a class-oriented conception of the ALP constituency was inadmissible to these ideals precisely because the whole program was to be financed by the continued, privately-directed expropriation of working class labour — the fundamental source of all the inequalities being dealt with.

This schema of reform produced a truly formidable theorist in Hugh Stretton. No one has formulated such an articulate economic and philosophical case for the suburban way of life as he; where the Palmers condemned and Horne and McGregor hedged their celebration, Stretton praises without reservation. His words are simple and, at first, plausible:

> You don't have to be a mindless conformist to choose suburban life. Most of the best poets and painters and inventors and protesters choose it too. It reconciles access to work and city with private, adaptable, self-expressive living space at home. Plenty of adults love that living space, and subdivide it ingeniously. For children it really has no rivals. At home it can allow them space, freedom and community with their elders; they can still reach bush and beach in one direction and in the other, schools to educate them and cities to sophisticate them. About half the lives of most of us are spent growing up then bringing others up. Suburbs are good places to do it, precisely because they let the generations coexist, with some continuing independence for each.[21]

Recently Stretton has turned his fire on a Left orthodoxy which he sees as being hostile to the development of private life and the private ownership of the things which really matter to people's daily lives. 'Seeing the masses seduced by capitalism, "hard" socialists respond by doubling their distrust of ownership. It does not occur to them that the house and garden and car turn people away from the party of equality chiefly because the party of equality officially despises the house and garden and car, and the life they allow.'[22] The Left, says Stretton, forms an unholy alliance with the economic orthodoxy, which refuses to count in the National Product the useful things which people do for themselves at home, and so neglects to direct social investment into areas that will improve the domestic quality of life.

Stretton's argument is on the one hand a very eloquent plea for things which Australia needs badly: better housing, town planning and transport policies. But it is also a blueprint for the consolidation of modern capitalism's domestic annexe. Efforts daily expended in the ordinary Australian home are vital to the reproduction of labour, both biologically and in the sense of a day to day fitness to work. The payment of a family wage takes this into account, but also makes assumptions about the amount of domestic work which is done unpaid by women taught to think of this as their duty. Moreover, programs like the Victorian government's 'Life, be in it' campaign attempt to confirm the domestic setting and leisure time generally as an arena of escape from the pressures of social life. For capitalism, the domestic sphere is both cheaply reproductive and privatised — a crucible of affluent quiescence. Any attempt to upgrade community life that does not challenge the relationships of capitalist production would thus cut two ways. Life would be genuinely better, for some; but at the expense of leaving unquestioned the social division of labour, between workers and owners, and between men and women. The 'ideal home' is still a gilded cage. And we need not take seriously Stretton's secondary argument that socialism could one day come through the ballot box. Stretton's conservatism lies in his defence of the separation of the 'private' world of consumption and sexual relations from the larger social processes, in work and in politics, in which this 'privacy' is ultimately articulated. His enquiry into this crucial nexus is bracing — he has made a case against the Left which it must answer firmly — but ultimately he confirms it as a necessary separation. In Stretton, we find Alf's apotheosis.

Throughout the different uses discussed here, the term 'suburbia' has developed in its idiomatic force its apparent authenticity as a description of the 'Australian way of life'. Beginning as an abstract Nietzschean dismissal, it enjoyed a career as the metonym of a half-accepted civilisation — stolid electorate or satirical object. Recently it has passed into a much more accepting sociological usage, connected to a program of reform which is sophisticated but fundamentally conservative of capitalist social relations. Inscribed in this career is the gradual acceptance by Australian intellectuals of their national civilisation as its urban and suburban self. The extent of this shift is marked strikingly at one point in Stretton's latest book:

> It is in private houses with storage space and some land around them that it is easiest to use more human energy in satisfying ways, and to manage with less powered commercial services . . . Environmental policies will always be determined chiefly by peoples' values; and urban houses and gardens are the nursery of most of the best environmental values. People who live in town but grow some foliage of their own, and keep a cat to deter mice, are the mainstay of all the movements which work to protect larger landscapes and eco-systems. Private residential land is both an environmental good which ought to be fairly shared, and a vital educator: a classroom for work-skills, play-skills, nature study and environmental values which an environmentally careful society could be mad to deny to any of its people. [23]

Palmer saw an unbridgeable antithesis between 'villadom' and 'the Bush';

Stretton sees in suburbia the nursery of a sentiment organic with the ecosystem.

But the continuities in the tradition of usage are stronger than this small upheaval in the geographical metaphors of Australian romanticism. All the authors mentioned have adopted a skeptical or disdainful attitude to revolutionary socialism as a movement based tenuously in an often unglamorous working class struggle. Each writer has been seduced by the relatively high degree of sameness in the lives that we Australians live outside the place of work. As Hancock said, with a playful mixture of banality and insight: 'There are no classes in Australia except in the economic sense'. He was viewing Australian society through the wrong end of a Marxist telescope. His use of the word 'except' trivialises the very processes which constitute ours as a class society, but it draws attention to the undeniably strong tendency for these divisions to be obscured in the forms of life led outside the workplace. Those who use 'suburbia' as a defining image of Australian society lend their support to this obscuring emphasis. As well they ignore the profound connections that exist between the exploitation of labour at work and in the home, a connection now being explored by Marxist feminists. Lastly, all of these social critics have defined the search for a better life in the same individualist and apolitical terms as has been recommended more brazenly in the acquisitive consumerist society which each of them would claim to criticise.

Number 1, 1979

Queensland: A State of Mind

HUMPHREY MCQUEEN

For a majority of Australians, Queensland is more a state of mind than a state of their nation. As such, 'Queensland' excuses them from doing much about what is wrong in their own states: 'If things are so bad there then we can't be too bad here'. A similar process works inside Queensland where the awfulness of Joh is occasionally used as an excuse for not doing anything about him. A mood of waiting for Joh to go has been broken by Aboriginals, by strikes, and most recently by opposition to the street march legislation. Yet a commonly encountered response is either a despairing 'Anything's possible in Queensland', or an incredulous 'Were you born in Queensland?', as if nothing radical ever came out of Brisbane.

Against Joh's attempt to convince Queenslanders that they live in a sovereign state and are in some way superior to the rest of their fellow Australians, ALP apologists push the counter-view that Joh is the odd man out and that Queensland is, and has been, very much the same as the rest of Australia. For party political reasons neither side in this argument can face up to the facts of the situation. The past is too embarrassing for present-day

Labor reformers, while the present is too revealing to be good propaganda for a premier seeking re-election.

On a number of important counts Queenslanders are different, although no one has yet suggested that, like Tasmanians, we all have pointed ears. As Byron implied, inbreeding is usually not the problem where the climate's sultry. The differences which exist are in population distribution, educational attainments and work-force participation, all of which are anchored in the primary industry bias of Queensland's political economy. Queensland's economic pattern is not unique; Tasmania's and Western Australia's are fairly much the same. What is unique is the spread of primary industries and population across so much of the state.

Brisbane is the only mainland capital to contain less than half its state's population: 857,066 out of 2,037,197. The percentage of Queenslanders living in rural areas is the highest for all mainland states: 20 per cent against a national average of 14. Brisbane is closer to Melbourne than to Cairns, and closer to Canberra than to Townsville. Compared with either far northern city, Kingaroy is just another outer Brisbane suburb.

It is the economic matrix and not distance which makes regionalism more significant in Queensland than in any other state. Even before separation from New South Wales in 1859, there were proposals to slice Queensland horizontally into three. The sugar industry's demand for Pacific Island labour was at the root of separatist, anti-Federal, and finally secessionist movements in the far north. Regionalism was bolstered by a rail system which spread inland out from a string of ports from Brisbane up to Cairns, which were not linked to each other by rail until 1924. Brisbane was never the focus of Queensland's economic life. Indeed, there never has been such a focus. As well as competing against Brisbane for the state's trade, eight ports battled their nearest neighbours for regional supremacy. Bowen's annoyance at the Cloncurry-Mt Isa railway ending in Townsville helps to explain why Bowen returned Australia's only acknowledged communist parliamentarian, between 1944 and 1950.

Twenty years of non-Labor rule have not altered the primary bias of Queensland's economy. With 13 per cent of Australia's civilian employees in 1976, Queensland had 19 per cent of the nation's rural workers but only 10 per cent of those engaged in manufacturing. Moreover, the structure of manufacturing is skewed towards rural products. Food, beverage and tobacco processing employ a third of Queensland's manufacturing workers, twice the national figure. The proportion of working wives is lower: 37.5 against 42 per cent. The population is very slightly weighted towards the under 20 year-olds and the over 55 year-olds, suggesting that people leave the state to work but go there to retire.

The reluctance to industrialise meant that fewer migrants went to Queensland. Between 1947 and 1961, Queensland's overseas-born rose by 56 per cent, against an Australian average of 139 per cent. The proportion of overseas-born remains substantially lower; 13 per cent for Queensland and 20 per cent for Australia; 16 per cent for Brisbane and 25 per cent for all major urban centres in the country. The percentage of Italians and Greeks in

Brisbane is 1.4, compared with a mainland range between the next lowest of 4.4 in Perth up to 7.7 in Melbourne.

Partly because of the economic pattern outlined, but more because of a complex cultural inheritance discussed below, educational levels are markedly lower: 36 per cent of Queenslanders left school after only five or six years, compared with a national average of 24 per cent; only 12 per cent of Queenslanders have more than nine years schooling, as against 18 per cent for Australia as a whole. Inevitably, the number of people with qualifications and degrees is noticeably smaller. And this pattern of early school leaving is continuing, so that while only 43 per cent of sixteen year-old Queenslanders are still at school, the Australian average is 57 per cent. . . .

Important as economic and geographic forces remain, they always have to work through politics, of which parliament is only one small part. Queensland is different because arrangements made out of rural circumstances largely held in place until the mid-1950s. Underneath the accommodations reached in the 1920s and 1930s with the major companies operating in Queensland — Colonial Sugar Refinery, Mt Isa Mines, Vestey's meat, and the London bond market — a governing stratum of Labor party politicians, Australian Workers Union officials, state public servants and Catholic clergy built a political culture that offered most Queenslanders some of what they then wanted most: for example, public instruction rather than education, and free hospitals rather than more of either. The repressiveness of this alliance grew as the old grouping was challenged by militant workers. When Bjelke-Petersen declared a State of Emergency during the 1971 Springbok football tour, he used a section of a strike-breaking Act that Labor had introduced in 1938, and had buttressed during the 1948 rail strike. The police bludgeoning of communist MLA, Fred Paterson, while he stood on the footpath watching a protest march against these 1948 amendments, is only the most notorious example of how Labor governed.

The linkages are clear. At root, there was a shared commitment to rural life as morally, politically and economically sound. The AWU machine was a prize in itself but its voting strength extended its officers' ambitions to the Labor Party, and through it to the government. Industrialisation threatened this power flow by strengthening craft unions open to 'communist' influence. The AWU believed that it could be secure as Queensland's one big union, covering all kinds of unskilled and all grades of semi-skilled labour, only if Queensland's rural bias was maintained. The Labor Party was Labor in name but represented more rural seats than city ones; its leadership was non-metropolitan and usually derived from within the AWU. The Catholic Church favoured farming as the best bulwark against the Syllabus of Errors, arguing that everything from 'race suicide' to communism was less likely away from urban industry. . . .

The potential for northern development to puzzle outside observers is indeed great, and several writers confuse it with the corruption practised in other states. In 1883, the premier, Sir Thomas McIlwraith, showed his faith in Queensland by proposing that his government allow a land grant railway company 12 million acres. In 1896, McIlwraith was acutely embarrassed by the unexpected death of the general manager of the Queensland National Bank, which had lent him £255,000 on securities of £60,700. This lesson in public finance was not lost on a subsequent Treasurer who, in 1899, concealed the colony's bankruptcy by using £500,000 of Government Savings Bank deposits without any authority. It was from this stimulating intellectual climate that E. G. Theodore emerged as a pre-Keynesian mine-owner, although his failure to anticipate the multiplying effects of public expenditure on his private enterprises cost him the Federal treasurership.

Not all Queensland politicians have been so large-minded. In 1946, Commonwealth police found 250 kilos of black market tobacco stored in the garage of the house occupied by the Minister for Health. Ten years later, a Royal Commission found the same minister guilty of collecting bribes for Labor Party funds. Magistrates acquitted him on both occasions. Most rumours and allegations of corruption were either not investigated or were dismissed. In 1940, when bridge contractors presented the premier with a portable radio, the main point of public dispute was the value of the banknotes inside: £10,000 being a favoured sum. The frequency and grandeur of such allegations made it too easy for the opposition to suggest that only Labor politicians operated with one hand in the till and the other in the ballot box. Time has not weakened nor coalition government stifled the venality of public life. In 1966, the state parliamentary Labor leader resigned on the day before the *Courier-Mail* announced that he had understated his taxable income by over $66,000 as a result of importing tin plates from Taiwan. The 1970 Comalco share handouts went to cabinet ministers, public servants, ALP officials and the Labor member for Gladstone.

Many of the checks on government available in the Westminster model have long been absent from Queensland. The Legislative Council was abolished in 1922 under Gilbertian circumstances and preceded by one of the most remarkable devices ever: a proxy voting bill which allowed Theodore to exercise personally the vote of absent members. In the words of an opposition squib, Whenever the government is found in a fix/My voice shall carry for those of six.

Significantly, Bjelke-Petersen has not demonstrated his loyalty to the British way by re-establishing a house of review. Two innovations which he has been forced to live with are a few parliamentary committees, and questions without notice, which are answered in kind.

Labor's grand old alliance was broken from outside in the aftermath of Evatt's splitting the Federal party, and from within when the AWU temporarily allied itself with the communist-led Trades and Labour Council following the 1956 shearers' strike. When Labor was defeated in May 1957, it was succeeded by Australia's only Country Party-dominated government, which had no more idea of how to break out of Queensland's malaise than had its predecessors. These economic difficulties were highlighted by the Federal government's 1960 credit squeeze and the 1961 swing to Labor which brought Calwell within one seat of forming a government. The credit squeeze blinded some commentators to the state's chronic unemployment, which had been much higher than the Australian average throughout the 1950s, despite (or because of) a relatively slower rate of population increase. In 1962-63, an investigation of Queensland's manufacturing industry found too few new factories to draw statistically significant conclusions.

The 1961 swing to Labor has been added to a list of alleged proofs that, despite the past decade, Queensland is inherently radical. To support this cheeriness, a long tradition is established from the armed camp at Barcaldine in 1891, through the world's first Labor government in 1899, Australia's first general strike in 1912, the anti-conscription stance of premier Ryan, forty years of nearly continuous Labor rule, Australia's only communist parliamentarian, and the militancy of certain Queensland unions in the 1920s and 1940s. Just as it has been shown that the Labor Party was in reality a country party, so it can be argued that most of the other examples cited are either misinterpreted or extrapolated out of context. For example, the militancy of the Twenties and Forties was directed against the Labor government's reactionary policies. Other dissenting highpoints were protests by depressed rural producers or disadvantaged regions, that is, by forces which today are marshalled behind Bjelke-Petersen's government. Change over time is history's divisive equation. Broken or blunted are the tough realities which once brought forth shearing-shed anarchism and bush populism, or determined railway workers in their militancy.

Likewise, the experience of Queensland's blacks is not only different from that of whites, it is also more of a piece than that of blacks elsewhere. Well before other colonies started, and long after other states stopped, Queensland's government took an activist approach towards Aboriginal management. Despite some recent window dressing, the philosophy of preservation and protection, first enacted in 1897, still prevails. The health of the whites was protected by locking away on penal settlements, like Palm Island, those blacks to whom whites had given tubercular, leprous and venereal infections. The wealth of pastoral companies was preserved by using other settlements as breeding grounds for cheap station labour. Blacks under this system acquired a healthy respect for a law which was custodian of such wealth as they were allowed to earn and able to keep from swindling police sergeants. Under this regime, Aboriginal numbers increased, the militant moved to Redfern, those under church control developed centres of resistance, and Uncle Toms abounded. Today, the militant are driven out of, rather than into, the camps which officially are hailed as the antidote to the apartheid of land rights. Within that old framework, change has moved slowly over time, establishing new forms of oppression before provoking fresh resistance.

Bjelke-Petersen is both inheritor and destroyer of these old ways. He uses ALP laws from the 1930s and '40s to bolster the transformation of Queensland from being a hillbilly Tennessee to become a Texas bonanza. The overused metaphor of a 'Deep North' entirely misses the point. Queensland is no longer like the Deep South, but is the New South. Its faults are those of progress, growth and development — as foreign monopoly capital understands those words. Under post-depression ALP governments, Queensland was indeed like Tennessee, or, more accurately, like County Clare in

Ireland. To label Queensland by its civil liberties is to ignore the substance of Bjelke-Petersen's regime, which cannot be as easily authoritarian as some of its Labor predecessors were precisely because it has unleashed on Queensland that 'constant revolutionising of production, uninterrupted disturbance of all social conditions, everlasting uncertainty and agitation' which Marx identified in the bourgeoisie.

History judges Bjelke-Petersen to be the farmer who killed rural idiocy, the lay preacher whose policies ensure that all things holy will be profaned. (Hasn't Joh himself started to take a little white wine with his meals?) From his first equipment-hiring ventures and aeroplanes to his current use of a professional image-maker, Bjelke-Petersen is stamped as capitalist moderniser, not as feudal throwback. He knows the relative significance of mineral and peanut oils, even if his opponents do not. The votes of a few small farmers help him to realise the interests of certain big corporations. His party's name change from Country to National and the votes won by National Party candidates in urban areas are the signs to read. It is the Liberals, not the ALP, who have lost most and have the most to fear, in parliamentary terms, from Joh's successes. Forget about Joh Bananas, and remember that his life-long hero has been Henry Ford.

Not that Bjelke-Petersen wants to industrialise. He ridicules southern manufacturing as a charge against Queensland's wealth. To the extent that he has any long-term economic plan, it is that growing mineral exports can lever overseas meat and sugar contracts; will need construction work; can support service industries; and be supplemented by tourism. As evidence he can point to state government expenditures which have quadrupled since he became premier in 1968, while mining royalties are twenty times greater. Beyond a pride in these superficial trends, he places his faith in foreign investors rebuffed by the Commonwealth, which has to watch the broader and longer-term interests of Australia and of capital.

As an advocate of states' rights, Bjelke-Petersen runs a poor third to Labor premiers Forgan Smith and Hanlon. His far greater success derives from those people whose rights he actually is defending, namely, anyone avoiding Commonwealth regulation, or with speculative capital: Utah and CRA; Wiley Fancher and the Moscow Narodny Bank; Mr Iwasaki's Yeppoon resort and — in time to come — Great Barrier Reef Oil Drilling (Aust) Pty Ltd. They are Joh's constituency. The book-burning bible-bashers who want to castrate poofs and shoot reds merely get the pleasure of playing with his gerrymander. States' rights have always been a mask for class interests, or more usually, for the interests of some section of capital which is on the outer at Melbourne and Canberra. United secession by Western Australia, the Northern Territory and Queensland would serve Japanese capital better than the old Brisbane Line.

In encouraging miners and speculators, Joh has attached himself to one predicted Australian future. The small farmers and bush workers who kept Labor in office are going, and Joh is using their dying resentment to reward the very people who have killed them off and who are already undermining factory and office jobs. The regrowth of massive opposition in Queensland is coming from such newly threatened groups, as well as from Aboriginals and mine workers, who are once more in the front line of the profit-making. Radicalism cannot be born again from the glory that was Labor's Portuguese-style fascism.

If mining is allowed to conquer manufacturing until all of Australia becomes, in Sir Roderick Carnegie's words, 'the Uruguay of the South Pacific', then fascist will be a far more appropriate description of all of Australia than it ever has been of Queensland. The rule of capital could not survive such a total economic reverse without open dictatorship. In such a pass we might be tempted to apply to Bjelke-Petersen, and even to his Labor predecessors, the *Bulletin*'s 1922 obituary judgement of an earlier Queensland Premier: 'We had no idea how good a man he was till we found out how rotten subsequent men could be.'

John Tranter to Jim Davidson

21 April 1977

Thanks for your letter of 19 April. About my proposed article — I think what helped to put me off the idea of doing an overview of the current scene is the number of mediocre talents around at the moment, and the amount of competent modern poetry I'd have to read carefully. I guess I'm getting old and crochety, but I don't want to read poetry that isn't important in some way.

My idea of doing a limited number of poets is partly the result of a wish to do something in some depth — my review of Adamson's *Swamp Riddles* in *New Poetry* a couple of years back is an example of the kind of article I'd like to write. I also got to thinking about the 'Generation of 68', and how the Revolution has developed and changed over the last decade. I would like to pick on say four poets who began writing seriously around 1967, and who each represent a slightly different approach, and do a historical analysis of their work over that period. I would have to bring in the work of other writers, in general, to fill in the background; and perhaps look briefly at the 'Generation of 45' as a comparison — Wright, McAuley, Webb, Harry Hooton, and so on. So I would hope to end up with a far more thought-provoking critique of Australian poetry than I could with a 'round-up' type of review. For example, I would probably start off looking at say . . . Dransfield as a fossilised watercolour mistaken for a de Kooning; and so on, using history as demystifying lens, or as a club. So it won't be your average *Southerly* article translated from a lecture. . . .

John Tranter to Jim Davidson

Sunday night 5 March 1978

You wouldn't *believe* the last few days, after my fleeing of Gomorrah on Thursday night: post natal depression (was my reading all that bad? Groan!); long alcoholic nights ie with Rae Jones and John Edwards; (Rae helped put the end of my article in perspective, such as it is; enclosed); son Leon (age 2) vomiting and screaming at three in the morning last night, rushed trip to Casualty, suspected meningitis (suspected by me, not the doctor); eventual total recovery of same Leon; vain attempts to write poem about obscure dream relating to the Adelaide River (Torrens?) and flowing wine in similarly large proportions, exhaustion; and a draft (final) of the end of my article, here appended.

Two things you must do with that part of my article which you already have: correct the spelling of Sidney Greenstreet (note the 'I' not 'Y') in my bit on Nigel; and identify the long quote from Adamson (the one ending with that memorable image of Courtly Fellatio) not with Adamson's name; we know, dreadfully, who wrote it; but with the line:

from 'Lancelot', p.136.

in the roman or italics of your choice.

Thanks for your long talk about my piece; your editing was both incisive and courteous, and helped aim the missile better. Do what brief editing you feel the enclosed needs; as you say, I will see proofs, and I'm sure you could trim here and there where needed to my satisfaction.

I will stagger to bed; and to the post tomorrow.

Number 1, 1978

Growing Old Gracefully: The Generation of '68

JOHN TRANTER

The October 1977 issue of *Australian Literary Studies* — a journal usually devoted to Aust. Lit. *minutiae* such as 'The Variation in Gender of French Solecisms in Patrick White's Grocery Lists' — consisted entirely of a survey of the 'new writing' in Australia, written mainly by those who have been involved in the development of prose and poetry writing or publishing over the last ten years; that is, the active members of the 'Generation of '68'. The essays and statements in *ALS* make it clear that the writers who have come to prominence in this decade are noticeably different from their predecessors, and owe little to their example.

Their work has flourished, and they have gone on to publish books literally by the dozen. Of the poets among them, some have matured and some regressed, some gone crazy and some terribly sane; and some have merely grown older, while others have died.

Ten years is a long time in the life of a literary movement, and I have a feeling in my bones that a decade has closed; that 1978 will see the end of an age wherein a coherent purpose was visible and acknowledged, that the brave young poets who rose up against the conservative establishment to struggle and finally triumph, only to feel the weight of the dusty mantle settle on their own shoulders, are finally drifting out from the hot centre of energy that burnt its message across the amazed countenances of a thousand readers and a dozen Aust. Lit. courses, and are now at last their own persons, writing the poems that the revolution helped them to devise but paradoxically held back from them until the larger collective work was done. I think we are now seeing the effects of a minor cultural shift of some significance — a revision of values that identified a large group of young innovative writers who are now not so young, and whose innovations are open to a more serious appraisal than was either possible or necessary during the experimental phase of their writing. I would like to discuss a dozen recently published books, partly from the viewpoint of the changes that I think are taking place.

It should have been the poetry publishing event of 1977 — *Cross the Border*, Robert Adamson's sixth book, a large and extravagantly produced 142-page collection of new poems.

Those who saw his *Swamp Riddles* (1974) as a turning point in his writing career hardly knew what to expect. A return to the outlaw themes of his earlier work? A further exploration of the Hawkesbury River landscape? In a way we got a little of both these things, though we didn't bargain on the 'Grail Poems'.

Not much need be said about the first group. They share many of the preoccupations of similar poems from his earlier books *Canticles on the Skin*, *The Rumour* and *Swamp Riddles*. Fast cars, drugs, lawlessness country radio, poets and the poetic life are the predominant subjects, and they are handled in much the same way, though generally with a looser grip on the form and with much less urgency than before. Adamson is rehearsing his earlier speeches here, and as with all forms of repetition, the voice eventually grows tired. At times he seems content merely to state the formula without the sustained effort needed to reach to the guts of the experience itself:

> I drive, and the lawless music I make clears
> the air, moving in no direction
> is a swift-flame dancing . . .
> . . . law is breaking
> into the imaginative cosmos
> and then out beyond order, language adrift,
> exploding, moving through . . .

Invocation may be the working mode of both magic and poetry, but a magician is only as effective as the real manifestation of his spirits. In these poems we often have merely the intention to evoke, and little of the substance.

This is also a fault in the middle part of the book, where Adamson once again claims magical dominion over almost every animal, vegetable and mineral form in the Hawkesbury River System:

> My arm is the arm around you . . .
> but it is also the river's arm . . .

The one exception to this catalogue of pretensions is the short poem 'The Mullet Run', a vivid and carefully-handled piece of naturalistic description.

The influence of Robert Duncan is again in evidence through most of the poems, but it would be too unkind to blame him entirely for the last section of the book, the 'Grail Poems'. In these sixteen pages Adamson really lets go, somehow exalting himself to the status of a member of the nobility of the Round Table, while at the same time holding other options open:

> Come, fill me with love for a maiden
> Show me the path to a desire that is carnal
> And offer me also the temptations and the fiery lust of
> Sodom.

The Grail legend travelled a long way, through many languages and several centuries, before it found its most moving embodiment in the work of Sir Thomas Malory. It is arguable that the English language was on the verge of its most potent stage of development in the late fifteenth century when Malory gathered, translated and re-worked the Arthurian legends. What is beyond argument is the dreadful decline in the power of this legend's expression from Malory, through Tennyson, Rosetti, and Hollywood to Robert Adamson:

> I draw the light from his death.
> I lose hold, lose my grip, the sword falls.
> I feel his arms about me, his warmth as I draw back
> from the memory. My needs flow through this female
> Hermes — a trick of Eros?
> What deformity held me back?
> We were knights, sucking our cocks
> by the Light of the Grail, furiously affectionate.

Like the Pre-Raphaelite painting it so much resembles, Adamson's art in the Grail poems is on the level of titillating decoration — baroque, effete, claiming for itself a profound human purpose while remaining vain and self-obsessed, and wasting its energy on tinsel emblems at the expense of the main design.

Adamson is too good a poet to wade further into this morass of coy self-regard. Some of the earlier poems in *Cross the Border* show traces of his old strength and wit; though it is worrying to note that in many places he claims virtues that the poems themselves fail to demonstrate.

Nigel Roberts has been around the new writing scene for some ten years, editing *Free Poetry*, organising the poetry side of the Balmain Prose and Poetry Readings, and generally stirring things up. He has only published one book, *In Casablanca for the Waters* (1977), and in its style and content it sums up an aspect of the poetry world in Sydney since 1968. There is plenty of dope, drink, fucking and sucking, poems about poets and painters, the Vietnam protests, big business, hippies on communes (treated very tartly) and John Wayne, Humphrey Bogart and Sidney Greenstreet.

It is not a catalogue of affectations; it is rather a mixture of tough and witty critique and generous celebration. The style he has made his own is jagged and clipped, littered with ampersands & slant lines (the printer's solidus, i.e. /) yet accurately fitted to his voice. The poem with the most ragged and chopped-up layout is also the one with the most self-referential stylistic wit:

so what
that it looks

like

cut-up
prose

go
find fault
with thistle
because it is not
rose.

Both Vicki Viidikas and Robyn Ravlich were associated with the early Balmain days of the new writing; both wrote out of a clear awareness of their female roles as poets, and while Ravlich appears to have gone on to other things after the publication of her book *The Black Abacus* in 1971 (among them, a degree from Sydney University and a role as ABC producer), Viidikas is still writing primarily as a poet, has avoided the academy and has travelled extensively through Europe and Asia. Her first book, *Condition Red* (1973), had many good poems in it, particularly four prose poems at the back of the book, and her collection of prose pieces, *Wrappings* (1974, and reprinted as a paperback in 1976), is in my opinion one of the most interesting books of the decade.

She has a new manuscript of poetry ready for printing with Wild & Woolley in Sydney, and I must confess I was disappointed with it. The flexible form of her prose is to my mind a more effective means of communication than her new poetry, which is a mixture of colourful scenery sketched quickly and without precise outline, and argumentative statement that often circles around the point without hitting it:

. . . My love, my blood
it is aeons of suffering
and the curtain before the sun;
O brother, O love
flesh the hands which hold the key,
O raise up the dead
and trust the spaces between the stars . . .

Her experiences in the underworld of dope and sex in Sydney and Asia are the materials of much of her poetry, and it looks as though the intensity of her emotional reactions is breaking the banks of her verse, spreading pools of bright colour across the page to little real effect.

John Forbes came on the scene during its second phase, when the drug-criminal experiments of Dransfield, Adamson and others were beginning to develop into a larger awareness of what poetry could do. When Forbes speaks of drugs, it is often to push only the word itself into place in the poem:

And we are as far away as ever from
The Perfect Carburettor. Drugs disappear
In the slipstream of a bright car, the
Windows are stuffed with menus but
They don't keep out the cold.
(from *The Sorrowful Mysteries*)

In fact, when he speaks of almost anything at all, it is with a careful eye on the poem's prospects rather than to do praise to the thing the word represents. Children, for example: 'Was that a baby/or a shirt factory?/no one can tell in this weather . . .', or rural landscape, that perennial theme of Aust. Lit.: 'I don't know much about bolts from the blue/But a house in the country spells death . . .' or even love itself: 'who loves at close range/ like they do thru a tube?'

There is a type of flip wit at work here, making mock of the great themes that poetry is supposed to worship, yet the lack of solemnity is also a lack of somnolence, and while the fresh air that drifts off his pages may not quite take your breath away, it is at least a refreshing antidote to the silly pompousness that a lot of poetry inflicts on us.

The two books he has published are both small (*Tropical Skiing*, 1976 and *On the Beach*, 1977) but it should be said that the energy of his working goes not into quantity but into quality, and that there is not a poem in either book that is a mis-fire. The accuracy of his selection of line and phrase is remarkable, and his effects are precisely calculated. His poem '4 Heads & How to Do Them' is in my opinion the most skilled and stylish work of the decade, and in its play with varied poetic forms (Classic, Romantic, Symbolist and Conceptual) it evades any notion of 'subject' altogether, while ably demonstrating that its real subject, the styles themselves, is more interesting than anything else the poet might have chosen. There are poems with subjects in Forbes' books, and even some with conventional narratives, though the path he chooses for his tales is a devious one, as in the poem 'TV':

don't bother telling me about the programs
describe what your set is like the casing the
curved screen its strip of white stillness like
beach sand at pools where the animals come
down to drink and a native hunter hides his
muscles, poised with a fire sharpened spear
until the sudden whirr of an anthropologist's
hidden camera sends gazelles leaping off in
their delicate slow motion caught on film
despite the impulsive killing of unlucky Doctor
Mathews whose body was found three months later
the film and camera intact save for a faint,
green mould on its hand-made leather casing

The poem, quoted in full, takes on the form and style of its content, with the 'action' inside the film inside the television set which the poet is not looking at, but asking the imperative object of the poem's request to describe for the benefit of the reader. And the poet's imaginary version of this answer that we never receive has a similar relationship to the reader that, say, the subject of Hamlet's ruminations (his father's ghost) has to the audience of Shakespeare's play: a non-existent subject of the imagination of a character in a manufactured story. We swallow Shakespeare whole but often baulk at poems such as these, not realising their familiarity or their lineage.

Laurie Duggan's book *East* (1977) collects the best of the poems he wrote from 1970 to 1974, and opens with the title poem, which won the *New Poetry* Award in 1972. It consists of eight sonnets that work in the collage form, and the portrait of Duggan's family and the East Gippsland area they inhabited emerges vividly from the artfully arranged fragments. The other poems are in a variety of styles; two of them recall John Forbes. 'Orient' gathers the detritus of a dozen Forbes poems and rearranges it in a mixture of parody, echo and homage: '. . . Thanks/for the postcard, the coconuts/ stun me continually. It's like the first colour movie/yes, but where are the ice-creams of last summer?' The poem 'Cheerio' is dedicated to Forbes, and in it flies 'crawl across the T.V. tube' where we remember meeting the unlucky Doctor Mathews.

The last section of *East* contains twelve anagrams, made up, after the manner of Jonathan Williams, of the letters of the names of poets, in this case, writers involved with the generation under discussion. Some are simply clever; others are dreadfully apt:

Ode's R.R. boatman
art demon robs a
T.A.B. or dreams on
sodom. Be arrant;
do a sombre rant!

('Robert Adamson')

Dead man chills fire.

('Michael Dransfield')

I? I? Vi vas I kick'd?

('Vicki Viidikas')

His later work, seen here and there in magazines and now collected for publication by Wild & Woolley late in 1978, has moved away from what Duggan calls his 'post-Modernist phase'. It is more personal, more relaxed, more narrative and chatty, and follows an honorable tradition that had a great deal of influence on the writing of the late 1960s; that of Jack Kerouac, Gary Snyder and Philip Whalen, itself a form closely influenced by Tang Dynasty poetry in Chinese and by some Japanese verse. Charles Buckmaster's work had this tone around the edges of it, and it will be interesting to see what Duggan, with his impish, dry and sometimes caustic wit, makes of his material.

The Melbourne poet Alan Wearne took a large step forward with his second book, *New Devil, New Parish* (1976). The first section of 23 pages is interesting enough, containing as it does many good and typically complicated poems, and on its own might be considered a reasonable advance on his first book, *Public Relations*.

The last 56 pages, however, contain the long poem 'Out Here', a feat of endurance as well as skill. It is 2,000 lines long, and consists solely of dramatic monologues spoken by nine people thrown together by a knifing incident at a Melbourne high school. Though the dramatic monologue is a form noted for its difficult inward focus, this poem reaches out through a varied range of suburban personalities and life-styles, painting a picture of Australian life that has enough violence, ambition, disappointment, anguish and love in it to fill a large novel, or (more to the point, considering the style) a gripping movie.

Wearne's one problem is voice. In 'Out Here' he has to build nine distinct personalities, and the variety of tone required for convincing characterisation stretches his vocal talents near their limit.

Nonetheless, the characters that people his story have so much to say, and say it with such directness and colour, that the supposed honesty of much contemporary personal and confessional poetry appears thin and hysterical by comparison. 'Out Here' is a very unusual poem, both because of the confident authority of its achievement, and because its only obvious antecedent is Browning (and a few currently unpopular Americans of the older generation). Wearne owes little to any living writer, yet his work is recognisably modern; his writing shows no trace of any local tradition, yet he is distinctively Australian.

Philip Hammial only arrived in Australia in 1972 (he's American) and didn't publish his first book until 1976. His work has much that is relevant to recent Australian poetry, though, and he raises interesting questions about style and its relation to content. His books are *Foot Falls & Notes* (1976), and *Mastication Poems*, *Chemical Cart*, and *Hear me Eating* (all 1977). There's not much a critic can say about the content or subject matter of his poetry; it's simply too hard to work out what it is from poem to poem. Who in their right mind would dare to venture an opinion regarding the subject matter of — for example — the poem 'Train Habits', which opens

> I shake to explain the wren.
> The tracks are covered for filial (not political)
>   consumption.
> The person is therefore beneficial, & threats are made.
> As pilgrim he is bridge, roman & spider. . .

It's not bird-watching, nor Roman aqueduct architecture, nor the study of arachnids. Nowhere in his work does Hammial do more than give us cryptic clues as to what he's talking *about*, and though there are clues in thousands, they point in a bewildering number of directions.

Yet there is a theme running through all his work, and it is that of mainly Christian religious doctrine and liturgy. Almost every poem contains at least one word or phrase with religious overtones and yet — the problem of elusive subject matter — the reader finds it impossible to know what to do with this knowledge even when he teases it out.

The other notable thing about his poetry is the extraordinary skill Hammial shows with rhythm, syntax and enjambment. His verse is so difficult that one might well say that we shall never know to what good purpose this talent is exercised; nonetheless it is there, and stands out clearly as both a gift and a discipline.

Rae Desmond Jones has continued to work in the area he staked out for himself in his first two books, *Orpheus With a Tuba* (1973) and *The Mad Vibe* (1975). His poems have often verged on the grotesque, and his latest volume, *Shakti*, contains plenty to make the reader sit up and take notice.

The opening poem, 'The Buddha', has its hero — yes, Gautama Buddha, centre of a vast and complex religion — being strapped into a fat Maserati and crashing horribly at Monte Carlo, and closes with the image of the car's pistons masturbating 'red hot under his feet'. The last poem in the book, 'The El Paso Restaurant', is a delightful game in the genre of old Western movies, but decked out in transvestite trappings — 'down on the street gary cooper hitches / up his stockings and checks the clock' — and these two extremes of grotesque ugliness and manic camp wit form the outer borders of much of the stylistic play in the book.

More important is the tension between the personal and the public, often seen in terms of private vision versus political cynicism. The poem 'Age', for example, is in two parts; the first is a quietly impassioned rumination on how our society strips away the dignity of age —

> all the disinherited &
> the suffering and stupidity of the oppressed
> beyond the cynical tolerance of the oppressor . . .

The second part is a nicely modulated poem about an old man sitting on a bench, that spreads out beyond the boundaries of a portrait to take in the cityscape and the harbour tides beating against the rock. No overt morals are deduced, nor is the scenery made to spell out a lesson.

The total effect of this poem is more than its surface suggests, and works finally in terms of the compassion that is always present behind Jones' concerns, a care that shows itself in his scrupulous honesty to his subject rather than by any overt claims. In poems such as 'Age' the poet is taking the side of the alienated proletariat against the impersonal forces that rob our society of its deeper values, yet while Jones' commitment has the ring of authenticity, it is notable that he avoids facile empathising, and makes no claims for the poet as a special advocate for the dispossessed.

It is difficult to sum up the effect of *Shakti*, so varied are the poems and the approaches used. There are two prose-pieces, poems about bizarre sexual episodes, poems about poetry, politics, movie stars and revolution. It is equally difficult to point to a clear line of influence — Rae Jones belongs to no identifiable school or group of poets.

He is clearly not several things: not typically Australian, though his tone of voice often is; not American, though some debt to Ginsberg appears from time to time; not Romantic, though he sometimes outlines the poet's role in neo-Romantic terms; and not taken in by the New York brand of flip poetic wit, though the poem 'Jungle Juice' (in which Tarzan minces up to take part in the 1936 Congo Fashion Parade) has much in it that is reminiscent of Frank O'Hara at his most irreverently camp.

What I think is developing in his work is a model of what is happening to the whole generation: the American presence in Vietnam, the music of Bob Dylan and the manic thrill of speed have all been replaced by other things, many of them distinctly less pleasant (Timor, punk rock and heroin?), and its poetry is beginning to widen out. As poets such as Rae Jones grow older and plot a personal life increasingly more separate from the issues that tied them together in their youth, so their poems follow this shift, paradoxically taking on a more individual flavour as the complex issues of both humanity and the writer's craft are absorbed.

Some — and I would argue that Adamson and Viidikas are among them — appear in their work to be regressing to a pre-socialised phase of ego development, seeing their writing as a means of forcing a stubborn reality to reflect a manufactured gratification of their psychic needs. The emphasis on magic and drugs and the denial of the claims of corporate social structures are the operative methods that the poetry both feeds on and attempts to authorise. Others — Jones and Wearne as examples — are using a more extravert mode involving social observation and critique to reach into and explore the varied world outside their personal concerns. The ego of the poet is still active in Jones' work, balancing, criticising and giving shape to the portrayed world, where in Wearne's writing it is subordinated to the needs of his characters.

The form of dramatic monologue used by Wearne is an abandonment of the poet's voice in favour of the speech that will emerge from the beings called up from the poem; in this sense, the evocation of spirits is demonstrated as the method, and their utterances as the substance, of the poet's art. The contrast with Adamson's thaumaturgy could not be more vivid — in Wearne, the voices come so clearly from the world around us that his best lines have the fascination of a well-shaped documentary; in Adamson we hear, beneath the loud accents of the poet, only the ghostly echoes of voices trapped in books for a thousand years.

Viidikas' writing has other purposes: a means of therapy, a form of self-expression and a celebration of a mix of sub-cultural life-styles. As she says in a statement in the *ALS* issue mentioned previously:

> . . . I like all writers who are out of step, and I guess that's what I try to write about myself, the realities of subcultures in Western society such as bohemians, junkies, criminals, prostitutes, atheists, homosexuals, or people who are just plain amoral . . . I'm only interested in creating out of the subconscious . . . Because intuitive knowledge is fast becoming lost in Western society, individuals are turning to extreme and aberrated behaviour, in order to express themselves . . . my writing started as confessional therapy and has remained so . . . (*ALS*, pp. 155-6)

In many ways the poetry revolution of 1968 was itself an alienated subculture, and Viidikas' emphasis on self-expression and unconscious forces strikes one of the notes that resonated through much of the writing of that period. The honesty of her commitment to her private visions is commendable, yet it is unfortunate that a species of writing that takes so little account of the broader society around it and of the average reader's inability to endure the unstructured outpourings of the subconscious mind with more than temporary interest should have so much of the writer's energy and belief invested in it. Writers like Viidikas — and since the invention of the Romantic Outsider there has been an endless stream of them — will always recall us to a proper consideration of the deeper urges that push up against the underside of our socialised gestures, and it is a pity that they should so often remind us of the bore who buttonholes us with the details of his dreams, recounted at great length.

As history is the analysis of change through the lens of hindsight, its character is often ironic. It is a minor irony that at a stage where the new writing of the late 1960s is beginning to be seen clearly as homogeneous, it is now also becoming obvious that the coherent purpose of writers such as Adamson, Dransfield, Buckmaster, Nigel Roberts, Rae Jones, Vicki Viidikas and others was merely the product of the constraining forces they worked against; in other words, they looked the same because they were all different from the established writers they opposed. And they *were* very different from, say, A. D. Hope, Buckley, McAuley, Wright, FitzGerald; long may they remain so.

Even as the picture comes into focus, its elements dissolve and disperse. I have pointed out the differences between Jones and Wearne on the one hand, and Adamson and Viidikas on the other; they are of course each different from one another, and there is more dissentience yet, various and profound enough to form the subject for a dozen dissertations. And it is not only the style and subject matter that is forming the basis for serious argument. Disquiet about the very teleology of poetic method is beginning to erode the fabric of community that once knit together a group of poets with an apparently common purpose.

It's hard to see a single direct cause for this shift, but it seems to me that the two major changes in Australian political feeling in 1972 and 1975 have a lot to do with it.

Whether the poets of 1968 were specifically articulate in political terms is beside the point. Their early work spoke loudly of a wish for change, and that change was duly achieved. Australian society showed a readiness to take on something new and untried, to abandon the safety of conventional established values in favour of a future that was unconventional, exhilarating and morally committed. But that experiment, in its larger social terms, was quickly crippled; after Whitlam, most Australians simply wanted to turn back to a less exhausting and more stable way of life. I think this engendered in the young poets not a failure of nerve, but a failure of purpose. Their disillusionment was pervasive; it was as though, in the stunned aftermath of 11 November 1975, the poets voted informal, came in off the streets and locked the study door.

The twelve collections of recent poetry considered in this article — with perhaps the exceptions of Rae Jones and Nigel Roberts — display a turning away from social and political commitment. Each poet has taken a different direction, but the paths all diverge from what was once common territory. It's not a happy prognosis for the poetry of commitment; but the poets are still writing, and getting better at it. A new range of styles is emerging, in these and other books, with a looser focus on the social realities and a closer attention to the voice of the individual. I doubt that the next decade will feature a group of young writers as energetically cohesive as those of 1968. What it might give us is something more valuable: a large number of varied individual voices, building on the achievements and hard-won freedoms of the past ten years, and leading poetry out into a larger and more generous field of experience.

Number 2, 1976

Ode to Stalin

JOHN RILEY/OSIP MANDELSHTAM

(154)

He still remembers my worn-out boots,
The worn-out grandeur of my soles,
And I remember his harsh voice,
Black hair, near Mount David.

Pistachio streets, tricky streets
Renovated with eggwhite or chalk,
Balcony, incline, clattering, horses, balcony,
Young oaks, planes, slow elms.

Yet the writing so curved so feminine it
Dazzles the eyes in its casing of light,
It's a good town, sunk back in its beams
In a young-for-its-age but aging summer.

(155)

Chained-down, nailed-down, groaning, where's
Prometheus, helper, and cliff's support?
Where's the black kite, yellow-eyed,
Hunting claws, sullen flight?

It can't be — tragedy can't be repeated.
But these lips about to speak,
But these lips lead straight to the heart
Of Aeschylus the docker, of Sophocles the forester.

He — echo and greeting, he was — milestone, no — ploughshare.
The stone-air theatre of times to come
Came of age, they all want a sight of the others:
The living, the doomed, those to whom death won't come.

(156)

Like Rembrandt, that martyr of chiaroscuro,
I've gone deep into ever more silent time,
But the cutting edge of my burning rib
Is guarded neither by those watchmen
Nor by that soldier, asleep in the storm.

Do you forgive me, magnificent brother,
Both master and father of black and green,
But the eye of falcon quill
And hot harem caskets at midnight
Excite the tribe disturbed by twilight's furs
To no good, to no good.

(157)

When my larynx is wet, soul dry, I sing,
When my eyesight's moderately moist, consciousness not cunning,
It is good for you, wine? Are wineskins?
The Colchidian heaving in blood?
But my chest is weighted, quiet, no language,
It's not I who sings now, my breath sings,
And hearing is scabbarded in mountains, my head is deaf.
A selfless song's its own praise,
A joy for friends, for enemies, pitch.

A selfless song, emerging from moss,
Single-voiced gift of a hunter's life
Sung on horseback, on high, breath
Honest and open, caring for nothing,
Honest and angry, but to get the young pair
To their wedding, blameless . . .

(158)

Rounded bays and gravel and deep blue sundered,
And the slow sail cloud-prolonged —
You're not here, I hardly knew your worth:
Sea grass bitter, a counterfeit of hair:
Longer than organ fugues, it reeks of the long lie.
Light-headed, an iron tenderness,
And rust gnaws at the sloping shore . . .
Different sand under my head.

Guttural Urals, burly Volga land,
Or this plain — these are what I have —
. . . Keep on breathing, where they are.

(159)

Armed with a vision of slender wasps
Sucking earth's axis, sucking earth's axis,
Everything I've had to face comes back,
I can say it by heart; and in vain.

I can't paint, I can't sing,
I can't draw a dark-voiced bow over strings:
I can only drive my sting into life and
Envy wasps their cunning and their strength.

O of sometime even I
Could be driven, past sleep, past death,
Goaded by wind and summer's warmth to catch
Sound of earth's axis, catch sound of earth's axis.

Number 3, 1976

Post-War

LAURIE DUGGAN

Lights burn in houses we are not, through
fear or ignorance, permitted to enter;
the hotel we visit in darkness
remains nameless   streaming from the balcony
expensive underwear of *ubermenschen*,
clown masks, balloons, whistles.
A blind accordionist floats across the suburbs
as if, from the brick and bone-dust, something
more than tangible can emerge.
In Berlin the balloons drift upward
on the pitch of a tide, as biplanes
descended on Lens.
Lost for images, we became the fleeing crowd:
a mouth swallowed the whole picture.

Years after the promise receded,
through the hard winter, men wander
aimlessly by the tracks, boxcars
branded by number,
convicted,
sentenced:

Scott's run, West Virginia 1937.
Figures in a caravan, huddled in pale incandescence
as whores who spurn commerce
summon a trite poetic.
The movement is into form;
the flux contained, the moment passes:
subject, object, fall into place as
starched gestures of shirts over the hotel.

Number 1, 1978

For the left hand (1)

JENNIFER MAIDEN

(Things gentle & are gentling.
A woman's face with qualities of servitude, refinement
& poignant ill-luck, the skeleton in it shadowed
superciliously beneath the cheeks & eyes. A reader,
a mistress, a victim, determined in all senses,
the voice scrambling but balancing, surviving
its rebellious march: small steps, back straight, hips in
across the obedience of its breath: a scrutinising voice,
low, knowledgeable, sly. Belonging to the kind —
the race, the family, the eucharist, the child,
the milker & the milked — the kind of being who could live
thirty years in a house with the bones
of something it had killed, & still obey it.)
There are compass curves of mirth but nothing
so arch as a dimple, the mouth corners set
in something too knowing for a smile, the lips
more relevant to people than to flowers. The dead
do sketch quirkish invisible lines on her face,
determining. The stubborn partial stars
dance like scalpels through the attic slates
& halo things in boxes, soft so quick.
If innocence were tangible & seen it would appear
as a natural fist: that of a baby or someone in torture or
a woman like her, observing. Long observed,
she provokes a petulance in nature, scalds herself
left-handling teapots & saucepans, & the taps
steam instantly from cold to hot, passim. The elements
in all the jugs are broken. The busy kettle boils
russet water. She implores like a musician, knuckling
the seamy sleep voluptly in her eyes. The dawn's a listless
undressed probing thing, with numb hips & crisp hands, a

circulator of dusk-whiskers in the cellar, & between
sinister attic avenues. The sinistral block,
the reversal, is most solid in daybreak, can be blithe
as an operatic arrest, sometimes. She never knew.
thirty years in a house with the boxes, gentling.

Number 4, 1979

The Home Conveyancing Kit

CHRIS WALLACE-CRABBE

Michael and Trish have bet their bottom dollar
on getting the house paid off, it is so sweet
they just fell in love with it from the start

so bought it, or began to, from Mario
still paying it off himself
who had a malignant growth removed before Xmas.

He it was planted the vegie garden
after handing over the deposit to Hugh and Min
who went overseas to try and save their marriage:

it failed, of course. The paint job and the sleepout
were the work nine years ago of dotty Neville Ryan
out of whose estate the balance was paid.

He had snapped up the then-quite-newish cottage
from a wolfish pig of a landscape painter
who mainly cared for what was under skirts

and collected it — till he suffered an amputation.
The place was originally sold by a dairy farmer
who never made it back from Armentières

as a building block within cooee of the station
before the city sprawled and gobbled it up.
Under the lemon are the bones of somebody's dog.

Number 4, 1979

Big time

ANIA WALWICZ

Wanted some good moments. Some hot times. Some sharp things that I couldn't forget. Hotter than life to feel like that. Something great. And proud. More or less like that. No small time low down. No just so and so. I was after bull's eye. And perfect. So it couldn't be more taut. That it was in the right spot. Want to be a star. Not the fourth girl in the back line of the chorus. But centre forward. Had enough playing half-back. Don't want to be half-back anymore. So I wanted to be right there in the front. And not necessarily strong. But feeling a lot more than most. Be the doer or have it done to. Didn't matter. I can play any role. As long as there is this one big moment for me there. As long as there is. I was looking for anything and everything to make me more than I was. And I was only small. And not much. Hardly anything. So I had no choice but to go looking for some good times. And something stronger than lemonade. And brighter than cream. And louder than a whisper. And warmer than luke warm. And bigger than my room that was too small. And better. I knew I could get better. For sure. You just know these things. Deep down. There was this pearl for the diver. Gold for the finder. Silver for the girls. Sparklets for the mister. Red for the bull. Big time moments for me. Fireworks for this girl. That lived at night. Ate chocolate.

Number 4, 1980

Yugoslav Story

SUSAN HAMPTON

Jože was born in the village of Loški Potok,
in a high cheek-boned family. I remarked
that he had no freckles, he liked to play cards,
and the women he knew were called Maria, Malčka, Mimi;
and because he was a 'handsome stranger'
I took him for a ride on my Yamaha
along the Great Western Highway
and we ate apples; I had never met someone
who ate apples by the case, whose father
had been shot at by Partisans in World War II,
who'd eaten frogs and turnips in the night,
and knew how to make pastry so thin
it covered the table like a soft cloth.
He knew how to kill and cut up a pig,
and how to foxtrot and polka. He lifted me up in the air.
He taught me to say *Jaz te ljubim, ugasni luč*
('I love you, turn off the light')
and how to cook *filana paprika, palačinka,*
and *pražena jetra*. One night in winter
Jože and two friends ate 53 of these *palačinke*
(pancakes) and went straight to the factory
from the last rummy game. Then he was my husband,
he called me '*moja žena*' and sang a dirty song
about Terezinka, a girl who sat on the chimney

waiting for her lover, and got a black bum.
He had four brothers and four sisters,
I had five sisters.
His father was a policeman under King Peter,
my father was a builder in bush towns.
Jože grew vegetables and he smoked Marlboros
and he loved me. This was in 1968.

Number 3, 1980

no love from Papunya

BILLY MARSHALL-STONEKING

Someone loves Alice,
she writes on the walls —
on the sides of sheds: 'one boy only him'
in white paint that drips and runs.

Two sisters, promised
to old men, giggle behind their hands
as the words dry —
laugh themselves to tears.

At the school, boys have drawn
phallic shapes on all the doors,
propped-up with giant balls —
at initiation time.

The new teachers furnish classrooms
with alphabet and number games:
A – C – D – C / Alice is prolific —
lifts her dress behind the hospital.

Two girls into old men goes once.

Number 1, 1981

Assignation with a Somnambulist

JOHN MANIFOLD

Walk in your sleep beyond Yeppoon
Out to the islands. Fear no wrong
From cone-shell, stonefish, or the prong-
ed lightning presaging the monsoon.

Call it a dream, and watch the moon
Casting your shadow straight and strong
With that of she-oaks. You belong
To silence, night and the lagoon.

Walk in your summer sleep. You know
There's nowhere that you cannot go
When you go thus. But understand

On the last island, there am I
Beyond the combers, high and dry,
Shaping our burrow in the sand.

Number 2, 1981

Ignaz Semmelweis, author of *The Etiology, the Concept and the Prophylaxis of Childbed Fever*, enters the Vienna Insane Asylum, 1865

JENNIFER STRAUSS

Not to be believed
What hands can carry . . . No, no!
No-one laid hands on me
To bring me here. No need.
I have never been so truly in the world,
Patient finally in the First Division,
Lying-in
To be delivered of a death.

You may place me with
My friend Kolletschka . . . Yes, yes!
He is here. I bring him in my hand — see!
Not to be believed.
I think myself Kolletschka? . . . No, no!
He is cold clay: I burn, I am ignited.
You make a note: it is noteworthy
I offer a pun: you take my sanity.
You say I have hurt my hand, it will be seen to . . .
Not soon enough.

I have in my time,
Like most *accoucheurs*,
Handled cadavers in the dissecting room
Extensively. Subtlest panders
Setting the flesh of the dead to living wombs

We breed morbidity. Professor Kolletschka
Died of pleuritis,
Peritonitis, meningitis, pericarditis.
In a woman we'd call it
Childbed fever.

Jesus the women die as if to spite us!
Their rose fevers bloom unquenchably.
At the clinic doors they scream for the midwives.
We lay our hands on them: they are not healed.
Not to be believed.
Accursed? That's it. From Eve downwards.
That's why the midwives must go,
They don't punish enough. Better believe
God vindictive
Than a doctor dirty.

Punishment interests you . . . Why I feel guilt?
In truth, dear colleague, because I am
Guilty,
Blood on my hands,
There is blood . . . in fact
Here, at the juncture of thumb and digit.
I have been telling you all this time
I cut my left hand in the cadaver room
Soon it will close
In peritonitis meningitis pericarditis
Childbed fever, dying proof
To be believed.

Number 1, 1982

from A Fear of Dying

ALAN GOULD

I

Quietly in a downstairs room
a nurse confirms the worst will come.
Upstairs you wear the china cool
composure of an heirloom doll,
so thin beneath the counterpane
illumined after weeks of pain,
and read-to from an ancient book
by someone with a troubled look
while elsewhere, angeline, remote,
the heady scents of evening float;

the woodlands shimmer like a sea
where warmer lives glide silently
and nightjars flit like atoms through
the tower that prepares for you,
the one-door little room wherein
you are the cornered heroine.

Now, leave the story's end unread,
dismiss the reader by the bed,
slip on your viridescent gown
and smooth the mirror's anxious frown.
Abandon your reproachful toys,
slip past the room of squabbling boys,
step through the copse of childhood thought
where all your naughty selves cavort,
the pilferer and chatterbox
who fall about in smeary frocks.
Go quick, yes nurse's cry is lost,
go quick, the garden wall is crossed,
the evening is immense and blue,
the moon, as though impelled by you,
is hatching from the high Tyrol
and rising milky as a foal
to follow at the pace you guide
along the jetblack riverside
toward a time that has no end
or harm, in which you apprehend
picture on picture of delight
which flicker briefly from the night,
— as this, the sudden festive house
wherein a lady and her spouse
arouse a company at hand
and lead them in a saraband,
while you, with others at a wall,
observe the stately dance as all
their swaying lords and ladyships
sail past your eyes like Spanish ships,
— as when you grant the rascal's boon
and dance with him a rigadoon,
and through the silk and tarlatan
you lead as though you are the man
and sternly tell him to amuse
and use the manners flunkeys use.
He will, he will, the darling boy,
but look, here comes the hoi polloi,
so snatch a parting kiss, then leave
and take the Colonel's proffered sleeve,

and take the horses he's prepared
to ride where no-one else has dared,
through forests and through gypsy camps,
through towns that are unserved by lamps,
past where the outmost farmsteads are
until one last particular
confronts you, say this iron gate
where you are told that you must wait
while someone goes to wake the host.
The lawns are vast and crisp with frost;
behind the trees dawn's thread of chrome.
Yes, you are aeons from your home,
your partner whispers all's arranged,
and nothing but his smile has changed.

II

It is today, you seem to wake to it
and sense there's nothing conscience won't permit,
no hazard the adventure won't refine
as light pours through your window like a wine
and islands melt like tablets in a glass;
The sun, today, will let no shadows pass,
and fiery parrots cackle in your ear
excuses that seem rash and cavalier,
there dash your children, they are running wild,
there broods your husband, he is reconciled
and there as well the mirror's sudden frown
but shrug that from you as you do your gown.

Put on the costly Adriatic blue,
put on the mesmerising necklace too,
leave by the front — of course you'll be observed,
but trust your contact; a table is reserved.

Now cross the dazzling midday plazas where
the fishermen and lazy soldiers stare,
mount streets of houses heaped like bleaching skulls,
pass fleeting inland views the haze annuls,
take alleys leading into alleys, through
the parts of town prohibited to you.
Here is the place. You're breathless. And you see
the table that was booked is laid for three.
The place is uproar, and the staff, inflamed,
have written out a list in which you're named.
Be cool among the lunches, be restrained;
someone will know you; all will be explained.
The ugly mood requires your unconcern
as do these voices speaking out of turn,
this thrusting face that fails to understand,

this kitchen knife appearing in a hand.
You've faced a mob before and seen it through,
nor will your consort fail to rescue you.
Now turn, to see in white your diplomat,
his limousine is purring like a cat;
his rakish chauffeur (you'd heard he was discreet)
is pissing like a bullock in the street.
He will not meet your eyes, and the other hands
uplift you from the door in which he stands.
So look away, be scornful, unaware
the makeshift surgery those hands prepare,
for somewhere near your throat has just occurred
a change that is both dreadful and absurd.

Number 4, 1981

At the Criterion

JOHN TRANTER

For Martin Johnston

I don't go to the pub much any more —
they pulled down The Newcastle ten years ago,
and the Forest Lodge is full of young punks
who can't hold their drink. But now and then —
say, some Friday night when my room
gets on my nerves, with its endless books,
with the pool of lamplight on the table,
the traffic outside my window,
the crowds, the rush and babble, then,
just for old times' sake, I go out.
And she's sure to be there, in the corner bar,
laughing with that young executive
who goes down to the snow in the winter
and has a town house in Double Bay.
They look happy enough — he seems
quite at ease and familiar with her,
though he's only known her a few months —
but does he know, for example,
that she had an abortion two years ago,
and still isn't over it? That
her mother won't speak to her now
because of the 'immoral things' she did
with her pretty room-mate at College;
that she likes Seafood Avocado, and can't stand

cats, or poverty; and when she makes love
with that awkward desperation, sad and hurried,
brief tears gather in her eyes: she's not crying,
not happy, just 'a bit out of it', as she says.
Well, he'll learn these things, if he's
attentive, and if it lasts long enough.

Even now — and I'm only on my seventh drink —
she's paying rather too much attention to that
academic type near the door — an older man,
good-looking in a rough sort of way;
a drunk, but with a charming line of talk.
And she prefers older men.
When I've had enough
I'll go back to the flat and pour a scotch
and read over my notes on Cavafy —
a Greek poet, dead long ago,
who lived very fast when he was young
then spent a lonely middle age remembering
his youth in Alexandria, the sordid affairs . . .
patiently sketching a portrait of his
beautiful, corrupt and much-loved city —
'its fever, its absolute devotion to pleasure.'

Number 3, 1981

Message
(Green Cape, N.S.W.)

Dimitris Tsaloumas

Tell her that I've made up my mind today that I
shall never die. They've cut a path
without a past in the hallucinations of captivity
and I thrust through the thickets of birdsong
and embroideries of light with the guileless snake
right to the heart of immortality,
I saw the wild duck beak strained forward
beating through the narrows of the ravine
and the hawk beautiful amid the frenzied squawks
rising deadly scaling
the slopes of heaven. Tell her that her son
came down to the spray-misted headlands
of the South and saw the onslaught of waves
huge as island hills and cried out
The sea! The sea! And tell her that he changed his mind.
She wasn't mean-spirited. She'll understand.

The Steel

LES MURRAY

In memory of my mother, Miriam Murray née Arnall,
born 23.5.1915, died 19.4.1951.

I am older than my mother.
Cold steel hurried me from her womb.
I haven't got a star.

What hour I followed
the waters into this world
no one living can now say.
My zodiac got washed away.

The steel of my induction
killed my brothers and sisters;
once or twice I was readied for them

and then they were not mentioned
again, at the hospital
to me or to the visitors.
The reticence left me only.

I think, apart from this,
my parents' life was happy,
provisional, as lives are.

Farming spared them from the war,
that, and an ill-knit blue shin
my father had been harried back

to tree-felling with, by his father
who supervised from horseback.
The times were late pioneer.

So was our bare plank house
with its rain stains down each crack
like tall tan flames,
magic swords, far matched perspectives:

it reaped Dad's shamed invectives —
Paying him rent for this shack!
The landlord was his father.

But we also had fireside ease,
health, plentiful dinners, the radio;
we'd a car to drive to tennis.

Country people have cars
for more than shopping and show
our Dodge reached voting age, though,
in my first high school year.

I was in the town at school
the afternoon my mother
collapsed, and was carried from the dairy.
The car was out of order.

The ambulance was available
but it took a doctor's say-so
to come. This was refused.
My father pleaded. Was refused.

The local teacher's car was got finally.
The time all this took didn't pass,
it spread through sheets, unstoppable.

Thirty-seven miles to town
and the terrible delay.
Little blood brother, blood sister,
I don't blame you.
How can you blame a baby?
or the longing for a baby?

Little of that week
comes back. The vertigo,
the apparent recovery —
She will get better now.
The relapse on the Thursday.

In school and called away
I was haunted, all that week,
by the spectre of dark women,
Murrays dressed in midday black
who lived on the river islands
and are seen only at funerals;
their terrible weak authority.

Everybody in the town
was asking me about my mother;
I could only answer childishly
to them. And to my mother,

and on Friday afternoon
our family world
went inside itself forever.

Sister Arnall, city girl
with your curt good sense
were you being the nurse
when you let them hurry me?
being responsible

when I was brought on to make way
for a difficult birth in that cottage hospital
and Cousin Robert stole my birthday?

Or was it our strange diffidence,
unworldly at a pinch, unresentful,
being a case among cases,

a relative, wartime sense,
modern, alien to fuss,
that is not in the Murrays?

I don't blame Robert's mother:
she didn't put her case.
It was the steel proposed
reasonably, professionally,
that became your sentence

but I don't decry unselfishness:
I'm proud of it. Of you.
Any virtue can be fatal.

In the event, his coming gave no trouble
but it might have, I agree;
nothing you agreed to harmed me.
I didn't mean to harm you
I was a baby.

For a long time, my father
himself became a baby
being perhaps wiser than me,
less modern, less military;

he was not ashamed of grief,
of its looking like a birth
out through the face

bloated, whiskery, bringing no relief.
It was mainly through fear
that I was at times his father.
I have long been sorry.

Caked pans, rancid blankets,
despair and childish cool
were our road to Bohemia
that bitter wartime country.

What were you thinking of,
Doctor M.B., B.S.?
Were you very tired?
Did you have more pressing cases?

Know panic when you heard it:
Oh you can bring her in!
Did you often do
diagnosis by telephone?

Perhaps we wrong you,
make a scapegoat of you;
perhaps there was no stain
of class in your decision,

no view that two framed degrees
outweighed a dairy.
It's nothing, dear:
just some excited hillbilly —

As your practice disappeared
and you were cold-shouldered in town
till you broke and fled,
did you think of the word Clan?

It is an antique
concept. But not wholly romantic.
We came to the river early;
it gives us some protection.

You'll agree the need is real.
I can forgive you now
and not to seem magnanimous.
It's enough that you blundered
on our family steel.

Thirty five years on earth:
that's short. That's short, Mother,
as the lives cut off by war

and the lives of spilt children are short.
Justice wholly in this world
would bring them no rebirth
nor restore your latter birthdays.
How could that be justice?

My father never quite
remarried. He went back
by stages of kindness to me
to the age of lonely men,
of only men, and men's company

that is called the Pioneer age.
Snig chain and mountain track;
he went back to felling trees

and seeking justice from his
dead father. His only weakness.
One's life is not a case

except of course it is.
Being just, seeking justice:
they were both of them right,
my mother and my father.

There is justice, there is death,
humanist: you can't have both.
Activist, you can't serve both.
You do not move in measured space.

The poor man's anger is a prayer
for equities Time cannot hold
and steel grows from our mother's grace.
Justice is the people's otherworld.

Jim Davidson to C. B. Christesen

31 March 1982

The wheel has now turned a full circle: it is my last day as Editor of *Meanjin*, and so I thought I would write to you.

There's not time to go deeply into the matters I raised briefly when we met last November — how the decline of the liberal assumption that the well-educated person should be as well informed as possible on as many subjects as possible, the decline of Melbourne vis-á-vis Sydney, the rising costs — how all these things have made it difficult for *Meanjin* to survive, but also — in a very real sense — more necessary.

So there have been adaptations: the cultivation of the concept of a cluster of constituencies, a more peripatetic editorship with a Poetry Editor in Sydney, and persistent cost-cutting to the bone. There is now half the office staff we had in 1974.

Despite this, I would like to think that the present *Meanjin* is a lineal descendant of all that has gone before: so I have said, and so I believe it to be. No doubt there are things you would disagree with that have appeared in it, but enough comments have been passed on to suggest that you have not been totally unhappy with what I've been able to do.

From tomorrow, there'll be a new editor. That, I think, should be a matter of pride to us both. I've no doubt that Judith Brett will make an excellent editor, though as different from me as I was from you. She has my full support — although I am retaining no formal connections with the journal —

and I hope she'll have yours. While there's been a slight upward trend in circulation figures lately, times have been bad, and may get worse: as a last-ditch stand, a public appeal might be necessary. I'd like to think, should that unhappy state of affairs come to pass, that all three editors could sit on a platform together. It ought to be possible, and would show that the journal had all guns blazing.

For the moment, let me merely say Thankyou. They have been eight difficult years, rich and memorable, and had you not designated me to succeed you, or handed over so impressive an artefact and asked me to share so important a calling, I would never have had them. In a very real sense I am in your debt, and gladly acknowledge it.

All good wishes

Jim Davidson

Part Seven

Who's On Whose Margins?

On Jim Davidson's departure in 1982 the editorship of *Meanjin* was taken over by Judith Brett, previously a lecturer in politics at the University of Melbourne. Like her predecessor, the new editor was committed to maintaining the magazine as a broad review of ideas with a strong contemporary focus — as a journal of Australian *writing* rather than a literary magazine in the narrower sense.

One conspicuous feature of *Meanjin* during Judith Brett's editorship was its extensive publication and discussion of the work of women and migrant writers. Beginning with a special issue on immigration and culture in 1983, *Meanjin* increasingly reflected (and promoted) the cultural diversification that was occurring in Australia during the 1980s. This was by no means *Meanjin*'s first foray into publishing the writing of hitherto 'marginal' groups, but over the five years that Judith Brett occupied the editorial chair there was a strong sense that the centre of gravity was shifting as new, heterogeneous creative movements rose to challenge the earlier nationalist project, with its promotion of a unitary, 'mainstream' Australian culture.

Number 2, 1983

Elizabeth Jolley: An Appreciation

HELEN GARNER

I first came across Elizabeth Jolley's writing in *Meanjin* in 1979. A story called *The Bench* (now retitled *Adam's Bride* in her Penguin collection *Woman in a Lampshade*) opens with these sentences:

> All small towns in the country have some sort of blessing. In one there is a stretch of river which manages to retain enough water for swimming in the summer; in another, the wife of the policeman is able to make dresses for bridesmaids, and in yet another, the cook at the hotel turns hairdresser on Saturday afternoons.

This is a perfect introduction to one of Jolley's dominant modes: the confident, attractive generalisation, the use of the word 'blessing', the easy feeling for the detail, both natural and human, of life in the country, and respect for the minor skills and generosities of ordinary people.

Jolley is sixty, was born in England, and lives in Perth. She has published six books of fiction in the last eight years: *Five Acre Virgin* and *The Travelling Entertainer*, short stories (Fremantle Arts Centre Press), *Palomino*, a novel (Outback Press), *The Newspaper of Claremont Street*, a novel (Fremantle), and in Penguin this year, *Mr Scobie's Riddle*, a novel, and *Woman in a Lampshade*, a collection of stories. I have listed the books in order of publication, but they have certainly not been published in order of writing: the order of writing, without consulting Jolley herself, would be hard to establish, for the world of her imagination is so unified, and her themes and images have been so thoroughly worked and reworked, re-examined, re-arranged and re-used, that one could dive in at any point in any of the six books and not be able to say with confidence, 'This is early Jolley' or 'This is late'.

Jolley operates with an inspired thrift. She returns unabashed to what she finds evocative and rich and not yet properly understood or exorcised. It's not just a matter of recurring characters, though that's part of it. Certain images, phrases, whole sentences, whole paragraphs, whole trains of events emerge again and again, in a manner which at first unnerves, like a half-remembered dream or a flicker of déjà vu, but which finally produces an unusual cumulative effect. She will take a situation, a relationship, a moment of insight, a particular longing, and work on it in half a dozen different versions, making the characters older or younger, changing their gender or their class, gaoling or releasing a father, adding or subtracting a murder or a suicide; and these repetitions and re-usings, conscious but not to the point of being orchestrated, set up a pattern of echoes which unifies the world, and is most seductive and comforting.

What are these images, so industrious but never threadbare? The timbered valley, the rooster which has just lost a cockfight and is too ashamed to peck at its food, the old man who designs his wine labels before he has even bought the land, the brick path made by the nine-year-old boy, unexpected rain coming into an open shed, the ribbed pattern of a vineyard, the old man whose 'freshly combed white hair looked like a bandage', the child's mouth 'all square with crying', the dream-like 'lawns made of water', 'the great ship with a knowledge not entirely her own', the half-eaten pizzas discarded in the laundry after a party, the person who crushes herbs in the palm of one hand and sniffs at them, the pile of firewood that the old husband lovingly maintains so that the housewife 'only had to reach out an arm for it', the father who, when his small daughter writes a sentence, 'kissed the page', the observation that 'water is the last thing to get dark'. These things are some of Jolley's icons.

Her characters, too, are part of this strange net of familiarity, and are held in it: that weird trio, always in paroxysms of laughter or rage, the mother who cleans houses for a living to support her feckless son and her anxious daughter — the daughter as often as not the narrator; mother as landlady or vice versa; pairs of sisters; pairs of lesbians, one much older than the other; migrants humiliating themselves to earn a living as salesmen; crazed European aunts who sob with homesickness and knit 'wild cardigans'; harmless impostors, simpletons and idiots; couples ill-matched intellectually; savage nurses with vast bosoms and shameful pasts. And running through all six books is the strong connecting tissue of land, land, land: the obsession with the ownership of land, the toiling and the self-denial and the saving for it with such passion that denial itself becomes the pleasure; land that people bargain for and marry for and swindle for; land with strings attached; land to be deprived of which can drive people mad; land that flourishes, land that is sour and barren; land that is stolen from ageing parents by children and sold; land with healing properties, land without which life has neither meaning nor purpose. 'All land', say her characters over and over, 'is somebody's land'.

But how can I have got this far without mentioning that Elizabeth Jolley is a very *funny* writer? The novel *Palomino* is the only one of the six books which is devoid of her weird humour, and this is one of the reasons for its failure. Her humour is not cruel, though some people have used this word to describe the novel *Mr Scobie's Riddle*. What makes us laugh in her books is the friction between humour and pathos. She is droll, sly, often delicate; not averse to the throwaway line ('Matron Price, while she had her scissors handy, bent down and cut off what remained of Mrs Murphy's hair'; a baby 'dressed with simplicity in a grimy napkin'); she is offhand, with a batty sideways slip that I find hilarious; and she is capable of the most skilful construction and priming, as in the first nine pages of *Mr Scobie's Riddle* which set out the whole ghastly, frantic moral sink of St Christopher and St Jude's Hospital for the Aged in a brilliantly comic exchange of official reports between Night Sister Shady (Unregistered) and the dreadful Matron Price.

Hospitals are rich mines of humour and pathos. The hospital in *Mr Scobie's Riddle* is almost a character in itself. 'Hilda's Wedding' (in *Woman in a Lampshade*), one of her most slyly funny, surreal and painful stories, is set in a hospital where the narrator is a relieving night nurse. In Jolley's hospitals, patients are helpless victims, and the lowly workers — cleaners, cooks, junior nurses, maids — are under such pressure from an unseen, wilful and corrupt authority that their lives become warped. Their struggle to maintain some form of dignity and also of fun takes strange shapes:

> 'It's very informal everywhere tonight', I told them. 'There's chocolate cake in Matron's office and someone's fixed a wireless in the broom cupboard, there's to be dancing later.'
>
> Smallhouse and Gordonpole . . . emptied the bins too and they were allowed to smoke which was fair enough when you saw what was sometimes thrown away from the operating theatres.

St Christopher and St Jude echoes with the strangled cries of the furious cook; there is always somebody crying somewhere at night; all night a card game is in progress in the dinette, where the hospital itself is being gambled away by Matron Price's feckless brother — a grown-up version of the charlady's son of many another story. There are only two medical treatments available: epsom salts and menthol camphor. Bowels are unreliable; there is lentil stew and lemon sago for every meal, burnt. Matron Price is engaged in a battle to get the senile patients to sign over their bank accounts to her. It is the most horrible place.

> Mr Scobie, allowed to take little walks, often passed by a bakery. Every day he stopped to admire the golden fresh bread displayed . . . He went inside. He bought a doughnut and carried it back to St Christopher and St Jude to eat it after tea.
>
> As he entered the hall of the hospital, Matron Price and the cook, leaving the office together, came towards him. He hoped they would

not see the little paper bag with the doughnut in it.

'Oh, Mr Scobie dear, you should not buy rubbish like that', Matron said. 'It won't do your bowels any good.' 'What's wrong with the food you get here?' the cook said. 'Anyone'd think you didn't get enough to eat here. At least it's home cooking here and you know what's in it. That's what I always say.'

Not wanting to be discovered eating the doughnut, Mr Scobie tried to find somewhere to put it in Room One. There really was no hiding place. He put the paper bag on the floor beside his bed.

Later, when he ate it, it was cold and heavy, lifeless. It tasted unpleasant, as if it had absorbed all the smells of the hospital.

Pathos is a risky mode. If the humour doesn't come off, the pathetic thing can be left stranded, wet and dripping. This happens: a little slide that's too easy, a too blatant twanging of the heart strings, a too convenient car crash. Sometimes she is a bit heavy-handed with the adverbs, or one of the family's comic brawls loses its rhythm and collapses. But even a clumsy, flustered, amateurish story will have a nugget of sense at its centre, an image that surprises, a simple — even a crude — stroke that comes off and almost saves it; or else she'll strike a note that only a woman of her age would have the nerve or the knowledge to go for: some low-toned remark that will flip a situation over or make a sudden quiet of acceptance. *The Shepherd on the Roof*, a story in *Five Acre Virgin* (out of print, I believe), shows this knack she's got, of letting one mood of a relationship suddenly overwhelm its opposite, while both are still sounding:

'You've got coleslaw in your beard', I told my husband after supper. He wiped it off before he kissed me.

'I do love you very much', he said. 'Even though you're such a nasty piece of work', he held me close to him.

'I don't know!' I said. 'Whatever keeps us together!

'Mutual contempt', he said and kissed me again.

I lay beside him and listened to him snoring. I thought of the children and how there seemed no place in the world for them. My husband often says he can't understand why they won't pretend to study, like Tessa's children, and get a government grant. But I think, like me, he does understand. And then I thought of Mr Stannard wanting his shed and not being able to have it. The kitchen tap dripped and I could hear the stream rushing and the unchanging noises of the frogs and I wanted to wake my husband and talk to him. I wanted to say, 'Let's not quarrel and argue any more'.

She is not quite at home with contemporary idiom. There is something irredeemably between-wars about the feckless son 'the Doll', Mr Scobie's racy nephew Hartley, and their ilk: you can't help seeing them in two-tone shoes and brilliantine, their slang is dance-hall, and she doesn't seem to be doing it on purpose. Sometimes these anachronisms jar; sometimes they have a shock effect that makes your head spin. This slight sense of uncertainty is compensated for, however, by her ability to make an unerring choice of detail:

> Like yesterday I had only two people in all day, just two little boys who looked at everything . . . spilled all the marbles . . . and then in the end they just bought themselves a plastic dagger each.

Because *Mr Scobie's Riddle* is about an old people's home, some critics have taken a sociological approach to it, as if Jolley were making an impassioned plea to the general public to soften its heart towards the aged. She's much tougher than that and much more of an artist. What she says about old people reminds me that one day I shall be one of them: she provokes not condescending sympathy but rushes of 'pity and terror':

> His hand, flapping, caught the door post on the way back. The frail skin, brown mottled and paper thin, was grazed and broken . . . Quickly she tore up a piece of old rag kept for padding up the old women and bound up the bleeding hand.

An expression like 'kept for padding up the old women' has the same effect as the half-understood references to adult sexual life that one reads as an eight-year-old: revulsion and fear, coupled with a sense of fate.

Life is pretty grim, in Elizabeth Jolley. People are disappointed, weak, frightened for their children, ill with homesickness, struggling against hostile circumstance, skating close to chasms — and some of them are right over the edge, dispossessed, helpless, deregistered, blackmailed, incontinent. But they are all battlers. Even if fantasy is the best they can do, they keep going. There is the possibility of love, of communion with land if no human being wants you; the regenerative power of land and of nature.

> In the quiet moments of soft rustlings between the bursts of singing, a noisy crow, flying over the neglected gardens of St Christopher and St Jude, cried the tragedy and the gift of half-remembered places, of distant towns and villages, of mountains and rivers and of wharves and railway stations. The crow, swooping closer, still crying, brought to the doors and windows of St Christopher and St Jude the sound of wind rushing across endless paddocks, the steady hopeful clicking of windmills and long country roads leading to serene crossroads. Another crow, in another garden, crying loneliness, seemed to answer the first one. When the crows were silent, the voices of the doves could be heard; a contented sound, perhaps a language of reason and of acceptance and resignation.

And in the last chapter of *Mr Scobie's Riddle*, when the old men have died and the mad woman has not been able to escape Matron's clutches, there is still the symbol of the tents, fragile, optimistic, temporary structures, clumsily erected in hope.

Number 1, 1983

Migrant Women Writers
Who's on whose margins?

SNEJA GUNEW

> No theory can develop without eventually encountering a wall, a practice is necessary for piercing this wall.
>
> We ridiculed representation and said it was finished, but we failed to draw the consequences of this 'theoretical' conversion — to appreciate the theoretical fact that *only those directly concerned can speak in a practical way on their own behalf.*
>
> Gilles Deleuze[1]

This essay will be about theory and practice as these relate to territorial boundaries, and about that 'voice of experience' and whether it can be authenticated.

Why should our concerns be with *migrant* writing?

For the time being let us assume that 'theory' translates, in this instance, into the territory of Australian writing, which in turn has long been a Tasmanian poor relation to British (Anglo-Celtic) writing. Not in the least does one wish to blunt that point, this shaft of practice which has pierced the walls of that institutional fortress, 'Brit. Lit.' Hurrah for anything that puts into question our hegemonic, monocultural assumptions. But perhaps the time has come also to question the category of 'Aust. Lit.' since it too has become a 'discursive formation' in Foucault's sense of the term. It too is now an institutional practice.

As a critic recently stated, Aust. Lit. is often loosely categorized as a 'corpus of travellers' tales . . . footnotes to the *Odyssey* and the *Aeneid*'.[2] This conjures up not just the picaresque Münchhausen yarns, but a whole coracle fleet of lone voyagers surrounding the unknown great southern land of the psyche. In turn, the interpersonal relations of voyagers and ocean have now spawned a new archipelago, that of migrant writing, a further set of cousins. But, as Jacques Derrida has pointed out (in *Of Grammatology*), the problem with supplements is that they tend to take over, insofar as they point to a lack or absence within the plenitude, in this case of the theory/territory of Australian writing. If something requires an addendum then it was incomplete from the beginning, and the supplement ends up supplanting the original. Here then, in the case of migrant writing, we discover a further set of travellers' tales which put into question, but also reinvigorate, the Australian literary paradigm of the exodus/adventus — the *Wanderroman* or *Wandergeschichte*.

The very term 'migrant writing' has been bestowed from within the *nouveau riche* walls of Australian writing. But how precisely was it arrived at and what is the nature of its taxonomic genealogy?

It is perfectly possible to argue that some distinctive objects are made by

> the mind, and that these objects, while appearing to exist objectively, have only a fictional reality. A group of people living on a few acres of land will set up boundaries between their land and its immediate surroundings and the territory beyond, which they call *the land of the barbarians*. In other words, this universal practice of designating in one's mind a familiar space which is 'ours' and an unfamiliar space beyond 'ours' which is 'theirs' is a way of making geographical distinctions that can be entirely arbitrary . . . Yet often the sense in which someone feels himself to be not-foreign is based on a very unrigorous idea of what is 'out there', beyond one's own territory.[3]

One of those 'fictions' underpinning the them-us binary opposition is the one which asks on just what authority 'they' speak to 'us'. Since the beginning of story-telling there has always been this question of *auctoritas*: who is licensed to hold us with a glittering eye? Invariably the answer comes: the witness, or the simulacrum of one. As Deleuze reminds us, the direct voice, the authority of experience is the most compelling. But as we also know, from seeing endless documentary interviews and being bored by lack of editing in the agonising search for 'what really happened', there are conventions for truth-telling. The use of the first-person mode is no guarantee of anything but that a convention has been mobilised.

Which brings us to the further refinement of why this is an essay on migrant *women* writers. That women writers have privileged access to truth or to the confessional mode is an assumption underlying much of what gets published in recent women's writing, so much of which is cast in the first person. The glittering *I* and its relation to the hitherto suppressed, to the voice from the other side of the barbed wire, is what permeates the following discussion concerning the nexus of migrant, women, and writing.

Until very recently migrants, like women, have signalled their oppression largely through their silence, at least for those who were prepared to hear it. Certainly both migrants and women have long figured as the metaphoric caryatids of many myths. The problem with this subordinate position is that it suppresses specificity. The line from a recent fine example of migrant women's writing comes to mind: 'For all persecuted people look like Ghetto Jews to me'.[4] But the sameness about the oppressed and marginal voice is largely the result of the undifferentiated way it has been situated by the dominant culture. It comes back to the question of who issues the licence to speak and under what conditions.

One of the seductions of speaking in the first-person, in one's 'own voice', is that story-telling, narrative shaping, gives an illusion of power and control over one's life. The last few decades have seen a proliferation of writings from the oppressed, the marginal, which have been 'adopted' by dominant cultures. Why not? Is this not another version (as Edward Said has shown in his study of the discursive practice of Orientalism) of colonialism? And isn't the central metaphor, once again, that of sexual conquest?[5] The first-person account conveys both strength and vulnerability. As Foucault has most recently demonstrated (in *The History of Sexuality*), hearing confessions can also be an exercise in sexual politics.

One can generalise (as Said does) about the oppressed position as having invariable affinities with the female condition but this generalisation, or homogenising process, is in fact a large part of the process of oppression: as a character in a novel by Antigone Kefala puts it, 'to steal one's perspective was equal to killing a person'.[6] The blending process finally serves only to reinforce the normative, what we already know. Look, for example, at the whole notion of 'multiculturalism' which was heralded as a necessary successor to the oppressive concept of assimilation.

Multiculturalism is the patented supplement, the addendum to Anglo-Celtic monoculturalism. But what really does it offer? Edward Said's contention that Orientalism (Europe's discourse about Islam and the Arab world) is an enclosed space, 'a theatrical space affixed to Europe', may cast new light on the domain of multiculturalism. Don't certain folkloric puppets glide easily into one's memory in the space reserved for migrants? For most New Australians growing up now and after the Second World War, wasn't the acknowledgement of their difference palpably recognised in a song and dance act in some school auditorium? And now can't we fill that theatrical space with even more public manifestations of multiculturalism — with multicultural television, for example? Contrary to the first conception of this project we have so far been offered very few local migrant voices. Instead the extra-Australian world has been ransacked for 'entertainment' which is defined by its alien and exotic characteristics. Even more than in the past the local migrants become further projections of this eternal repetition of the colourfully costumed singing dancing migrant. That's entertainment; with subtitles. And that whole issue of subtitling, interpretation and translation deserves an essay in its own right.

From 'a whole world of migrants' we turn to another system of catching and classifying the authentic voice of migrant experience. A recent annotated bibliography of migrant writing[7] being promoted in secondary schools has chosen to include only those writers born outside Australia in a country which does not have English as a first language. The rationale for the publication is that it will promulgate cultural diversity and that 'it will have the ring of truth about it'. The venture is to be applauded but one cannot suppress the uneasy query: whose truth? By choosing to include only those authors born outside Australia and the English language it may be that the editors have, in spite of their stated intentions, guaranteed a limit to diversity. For example, for a writer who needs to break into not only a culture but also a language, success may well be synonymous with *writing like the Australians*. Success may mean *not* rocking the boat, abiding by the prevailing conventions in order to prove one's competence, not being master but mastered. Then the authority of experience will amount to suffering in distant parts and relief at being here in a safe territory — the will to assimilation in fact.

A more empirical objection to the bibliography is that one of the finest accounts of children passing from one culture to another, Zeny Giles' *Between Two Worlds*[8] has not been included because Giles (Zenovia Doratis) was born here, though of Greek-Cypriot parents. Also excluded, because not so 'accessible', was poetry. The innovative language experiments of poets like *Π.O.* and Ania Walwicz, who interrogate prevailing linguistic conventions far more profoundly than on the merely thematic level, are absent. This is another version of the blending process which shepherds migrant writers through a narrow gateway of the authentically ethnic.

If an enterprising publisher catches the bona fide migrant from overseas, the witness for the *Wanderroman*, then the most readily recognisable (and presumably saleable) mode of truth-telling is the first-person account. Even better if the illusion is heightened by the further subtitle that this is an autobiographical account. (What writing is not?) Further, the desire to associate the first-person with the autobiographical in the sense used above is so strong that it will not be deterred by overt expressions to the contrary. For example, in that same bibliography a reviewer of Antigone Kefala's novella *The First Journey* persists in seeing the narrator (whose name is Alexi, amongst other references to the masculine gender) as a 'girl' on the sole evidence, one assumes, that the story is in the first person and the author is a woman. But the first person is open to anyone:

> The 'I' is an empty signifier available to anyone. The mere use of 'I' does not answer the question of who or what that I actually stands for.[9]

That 'I' guarantees nothing, just as the fact of being born overseas into a language other than English does not guarantee that one speaks from a place different from that taken by writers placed within the host language. Writing from a female position, writing from a migrant position, need not be coincident either with being biologically consigned to the female of the species, or with having come in on a foreign passport. One is not thereby magically freed of the conventions associated with the way the migrant is metaphorised in writing. Both women and migrants internalise the process whereby the culture constructs them, and it requires a great deal of selfconscious analysis before they are able to step (and only ever in part) outside these constructs. Therefore, as has been suggested, the pressures to conform are inevitably much stronger in the case of migrants of the first generation. Nonetheless, returning to Deleuze, theory needs to be pierced or extended by a practice and such a practice does derive from a material reality, among whose elements are both lived experience and its mediation by conventions of representation. There are no 'right answers' for detecting the authority of authenticity; I am merely advocating a scepticism towards equating certain conventions with truthtelling. Rather than expending energy on the quest for a pure-bred or authentic migrant voice, perhaps there is more to be gained by pursuing another kind of lateral approach, Foucault's notion of the transgressive.

> The limit and transgression depend on each other for whatever density of being they possess: a limit could not exist if it were absolutely uncrossable and, reciprocally, transgression would be pointless if it merely crossed a limit composed of illusions and shadows . . .
>
> Transgression carries the limit right to the limit of its being; transgression forces the limit to face the fact of its imminent disappearance,

to *find itself in what it excludes* (perhaps, to be more exact, to recognize itself for the first time), to experience its positive truth in its downward fall .

Transgression, then, is not related to the limit as black to white, the prohibited to the lawful, the outside to the inside, or as the open area of a building to its enclosed spaces. Rather, their relationship takes the *form of a spiral which no simple infraction* can exhaust.[10]

It is possible that it is not so much a question of 'being' a migrant but of writing from a migrant position, and this in turn could be a matter of choosing to interrogate — a will to alienation. Admittedly this is also, in the long run, going to mean being subject to metaphorisation since anyone can mimic forms of rebellion. It is not just a matter of which 'I' but of what sustains the various 'I's: what are the conditions of speaking? 'I paid for this. I am pleased. I am my own . . . When I open the door, I open me'.[11] How many 'I's are offered here? The authentic voice, the practice which extends the theory, is always a problematic category which can only ever be partially defined. In the case of migrant writing it is not synonymous with the discursive formation of 'multiculturalism'. Neither is it merely reducible to the rhetoric of conviction, the first-person mode. It is not exhausted, for example, by the voices of migrants contained in the oral history collections by Lowenstein and Loh.[12] If it were, we would never need to move beyond such oral history. It is only one area of the archipelago of migrant writing.

To explore other aspects, I would like now to focus on the work of four writers, to show their differences from each other as well as their difference from Australian Anglo-Celtic writing. Antigone Kefala is a Rumanian Greek who emigrated to and spent her youth in New Zealand before moving to Sydney. Zeny Giles (Zenovia Doratis) was born in Sydney of Greek-Cypriot parents. Ania Walwicz was born in Poland and arrived in Australia in her adolescence. Anna Couani is a second-generation Australian of Greek-Polish extraction (a Polish grandfather arrived here in 1860). On the face of it Couani does not belong in the category of migrant women writer yet she chooses to speak from various migrant positions, as we shall see. All four writers are transgressive in ways that interweave the voices of women and of migrants: testing the limits of languages, the limits of gender.

Unity is conferred by the gaze of the other, the parent culture. This corresponds to the homogenising process we have already observed. But the notion of a unified subject is very much in dispute in recent times. Where, if not in marginal territories, might we seek conventions which represent the fragmented subject, the splintered ego? If it is to succeed in being compelling, the glittering eye must, at the very least, reflect the eye of its listener. Here, as in so many other places, Lacan's account of the mirror stage in the formation of the subject is helpful, in this case, for understanding the notion of the fragmented subject.[13] In this fiction, the child's first encounter with the mirror endows its fragmented sense of self with a spurious unity; endows but at the same time imprisons and at the cost of several other aspects of the potential 'I' which need subsequently to be suppressed. The mirror stage is analogous with that process which includes the entry into language, into socialization, the prescriptive gaze of the other which succeeds in splitting the subject into perceiver and perceived, subject and object. That schizophrenic perspective, sometimes overtly attached to the image of the mirror, but always indicating the network of contradictions which invade the enunciating subject, is a trope of migrant writing. One common manifestation is in connection with names, those social labels for the unified subject which, when questioned, or changed, or mutilated, throw everything concerned with identity into question.

> She could see that Manoli was right — they had to learn to live in two worlds. At school they would answer to Nina and Herb. They would speak English, trying to copy every characteristic of the accent around them. They would join in lessons and sport and play with their Australian friends, trying in every way to fit in. But as soon as they stopped at the back door of their house, they were different people. Herb would become Manoli, Nina would become Finnaki or Chrisaphina, as Father called her.
>
> (Giles, *Between Two Worlds*)

How does one project the self onto a world when the prime signifier, the personal name, has either disappeared or become multiplied? Mirrors, as in Lacan's account, reflect more than surfaces.

> And I stayed alone in my room watching my face in the mirror. Caged in myself. Petrified in this frame out of which I could never hope to come except by a definite act. A positive act of will that would destroy me at the same time. And in the meantime the other one stayed inside me unimpressed. For there were always two inside. The one that moved and laughed, cried and was angry, had attitudes and demanded things and was stubborn in wanting, that felt the vacuum and was afraid. And there was the second one. The one that undermined every effort towards an involvement. The one that dwelt somewhere at the roots of my being and knew with an absolute certainty that everything was futile. That I was making far too much noise about all these not very important matters. The second one that could see through everything. That was merciless. Absolutely indifferent. That watched the very movement of people with a sharp clinical eye, when I, the other one, was totally involved. So that the moment became split, between a doer and a watcher, and the watcher being the stronger, the doer tried to maintain such a level of concentration and involvement leaving no room, no crack, for the second one to insinuate itself.
>
> (Kefala, *The First Journey*)

That second 'I' perceives the fragility of the constructs of the self as they impinge on the equally fragile surrounding world. In Giles' *Between Two Worlds* the mirror functions to confirm a past socio-cultural self that has been interrogated too soon.

> Before he'd started school in Australia, he had always fitted in so comfortably that he'd never even thought of what he looked like. He

> didn't remember even bothering to look in a mirror in Castellorizo, except perhaps to pull a funny face. Now he would stare into the bathroom mirror and he was ashamed of his brown skin and his short black hair. He was determined never to allow Maria to cut his hair again. But most of all he hated the old-fashioned knitted suit Maria had bought in Port Said. It made him look so different from the others. He had been at school for well over a month and he still dreaded the time each day when one bully or another would poke fun at him. And the terrible part about it was that although he despised these bullies for making fun of him, he wanted to be like them. He wanted light hair and fair skin and, most of all, he wanted to wear not-good clothes.
>
> (Giles, *Between Two Worlds*)

Implied in both these quotations is the arbitrary nature of these social images which in turn reflect, or cast doubts on, the nature of the larger social structures which prescribe certain conventions of behaviour and speech. Compare this with Ania Walwicz's two prose poems: 'I' and 'Sitting Pretty'.[14] In the latter there is once again the splintering of the self into the social selves of certain kinds of female stereotypes: an amalgamation of doll and child. Again, as in the Kefala extract, there is the caged self but in this case, paradoxically, because the images are so definitive, so definable, it is possible to escape them. The enunciating 'I', from a third place (not doll, not child), discards them. 'And I was nice and quiet and no trouble to anyone. And clean and tidy. And I left me.' In the poem 'I' there is a reverse movement of Rabelaisian (or Whitmanesque) inclusiveness where the 'I' finally (and in a fundamentally truthful phenomenological sense) engulfs everything, but also remains 'I'. 'My objects are pieces of me . . . They speak my words. I wrote them.' Although it embraces the universe, the 'I' is subject *and* object still. Compare this with the fifth section of Couani's prose poem, 'Untitled'.

> The two white chiffon curtains are being blown into the room by the wind from the open window. They are twisting like cigarette smoke and obscure the view which is of a hazy grey block of a building. Through the open doorway to the next room can be seen a mirror which reflects the mattress on the floor and some pillows, sheets and clothes. There is a small tinkling sound and then a door closing softly. The curtains are blowing over the table just touching the top of a glass without moving it.[15]

Here the 'I' is displaced by the description of objects, akin to the putative objectivity of a camera eye. Gradually, in succeeding sections, across the fixed frame of the mirror, there drift further details, including limited human statements. In this case it is the reflected listener, the reader, who is left free to draw connections between these fragments. In a later poem sequence in that volume, 'The View', the various sections keep re-playing the same perceived sequence of events in order to tease out various meanings. In this case more of the process is completed for the reader but, nonetheless, there is never a total unification or closure. The ends are not tied up. It is never a question of a unified perspective mediating or enclosing an event. This refusal of closure, this interrogative approach, reinforces the notion of language itself as a network of territories where boundaries keep shifting in accordance with prevailing ideologies. *These transgressions query constantly the concept of a 'natural' language in which one gains competence*. 'You step outside convention and then you forget it. The convention seems arbitrary — for anyone who does it anywhere in the world.'[16] Amongst other things the migrant voice can alert readers to the arbitrary nature of place, that the mother or father land amounts to an imaginary territory perilously shored up by conventions which may melt away on close scrutiny. In an interview about her writing, Ania Walwicz stated:

> As both woman and migrant I have been given no sense of belonging in the world, no set place. I have to state my identity. I have to reconstruct the world . . . I join me to the world.[17]

This awareness, that the 'world' comes into being through the 'I' is echoed by the narrator in *The First Journey*:

> The old fear in me again that they might all disappear some day because of a negligence of awareness on my part. A moment when I would fail to lend them my *constant* support as an onlooker, that gave substance to their limbs.[18]

At the same time, since communication needs to involve the recognition of a shared base, that 'I' is the result of construction in and through language. In *Between Two Worlds*, Manoli is unable to articulate his sense of self in the alien language but breaks through when he recognises a familiar place in the universal language of numbers (p.50). Later, the book includes an important section where Greek and English words are juxtaposed so that the shared base is extended by means of this either/and rather than either/or approach. In Kefala's story 'Alexia' the eponymous protagonist is introduced to the vagaries of the English language by a teacher who demands:

> 'Are you happy?'
> Alexia went immediately into a panic. For she felt HAPPY to be an Enormous Word, a word full of flamboyant colours, which only people who had reached an ecstatic state had a right to use. She saw it as the apotheosis, so to speak, of a series of events which, as far as she could see, lay totally outside her life. But she could not explain this, for everyone on the Island kept asking, as if this Fantastic Word was the basic measure of their days . . .
> And the more she thought about it, the more confused she became. Did Miss Prudence mean:
> Was she happy eating her mashed potatoes?
> Being in the house with the grandfather clock chiming? Happy living on the Island?
> or
> Happy living in the world?
> There she was, with the salt cellar in her hand, which she had been asked to pass on to Mary, not knowing what to say, getting more and more confused between Happiness and Salt.[19]

What can be more transgressive than such comedy? Almost comparable in the sardonic confusion of meaning and representation is Lucija Berzins' story 'The Berlitz Method'[20] in which an earnestly conducted English language class is anarchically sustained by the promise of a strip-tease.

Edward Said has explored in detail how the Orient becomes an object constructed by the Orientalist. So too the migrant becomes an object constructed by Australian culture, in particular, by its officialdom. Paternalistic institutions reduce the migrant to the status of child as is seen in Walwicz's poems 'So Little'[21] and 'helpless'[22]:

> before they were big i was small they could do things more than me they were something now they are nothing he was a doctor of animals now he was learning to speak properly he talked funny they made mistakes she was clumsy she works in a factory he cleans the floors of the serum laboratory now life can be everybody clean and nice and we are all wrong here i was the translator i was the mother of my mother they were more helpless they were useless nervous didn't know what to do i was too serious for me it was too early to be like this we walked lost on the street we were looking for john street i was bigger than them my parents were again small old children they were heavy for me they couldn't do much you are helpless useless.

So that another trope in migrant writing becomes, not surprisingly, the government institution, be it a hospital (as in Kefala's 'The Waiting Room'[23], Walwicz's 'Hospital'[24]), or even the academy, as in the following extract from Kefala's unpublished novel, *The Island*:

> I spoke. One could see from his face that he had not the faintest idea what I was saying, the meaning stopped somewhere mid air between us, he incredulous that he will ever understand me, I incredulous that he will ever understand me. He was busy swallowing thin mouthfuls of vinegar, watching me with preoccupied eyes, rubbing his hands as if drying them of sand, trying to get rid of it. One could see in his whole attitude the immense surprise of being confronted, here in his own room, at the University, by something as foreign as myself. The implied extravagance of my voice, the rapid nervousness of my movements, my eyes that looked too directly at him.

As well, however, there is a reversal of this process of objectification when the migrant, in turn, transforms the Australian experience into an object. Compare, for example, Walwicz's poem 'Australia'[25]: 'You big ugly. You too empty. You desert with your nothing nothing . . . You don't like me and you don't like women' and its counterpoint poem 'Wogs'.[26]

> you can't speak to them why don't you learn to speak english properly they are not like you or me they're not the same as everybody they change us is your child educated by an australian? is it? do you know if? you don't know what they think you don't know what they can do here they change us they paint their houses blue green have you seen blue houses who ever heard of that they live too many together they're too noisy they

In a sense the 'you' addressed in the former is the speaker of the latter. In the former the speaker is oppressed, migrant and female and attacks the assumptions of the 'you' which is loosely defined as Ocker and male but also, strangely, oppressed. 'You go to work in the morning. You shiver on a tram.' In the fourth chapter of Couani's *Were all women sex-mad?* there is a long section of Australia as object for scrutiny by, presumably, the 'citizen of the world' mentioned elsewhere:

> It's unique I'll say that. Anyone can feel at home there because it has a strange character or atmosphere which is like an absence of character, a kind of neutrality. I think it's very tolerant or maybe just very anonymous. No really, I do *like* Australia. When I lived there I liked it. But I realize coming away again that there's some strange pressure there. It's subliminal, very subtle. I don't think I could describe it exactly because it's an abstract quality which pervades everything there, the work situation, the politics, the social life. It's a place that gets you down. The amount of drinking the people do is phenomenal. And it's as though everyone's bitten by the same bug — some kind of desperation or hysteria which is never expressed. They're stoics, the Aussies. The most cynical people in the world. Beyond morality — like the English but more sophisticated because they never say *anything*.

And later, even more damning:

> But now it's changing a bit at last. They're starting to come in from the cold like the old stockman returning to the bright lights of the station after 2 weeks riding the fences in the cold and the dust. While he's away he has to remember the warmth and light of his home but when he comes back he can forget it.
> — He says, And then I get home and wouldn't you know — the wife started her period today. Forget it.
> — I think you're starting to understand.

Looking at migrant women's writing is a way of questioning literary taxonomies. Such writing speaks from positions which interrogate socio-cultural conventions, notions of linguistic competence, and gender certainties. Migrant, and women's, and migrant women's writing are the 'excess' of Anglo-Celtic writing, a luxury which is an index of what? Civilised scepticism? The mining rights to an unknown territory? New histories or new subjects?

> He claimed that in order to understand history, one needed a type of vision that only people placed at the crossroads could provide. That is, people that lived between cultures, who were forced to live double lives, belonging to no group, and these he called 'the people in between'. This type of vision he maintained, was necessary to the alchemy of cultural understanding.
>
> (Kefala, *The Island*)

For those inclined to take territorial metaphors for certainties, migrant writing indicates that Australia is really off the planet.

Poem

ANNA COUANI

We could smell the salt in the air at Parramatta
That was where the city began in those days
Then everything had a kind of sameness until we hit the city
Everything seemed old and dirty, running beside the tram tracks.
Newtown seemed particularly old and Redfern not at all red or fern-like
This was one idea of old, but not like the mountains which were ancient.

And in between this old and this ancient was European old and the ancient
Of the Mediterranean and Asia. But I didn't know that, it was a blank for me like Parramatta
Was till recently. And I never thought I'd find people I could like
Not in the enduring way I love the mountains and the city, where days
Counted for nothing against 'forever'. Bush love like bush tracks
And city love I could trace back to Sydney's birth as a city.

My memories are my grandma's memories of the city
And my mother's talks looking at the mountains, talking about The Ancient
About the beginning of the world like a 2001 movie track
But more serious. And Dad feeling alien anywhere west of Parramatta
Or Broadway even. I felt his sense of relief on the days
We came down to the city and he showed me what his Sydney was like

Where we saw salami and olives in shops I now realise were just like
Ones in Greece and definitely unlike the big Franklins in the city
Which sold DEVON (a word my parents pronounced like POISON). There were different city days
With Mum, more anglo. Sitting in the Cahills coffee shop looking at the ancient
Egyptian motifs etched on the amber mirrored walls. Stopping at Parramatta
For a sandwich and having a talk about the Great Western Highway when it was just a track.

Just as Mum knew the mountain tracks, Dad knew the city tracks
Not just the steps and pathways around the Cross for example, but he had a mental picture like
A map. The shortcuts all the way from the coast to Parramatta
Which makes me think of Sydney as like a middle-eastern city
Multi-layered and only really knowable by people with that ancient
Knowledge which is still applicable in the cleaned-up version of Sydney these days.

I had a dream of finding parts of Sydney I'd forgotten and rediscovered on summer days

In the dust and heat. Suddenly finding a lane like a track
Leading between some buildings. But that's ancient
History to me now, that personal approach to writing. Now I like
To write about the things happening around me not to me. About the city.
And I want to start from the centre I know and work outwards past Parramatta.

Even trying to avoid nostalgia, my childhood days
Seem ancient and thinking about them is like archaeology
Tracking down connections and making them
Till they stand out as strongly and clearly as the arterial roads
Between the city, Parramatta and the mountains.

Number 2, 1985

My Sister's Funeral

ROBIN SHEINER

The grapes arrived on the day of the funeral. We loaded them onto the back of the truck with the beer then everyone climbed on afterwards. My Japanese friend had to be helped up, Billy on one side of him, and Rosa on the other. He is a very old man now but still he doesn't speak English. He was pleased about the grapes, though. I could tell by the way he smiled. Since he had his teeth pulled out he doesn't smile very much because he can't enjoy a good feed of meat. He always liked a feed of meat but now he has only five teeth at the top and three at the bottom. I think he'll like the grapes.

He came here in 1920 to dive for pearls. They all came then, the Japanese, because they wanted the pearls, and knew how to get them. No-one else did. They liked the coloured girls and were nicer to them than white men were. They made the girls dive but didn't beat them or make them lie down with them afterwards.

I didn't know my old Japanese friend then, even though I lived in this town. Well, not really in the town. My husband and I lived in one of the old boat sheds, with all our kids, out across the mangrove swamp. At night we could hear the swamp gurgling beneath us and sometimes the big mangrove crabs climbed in and walked across us sideways. Our kids had a lot of fun chasing them around the shed. It was all right until the hot came and then the mozzies, ouch, you should have seen them, as big as dragonflies. At least we had shelter, not even the mozzies could drive us out to join other coloured people who slept along the gutters.

There are black and white and yellow people in the town, there are others half and half, and there are others all mixed up so they came out cream. My father was a very important white man. He owned a big station and had three black wives and one Malayan wife. My mother was one of his black wives. He loved her and he loved us, his kids. When they came in a car and took all of us kids away to the mission he wasn't there because he had gone down to the big city to visit his relations who are the people who grow grapes. They have lots of land in the city with grapes like you've never seen — red and glittering like rubies, black like opals, white and shiny like pearls with no seeds. I know this because some of my cousins' kids went down there once. They went all the way. Don't ask me how they got there but they did, and they went to work on the vineyard picking grapes but they weren't treated so good. I told them they should have told the owners they were their relations. Nobody makes their relations live in kerosene tins that let in the sun so bad, and the flies. Some people say black people like the flies. I tell you now, while my sister Rosa writes, we don't like the flies. They get in our eyes and make us go blind. Even now I don't see so good and I am telling this story to my sister Rosa to write down.

Rosa is married to a Malayan, his name is Kim Bin, and she has electric fans in the ceiling of her house to keep her cool. There are only two of us sisters left now because of the funeral. It was three days ago. The beer flowed for two days and Rosa and I were the only ones who didn't drink. Now we are home again and tired and I am asking my sister Rosa to write down how our sister Marcellus is gone. The nuns gave Marcellus her name but our father gave us ours — Clara and Rosa — pretty names to show he cared for us. I have found out from Billy's uncle, who knows everything, that our father died on the other side of the country, a lonely old white man. Where he lived they used to call him the captain and he would walk along the beach with pockets full of lollies for the kids who followed him everywhere. I think he was wondering all the time about us, his own kids who were took away young to be brought up at the mission.

Our sister Marcellus who died never left the mission, she stayed on as a helper in the kitchen to the nuns for forty years. For her funeral everyone, all of us, except the white relations from the city, came. We all went up from here and you should have seen us on the back of the truck. I wouldn't let anyone sit on top of the grapes. It was funny that we didn't ever ask who'd sent them or how they'd known that Marcellus was gone. We were so sure they'd been sent for Marcellus' funeral that we didn't bother to ask. We have learned not to ask questions, especially my old Japanese friend. He could learn English easily if he wanted to but he doesn't try. They tried to make him talk when he was sent away from here to be kept wired-in during the war. They tried to get him to say that he knew who was bombing us. Still he didn't talk. They thought he might be dumb. Big bombs came. We were lucky in the boat shed over the mangrove swamp because they didn't hit us. My husband was sick during the war. Too many mozzies. I couldn't do anything except wring out his singlet in the cool swamp water and lie beside him. There were no Japanese around then, they were wired in, so the pearl luggers were sitting empty not far from our shed. There were lots of sea planes on the water, too, funny looking things like giant birds, and when the bombs tried to hit them they hit some of the luggers instead. I don't think if it was the Japanese dropping the bombs on us, they would have bombed their own Japanese boats that only wanted to look for pearls.

I was pleased my Japanese friend came for Marcellus' funeral. She would have been pleased, too, because she loved everyone like the nuns had taught her, even Japanese, because Jesus would have done, she said spitting on her hands and rolling out the pastry for the nun's steak and kidney. I didn't care much for Jesus when I was at the mission even though the nuns crammed him down my throat. Our mother would come to the mission gate every day and cry for us to come back to her and cry and cry when the nuns wouldn't let her take us out. So much for Jesus. I could see her crying behind the fence that kept us in and I know what my Japanese friend must have felt like, all wired-in but no-one cried for him to get out. People were glad. So, when he had his teeth out I sat with him and made him warm cloths to put across his cheek because I can guess what it feels like, when all your teeth are gone.

He looked comfortable in the truck, squatting on his heels near the beer crates. We hid the beer when we got to the mission. Some had been drinking on the way and fell over at the mission and couldn't walk straight. It didn't worry us. We were used to it but the nuns didn't like it, especially at a funeral. They let Rosa and me look at Marcellus when she was lying in the coffin, open, and they had done her up nice and put a flower in her hand and dressed her in her best white dress that she wore for Holy Mass. Rosa started to cry so I stood up very straight and was glad for her sake, and for Marcellus', that I had worn my hat and white gloves. Some people in our town say what does a coloured woman want with hats and white gloves but it doesn't worry me if I am dressed up. Let them worry. My father who owned a station would have been proud of us: Rosa who married a Malayan and Marcellus who worked her life to the bone for the nuns, and I who wear a hat and gloves because they don't think I'd dare. I looked down at Marcellus and she was still the blackest of us three sisters.

Some of the others outside the room with the coffin in it were starting to make a lot of noise, especially the drunk ones who had started wailing and the nuns couldn't quieten them, even when the priest said the holy dedication. The nuns are not happy because the mission is going to close now that there are no more half black children they can bring. No-one these days will let kids be snatched. They used to bring all the ones who had white fathers and black mothers. There weren't any who had black fathers and white mothers because the black men didn't go near the white women. They didn't like them smelling of soap and stiff with corsets, and they would have been hanged if they did. My father's brother, my uncle, hanged lots of people. He was the magistrate in our town and lived in a big house and had black people fan him with banana leaves. Lots of them would run fast past his house because they thought he was the devil, and the nuns had scared them of the devil.

My Japanese friend is not scared of anything, even when he dived for pearls and saw crocodiles as big as boats and great big sea snakes with yellow stripes like lightning. He was not wailing like the others when Marcellus' coffin was wrapped up in the ground but was sitting down on a little stool I had brought for him and he was smiling because in his hand he had a bunch of grapes and it didn't matter with grapes that he had no teeth. Soon someone brought out the whole box of grapes because they were too scared, even the drunk ones, to bring out the beer in front of the nuns who could be very fierce if they wanted, especially now their mission was closing. Next thing, all the grapes were gone, the juice of them dribbling from our mouths as we stood there and the sun opening up the sky to let in all the light across Marcellus' grave. My Japanese friend lay a bunch of grapes next to the flowers my sister Rosa had brought, across the sun on the grave. The flowers were withered because we had come such a long way in the truck and it was a hot day but the grapes were firm and shiny. My Japanese friend said the gods would like them and they would be kind to Marcellus but I didn't think Marcellus would be happy about it, so when he wasn't looking I picked them up from the grave and gave them to the twins, my grandchildren who are growing tall and fat. The priest gave a talk about how nice it was that all of us who had been half-caste children at the mission, and looked after so well, had come back to see one of our own buried with the grace of God. Then he said much louder, that drink was the temptation of the devil, and we should cast it from us. But I knew from what Marcellus had told me that the priest drank the altar wine when he could and that she had seen him without his cassock and with his fly undone, and had been so frightened she had said ten holy Marys, then burnt the cup cakes that she was going to cut up to make angels' wings. When she went to confession and told what she had seen the priest said she was very wicked and must scrub the big black pots every night until she washed away her sins. Marcellus was obedient, not like Rosa and me. We were proud and did not let anyone put us down or call us half-caste good for nothings. Rosa learned to swear at them in Malayan if they did, and I would walk on past, knowing how much it annoyed them to see me in my hat and gloves.

'Why do you think our father let them take us?' Rosa asked when we were trying to get everyone back into the truck. I couldn't answer her because I knew he could have got us back if he wanted to, an important man like that who had relations who almost owned the city, so my cousins' kids, who went to work for them down there, said. 'It broke our mother's heart,' Rosa told me as we hugged each other.

The sun was going down and everyone was tired. It was good the grapes were gone because it made more room in the truck. As we went along we saw something very funny. There were a lot of emus trying to get through a wire fence, getting very mad and tangling themselves up. We all giggled so much we rolled about the truck and one fell off and we had to stop but he wasn't hurt, so we lifted him back on. It was my cousin's son and his name is Billy. He has seen the city, picked grapes for our relations and come back, drinking worse and worse, sometimes beating his wife who is the daughter of my second cousin Mary.

My Japanese friend squatted on his heels in the middle of us all like that, so quiet with his eyes squinting. He is a good man and never minds being with us half and halfers, neither one thing nor the other but in the strip between. His wife was a mixture, cream coloured. He had married her in a Japanese ceremony, that was when there were lots of Japanese here because there were so many pearls. They had their own temple, even their own graveyard. It's still there with Japanese writing on the headstones. His wife had been a beauty, like all the cream coloureds, and she had run off with a white man, down to the city in a ute. They didn't have no kids. Just as well. He lives with me now in the house the government sold cheap when they were trying to do something about us, tidy us up. In the drawer of the cupboard he made for me he has two big pearls and sometimes he takes them out to look at them. I think he's keeping them for if his wife comes back.

He has given me some pearl shells and I wanted to send one to our white relations when I thought they were kind enough to send us grapes for Marcellus' funeral. I only found out about the grapes when I went down to the big store to buy some powder so my nose wouldn't be red if I cried. 'You,' the shop man said. 'Them there are for you.'

'How do you know?' I asked.

'Ask no questions and you get told no lies,' he said. He is a white man who has been hit on the head with a black man's bottle and he sometimes acts up stupid. But there it was blurred across the side. Even with my eyes blinded from flies I could see it, Clara my name. I held myself proud. 'From my relations in the city for my sister's funeral,' I told him. 'I'll call my cousin's son to carry them. Hoy there Billy, come over and carry this box of grapes for your aunty.' He came across from the hotel where he had been playing snooker with some white friends, just to carry it for me, back home so it could be loaded onto the truck. He's the one who fell off the truck and I'm glad he wasn't hurt through laughing so much at the emus. We have a lot of fun. It's the black side of us. I don't miss out on much. My father laughed a lot but he wasn't like other white men, having all us black kids made him different, and anyway I don't think he could have laughed too much after we were gone. Blacks can laugh at anything, birds dropping shit from the sky, bungarras racing up white ladies' skirts looking for the trees.

It was a long trip home from the funeral and very dusty so we stopped a lot even after Billy fell off and soon all the beer was gone and half the men were snoring on the back of the truck. I was glad my cousin Paddy was driving because he can drive straight even when he is drunk. When it got dark we stopped and all curled up warm together there on the back and my Japanese friend rested his head on my knees. It was nice there looking up at the stars and all together, though I felt sad about Marcellus who had never got away from the mission and was so small, smaller than Rosa and me, when she was taken that she couldn't remember where she had come from.

In the morning we washed ourselves in a pool left by the dried-out river. My cousin Paddy always follows the river road, when it's not flooding in the rainy season, because his truck overheats all the time and needs water for the radiator. There aren't any garages on the way to the mission and if there were there are lots of whites who wouldn't even give water away to blacks. It was nice to be clean. My Japanese friend washed his feet and slicked down his hair. I put my hat and gloves back on so I would be ready when we arrived back at the town to see anyone and look them in the eye. That's my white side. It doesn't bother me if a white man puts his evil eye on me because I give it to him straight back again. Except I wasn't ready for the policeman who met us at the door of the house the government sold to me, and I wish they hadn't, it's damper than the boat shed in the rainy season.

'Which one here stole the box of grapes?' he asked, and we were all struck dumb.

I climbed down from the truck first. 'They were my grapes,' I said, 'sent to me from my relations who grow grapes in the city.'

'Garn. Tell us another,' the policeman said, 'they were addressed to Mrs Clare, the station owner's wife and she gets them sent up regular. Seen you before, haven't I? Hanging about with whites in the hotel?' He moved across to Billy. We knew what that meant. Billy melted into us and we closed up tight around him. Everyone had climbed down from the truck, even those with hangovers so bad they couldn't make any sense of day or night; the children glad to be home had run off whooping.

'You pay for the grapes, or else,' the policeman addressed us all.

It wasn't pension day but that didn't worry me. It was that my relations hadn't known about Marcellus' funeral after all. They hadn't cared that she'd died there like that in the mission, that she'd never got out not for forty years and now she was there forever, buried in the ground. So the grapes hadn't been for her, they had been for the white lady who ordered them regular. A mistake had been made.

I took off my hat and crumpled my gloves up small inside it.

My Japanese friend knows what it's like to be wired-in, and I know for certain he didn't scream when the dentist pulled out his teeth. He stood forward, separating himself from us half and halfers, and he spoke his first words in English. If I hadn't heard it with my own ears I wouldn't have believed it. 'Fuck your grapes,' he said.

Judith Brett also brought to *Meanjin* a sharp understanding of politics and political theory. She maintained political commentary as a strong current in the magazine's pages, publishing essays on such subjects as land rights, contemporary political economy and the Blainey debate over immigration, as well as two incisive psychological analyses by Graham Little of Fraser and Hawke.

In the 1980s some still saw the political and the literary as opposed, and in 1984 Judith Brett took on a new version of the old argument that politics is out of place in 'literary' magazines. The following piece is an edited version of her response.

Literature and Politics

JUDITH BRETT

In a recent issue of *The Age Monthly Review* Paul Carter, freelance writer and reviewer, and Martin Harrison of the ABC's 'Books and Writing' express their dissatisfaction with Australian literary magazines; one of the sources of this dissatisfaction is that such magazines do not take literature seriously enough and that, conversely, they are too political. Such attempts to confine literary magazines to the literary are not new. The outspokenness of *Meanjin*'s founding editor, Clem Christesen, on political issues, particularly on questions of civil liberties, earned him continual criticism. The understanding of the relationship between politics and literature continually changes. During the 1950s, with the attempt to ban the Communist Party, the Petrov Affair, and demands for security reports on individuals and organisations, issues of civil liberties were at the centre of *Meanjin*'s political concerns. Issues of civil liberties are issues about the freedoms of the individual. The individual is also the centre of a corresponding literary position which reads literature for the expression of individual experience, whatever political regime the writer lives under. Censorship, political or otherwise, is anathema to such a position. It was in part Christesen's refusal to judge writers according to their political colours that drew criticism to *Meanjin*. This belief in the integrity of the individual's experience creates the field in which political concerns like those of civil liberties or freedom of expression are unified with a commitment to literature, and in Christesen's case with a dedication to providing a place where the best literature could be read.

While this way of understanding the relationship between politics and literature is still important, *Meanjin* now embodies other equally important ways of understanding this relationship which focus not on the individual but on the social or, more broadly, the cultural. *Meanjin* is now concerned with cultural politics and with what can be called the politics of representation, and both these challenge the possibility of keeping political and literary questions apart just as surely as did the earlier conjunction. Where *Meanjin*'s political and literary preoccupations were once linked by the concept of the individual, they are now linked by the concept of culture. Different forms of writing embody different commitments to the distribution of social, political and cultural power; different forms of writing support or challenge the position of particular classes and élites, different ethnic and racial groups, and the two sexes. They embody different answers to the questions who owns culture and who should own it. All literary practices imply answers to these questions, whether they admit it or not. Cultural politics is about the way different cultural forms speak to and support particular social groups in various positions of power, and about the ways marginal groups attempt to develop cultural forms with which to express and reflect on their experience.

Until recently in Australia, the domain of the 'literary' has been predominantly the domain of middle-class white Anglo-Celtic men. Because of their prior occupancy of the domain their maleness and class position has been relatively invisible and so they have been able to claim that their literary activities embody universal values, that their writing is literary. The particularity of such men's writing has thus remained unnamed, unlike the writing of those challenging the claims of those who hold cultural power: 'women's writing', 'black writing', 'working-class writing', 'ethnic writing'. To keep politics out of literary magazines is thus to exclude the culturally marginal, for it is to ask that only that writing which does not show its politics be included. How, for example, can writing by Australian blacks ever not be political?

Some of the problems of a marginal group making a bid for a cultural place are seen in the new magazine *Outrider*, which is subtitled 'A Journal of Multicultural Writing in Australia'. The subtitle's naming of the magazine's province indicates the modest stake it is claiming within Australian literature, and the limitations it is thus imposing on itself and on the writers to whom it wishes to give a voice. The editorial sees the magazine as adding another dimension to mainstream Australian culture, but assures us that this is not to imply shortcomings in the culture, 'but merely to affirm that cultures, like oceans, can have many streams'. But why not criticise the mainstream? Doesn't the fact that such a magazine has been felt necessary deserve anger rather than this apologetic request to be allowed to make a contribution? But more importantly, can migrant writing, conceived of as a contribution or addition, ever deeply affect Australian culture?

In the special issue of *Meanjin* on immigration and culture it was argued that writing by immigrants to Australia, particularly those whose first language is not English, has the potential to transform Australian literature, not just add to it. Minorities only exist in relation to majorities, and the presence of people from different language groups and cultural backgrounds changes the host community's perception of itself, just as the process of immigration changes those who experience it. In both cases awareness is heightened of the individual's relationship with language and culture, of the frailties and strengths of cultural traditions, and of the inevitability of separation and death. This issue of *Meanjin* was not merely suggesting that writing by immigrants might enrich or add to the mainstream, but that it might transform our understanding of Australian writing such that we no longer think in terms of images of homogeneity.

Politics and literature also come together in the politics of representation, which transcends any simplistic opposition between literary and non-literary language. Although this opposition has been subjected to a barrage of attacks from philosophers to semioticians, it seems that it must be said again — that all language constructs ways of feeling, thinking about and acting in the world; that there is no such thing as a language of pure description; that all language, political as well as literary, in some sense deals in fictions. Political language embodies certain ways of understanding the world, as does legal language or the language of advertising. The opposition between literary and non-literary language thus dissolves into the general problem of the construction of meaning in language, and this is one of the key sites for the meeting between politics and literature in *Meanjin*. It is also what links the various forms of writing published in *Meanjin*. To ask, as Carter and Harrison do, that our literary magazines be less political and more literary is to ask us to go back to a time when the power of literary élites was unchallenged by writing from less privileged groups, and when everyone assumed that literary and non-literary uses of language were quite distinct. And it is to ask *Meanjin* to deny its past. *Meanjin*'s interests have always been broadly cultural and political, and they will remain so.

Number 4, 1983

Invisible People: Homosexuals In Australia

Bev Roberts

Margaret Bradstock, Gary Dunne, Dave Sargent, Louise Wakeling (eds.), *Edge City on Two Different Plans* (inVersions, Sydney, 1983), pp. 223, rrp. $8.50.

In an article written ten years ago Dennis Altman discussed Australian media reporting of homosexuality and concluded that

> The worst form of media coverage . . . is neither distortion nor misrepresentation, it is sheer omission. Once the specifically homosexual story has been filed we become invisible people.

There has been no noticeable change in this attitude in a decade which, if not exactly characterised by enlightenment, has at least seen some change in the understanding and discussion of sexuality. Whilst the phenomenon of homosexuality is freed from taboo as a debating topic, the homosexual as a person has no public existence, is still treated as invisible and condemned to silence. To be homosexual is to experience absurdity as well as insult.

It is by now well-known — though it obviously needs to be constantly asserted — that statistically, homosexuals form a large proportion of the Australian population; that homosexuals are distributed over the whole range of occupational and social groupings, from legislators to labourers; that homosexuals are in outwardly conventional marriages, are parents, grandparents, aunts, uncles, and so on. But what is commonly known cannot be formally sanctioned. Myths and stereotypes prevail over known facts: homosexuals are a threatening guerilla force, terrorists in the battlefield of morality, subversive of everything from The Family to national security (especially, of course, in Queensland). Yet most 'straight' Australians probably know at least one homosexual as a relative, friend, colleague or acquaintance, and somehow manage to exempt that person from the myths and stereotypes. The proviso attaching to that exemption is usually that 'it' is never mentioned; thus the absurdity that it is not homosexuality which is the subject of taboo, but the naming of it. This is most commonly experienced within the family: 'My family knows about me [my sexuality] but doesn't want to talk about it.' For many homosexuals, therefore, life is like a silent movie. Or a perpetual extension of the old childhood rule of being seen but not heard.

Breaking the silence is a social and individual necessity — not in any defensive or didactic way (as in Altman's reference to reportage invoking 'the sort of breathless amazement with which homosexuals are revealed to be people just like you and me'), but with the aim of legitimising and recording the homosexual experience. As the editors of *Edge City on Two Different Plans* recognise, it is necessary 'to counterbalance the heterosexist and masculinist literature which still predominates in Australian culture', and their book, described as the first Australian collection of lesbian and gay writing, is, as they say, long overdue.

It is, however, a slightly disappointing book, presenting problems which suggest that the editorial collective could not reach consensus — or perhaps that the response to what they rather unfortunately term their 'coo-ee for contributions' did not produce the kind of material which had been anticipated when the book was planned. Despite the growth of gay consciousness, the increasing politicisation which is transforming homosexuals into gays, work collected in *Edge City* is largely apolitical, more defensive than combative or angry, and preoccupied with self rather than society. The editors have attempted to provide an ideological context for this writing through their Introduction, Dennis Altman's Foreword, and the inclusion of a number of songs from the gay movement, but the end result is a book which hovers unhappily between the categories of literature and polemics. The sense of ambivalence is also evident in the nature of the contributions; most of them are *about* gay experience, but a number are on other themes, presumably being included to represent writing *by* gay people, implying that gay identity is central in the consciousness of at least some writers. This makes the book rather difficult to deal with as a collection: it would be easier to respond to and assess a cohesive collection of writing which was directly or indirectly about the experience of homosexuality. Writing on general themes by gays is more like, say, writing by people with red hair than like writing by another particular group — women — with which the editors associate their volume. The primary determinants of 'difference' in writing are the social constructs of gender and class rather than sexuality.

The rationale for a volume like *Edge City* should be its distinctive subject matter. As the editors declare, 'a shared history of oppression, artistic denial and on-going censorship has produced the need for a collection like *Edge City*', and it seems valid to assume that the chief criterion for selection should be, as Altman puts it in his Foreword, that it is writing which names the previously unnameable.

While the collection is not firmly linked by theme, there is an overarching feeling which is reflected in the well-chosen title (a line from Lee Cataldi's poem 'Gay Liberation'). There is a general sense and expression of alienation, of marginality to Australian urban life, and of the particular introspection which is imposed by awareness of the social ramifications of sexuality.

There are also marked differences between the writing of female and male contributors, indicating the 'different plans' of the experience of lesbians and gay men. For the former, the city blurs to backdrop, to setting for the exploration of social and personal relationships. For the latter, there is an emphasis on the physical: the city is firmly present as playground or battleground, the territory of sexual encounter. It might also be noted that male writers are on the whole preoccupied with the male world and male relationships, whereas female writers explore more widely. This suggests that the male gay world is self-contained and self-sustaining, a sub-culture, whilst gay women are able to relate to the broader culture and concerns of the women's movement.

Edge City is a pioneering book, a ground breaker, and has the roughness and unevenness which those metaphors suggest. It is tempting to argue that, as in the case of the first collections of women's writing, the act of writing and the production of the book are of more significance than literary quality. For several contributors these are first attempts at writing about gay experience; as one writer noted, this was her first story 'which she began because she wanted to make sense of something'. The best and most interesting works are those which have the same concern, even if they are not first attempts; they are more moving, more powerful than the self-consciously literary or self-indulgent campy pieces in the book. They are also marked by bitterness as many writers deal with that naming of the unnameable, and its usually traumatic consequences, which is a central and wounding part of homosexual experience. Most of this naming, as statement rather than confession, appears in writing by women, and covers a range of situations and relationships.

A potential landlady:

> . . . By the way, in case you should decide on me, there's something you should know. I'm gay.
>
> That word sounds so falsely together, so slick. Bright and fragile as a soap-bubble. Not her word, but you can't use the others. Good evening, I'm a female homosexual/lesbian/dyke come to share your lifestyle. . . The word reverberates on the stairs. It feels like a loose tooth, making her wince as though her tongue has probed it.
>
> That's alright by me, Rabbit says.
>
> Her face is cold, shut off.
>
> (Louise Wakeling, 'Getting the Right Person')

A friend:

> 'Actually it's been a strange year. I found out I'm a lesbian and it's great. Ummm . . . but it's hard too . . .' Ordinary words, ordinary voice, ordinary silence. 'I hope you're not shocked or anything . . .' Her hands pick at the dog hairs in the car seat cover. She had caught Vicki's face. Blank.
>
> Opaqueness concealing a mental lunge — lurch and recoil. Only her eyes had leapt at the news. 'No, that's great.'
>
> (Jane Elliott, 'Holiday at the Farm')

A mother:

> 'Jane and I love each other, mother. We're lovers! I'm starting my family with Jane.'
>
> Great gasps of air sucked in to fill the roaring, whirling emptiness inside her. 'Don't be ridiculous! That's disgusting! You don't know what you're saying.'
>
> (Jan Prior, 'Release')

A grandmother:

> She brews a poultice
> to draw the glass from my foot.
> I walk more evenly now
> and before I know it,
> such herbs and warmth
> have drawn from my mouth why it is
> I'll never need a bride . . .
>
> (Tony Page, 'Like That Hill')

And finally, in a different tone,

> let me introduce you to
> someone you probably don't know
> it may come as a surprise to you
> but this is my lover Jo
>
> (Lee Cataldi, 'To the English Department of the University of Bristol a Song in Two Parts to be Sung at my Farewell Dinner')

Despite representing a variety of forms and styles, most of the writing in *Edge City* is fairly conventional and conservative. There is however variation in quality, from Jenny Boult's three excellent poems and Sasha Soldatow's beautifully controlled story 'Intimacy' to verbose and pretentious verse and the song lyrics which mar the volume. It is probably not surprising that in a collection like this there is overall a rather sombre tone; there is not much humour (though there is a kind of brittle wit) and not much celebration of love. But there is great strength of feeling and the honesty of experiential writing which makes an important contribution to the Australian literary record. *Edge City's* main achievement is in breaking the disabling silence imposed upon homosexuals, in revealing the reality of life for those forced to the edge, and in exposing the double standard which creates the situation where, as Geoff Pearce says in his poem 'Australian Experience',

> being gay is not
> as widely accepted
> as
> we are led to believe.

The Fishermen

JUDITH BEVERIDGE

The air's a torn weave
of sea-spray,
the wind lifts my blouse
a little from my shoulders.
I see birds thin as apple-cores,
the sun eating what life
there is. I listen:

the wind and the sea
move the same sound through broken shells.
And sometimes that sound
will never leave your hands;
it will trail like something
caught on the tips
of your fingers.

All night here, all you can see
are the faint white casts
of the fishermen
and a shore that seems
to be drifting.
I cup my hands,
hear my blood in shells

dead voices spill into.
The fishermen stand
with one artery open
to the sea. The moon glows
in their breath
starched by the cold
and white water flares up.

I hear the gasp in the shells
when the shore drifts.
I stand right at the edge
with the men,
but at a distance
and threads pump back
a secret voice

into my open hands.
We don't call, the one
tense strand is enough.
All night, our white breath
crosses into the cold
ouija-world of the sea.

Number 2, 1983

old man at raglan

ERIC BEACH

his face has finally made itself at home
with th trenches & shell-holes of th great war
now he's not so much blasted as furrowed
braving th camera for th first time in 60 years
retired to th bottom of th hill, th soldier's selection
he lost in th depression, he still checks to see
if his fences are standing, th road to th top
no longer 'Beach Road'; 'too many bewildered surfies'
th farmer pleaded to th council, his life's a trickle
(he lowers th pressure so that visitors don't use too much hot water)
& now he writes letters both sides of th paper
chipping at 'Bullheads' & 'Leather-lungs', those who love war
talking of 'communist' brothers who got lost in Paraguay
10 years getting back because they had no money
idealists in th family (their father alcoholic)
tales of Gloucester, Park House, Redmarley,
in th cellar, passing round th bull's horn of cider
welcome & wounded, secure behind 2 foot walls of wattle & daub
with th birds singing & th church tithing
while th grand-children counted out shillings from a brown jar
— grand-dad's farthings, bumped over pot-holes, taupo road
400 miles in a baby austin at 25 miles an hour
we never saw him as ugly, with his lop-sided grin & tics
that bounced like his old indian bike across rough country
to claims that were jumped & pegged in, buildings that killed men,
a life of work, & only th body complaining, retiring at 75,
I've 30 years of letters, & only 2 lines on th war,
when he copped a packet, & his mate lost th top of his head

Number 3, 1985

Rainbow

JOHN JENKINS

Above the gravity that pulls everything down
are words that float like a morning rainbow.
Looking up, the ticket you hold in your hand
turns liquid in the red wind. And you are
suddenly set into the fragile form time
erodes. There are also gulls which turn
liquid on the wing beyond the orange river
where the silver fades and the sun smothers
docklands and a heart full of daisies.
You look above yellow rails and the slight
morning mist rising as if from the corner
of a painting and it softens the glare of
existence; watching death-bright passengers
alight, caught in the green air they embrace.
The skyline burns into blue surrounded by
nothingness and we move along its indigo veins.
As intense as the violet sky, yet cloudy and often
hopeless, your luminous and incorrigible mind
flowers towards the cold light: a thing of
adjectives afloat above the day, perhaps
a bruised rainbow burning in the air
beyond the gravity that pulls everything down.

Number 4, 1985

The Killing Fields, nominated

GIG RYAN

The journo heroically watches the bomber planes dive
His mawkish face backtracks, sees headlines
that is, money, a Pulitzer Prize chops its knife propellers on the Asian air
Back home, he flips through the video
stalking news, his hands full of gore he didn't cause
Wisely he writes 'the despicable Khmer Rouge'
the ditch of bones fired by fervour
for an inhuman ideology. His feature article chalks the hand back
that 'Communism's' removed
between the stick parent and its brood
He's artistic, un-involved
weeping for the source's loss. His big American heart throbs
and gets paid

Number 4, 1986

geographic

JENNY BOULT

we tie off loose ends like tourists
as our senses focus on the landscape

of each other's flesh. in a few hours
it will be history. i don't ask

questions. you tell me i make love
like a ballet dancer. i don't know

what you mean. i deify the act of sex
salt slicked & slippery ready to drown

in the quarry of your eyes. these
are writhing couplets

caught in the flow of cloud
over mountain. you leave your phone number.

we kiss & night dissolves into the deep
blue screen of dawn. we're civilised

like actors playing roles. you say
'see you soon. later.' i say 'sometime'

when i mean 'yes. yes.' after days
of preparation this scene still feels strange

the taxi driver's waiting
you have a plane to catch. i have a life

to catch up with. the door slams. there are
no photographs. i hear rocks

falling

Another strand of intellectual debate that found expression in *Meanjin* in this period was the continuing reassessment of the legacy of Australian radical nationalism. The debate was initiated in true angry-young-man style by Humphrey McQueen with *A New Britannia* in 1972, but by the mid-1980s it was developing a more thoughtful, reflective tenor, and was informed by new ways of thinking about cultural politics. Among the contributions to this debate that appeared in *Meanjin* were two essays by David Carter on the Australian left in the 1950s, and the following piece by Graeme Smith, which reappraised the 'folk' tradition on which Russel Ward and other proponents of the 'Australian Legend' had placed such reliance.

Making Folk Music

GRAEME SMITH

> Long study of folklore and folklorists has convinced me that there never were any folk, except in the minds of the bourgeoisie. The entire field is a grim fairy tale. By an act of magical naming, all the peasantries and technologically primitive people of the world can be turned to 'folk'.
>
> Charles Keil[1]

The Department of Arts, Heritage and Environment has recently released a directory of Commonwealth resources and activities entitled *Folklife and the Australian Government*, and at present the Policy Co-ordination Branch of that Department is developing policy relating to 'folklife'.[2] The scope of 'folklife' in this guide is very broad, ranging from Aboriginal culture, through various forms of Anglo-Australian oral folklore — sayings, yarns, songs and so on, and in fact including the Australian language, accents and dialects — to the cultural activities of non-English speaking groups. The terms 'folk arts', 'folk crafts', 'folk architecture', 'folk customs', 'folk poetry' and 'folk music' all appear in the document with no suggestion that the meaning of these terms is in any way less than self-evident, in either the range of practices referred to or the social place ascribed to them.

'Folk' has always been a term applied by one group of people to another, usually distant from them in time or social status, generally to give value and legitimacy to cultural practices which have previously been ignored or regarded as vulgar by the cultural élites. It is a term which attributes value to lower class cultural practices, but in so doing it shapes them in particular ways. In this essay I want to look at the Australian folk revival and its shaping of that genre of music which is now generally known as Australian folk music, although recently out of recognition of non-English speaking cultures it may be referred to as Anglo-Australian or Anglo-Celtic-Australian music. This genre was largely defined by left-wing cultural activists in the 1950s who drew on ideas developed in earlier folk revivals in England and America to assert the existence of an Australian folk song. This assertion was part of the left's preoccupation with nationalism at the time, its search for something distinctive in the Australian character and experience which could sustain its hopes for a more socially just Australia in an increasingly conservative political world.

The term folk has always been closely linked to the discourse of nationalism, first emerging with German Romanticism as intellectuals like Herder sought among the lower classes for a distinctive culture which could be seen to embody the essential features of the emerging German nation. It is a consensual term, used to assert a unity of national experience over and above class and regional differences; the Hungarian musicologist János Marthy has argued that folklore studies were born from the bourgeoisie's need to construct a nation in the face of increasing polarisation between the proletariat and bourgeoisie.[3]

Under the influence of German studies of the *Volk*, the term folklore was introduced into English in 1846, in an attempt to regularise what was then called the study of Popular Antiquities. The term folk music became current about forty years later, but interest in English folk music among folklorists was not strong until the English Folksong Movement of the turn of the century.

The theorist of this movement, Cecil Sharp, was influenced by the marginal position of English composition in relation to German composition and the growth of German imperial power in the late nineteenth century, and was looking for the unconscious and racially authentic expression of a pre-urban peasant class in the material he collected. His fantasies about this class had little to do with the material conditions of life of his informants, and guided his selection of both informants and types of songs and the way he presented his material. Though founded on very shaky evidence, Sharp's ideas have been extremely influential on the development of thinking about folklore in the English speaking world.[4]

The next important revival of interest in folk music in the English speaking world was the People's Songs Movement of the USA in the 1930s and 1940s. This was a movement of left-wing singers and collectors which started as a musical expression of the radical populist politics of the Popular Front phase of communist politics and had considerable influence on the Australian folk revival of the 1950s. In the late 1920s and early 1930s the Communist Party and the left in general had little interest in folksong, regarding it generally as a backward musical form. In 1934 an American communist music critic could write:

> Not all folk-tunes are suitable for the revolutionary movement. Many of them are complacent, melancholy, defeatist — originally intended to make slaves endure their lot — pretty, but not the stuff for a militant proletariat to feed upon.[5]

With the institution in 1934 of the Popular Front in international communist strategy, Communist Parties were called to co-operate with left-wing reformist parties, such as labour parties, in the fight against fascism. As Communist Parties around the world began emphasising the themes of national identity and national history, and playing down the importance of class differences, the idea of the folk again came to the fore.

Communist intellectuals participated enthusiastically in the growing interest in American culture and folklore, and were able to find within it expressions of an autonomous workers' culture. This change in attitude is clearly seen in the writings of the then radical musicologist Charles Seeger. In 1934, a few months before the inception of the Popular Front policy, he wrote in 'On Proletarian Music', 'Needless to say, the proletariat has not produced any music of its own as such'. Several years later, after some experience as Deputy Director of the Federal Music Project of Roosevelt's Works Progress Administration, he was enthusing in the same journal about native American music as the way forward for contemporary composition, and talking of the musical richness of the American people and the incorporation of its folk music traditions within the labour movement.[6]

Until the 1950s there was almost no awareness of any comparable folk music or song traditions in Australia. Wendy Lowenstein has noted that when she and Ian Turner set up the Victorian Folklore Society in 1955 they knew exactly three Australian folk songs: 'Click go the Shears', 'The Wild Colonial Boy' and 'Botany Bay'. Australian folk music as we know it today had scarcely any public currency.[7] A few collections had been published prior to the 1950s, beginning with Banjo Paterson's *Old Bush Songs* (1905), assembled from responses to a request published in the *Bulletin*. It included vernacular poetry as well as texts clearly intended for singing, but until the 1940s little interest was shown in the music the songs were performed to, or in the social context and style of performance. By the middle of the twentieth century active performance of traditional music was fairly rare in Australia; there were still individuals who remembered songs from around the turn of the century, but the style of singing had fallen out of use, even among those who came from the social and occupational groups which were actively creating the old bush songs but two generations ago. When, in the 1940s, interest began to develop in traditional Australian songs, the form was already of historic rather than current significance.

The first conscious collecting of this material as Australian folk song, and the noting of words and texts in conjunction, was by Dr Percy Jones in the middle 1940s. Jones's article, 'Australia's Folk Songs', published in 1946 in a Catholic quarterly, was probably the first article to discuss this song genre as folk music, though he is little interested in the social context of the songs and is content to see them as belonging to an earlier rural Australia: 'The easy going nature of the people and the timelessness of the country can be heard in these droll lilting tunes of the early Australian ballads.'[8]

In 1950 Vance Palmer and Margaret Sutherland issued a collection of thirteen songs remembered by Palmer and associates.[9] Though Palmer had lived much of his life in the country the significance of an indigenous music did not interest him until then, and he may have been influenced by Jones's work. The melodies in this collection are described as having been 'restored' by Sutherland, but comparison with later field recordings shows substantial differences in melodic style and detail.[10] The next song publication was the *Bandicoot Ballads* by Ron Edwards and John Manifold, and like Palmer's, the songs in this collection were also initially drawn from the memories of the compilers.[11]

The published collections of Palmer and Edwards and Manifold contained a total of twenty-one songs and were the extent of the published folk song repertoire in Australia in 1953. In South Australia Russel Ward was researching the social history of the nineteenth century working class, and was collecting some song texts as historical evidence. John Meredith, another young radical from a rural background, had started searching for tunes to the old bush ballads. About the same time other individuals like Edgar Waters and Alan Scott were also beginning to gather together remembered tunes and texts to bush ballads. The idea of an Australian folk song had become firmly established.

All of these individuals were inspired by ideals of cultural nationalism and radicalism, and most were members of the Communist Party. But they did not yet form a movement. It was not until the staging in 1953 of *Reedy River* by the New Theatre that the isolated activities of these individuals were transformed into a social movement asserting and defining Australian folk music. After this Australian folk song was wholeheartedly embraced by the left.

The New Theatre was closely linked with the Communist Party of Australia, though not all of the people associated with it were members of the Communist Party. In 1953 Dick Diamond, in association with other members of the company, began to assemble a musical play based around the Queensland shearers strike of 1891. They used the songs from the Palmer and Sutherland collection, though they were denied access to material Percy Jones had collected, no doubt because of the company's overt political identification. The resulting play, *Reedy River*, was interspersed with songs and dances suggestive of the period, a couple of which were contemporary compositions. It probably owed a certain amount to the current Rodgers and Hammerstein musical *Oklahoma*, a folksy celebration with quite different musical style and political intent. In theme and setting *Reedy River* looked backwards to the historical roots of the Australian labour movement, and the incorporation of music into the play suggested a unified working class culture of which this radicalism was part. Its particular mix of nostalgia and radicalism struck a responsive note with a large number of people, and the production was a resounding and somewhat unexpected success, inspiring the establishment of music groups to continue to play music from the show, and the formation of folk music and bush music clubs in both Sydney and Melbourne. Collecting activity increased and recordings of Australian folk songs were produced, including one important recording of traditional singers.

Why was the left so receptive to the idea of an Australian folk music at this time?

The Comintern's change to a Popular Front policy in 1934 had similar consequences in Australia to those already mentioned in relation to the American People's Songs Movement. From ideas of a revolutionary proletarian culture forging the weapons of class struggle, Communist Party cultural policy came to stress consensual, populist notions of culture, and emphasis on national traditions came to pervade all communist discussions of art.

After a position of considerable influence during the war, supported by the Russian alliance and drawing in thousands of new members, the Communist Party of Australia was a party besieged in the cold war atmosphere of the late 1940s and 1950s. In 1951 Menzies only just lost the referendum to ban the Communist Party, and its membership had shrunk from its war-time peak of 23,000 to 6,000. Throughout the cold war, the right used the language of national unity to define the communists as treasonous, a potential fifth column inside a united Australia. The communists, on the other hand, proclaimed themselves to be the true inheritors of the Australian tradition. Their 1951 programme announced itself as an

'Australian Path to Socialism', opening with a nostalgic reference to the nineteenth century 'Australia of which our poets sung'. And just as the conservative attack stressed the unity of Australia against a small treasonous faction of communists, the Communist Party was able to condense the Australian bourgeoisie to '50 monopolist families in Collins House', against whom the whole of the Australian people could be arrayed.

The cultural implications of this extreme populism can be seen in J. D. Blake's article from the *Communist Review* of 1951, 'Folk Culture and the People's Movement'.[12] In this article the key enemy of the Australian people is American imperialism and its cultural propaganda. Blake criticises 'cheap degrading literature, ideological filth from Hollywood and drooling songs churned out day by day by the imperialists'. These are criticised not just for overtly reactionary content and lack of realism, but also for 'introducing the spirit of cosmopolitanism'. Blake finds comfort in 'an important characteristic of the Australian people . . . that they love their country', and he urges party artists to develop the people's 'folk-pride and strength'. The concept of a folk culture is accepted here without any consideration of its relationship to conflict in the nation or to class and is clear heir to the ideas of Herder and the German Romantics.

As its nationalism became more insistent, the Communist Party was able to embrace more unreservedly the ideas of radical nationalism which had been espoused by Vance Palmer and others since the 1920s. In the 1950s the greatest threat to the possibility of a radical Australian culture was seen to be American mass culture. The rapid change in the face of popular culture after the war and the access of the broad mass of the people to these new forms disturbed conservative and radical critics alike. Docker describes the Communist Party's reaction to comic books, and stresses that the communists' opposition was not very different from that of conservative or religious critics.[13]

Docker argues that the radical nationalist arguments of this time were anti-working class. By standing so strongly against the undeniable popularity of the newly available mass cultural forms, radicals were in danger of cutting themselves off from 'a popular urban culture that the working class had made its own'. While not wanting to agree completely with Docker's argument that urban popular culture becomes a distinctly working class culture merely by use, I think he is right to point to the serious failure of radical nationalists of the 1950s to discuss popular culture in any terms other than those of corruption and alien influences on the one hand, and a pure national tradition on the other.

The left's failure to consider contemporary popular culture seriously was part of its much larger failure to come to terms with the contemporary working class. The growing power of right wing Catholics within the ALP and the union movement, the increasing affluence of the working class, and the influx of postwar migrants, many from the 'people's democracies', had changed the political and social face of the Australian working class. Just when the hostility of the international and domestic political climate was increasing, the class for whom they were fighting seemed to be deserting them. Politically besieged, the Communist Party, and many on the left generally, turned to an image of a working class which was free from cultural imperialism, suburban affluence and Catholic and European anti-communism. This defensiveness, as much as any positive affirmation of Australian culture, inspired the popularity of Australian folk song on the left.

It also shaped the way the genre was defined. The participants in Australia's first folk song revival constructed a musical genre, giving meaning to certain musical practices by placing them within a cultural framework and asserting their social and historical significance. Such a process is not unique to the construction of folk music as a genre, for all musical genres are socially defined and such definition always takes place in relation to other musical forms. To say what Australian folk music *was* involved saying what it *was not*, the ascription of meaning involved the drawing of boundaries; and one thing it was not was contemporary Australian country music.

Country music, originally known as hillbilly music, first became popular in Australia in the early 1930s with the release and radio play of the recordings of early American performers such as Vernon Dalhart and Jimmy Rodgers. It had an immediate impact upon rural listeners around Australia, particularly on small dairy farmers, who made up a large proportion of Australian farmers. When Australians started performing in this style from the late 1930s they played both copies of American songs and self-composed material. Some of this held fairly closely to American models, but much drew upon other musical genres, including the sung bush ballad and nineteenth century popular song. Indeed some early Australian country music recordings were of old bush songs, performed in hillbilly style with guitar accompaniment. While the American origin of Australian country and western music is undeniable, the Australian performers and song-writers were also drawing on just those musical traditions which the folk song revivalists were now struggling to preserve.[14]

Rural Australia's enthusiastic response to country and western music was by no means unique. The first American recordings of hillbilly music were intended merely to tap the potential of poor Southern whites as a record market, but the genre quickly spread beyond this enclave, becoming popular among rural and urban lower class groups in many countries, and it has generally retained this popularity. It is tempting to speculate whether this working class popularity arose from a vague recognition of the origins of the music, or was a response to its narrative and emotional strategies, but whatever its origins, it has been accompanied by a complementary rejection by metropolitan, educated, middle class taste. While such taste has been able to define Afro-American music as serious, its reaction to country and western forms has ranged from patronising dismissal to disgust. . . .

By the 1950s, the popularity of Australian country music had reached a peak, yet it was almost totally disregarded by urban radio stations. Similarly, the urban-based folk song revival movement ignored its existence and could see no relationship between it and the failing historical genre which they were determined to rescue. They merely saw in country music the American cultural penetration they loathed and feared, and it is ironic that here was a contemporary form close to the myth of organic musical expression which they espoused. It is not, however, surprising. The concept of folk emerges from the vast differences of cultural power between one group and another, and what presents itself as a preservation or revival is really the expropriation of a cultural act. Active contemporary lower class musical practices, such as country and western music of the 1950s, do not easily submit to the massive mystification which 'folk' requires.

We should not see this blindness to the significance of country and western music as the folk song revival's lack of scholarly precision. Folk song scholars have often been criticised for ears which failed to note the subtleties of alien musical systems, for sensibilities which expurgated sexual texts and so on. But such criticisms, implying as they do the possibility of transparent cultural mediation, are misleading. Not only are all musical genres socially constructed, but folk music, as should be clear by now, has always been a particularly politicised musical genre.

The achievements of the folk song revival of the 1950s are usually seen in songs collected and published, performances and recordings produced, and the general public promotion of this material. But ultimately, more important than all of these activities was the demarcation of a genre. This defining occurred within particular social ideologies and historical circumstances and has determined the way in which individual items and musical forms have since been heard. The ideas we now have about Australian folk music are a direct result of this activity, as is our general perception of it as a self-evident musical genre.

But though a group can be dominant in the definition of a musical genre, once defined the genre enters the public domain to become the site of competing social interests and open to the imposition of new meanings. I now want to trace briefly the further developments in the concept of the folk since the 1950s.

The first folk song revival lasted till about 1963. The second revival, based in coffee-houses and clubs, attracted a young middle class urban population, half a generation younger than the earlier revivalists. There was a considerable social distance between the older bush music clubs and the newer folk clubs. The radical nationalism of the older activists was generally seen as irrelevant by the new enthusiasts, and performance replaced preservation as the focus of the movement. The new clubs and performance venues built up a core of semi-professional performers who were much more musically committed than the activists of the 1950s. Models of both musical style and performance context were largely borrowed from Britain and America, and, as in other areas of Australian popular music in the mid-1960s, young emigrants from the British Isles dominated.[15]

With this second revival the mythologised and historicised bearers of a 'folk culture' give way in importance to performers of an established genre, who themselves assume the mantle of the legitimate bearers of a specific, though not clearly defined, relationship between art and community. The idea of the folk no longer simply refers to past social experience but comes to express an ideal of a community which is socially authentic and organically related with its cultural forms and its past. As folk music took its place as an established, if minor, popular music form in the English speaking world, folk could become one of the terms in a public debate about the relationship between popular and mass culture. In this it was not limited to the underwriting of 'folk song' as culturally authentic, but was given more general applications.

One of the few people to have written seriously about contemporary popular music, Simon Frith, argues that during the Woodstock era the mythology of folk was taken over by the rock music ideologists of *Rolling Stone* to assert the difference between counter-cultural rock and commercial pop.[16] Counter-cultural rock was seen to emerge from a closeness of experience between performer and audience in comparison with the imposed, alienated musical forms of commercial pop. The idea of folk music as the music of a community has thus become an important, if obfuscating, part of the sense of possible relationships between popular cultural forms, their audiences and their producers.

As would be expected, the concept of folk continues to be used vigorously by the folk song revival movement itself. In spite of its decline over the last decade, to many of its staunch adherents the revival movement has become 'the folk community', and finally the 'folk' itself. There is an historical irony here: as this taste group becomes smaller and more inward looking, it is able, through its unity, to define itself in more universalist terms. At the same time, the historicist definition of the folk still holds its place in the discourse of Australian nationalism, and the folk song revival movement can invoke this to seek recognition from a Labor government whose last claim to radicalism is in the vigour of its nationalist rhetoric. . . .

The last generation of enthusiasts and performers from the late 1960s do not seem to be attracting a younger group, and the scene has that ageing character reminiscent of jazz clubs some years ago. However, in another irony of history, many of these older enthusiasts, now with professional or semi-managerial occupations, are discovering ways of gaining a powerful voice in lobbying government authorities. So when the folk revival movement is at its lowest ebb creatively, it has suddenly gained a strong public voice.

As has been argued above, folk music is not an analytical description, but a legacy of a series of historical practices: various interventions of cultural élites upon selected lower class musical genres. Alongside folk stands the concept popular.

In a paper on the conflicting interests for the funding of music, the Music Board of the Australia Council had the following attitude to popular music:

> *Popular Music*: It is reported that the first two records made by the rock group Men at Work grossed $130 million. This is over thirteen times the annual grants budget of the Music Board. On the face of it, there can be no rationale for subsidy of an industry which can bring such enormous financial rewards. This is basically the Music Board's position.

> However, keeping in mind that popular music of various kinds is really the folk music of our day, occupying the musical interests of the great majority of the population, the Board has felt it incumbent upon itself to look below the surface of all this success. This process is just begun.[17]

This Music Board document shows an almost total unawareness of the complexity of popular music. It stresses that the pop music industry was 'in some ways fairly brutal . . . and aspiring musicians need to pass through the bath of fire in Australia if only to be able to survive an international scene where no quarter will be given'. One wonders how a Board of the Australia Council, whose primary reason for existence is to enable art forms in Australia to achieve some independence from international markets, can make such a statement unless it feels that popular music is by its very nature quite unsuitable for assistance. However, one possible reason for assistance has been noticed by the Board. They have read *Rolling Stone*, and know that popular music is really 'the folk music of our day'. The mere involvement of a large number of Australians with popular music does not seem significant in itself; only on the basis of the 'folkness' of popular music might it warrant some support.

Cultural élites who spend so much mental energy on the justification of specific art forms occasionally have to reshuffle the hierarchies of taste and seriousness. Thus what was once trivial or vulgar can become historically significant or meaningful as the political context of a cultural world shifts. It is within this cultural discourse that the folk have existed. If, as Keil maintains, the bourgeoisie have always needed the folk, so too have other groups in less powerful social positions who want to redraw a cultural map. The term can be taken up by diverse interest groups. The Music Board of the Australia Council, confused and hesitant before the universe of popular music forms which swims before its classically focused eyes, sees it as a way of accommodating these forms. To the Department of Arts, Heritage and the Environment it is both an expression of the new nationalism of Australian right wing social democracy and a convenient way to avoid any real attempt to develop a socially informed aesthetic.

As Tim Rowse pointed out in a recent *Meanjin* (2/1985), a democratic cultural policy needs to recognise the legitimacy of a pluralism of cultural forms.[18] One step in this is to examine, and I would argue, ultimately to reject, such terms as folk which, by assigning a preeminence to certain cultural forms at the expense of others, legitimise the process of the construction of aesthetic hierarchies which merely disguise relations of cultural power.

Part Eight
Pressure Points

When I try to recall my first days at *Meanjin*, I often think of the title of Albert Maori Kiki's autobiography: *Ten Thousand Years in a Lifetime*. The time-scale is shorter, but the ratio is about right. Certainly February 1987 seems a very long way away. In thinking about this sense of distance, it is hard for me to disentangle the autobiographical elements from the changes in the wider world; in my line of work, engagement with the outside world is both compulsory and compulsive.

Before I came to *Meanjin*, I had followed a path that was fairly typical of the cohort of students who graduated in the middle of the economic and political crises of 1974–5. As there was little academic work offering, I had oscillated between other kinds of paid work, further study and child-rearing; I had shifted from Canberra to Melbourne, and moved house five times in as many years.

I remembered *Meanjin* from my final years of high school in Tamworth, where the magazine had been a kind of intellectual lifeline; but, having opted to study history rather than literature at university, I had lost contact with *Meanjin* and the cultural stream it represented. As of February 1987 I knew little about Australian literature in the 1970s and 1980s, very little about critical theory, and nothing at all about magazine production. Living with the knowledge that every mistake I made would march back through the door three-thousandfold, I had to learn fast; it's a pretty drastic way to serve an apprenticeship.

Fortunately there was no shortage of mentors. As assistant editor, Bev Roberts and then John Bangsund acted as safety nets on the production side, and a lot of other editors, including my three predecessors, were generous with their advice. Among these encounters, there is one that I will never forget. In the spring of 1987 I was summoned to lunch by Stephen Murray-Smith. Absolutely deadpan, he informed me that it was 'vital to the future of Australian culture' that I make a success of *Meanjin*. At the time I was in the throes of getting the magazine computerized, trying to put an issue together, and hoping that my children weren't going to get sick. Also, I wasn't entirely sure that what Stephen meant by Australian culture was what I understood by the term, or that it *deserved* to survive if it needed me to do the job. Thanks, mate, I thought. Right now I need this like a hole in the head. But later I was grateful; I probably needed to be provoked into thinking about the responsibilities that lie behind the day-to-day slog, and about where I was going.

Where I was going at the time was into 1988 and the bicentenary of white settlement; and, like many others on the intellectual left, I was facing the prospect with some trepidation. The task was to turn the inevitable nationalistic brouhaha to some useful purpose — in particular, to provoke a greater awareness of the need to redress the harm that had been done to the original inhabitants and to their continent; and, more generally, to use the opportunity to subject Australian nationalism to a closer critical scrutiny.

Essay on Patriotism

PETER PORTER

Compared with my true patriotism,
the imperialism of my legs and bowels,
the suzerainty of my eyes,
grave hemispheric rulings
of the wide Porterian Peace,
my love of country is a pallid passion.

So when they say
we've dwindled to a Third Class Power,
a Banana Republic without
a decent satellite to spy from,
I recall those old inheritors
of fear, dirt, sickness, snot and rickets
who crawled out of their burrows
to hail Ladysmith's Relief
and bray the victories of their rulers
on air they couldn't warm.

Let us therefore handle the word 'great'
with circumspection. It fits Blake
and Milton, is much too big for Cromwell
and generally should watch itself in mirrors,
bearing down like Yeats's Nobel head.

When commentators write about
'the patriotic proletariat',
imagine week-end articles —
'from flat-cap to cat-flap
in one generation', 'Dinkies
are not toys today', 'Designer
Murder comes to Sicily' —
and hang wild garlic round your ears.

Let what people really love
invent an island tongue:
'a gemstone cantilever . . . .
hearing it in Noel's SOTA/
Dynavector/Spectral/Threshold/
Acoustat/Entec . . . .' no wonder
Rambo gobbled up the gooks
if he had such voices in his head.

Patriotism is not enough
of a scoundrel's last refuge
even if you love
your neighbour as yourself.
When I fell from the long tree of light
I didn't know it was going to be me
or I'd have checked all these quotations.
Where I landed I named ours
though it was never mine.

True patriots all,
the still-swimming lobsters in the tank,
the lambs that face the ocean through steel bars,
the opals in the open-cut —
I left my mother's and my father's house
and stepped on to a road beneath the stars.

Number 4, 1988

Oyster Cove 1988

CASSANDRA PYBUS

In April 1855, J. E. Calder, Surveyor-General of Tasmania, set out to walk to the old convict station at Oyster Cove. So lovely was the day and so beautiful the terrain that Calder made detailed notes of his impressions for a Hobart newspaper. After passing through the hamlet of Snug on the southern edge of North West Bay, Calder followed the road upward into heavily wooded hills from which he caught the occasional glimpse of a spectacular landscape.

> Now and then only, when an opening occurred, . . . we greatly admired the varied and magnificent picture which lay before us. The dusky eminences of South Bruny stretched along the horizon, terminating in the bold and beautiful cliffs of the fluted cape. Adventure Bay on the east of Bruny — the place of anchorage of the famous old navigators Cook, Furneaux and Bligh, last century — lies fully in view, separated from the nearer waters of the D'Entrecasteaux Channel by the long, low thread-like isthmus that unites the two peninsulas of Bruny Island . . . and a vast extent of undulating country in the east and north east, fronting on the most varied coastline in the world, forming altogether a picture which well repays the toil of a long journey to see it.

The huge eucalyptus and myrtle forests have now gone, but in essence the majesty and extraordinary beauty of the scene remain as Calder encountered it in the autumn sunshine a hundred and thirty-three years ago. This is the channel country, the home of my family for six generations. From where Calder stood he could possibly have made out the homestead Sacriston, built by my great-great-grandfather, Richard Pybus, who took up a large land grant on North Bruny Island in 1829. Below him, nestling at the very tip of Little Oyster Cove, but hidden from view, was the house and orchard of Calder's brother-in-law, Henry Harrison Pybus. This house, inherited by my great-grandfather, is still there behind its screen of trees, but only a huge scarred mulberry tree remains on Bruny to testify to the good fortune of that first immigrant from Northumbria. Not that physical presence matters. On my morning walks over the old station road I can feel my ancestral bonds to this place. It is my place: the landscape of my dreaming.

As I follow the path of my distant kinsman over the steep hills that divide North West Bay and the D'Entrecasteaux Channel, I have the same destination. It is a good long walk for my dog, while for myself it is a profound and constant source of psychic renewal. Like the tall timber, the old station is long since gone, and until recently the site was overrun with a tangle of bracken and blackberries. It was always sour and swampy ground, too low and damp for prolonged dwelling or productive use. Now it is cleared and signposted. The marker, pockmarked with dozens of bullet holes and defaced with spray paint, carries the Aboriginal flag. It is still possible to make out the words, a quotation from Xavier Herbert:

> Until we give back to the black man just a bit of the land that was his, and give it back without provisos, without strings to snatch it back, without anything but complete generosity of spirit in concession for the evil we have done to him — until we do that, we shall remain what we have always been so far; a people without integrity; not a nation, but a community of thieves.

The clearing and sign are the work of the Tasmanian Aboriginal community who have a repeatedly unsuccessful land claim on the old convict station site. Their reasons for such a claim are simple and unassailable: this damp glen and swampy inlet are where the remnant of the tribal people of Tasmania was brought to die. On that April morning in 1855, Surveyor Calder was on his way to visit the few Aboriginals who still remained at Oyster Cove.

Nearing his melancholy object, Calder found the glory of the landscape quite diminished by the forlorn spectre of the station. 'But if the view were a hundred times more prepossessing than it is', he wrote, 'its attractions would be scarcely observed . . . when we know that within the walls of that desolate-looking shealing are all who now remain of a once formidable people, whom a thirty years war with our countrymen has swept into captivity and their relatives to the grave.' Within this dreary edifice, Calder found sixteen Aboriginal people living in a state of abject neglect and degradation, denied all but 'a naked sustenance . . . to prevent them dying from want'. Mindful of 'the duties of man to his fellows', Calder was indignant that 'even at this late hour' something should be done to improve the conditions of this pitiful remnant, 'for we cannot by mere maintenance in life repay the debt we owe a race whom we have forcibly dispossessed of everything but mere existence'.

Did this desire to soothe the dying brow, I wonder, bring with it any sense of culpability? Was Calder moved to reflect on the role he might have played while on his surveying explorations into various parts of Tasmania? Did he have cause to consider that, as a recipient of an original land grant on Bruny Island, he had actually dispossessed one of that remnant whose plight now so moved him? As he admired the impressive terrain of the D'Entrecasteaux Channel, did he observe that this temperate paradise contained both the beginning and the end of the fatal encounter of European and Aboriginal peoples? Did it matter to him that the virtual genocide of the Tasmanian people occurred within his own lifetime and that he was both witness to and participant in the process? Sadly, these are not the kinds of thoughts to which Calder's readers are privy.

It is a perverse desire to make the past bear witness, to own up to its grievous acts. After all, what difference could it possibly make now? What was done is done, the newspaper letter writers remind me. Those early settlers, my ancestors, were simply creatures of their time, which is to say they were men like other men; no better, no worse. The past is another country, things are different there. Ah, but that is not how it seems to me on this morning, when a delicate shift of wind across the channel brings me the smell of broom on dancing white horses. In that instant of pure joy I am awash with memory reaching back to smallest childhood and beyond to the accumulated memories of my father and grandfather. We have been very happy here in the territory of the Nuenone people. Has any one of us stopped to do a reckoning?

On 26 January 1777, Captain James Cook brought his vessels *Resolution* and *Discovery* into calm anchorage beneath the great fluted cape at Adventure Bay on Bruny Island. Here, as elsewhere in the Pacific, the great navigator was keen to cultivate friendship with the native people. He seized his opportunity when a party of ten Aboriginal men was sighted on the beach. Cook was agreeably surprised to find the men approach his party unarmed and confident. They showed little interest in the trinkets he proffered or the varieties of food with which they were tempted. Cook noted that the Aboriginal men were naked, with ornamental punctures and ridges on their skin. He found them to be sturdy, healthy and 'far from disagreeable'. There was nothing in this encounter to make him revise the opinion he had formed in New South Wales, that the Aboriginal people laid no claim to the land and would not oppose British settlement.

When d'Entrecasteaux sailed into the channel that bears his name almost exactly sixteen years later, he and his fellow scientists were also on the lookout for the local inhabitants. In a charmed encounter with a large mixed group, the naturalist Labillardière found them to be a spartan and friendly lot, with an openness he found most disarming. But his enthusiasm for these noble savages was not echoed by Péron and other scientists aboard Baudin's expedition, which called at Bruny Island eight years later. After an encounter with some twenty of the inhabitants, Péron described them as a miserable horde in a state of extreme primitiveness. This assessment concurred with the observations Péron had made elsewhere in Van Diemen's Land. In concluding that the Tasmanian Aborigines were further from civilisation than any other human race, Péron unwittingly provided scientific justification for their dispossession.

The presence of Baudin's expedition in Van Diemen's Land also provided justification for the occupation of the territory by the British, who feared the intentions of the French. Woorredy, a youth of the Nuenone band from Bruny, saw these first white settlers arrive:

> we watched the ships coming and were frightened. My people had seen ships like these before and knew about the white men and their pieces of wood that spat fire and killed. I was very young and I thought the ships were the Wragewrapper — the evil spirit my parents had said would come and get me if I did not behave well. Although we were frightened my people did not leave Nibberluna [Derwent]. We stayed hidden for a long time watching the strangers as they cut down trees, built their huts and planted their crops. (Reported to G. A. Robinson on 11 July 1831)

Woorredy's sense that these ships bought the evil spirit was not misplaced. Within twenty-five years of the first settlement at Risdon in 1803, the newcomers had taken all but the most inhospitable parts of the island for themselves, reducing the Aboriginal people to trespassers on their own hunting grounds. Though initially courteous and hospitable, Aboriginal reaction turned to violent resistance in the face of mindless killings, kidnappings and wholesale expropriation. Outraged at Aboriginal retaliation, the settlers declared an open season on killing the 'crows', as they commonly called the Aboriginal people.

In the midst of the lethal hostilities of the 'Black War', the channel district could still present an image of racial harmony. On 11 April 1828, a Captain Walsh reported that a party of about fifty Aboriginals from Bruny and the channel always gathered when vessels called at Recherche Bay, and would enthusiastically join the crews, hunting, fishing and making themselves useful. That the Nuenone people could be so benign is quite remarkable, as they too had suffered untold depredations and cruelty. On several occasions Nuenone men were captured and taken to Hobart as sociological exhibits. One man had escaped the Governor's pleasure to return to his people with a ball and chain still attached to his leg. Mangana, an important elder, had experienced the murder of his wife by whalers and the abduction of his two eldest daughters by sealers. His youngest daughter, Truganini, had been raped repeatedly by convict sawyers, and borne horrified witness to the gruesome murder of her betrothed and his friend by these same men.

Neither were the Nuenone free to regard Bruny Island and the channel as their hunting and fishing grounds. Whaling and logging had been established in the 1820s, and the government magnanimously parcelled up large sections of the island to be granted freehold to settlers. One such beneficiary was Richard Pybus, who arrived in the colony in 1829 with some two thousand pounds in gold and stores to be promptly granted title to 2560 acres of the fertile northern part of Bruny. There is neither surviving record nor family lore as to how this first Pybus regarded the dispossessed people who still clung to their traditional territory. Perhaps he gave them handouts of tea and flour, as did the overseer at Captain Kelly's farm on the point. Perhaps, like so many of his kind, he found them just a damned nuisance. I don't know. But I do know about his loquacious neighbour, George Augustus Robinson, whose voluminous and self-regarding journals represent almost the entire written record of the tribal people of Tasmania.

Lacking the social standing and material assets to guarantee him a land grant as an automatic right, Robinson was given 500 acres and a cottage in addition to his salary as the government-appointed storekeeper of an Aboriginal establishment on Bruny. Robinson had left his trade as a bricklayer to take this post, 'actuated soley by a desire to serve the Aboriginals, to do them good, to ameliorate their wretched conditions and to raise them in the scale of civilization'. To this end he proposed the establishment of a native village where the principles of European civilisation could be learnt and Christian instruction given. As he explained in his journal of 30 September 1829:

> Though in point of intellectual advancement the aborigines of this colony rank very low in the savage creation, yet this defect is amply counterbalanced by the many amiable points which glitter like sunbeams through the shroud of darkness by which they are enveloped, and operate most powerfully in calling forth from the discriminating and philanthropic observor an irresistable feeling of sympathy on their behalf.

The concept of an Aboriginal settlement which would afford some protection to the indigenous people, and possibly some token recognition of their right to land, was part of Governor Arthur's strategy to find a solution to the native problem short of the genocide proposed by many vocal sections of the white community.

Arthur's strategy also included the deployment of roving bands whose mission was to capture blacks for a bounty of five pounds per adult and two pounds per child. Presumably Arthur intended these captives to be repatriated to Robinson's care on Bruny. Indeed, two Nuenone people, Jack and his wife Nelson, were used as trackers for one roving party in the central plateau. Their experience yields some clues about such parties' *modus operandi*. While Jack was repeatedly beaten by the soldiers, Nelson was forced to have sex with them. Jack was callously shot on attempting to escape, but Nelson managed to return to Bruny in a shocked and dazed state. There is no way of knowing just how many Aboriginals were killed by these bands. Certainly no-one grew rich on the bounty. According to Backhouse, such a successful operator as John Batman had killed thirty in the process of capturing five.

Some indication of the Governor's intention can be gleaned from the newspaper editor Henry Melville's report of a bizarre conversation between Arthur and Black Tom (Kickerterpoller), a guide for Gilbert Robertson's roving party. After an exchange concerning the policy of confining Aboriginals to specified areas such as the islands of Bass Strait, the conversation continued:

> Tom — You send him to dat hyland, and take't all him own country — what you give him for him own country?
> Governor — I will give them food and blankets, and teach them to work.

By mid-1829, Arthur seems to have decided on Bruny Island as the site. He ordered that all Aboriginals living with Europeans were to be sent to Bruny and soon after dispatched the few captured Aboriginals to join them. He was prepared to be generous in assisting the experiment. To Robert, an industrious fellow raised by settlers since a baby, he made a grant of twenty acres, as well as a boat, cart, bullock and farm implements. Likewise, Kickerterpoller was promised land and a boat. Perhaps these two, having learnt the rewards of European labour from childhood, were to be models for their fellow countrymen.

Whatever the intention, neither Robert nor Kickerterpoller became farmers. By the time they reached Missionary Bay, Robinson had despaired of Bruny for his Aboriginal establishment. Death had rapidly overtaken the Nuenone since Robinson's appearance among them. Mangana, on whom he had relied, had taken his second wife and son on an annual trip to Recherche Bay in August 1829. There his son was killed and his wife seized by mutinying convicts on the brig *Cyprus*. He returned to find that in his absence eleven of his people had died, as well as eleven visitors from Port Davey. To Mangana's further dismay, Robinson had shown himself to be unable to restrain the women, Truganini, Pagerly and Dray, from cohabiting with the European men who supplied them with tea and sugar, and all three were debilitated with venereal disease. Mangana himself died in December.

Not to be daunted, Robinson hit upon the audacious idea of taking the five surviving Nuenone — Woorredy, Myunge, Droyerloine, Truganini and Pagerly — as well as Dray from Port Davey, to conciliate the tribes of the west coast and bring them under the umbrella of his protection. To this group he added the newcomers Kickerterpoller, Eumarrah, Trepanner, Maulboyhenner, Pawaretar and Robert. They left Bruny Island on 28 January 1830. The Aboriginals never returned. What became of Robert's twenty acres, I have no way of knowing. Probably it was absorbed into the estate of some enterprising settler, to be passed on to his descendants and defended with the fierce determination and full force of the law that is so endearingly British.

Robinson did return to check on his own land on 5 April 1833. He dined with Richard Pybus, and they discussed property values and the cost of improvements. That evening in his journal Robinson had reason to query the veracity of Pybus's assertions on this score. They remained neighbours for another five years, although Robinson was perpetually absent. In 1838, when Pybus sold 1880 acres, Robinson's interest was aroused at the prospect of capitalising his property also. But it was not until 1848, just before he departed for England, that Robinson sold his Bruny Island holding, by then one of many land grants he had received.

Not Bruny but Flinders Island became the site of Robinson's philanthropic enterprise for the approximately three hundred Aboriginal people he was able to track down and conciliate between 1830 and 1835. There, at the dreary settlement at Wybalenna, he set about making them over into a Christian peasantry who laboured for a master and had no rights to the land they occupied, or to its products. 'Had the poor creatures survived', he wrote in his retirement at Bath, 'I am convinced they would have formed a contented and useful community.' Perceiving that Flinders had become one great graveyard, he threw in the towel in 1838 and took himself off to more lucrative prospects as the Protector of Aborigines in Port Phillip.

In October 1847, the forty-six survivors of Wybalenna made the longed-for return journey to the Tasmanian mainland. Among them were Truganini and Myunge, returning after seventeen years to the familiar territory of the Nuenone. The convict station at Oyster Cove was damp and dilapidated but it was in sight of their birthplace, their spiritual homeland. It was the proximity to home, much more than the beef and damper, that sustained Truganini for the next four decades of her increasingly lonely life.

Sir William Denison, the governor who had delivered the Aboriginals from their misery on Flinders, had his anxieties about the return to the mainland. Public protests had been held in Launceston; there was widespread concern that the blacks would endanger property. Having surveyed the thoroughly inoffensive group, Denison wrote to the Colonial Secretary: 'the mountain is delivered of a mouse indeed'. He gave instructions that the survivors be paraded before the citizens of Hobart and that 'respectable persons' be invited to visit Oyster Cove to observe them. In December 1847, Denison organised a Christmas party at New Norfolk where he entertained fourteen Aboriginal guests, and the following year six men were taken to visit Government House.

At Oyster Cove, however, the Aboriginals were largely left to their own devices, while the children were removed to the orphan school at Hobart. Occasionally there were hunting sorties as far afield as the Huon, which provided great pleasure in contrast to the chill and idleness of the station. Walter Arthur, undisputed leader of the community, attempted to farm the sour ground, and received a grant of fifteen acres near the settlement. He employed a European labourer to help him clear the land, but his later request for an assigned convict was refused. Subsequently, a request for more fertile land near the Huon was also refused.

Except for the social outings when the residents at Oyster Cove were dressed up in European finery, parsimony was the watchword for all government dealings with the Aboriginal settlement. By April 1855, only fourteen people remained at the station. Thirty-one had died. Fanny, daughter of Nicermenic and Tanganutura, had married a European, William Smith, and had gone to live with him at Nicholls Rivulet. Despite complaints from both Calder and the visiting magistrate, the settlement's funding was pared to a minimum and nothing was done to repair the filthy, derelict buildings. Meat rations were often inedible, and blankets and clothing were traded for supplies, including 'strong drink' from local

Europeans. Mathinna, once the pride and joy of Lady Franklin, who had taken her from Flinders to the pampered inner sanctum of Government House, drowned in a shallow creek beside the station in May 1855, having fallen face-down in a drunken stupor. She was twenty-one, but no longer anyone's pride and joy.

In 1859, *Hull's Royal Kalendar* listed the occupants of Oyster Cove as 'five old men and nine old women . . . Uncleanly, unsober, unvirtuous, unenergetic and irreligious, with a past character for treachery and no record of noble action, the race is fast fading away and its utter extinction will hardly be regretted.' Such sentiments were not uncommon and helped to fan official concern for the cost of maintaining this despised remnant. Walter Arthur, already defeated by disappointment, drowned when he fell from a boat in 1861, leaving the eight remaining Aboriginals with no-one to represent their interests. Alternatives for their care were canvassed, including an intriguing offer from Henry Harrison Pybus to look after them for five hundred pounds a year on his adjacent property at Little Oyster Cove.

Henry Harrison and his sister Margaret, probably children from an earlier marriage, emigrated with Richard Pybus in 1829. Margaret married the surveyor J. E. Calder, and Henry Harrison prospered in various entrepreneurial enterprises, including the logging operations and saw mill he owned jointly with William L. Crowther at Oyster Cove. He was certainly not in straitened circumstances, so I might assume his offer sprang from benevolent impulse rather than mercenary considerations. It is possible that he remembered Truganini from his youth, or that his proximity had stimulated an affectionate concern for his Aboriginal neighbours, though he does not seem to have ever made a visit to the station. Maybe he was concerned about the moral tone of the neighbourhood, since he undertook to keep his charges from public houses and 'intimacies of an objectionable kind'. Yet another possibility is that it was his partner, Crowther, who instigated the offer.

Dr Crowther, among his varied pursuits, was a man of science with a particular interest in the original Tasmanians. He already had a collection of skeletal material and was keen to secure the skeletons of those he believed to be the last of their race. As joint owner of the property to which they were invited to move, Crowther would certainly have had prime access to the Aboriginal skulls and bones he coveted. With an arrangement of this kind, Crowther may not have needed to resort to breaking into the morgue to steal the skull from William Lanne's corpse, as he did on 4 March 1869. The *Examiner* reported a rumour that Crowther had taken a prospecting lease on the old convict station in 1867. His son, Edward, who had assisted with the operation on William Lanne, acquired the site in 1900, and with his own son proceeded to dig up the graves of its Aboriginal inhabitants in 1907.

Speculation about motives aside, Pybus's price was still too high for the Tasmanian government to pay. Instead, the settlement was allowed to continue in its deplorable condition under the despairing supervision of John Strange Dandridge, who did what he could with his meagre provisions. Despite the appalling conditions of their domicile, the remaining Aboriginals were increasingly being recognised as rare and valuable. William Lanne, who had joined a whaling crew, had been given the quite erroneous title of King Billy as a recognition of his importance. In 1864 the four women still living at Oyster Cove — Truganini, Wapperty, Goneannah and Mary Ann — were dressed up and taken to a ball at Government House. A newspaper social columnist reported the women to be 'charmed beyond measure by the position they occupied'. Along with Lanne, they then had their photograph taken so the Museum could record them for posterity. In 1868, William Lanne and Truganini, now called Queen Truganini, were presented to the Duke of Edinburgh as fellow royalty.

William Lanne died in 1869, having progressed from being a despised outcast to itinerant seaman to immensely valuable property. After Crowther and son stole his skull, the Fellows of the Royal Society cut off his hands and feet, then returned to the grave to cart off the rest of his remains after they had been buried. Such grisly scientific endeavour had a profoundly unsettling effect on Truganini, who was quick to perceive the interest her own body might excite. It was her fervent wish, reiterated to several people, that she be buried in the deepest part of the D'Entrecasteaux Channel in order to escape such a fate.

In 1874, after three years as sole Aboriginal resident at Oyster Cove, Truganini was transferred into the care of Mrs Dandridge at Battery Point and the settlement was closed. Truganini, last of the Nuenone, died on 8 May 1876, ninety-nine years after her people had their first fateful encounter with the inquisitive Captain Cook. She was buried at the Cascades in Hobart, and the following year her body was illegally exhumed to serve the interests of science. It was a further ninety-nine years before Truganini was to get her wish to be buried in the territory of the Nuenone. Her skeleton was on display in the Tasmanian Museum until 1947, then stored in the museum vaults. After considerable public pressure, Truganini's remains were finally cremated on 1 May 1976 and the ashes cast upon the waters of the D'Entrecasteaux.

On the other side of Mount Wellington, well away from the public debate about the proper disposal of the body, Truganini was mourned in the traditional way by her friend Fanny Cochrane Smith, who had been born at Wybalenna and lived with her family at Oyster Cove. For many years Fanny had lived inland from Oyster Cove at Nicholls Rivulet, on a hundred-acre allotment granted to her in 1856, along with a lifetime annuity of twenty-four pounds. There she escaped public interest because of her marriage to William Smith, and because there was a suspicion that, like her sister Mary-Ann, Fanny was a half-caste and of no scientific value.

Along with her husband and eleven children, Fanny ran a successful farm and timber business as well as continuing the traditional pursuits, hunting and gathering wild foods. Until 1874 she was often accompanied on her hunting trips by residents from Oyster Cove, especially Truganini. Until her own death in 1905, Fanny Cochrane Smith nurtured and promoted Aboriginal culture and traditions, giving performances of the songs and stories of her people. These she also passed on to her many children and grandchildren. Thanks to the wonders of technology, I can still listen to Fanny singing into a recording machine in 1903. She sings in honour of a great leader:

Papele royna ngongna	Lo with might runs the man.
toka mengha leah	My heel is swift like the fire.
Nena taypa rayna poonya	My heel is indeed swift like the fire.
Nena nawra peyllah	Come thou and run like a man.
Pallah a nawra pewylla	A very great man, a great man.
Pellanah, Pellanah	A man who is a hero! Hurrah.

The recording quality is very poor, but Fanny's strong voice never fails to make the hair rise on the back of my neck. Her photographs show a handsome black woman, assured and elegant in Edwardian clothing which she has adorned with shell necklaces and possum skins. By all accounts, Fanny Cochrane Smith was an impressive woman. She so impressed the Tasmanian Parliament that in 1884 they agreed to increase her pension to fifty pounds a year and give her full title to 300 acres. The land was actually granted in 1889. There is no doubt that both Fanny and the parliament regarded this grant as compensation for the expropriation of Aboriginal land.

While 300 acres was small cheese compared to Richard Pybus's 2560, there were those who felt that Fanny's claim to land was fraudulent. In the late 1880s, opposing voices raised the issue of her parentage, insisting that as a half-caste, by which they meant non-Aboriginal, she could have no claim on the land. Fanny's mother Tanganutura, known as Sarah, had lived with sealers for some years and had one child, Mary-Ann, by a white man. Though Fanny was born at Wybalenna after her mother had married Nicermenic, there was always a suggestion that she too was 'half-caste'. The Aboriginal people all regarded Nicermenic as Fanny's father, just as he was the father of her brother Adam. Fanny and her husband always maintained both parents were Aboriginal and presented convincing evidence to the parliament in 1889.

This would have been the end of the matter but for the Royal Society, which was never far away when Aboriginal issues were at stake. A paper read at the Society by Mr Barnard 'threw out the challenge to ethnologists' with the assertion that Fanny was of pure Tasmanian blood. Science rose to the occasion to prove she was not. Ling Roth, working from photographs and a lock of hair, definitively proclaimed Fanny a half-caste in 1898. His 'proof' was accepted over Fanny's own evidence and has been ever since.

Fanny did not lose her grant and pension, but the denial of her identity must have dealt a cruel blow to her, as perhaps it was meant to. Entering the twentieth century, Tasmanians were disinclined to dwell on the moral responsibilities of their past. Modern Tasmania had no place for Aboriginality outside of the classroom and the cherished story of 'Queen Truganini — Last of the Tasmanians'. By proving that 'half-castes' were non-Aboriginal, Ling Roth's curious science provided the underpinning for a continuing policy of denying Aboriginal rights in Tasmania. In granting land to Fanny Cochrane Smith, the government acted in error — so the logic runs. Since then, however, science has been on hand to ensure such errors are not repeated.

Leaving the grand sweep of vista, my walk descends into a perpetually damp gully of man ferns and musk trees, and I am conscious of the melancholy that always seems to emanate from Oyster Cove. But on crossing Mathinna Creek, named for Lady Franklin's darling, I catch sounds of revelry from the old station site. Smoke rises above the trees, and excited, high-pitched voices carry to where I stand, taken by surprise, with my dog. Closer scrutiny reveals a kids' barbecue, organised by the Tasmanian Aboriginal Centre. A game of rounders is in progress on the mudflats while huge quantities of chops and sausages are charring on the grill plate. My dog, keen to play, darts off to chase the ball, leaving me, the intruder, unsure whether to advance or retreat. I know these people, some of them at least. Several whom I recognise are the great-great-grandchildren of Fanny Cochrane Smith, who lived here with her parents, her brother and sister, all those years ago. We were close neighbours then, my family and theirs, but I fear I am not wanted here at this family picnic. I wave, call my dog and leave, somewhat belittled by the feeling that I have nothing to contribute.

On the homeward path, I crush leaves from the musk tree to immerse my senses in their pungent aroma. I do not know how to pay the dues I owe for my charmed existence in this place. I do know we cannot remake the past, but the promise remains that we can remake the future. With a head full of musk scent I remember the words of the American poet Robert Penn Warren, reflecting on his own country's brutal history:

> But if responsibility is not
> The thing given but the thing to be achieved,
> There is still no way out of the responsibility of
> Trying to achieve responsibility.

From the first I had decided to focus at least a part of each issue on a particular theme. This was partly a matter of learning from my predecessors' experience: I had noticed that their thematic issues had far more impact than those that didn't have a particular focus. It was also partly a question of devising a means of opening the magazine up and keeping it open. Oddly enough, the thematic issues I have produced, however highly structured they might seem, have usually involved a minimal amount of commissioning. I spend a lot of time reading the unsolicited material that arrives at *Meanjin*, and often the idea for a theme comes from that rather than from any inspiration of my own. On other occasions someone else has offered to act as guest co-editor of an issue. And, once a particular hare is set running, the word spreads fast. This editorial style has something to do with my preference for working collaboratively, but there is more to it than that. It also represents a response to the increasing

plurality of Australian literary and intellectual life, and an attempt to make *Meanjin* into a bridge between the different streams without trying to subordinate them to any programmatic editorial control.

A similar policy has ruled in the selection of poetry. From my first day at *Meanjin* I was blessed with a poetry editor who had an encyclopaedic knowledge of contemporary poetry, and was also prepared to act as a kind of industrial advocate on poets' behalf without pushing a barrow for any particular faction. His selection of poetry has reflected the diversification of Australian poetry in the 1980s. While poetry now is still fuelled by the energies released in the 1970s with the emergence of the New Poetry, the divisiveness of that time is gradually yielding to a new plurality, an awareness of the multifarious possibilities of contemporary poetry. This plurality has been supported by a continuing American influence and, more importantly, by the emergence of poetries of difference within Australia. Poetry by women and by poets of non-Anglo-Celtic origin has broken down many of the earlier constraints on the development of Australian poetry. With a growing contemporary interest in poetry in translation, Australian poetry seems set to diversify even more extensively in the 1990s. At the same time, since the advent of poetry readings in the 1960s, poetry has continued to 'go public'. Live performance has become increasingly popular; poetry has shed much of its esoteric image and reasserted its central place in cultural life.

Number 3, 1987

the stunned mullet

JOHN FORBES

lips bruised blue
from the impact of the shore
form words you applaud
because, after all, a fish is speaking
it's perfunctory though,
like the scattered clapping
a bronze medal at the Olympics gets
as you just pass muster
under a distant, benign regard
only the fish thinks odd, because up close
the scales are false
in fact a cunning mechanical contrivance,
like Bob Hawke's hair —
they glitter, exposed to the atmosphere
instead of dying, being alloy not flesh
& down below Captain Nemo, a fussy, European
judge of a good cigar

nurses the elaborate grudge
that brought him here, a picture of Wendy Hughes
taped beside the art-nouveau controls
while above you
Alan Bond's belly coloured airship
inspects Sydney like a stupid beach.

Number 2, 1987

convenience

JOANNE BURNS

consider the plastic bag.
consider the plastic bag full of the week's shopping from the supermarket. jars of jam. bottles of sauces. packets of noodles. rice. brand new.
consider the shape of the bags. the way we can call them singlets. the way they resemble well fed, bloated bellies when they're full of the week's shopping. the way they can cut into your fingers with their weight.

consider the ease with which a plastic bag fits over a human head. long lasting. airtight. these are the features a consumer looks for. is told to look for. remember the sight of such bags in the skull supermarkets of pol pot. the open air markets of the killing fields. pre-packaging at its most contemporary. these cambodian bags were not disadvantaged by the splitting of their sides from a restless carton of milk or an overload of shopping poking through.

consider the silence of the plastic bag as it lies flat in the checkout drawer neatly compressed with a hundred others into a pile as deep as a jackie collins paperback. consider the noise your shopping bag makes as you carry your purchases to their destination. think about how these plastic bags resemble skins. think about what happens to your ears when these bags make contact with small breezes.

remember your friends who said the killing fields was 'too american a movie'.

discuss how angry you get when you find the pile of new bags passed to you with indifference by the checkout operator are sometimes so hard to open. and occasionally even faulty.

but never neglect to remember the convenience of the plastic bag. the difference it has made to your life.

Looking For Some Tracks

(instead of making them)

J. S. Harry

The best poem you have ever written
hides like the Emmaville panther
dark/myth/uncomplicated by existence/
in a huge blackberry tangle
up the valley
beside the river.

You can hear it cough,
hear the dry snarl
as it moves its slight
animal's bulk, over sticks,
in the thicket's middle.

When your heart
stops pounding panic
& slows to an even
beat, you walk closer
& find the cat-tracks entering or
                                        leaving?
larger
        than any you have ever seen.

You cannot tell, still,
with your nose stuck into spoor,
the tracks going into the thicket
from the tracks going out of it.
You've always been
a bad
reader of signs.
The surreal   has been padding
to & fro
tearing up
the ground all night.

Your poem, like the panther,
fails to emerge.

Giving up, on the idea of hunting
a poem as if it were an animal,
you decide to study hunting
in general.

A poem about hunting
will become a poem about processes.
The process will *be* the poem.
There will be no 'one-only' 'object',
or objective reality, that the poem
will be trying to 'catch'.

Going home, through the ordinary scrub,
towards Emmaville, your head
lost in abstraction,
you meet an
unimaginative, non-drunk,
bush-walking,
disbeliever-in-panthers

who describes to you
in hair-crisp detail, perfect
down to dimensions of paw-print,
the objective correlative
to your unseen panther.

It is now
his panther   quietly padding off
to kill some sheep
over in Deepwater.

Perhaps once   a pair of panthers
did fall, out of a travelling
circus truck (springing
out of their cage
that was smashed
by the accident)
& escape   into the real bush
round Deepwater or Emmaville?

You will be unable
to make your mind
move your feet
from the blackberry tangles
round the bad
simile of the panther
for at least
the next week.

Number 1, 1988

Home Life, 1975

R. A. SIMPSON

I drowned myself at dinnertime
nearly every evening
with chablis or with claret
from fat McWilliams flagons

After that came the brandy
three or four at first
but then with two barbiturates
I was drinking a bottle
and sinking to sleep in a chair

My family watched TV for hours
but finally crept to bed
my wife alone
my children alone
and me as good as dead

We said goodbye each morning
as I left to teach baloney
about the Graphic Arts

I walked there almost daily
with my feet encased in lead.

Number 2, 1988

Landlocked

VINCENT BUCKLEY

It was like the mockup of a suburb,
and you were inside it
almost mute, totally indoors;
except for glimpses of duckboards
and the ends of walkways.

There I lasted into summer,
hospital summer, in the western suburbs,
fans caught in the air
like flies in a spider web,
a tree stiff with heat at the corner,
and the wireless playing 'Paper Doll'
while the hearts of the new arrivals
went thrum, thrum, tharrumm,

all through the dark night
of the soul and the anarchic organs.

You heard the wind, but saw no branches,
you saw sun-bleach on the windowsills
but no sun climbing or delaying;
your speech was all of yes, yes, and no, no,
you met the tours of inspection every day;
you nodded like a toy, you leaned back on the bedrail,
getting better, being cured, endlessly,
they told you with careful eyes.
Someone had lent you photographs of Manly.

That was 113th AGH, Concord,
not seed but cutting time,
thin whiplike branches cut from the red hibiscus,
seasons cut from your life,
blood cut from the heartbeat.

*

None of us learned understanding
or got wisdom.
And the great shade is fallen about us,
striplings and old soldiers,
young crocks and old hopefuls,
all, in the middle of our journey,
relieved to be bossed by women.

For we have no landscape outside or inside us;
the heart limps round its territory;
put somewhere, but not placed anywhere,
we have no answers
for one another's questions
except the fumbles of our pasts.

*

If I had known
how close we were to water,
the brackish, the flowering, the breeze-caught,
how that breeze came from Yaralla Bay,
those cool airs and swirls of rain
from Rocky Point and Kissing Point,
that faint musk from the bends of river,
I would have sent my soul out
like a sightseer on a wharf
to look for hours across the water,

to query and consult tides,
the light inside them red as resin.
But so far as I knew we were landlocked.

The wise healers nodded, and I nodded,
the handmaidens smiled, O do smile,
show you are grateful, O *be* grateful.
I nodded stiffly, like a toy.

Number 4, 1988

Dreaming Up Mother

ROBERT ADAMSON

Understanding is all, my mother would tell me,
and then walk away from the water;

Understanding is nothing, I think, as I mumble
embellished phrases of what's left of her story.

I carry her about like an old lung.
There is nowhere to go now but inside

though I keep battering myself against sky,
throwing my body into the open day.

Landscapes are to look at, they taught me,
but now the last of the relatives are dead.

Where do these walks by the shore take us,
she would say, wanting to clean up,

after the picnic, after the nonsense.
I've been a bother all the years from my birth.

Look out — the river pulls through day
and Understanding, like a flaming cloud, goes by.

Number 4, 1989

Letters on a Bridge

IRINA GRIGORESCU PANA

I was writing letters on a bridge,
It must have been in Budapest, in summer
And it must have been the war.
My father was also there, in uniform
Young, smiling, unafraid.

We were alone in the huge theatre,
But when we spoke it was not with words.
Letters poured out of our mouths,
Pages in black and white fell off my breast,
A diary, too, and more epistles.
We were both wandering scholars,
Whirlwinds of ink swelling in the mind,
Sleepwalking over roofless bodies.
When in the glass our eyes met,
Feverish adjectives kept darting and flashing.
It was a summer colonised with writings
And, as in the war, another life had gone by,
Leaving tiny marks on the retina,
But letters were a hospitable home
And we were glad of more and more
Flapping in the wind. We squandered memory,
Used it up, sealed it up in a night dress
I had come to wear day and night.

Number 1, 1990

Imagine This

JULIE COOK

That the day is hot.
There's an old iron fence at the end of a long yard.
A wide open gate.
At the top of the yard is a house.
A house on stilts with wide wooden verandas.
Lazy ceiling fans that lick the heat.
Imagine you're on that veranda, eating.
Say, your lunch.
Adult voices and laughter drift to you from further inside.
Bottles pop and glasses clink.
Go back now to the open gate.
At just the moment a bottle pops, a group of people passes through the gate.
Adults, children, and imagine even a baby.
About a dozen people altogether.
There's one main difference between the two groups of people.
But imagine for a moment you're unaware of that.
The Fence people move closer.
The younger children skip right up to the house.
Calling 'please miss, bread'.
Of all things.

Pointing to gaping mouths and tight protruding stomachs.
Imagine they're looking straight at you.
You with your lunch.
Then a big topless pale male rushes out from the bottles and glasses.
Neck veins taking the strain,
'Piss off or I'll set the dogs, call the police. Buy your own food you lazy buggers, the lot of yous.'
Try to imagine that, that Fence people were able to get jobs to earn money to buy food.
House people did.
That the bellowing pale picks up a stone and throws it.
One of the children is hit.
And you can imagine the scream that pierces the air.
Now imagine none of that ever happened.
House people do.
Move forward now to many years later.
A young person dies in a small locked room.
Then another.
Imagine quite a few if you will.
That those minding the rooms are all House people.
Even further,
That all of the dead are Fence people.
And try this,
The House minders have to answer some questions.
And I quote:
'As far as I'm concerned, I'm right behind the police'
'It's simply that they're not used to living in custody, they're used to wide open spaces'
'As police officers we just cannot be expected to constantly watch every prisoner. Or to be responsible'
And imagine this:
'Yes he could have done it with a towel by himself'
Fancy that, powered by imagination.
House people thrive on overdrive.
The questions aren't so hard.
Imagine their imaginations.

And if you can't manage that,
Imagine what a Fence person might say.

Early in 1988 Gerald Murnane became the first fiction writer to act as fiction consultant at *Meanjin*. From the outset it was agreed that we would avoid lowest-common-denominator decisions. When in doubt, rather than publishing stories that we both *quite* liked, each of us would reserve the right to overrule the other. So there have been two pairs of hands at work in the selection of fiction, both for the magazine and for

this anthology. The explosive potential of this arrangement has been kept in check by a lot of good talk (largely by courtesy of Telecom) and the shared excitement of discovering, among the mountains of unsolicited manuscripts, the occasional distinctive voice saying something that needs to be said, and read.

Gerald and I also agreed that, rather than taking the easy option of pursuing writers with established reputations, we would give particular attention to previously unpublished writers. The short stories that follow were both their authors' first publications.

Number 2, 1988

The Characters of Nineteenth-Century Fiction

LOUISE DAVENPORT

She wanted to squash the characters she read about in nineteenth-century fiction. She wanted to put an end to their wholeness, the bodies given to them by an author. They had histories, motivation and denouement.

She kept the characters in matchboxes. They were small but they were real. They had bodies.

One day she took hold of an axe. It was a toy axe with a head one centimetre long and a handle four centimetres long. It was small but sharp. She opened the matchboxes one by one. She looked at the characters she'd read of. One by one she killed those fictional people.

She held the miniature axe in her giant's hand. The boxes with characters of fiction in them lay open on the bench top of the vanity basin in her parents' bedroom. Anna Karenina with her deep grey eyes. Heathcliff with his brooding brow. Rochester with his stern face just beginning to gentle at the corners of the mouth. Tess with her torn and bloody dress.

She looked down on those bodies, creatures of the imagination. She lifted the axe five centimetres above the first box. She hesitated, then brought the axe down firmly. One at a time she killed those characters. With her little axe she chopped each in turn into three pieces — head, torso and legs. She watched the blood soak into the matchboxes. The matchboxes swelled with the wet of the blood. The blood stained the white surface of the vanity bar and ran in rivulets into the basin. She picked up the matchboxes and dropped them into the small white plastic bag that lined the bedroom rubbish bin. The bin was made of metal. It was coloured red, green and white. The bin had a painting of roses on it. The roses were scattered around the centre of the circumference of the bin. She washed the bench and basin of the vanity bar.

She picked up the white plastic bag containing the dead and bleeding bodies of the characters of fiction and walked out of her parents' bedroom. She walked down the hallway. The floor was covered in a square geometric pattern with orange-brown and beige cork tiles. She walked across the TV room, which opened out, without a wall, from the hallway. From the TV room she walked to the bathroom and from there to the toilet. The toilet had two doors connecting it to the bathroom and laundry. She walked through the toilet into the laundry and from the laundry she opened the back door and walked out into the back yard.

It was mid-morning of a hot summer day in central Victoria. The gum trees in the back yard stood tall and grey-green against a blue sky. The air was shimmering, bristling with the noise of a hot summer day. Cicadas crackled in the heat. Blowflies and bees bumbled, hummed and hissed in the heat.

She walked across the back yard towards the fence that divided their home block from the neighbouring farm. Along the fence was a channel. She hitched up the skirt of her dress into the legs of her underpants and waded into the warm, brown, muddy waters of the channel. She was still holding the white plastic bag with the dead and bleeding bodies from fiction in the separate matchboxes.

She waded through the waters to the bulrushes. The yellow-green leaves were long and narrow and sharp. They grazed her legs as she pushed a path towards the centre of them. The bulrushes themselves were soft and beige in colour. They were beginning to open and would scatter soft seeds when the wind rose.

She stopped in the centre of the channel, surrounded by the bulrushes and hidden from view. She rested her bundle against the reeds of the channel and untied the double knot in the white plastic bag. She picked up each matchbox in turn and opened it. She gently placed the little heads, torsos and legs of the characters of nineteenth-century fiction between the reeds. The pieces of the bodies floated and then slowly sank into the muddy waters of the channel.

She bent over and gently swirled the pieces of the characters in the muddy waters and then pushed the pieces softly into the sandy soil at the base of the channel. Then she stood and bent down again to swirl her empty hands in the water. She stood up again and dried her hands on her dress. She bent over and picked up the white plastic bag, rinsed it in the muddy waters and watched the darker brown bloody liquid pour back into the channel. Then she walked back through the bulrushes to the edge of the channel.

She scrambled up the bank of the channel, still holding the white plastic bag. She walked across the back yard, under the gums to the back porch. She placed the plastic bag in the big metal rubbish bin that was standing by the back door.

She walked from the back door along the path that led around the house to the front yard. Her brother was cutting the front lawn. She picked up the rake and followed him in the mown path he had made. She raked the fresh green grass in piles and felt and smelt the clean grass at her feet.

Recollections of Ludowyck B.

LAURENT VITEL

> It is something to be at last speaking
> Though in this No-Man's language appropriate
> Only to No-Man's-Land.
>
> E. Malley

> The face of the *hard trying* writer does not conceal anything.
>
> L. B. (Notebooks and Conversations)

Regardless of mental and physical expense, regardless of time, he would write, write, write. This activity, 'which now so many look down upon as vain', would consume all his life force, all his energy. He would often go home late at night and sometimes, when his wife had guests, was barely able to speak. Their embarrassment would slowly become obvious. 'I am also this stut-stuttering writer,' he once said.

*

As long as he did not feel an urge to justify his work, which he occasionally referred to as 'useless attempts at proving that I am alive', he could be the best of company. But any superficial remark about literature, any comment made about a book in a careless way, could alter his mood — he would almost instantly slide back into sullenness, seek refuge in silence.

*

During the winter of 19—, he decided not to work in libraries any longer, not so much out of a feeling of the aimlessness of it all: 'this business which consists of trying to add a book to the already unlimited ocean of books . . .' In fact, he did not really suffer from such inhibitions. 'One day,' he said, 'I realised that members of the staff, and some students too, were convinced that I was day after day plodding along on some difficult subject and that, dedicated to Knowledge, I had accepted the burden of a long-term research project, the completion of which I might not live to see. Now this is partly true — I will never see the end of it — but I could not stand the respectful looks and attitudes they felt compelled to reward me with in advance. What I am at heart trying to do is tear apart the layers of awe under which the written thing threatens to choke.'

*

'In a state of immense weariness I would sometimes wake up and immediately the idea that the passive fight should begin so early in the day would crush me.'

*

He had decided to, as he put it, swim against the tide of his own language. Somebody called to mind, about a certain pattern recurrent in his sentences, the 'clumsiness of literal translations', but no-one could tell which language they could have been translated from.

*

'As far as I can see,' he used to say, 'the idea of a book has no bearing on my day-to-day writing rhythm. If such was the case, I would have to publish one book a day (not to be continued).' 'Some journalists might do it,' he added.

*

At the end of the war he had worked as a freelance translator. Each morning during his breakfast, rain or shine, he used to count the words in the letters he had to translate for some gum importers. Their number would determine the duration of his working day and allow him to make a rough estimation of his income. It was a very practical daily ritual. But these accounts had developed into a strange incentive to work: after every 5000 words he would stop, have a complete meal, and call some member of his extended family in Europe, confident he would have no difficulty with the phone bill.

*

He had made a vow to stop reading. He used to say: 'You have to make clear which side of the fence you're on.'

*

At one point he had set for himself the aim of writing a detective story, the hard-boiled stuff. His work was moving fast — too fast maybe. He kept losing his characters. 'They were not tough enough and would either not survive the action scenes or decide they did not want to have anything to do with such a risky business. The few who agreed to go along had too many scruples.'

*

He had a lot of tricks in his trade. One of them was, when having reached a dead end, to keep writing the same word over and over again. Sometimes another one would appear out of the irregularities of his handwriting. Between the two words there would lie a sentence. Once written, it would allow him to get round the wall.

*

Once, during a discussion of his notes about bilingualism, he talked about his own exile. It had never been a painful experience to him. 'I am rather at a loss to understand the mental processes of people who speak only one language,' he said, 'and this feeling extends to the people who have always lived in the same country. When I left Europe, I had just taken to Danish. Beautiful language! *Så for helvede!* Oh hell! I wish you could speak it too.'

*

Totally unable to make any plan, he refused to arrange for any appointment earlier than half a day ahead. And he would always reserve the right to cancel, afraid of being forced to leave his work in the course of a promising flow. He tried as much as possible to keep his life in what he termed a 'state of unexpectancy', a state out of which, he would specify, 'the best lines are drawn, not to be known again'.

*

Questioned one day about the year he had spent in Scandinavia, just before leaving Europe for good, he talked at length about Göteborg's waterfront and the long walks he used to take there after nightfall. 'I could spend hours walking on these wharves,' he said, 'back and forth between the cranes, yes, back and forth, lending my inner voices to these giants' mute dialogues. And I was not the only nightbird hovering round them.' He told us about the friendly relations he had developed with a few Swedish tramps. 'I was looking for some kind of intimacy,' he said, 'and it was only fair to try to share it with the destitute ones.' He explained how much he despised patronising attitudes. 'Being destitute of writing — a nakedness which can only compare with the stripped bare and agonising selves of the downtrodden. Think of the joy one can experience down there too.' He mentioned an intimate complicity: 'Like members of the same family having been separated for years, you do not have to like each other. You belong to the same tribe. It is a fact.' In his later years he became obsessed with the memories of some of the men he had known there and even tried, through numerous letters, to convince European friends to investigate them. He felt, with a growing sense of urgency, that he *should* know what had become of them.

But he could only remember first names, and none of his correspondents ever took his request very seriously.

*

He liked writing in English. 'It allows me not to try to understand what writing is all about,' he said.

*

He neglected a lot of information which would have been important to the narrative included in his last book. He turned his back on studies deemed indispensable by well-meaning advisers, and his ignorance of basic scientific notions was heavily criticised — it was 'presumptuous of him to pretend to be dealing with matters affecting the scientific community at large'. When the book was published, in fact, the only review which commented on his literary capacity appeared in a scientific periodical.

*

When the four little volumes of the hard-bound edition of his Collected Writings finally came out, he was still alive. There had been a lot of disagreement over the selection of texts, some of which had already appeared in print. He considered that he should have been allowed to forget some of them before dying. When the publishers first sent him only five copies of each volume with an accompanying letter advising him to get in touch with them 'should he be interested in purchasing extra copies', he could not believe it. He pretended to faint: 'This is the last blow. I will never get over it. I'm through.' Then he started to laugh: 'I guess they are afraid that if I have too many I might use them for firewood,' he said.

*

Returning from H. once, he said that his decision to leave the city for a month had been an excellent one. He walked to the orchard every day, looked attentively at the fruit, fed the hens, thought of his grandparents, of the farm they had owned back in Europe. He never sat down in front of a desk. When questioned about his output there, he said: 'Each morning, on my way to the orchard, I was thinking, arguing with myself about what should be the first line of the day. By the time I had checked all the fruit, whatever I had made up my mind upon was gone. The hens never seemed to care about this loss.'

*

On one occasion, he compared himself to a croupier at a gaming-table, shuffling the cards, dealing them and picking them up at the end of each game without a smile. 'Win or lose,' he said, 'you will never know whether he is corrupted, however long you play.'

*

Here is an anecdote he liked to recall: On the night of Easter 19—, he came back home violently upset. He had been invited to a dinner by a friend who, aware of his last-minute habits, had called just before dusk. When the phone rang, he was dozing in an armchair, both legs stretched, pen in hand — caught off guard, he could not refuse to go. In his friend's house he realised immediately that some importance was attached to this particular night. The number of guests was unusually high and a few details, like the way he was introduced, the strange look on an old man's face, the readiness with which, from all sides, he was offered a new drink as soon as he had gulped the first one down, made him slightly nervous; he decided he might have been announced to some of the guests as a curiosity worth exchanging a few words with — this kind of praise. The well-to-do, he had learnt, are always superficially fond of *émigrés*. 'So predictable — and so paradoxical.' Taking discreet steps towards an emergency retreat, he was cornered by 'you know, one of these nasty self-righteous university dwarves, pondering about any subject with the loudness of a lynching mob' (this is how angry he was — fuming). As for the cause of this anger, it took us a while to unravel it. The spark which set ablaze an otherwise moderate temper turned out to be the use by a university lecturer of the phrase 'identity problems' in connection with exiles or displaced persons.

*

'The necessity to work slowly', he said, 'has to do with the illegal character of the work. Move one cautious step forward, stop, listen — same thing again and again but an ever-changing rhythm. Some light might flash into your face, some noise develop into a threat, some lock take too much time to force. One sometimes forgets the tension of this, the lasting fright, but never gets used to it. You see,' he added, 'I am at heart a law-abiding citizen.'

*

'I would like to write stories whose meaning would seem perfectly obvious to all but *myself*.'

*

He never showed any real concern for the future of his texts. But whenever he was approached to have some of them published or republished, he would go to great lengths to convince the adventurous publisher of the necessity to shorten them to such an extent that a complete rewriting was obviously preferable, or oppose the publication altogether a few weeks after having approved of the project with enthusiasm. 'Why give away pages which are not *au point*?' he would say. 'There is no hurry. I am only beginning to learn to write. Learning to read took me . . . well, in fact, I can tell you, I gave up. No, I am not ready yet.'

*

He seemed to enjoy in a special way the moments devoted each morning to the reading of the mail, as if they were essential to his balance. His table was always covered with strangely shaped, beautifully stamped envelopes. We assumed that they were his only opportunity to practise some of the languages he had studied in Europe and most certainly had been fluent in. Therefore we were very surprised when we heard him complain about his 'daily obligation, probably the last I have not managed to run free from'. His numerous correspondents had long since lost all reality for him. They were mentioning in their letters events, human beings, places with which he no longer had any ties, assuming he had ever had anything of the kind. But their tone, their warmth, the concern which they expressed about him implied that they had never doubted his reality, his precise necessity to them. So there he was: unable to take upon himself the responsibility to stop the exchanges, he had to deal with a large collection of characters for each one of whom attentive replies were needed as well as new questions and new comments to keep the letters alive. This thing had grown terribly on him. He arranged some kind of alphabetical file with several entries for each letter; he called it the 'extended family file', though he might not have been related to any of the writers from abroad he considered it his duty to answer. We soon learnt to avoid any mention of *the file*, unless we were ready to face an enduring irritation. 'I was not meant for this,' he would say. 'When I was still reading novels, I never could remember the names of most of the characters. Not a very convincing background for a writer, I have to admit, but tell me: do you still believe a bucket of surnames is essential to fiction? My difficulty with fiction might have stemmed from that — I will never be able to remember all those names! — hence the urge to write.' In the last years *the file* was getting thicker, the family and its writers obviously expanding, and he came to a different view. Pointing at the folders on his desk, he would say: 'They all deserve to be published. Compared with their ability to keep track of names, my own stuff is just amateurish scribbling, a joke.'

*

He often sneered at some writers' 'supposedly overpowering display of rich imagery and intertwined symbolic figures which are meant to drag you down into deeper and deeper layers of meaning and seduce your mind into the restless and indefinite movements of interpretation'. If he showed any interest in the reader's point of view, it was only to suggest that 'obviously overfed, this fellow deserves a diet prose: fish-bone sentences with pinhead tasteless words'. And also: 'Which century do you think you live in? Can you forget decennaries of language orgy? The skinnier the prose, the better.' He dreamt of an obituary which would mention his effort to put an end to the 'writing party' and would dwell on his 'contribution to the cutting down of the production of language waste — but,' he said, 'it does not have to become a funeral party'.

*

Another trick: when suddenly paralysed halfway through a page, dreading a long and sterile immobility, he would write at random on the white bottom half four common adjectives and wait for some relation to appear, some connection to take shape between these and the last sentence above. This way he would fill up the gaps. 'It usually works,' he said. 'Adjectives are incredibly attractive and sticky. They draw you forward. But it is terrible to have your luggage full of them.'

*

He drew a crossword pattern and held it out to us. 'Now, most of your questions assume that this is what I should end up with. Maybe *you* would. In which case you'd better start learning to read. Long and tedious work — worth the pain though. Anyway, *this* is a hobby for the truly illiterate. Coincidences, correspondences are never of that kind. However, if such was the case, misunderstandings would keep protecting us from these nuts' knots.'

*

One day he tried to deprive his critics of their main argument against his method. He said: 'My work is made of long *palabras de justificacion*, as the Spanish put it.' And immediately: 'See, once again, you have forced me into another language.'

*

He was also rewarded with a few moments of intense fulfilment. 'I can describe it this way: I would be seated, from time to time aware of a stiffness in the back, arguing with my own impatience maybe — how dare you call such a slow pace work? etc. — head held high, watching the students up and down the stairs to the mezzanine, or the leaves waving at me through the window, or not looking at anything special — does it matter? I would be visited by what we term anxiety — though it is impossible to know whether we speak of the same thing whenever we use this word — I would be overwhelmed by it. Any seemingly precise description would be banal, I suppose. A painful belly and my head like an abandoned hydrogen balloon whistling somewhere over me. No euphoria in all this, just a physical illusion: writing about events which I had no memory of, I would witness the unwinding of the lines of writing I am made out of — rather like the unwinding of these lines children are often compelled to copy, a hundred times, five hundred times. Do you remember? Did they really read carefully each one of them after us?'

*

Standing up with a threatening voice: 'I have found a general title. This title will be the first of a series of conditions with which whoever will be responsible for the edition of my writings will have to comply whether they find it appropriate or not — OK, let's save the rap,' he giggled. 'I just thought *Namesakes* would be appropriate. If I have to ground my work somewhere, this is as precise as I can be. Besides, my family would have approved of it.'

*

He always denied having been politically involved in the European postwar turmoil. Other exiles would state his precise activities, the names of organisations he had belonged to, articles he had written under a pseudonym. Travellers from his country were even reported to have said that one of his articles, dealing apparently with a peculiar blend of ethical purposes with a view to action, was still highly thought of and often quoted in the publications of a minority whose name no-one here had ever heard before, not even the university people who were always trying to approach him on account of his alleged past. He managed to avoid the subject most of the time by making this avoidance a sort of unspoken mutual condition to any relationship. To direct enquiries he would answer: 'Shall I hand out to you bits of guilt about my particular shortcomings? Is that what you want? Will they ever make up for your misunderstanding of that time? We are still at a loss to explain it.' But he was also forgetful; he would not hold a lasting grudge against the trespasser. 'The now impressively common blindness through those years', he once said, 'seems to belong to other cultures, quite different from those that allowed so many decisive insights. But we know that things cannot be divided in that way. At least I do not make any historical statements. Thank God.' And also: 'It is always this readiness for criticism — backstage people deluding themselves, relishing crumbs of self-criticism.'

*

From his last notebook:
'I spent the entire morning rummaging about among old drafts — the

certainty somehow that I will not be able to make any use of them, that I will fail to arrange them for publication, that I will not have the time, the energy. The still strong emotion when rereading some pages could explain the foreboding — they were burning my fingers!

Something deceptive also about a collection of handwritten notes, preciously kept over many years, through several countries — with the memory, which remains attached to them, of long hours of hard work. Is there a necessity for anything sensible to emerge from this heap?

I used to think, it's true, that I had better delay the harmonisation of these bits and pieces as long as possible. I had endless justification for this — I have in fact delayed the attempt all my life.

The change of country made it easier in a way. I kept looking forward. In front of these piles of paper today, standing as if accused by them, I thought: that's it, there will be no reconciliation — it will not happen, the meaningful moment of Form. Exile!

But I do know that I will open the old cardboard boxes again, pull out the dusty sheets, devise some sort of provisional order for them, and that again a whole series of text will arrange itself in my mind with something like obviousness — I might even, next time, go as far as planning a conclusion . . .'

*

'Words . . . words and weapons, they're the same, they can kill the same way.'

*

When overwhelmed by doubts about his stance ('I am just another European *poseur*, I am afraid'), he would always tell the same memory: 'I was sailing into Helsingør once. It was a beautiful day. Wonderful short journey from Sweden. The ferry had to slide between two high columns in order to touch the landing. On top of them, waving and dancing, faces turned towards the inside of the harbour, two little stone angels. I was back in my compartment when they appeared briefly over the boat's railing. I will never forget their welcoming sign. I decided that they were waving at me — I was immensely moved. During the following week, in Copenhagen, at a café table, I began writing again. From the boat's deck, I could not see what they were looking at. One of them at least was and remains my *Angelus Novus*. Probably looking at us, ruins.'

*

During the last week, he asked for Ravel's *Bolero* to be played again and again on the tape-recorder next to his bed. Nobody dared to question him about this sudden taste for musical *espagnolismes*. He finally explained to one of his visitors: 'I hate the *Bolero* so much, I always had a special and consistent dislike of this music, I figured getting used to hearing it all the time might be good training. I have a feeling that I will not enjoy much whatever is coming next.'

To return to the question of that sense of distance from 1987: While I have been serving my apprenticeship as an editor, the world has changed with astonishing rapidity — so much so that it is hard to remember what life was like before the stockmarket crash of 1987, the recognition of global warming, the demise of the old regimes in the Eastern bloc, the Gulf crisis and the rest. These are not isolated events from which one can draw simple lessons. They are interconnected in unexpected ways; many of their effects are contradictory, and the tensions they have set up will probably take decades to work through. But it is reasonably safe to say that one of their first casualties has been the particular construction of the 'good life' that the Western media were purveying at the height of the boom — a heady concoction of Porsches, polo parties and pink helicopters on an adrenalin base. Today, with the demise of the entrepreneurs, the dominant image of the good life is more restrained: domestic, environmentally aware, even a trifle austere, and marginally more democratic in principle, if not in practice, than its 1987 equivalent. It is now chic to have a penchant for gardening, as long as you don't appear in public with dirt under your fingernails.

As a historian I have watched this whole scenario unfolding with a rising sense of dread. The very knowledge that the situation is so critical seems to induce a kind of paralysis. What happens in these conjunctures has a terrifying amount of historical leverage; if you make a mistake, you may have to live with the consequences for the rest of your life.

As an editor, however, I cannot afford to succumb to paralysis; and within this scenario there are still many points of pressure. One is on the question of education, where government policy has become increasingly narrow and instrumentalist just as a more flexible approach has become vitally necessary. Another is on the environment, where the small gains of the past few years are in danger of being swept away by a resurgence of progressivist ideology in the guise of 'sustainable development'. A third is on the issue of how Australia should conduct itself in relation to the rest of the world, and particularly to its immediate region, in an age when it can no longer be assumed that to be white and of British heritage automatically confers a cultural advantage.

These are all issues that go to the heart of our culture, in the broadest sense of the term; they are also questions on which intellectuals and cultural theorists potentially have a lot to contribute. Here, *Meanjin*'s long-standing project of fostering an interdisciplinary intellectual culture gains a new urgency. In a sense, we have come full circle, back to Clem Christesen's project of 1940: reasserting the need to 'talk poetry' — and culture — in another age that is governed by the 'stomach-and-pocket view of life'.

Number 3, 1990

Professing the Popular

SIMON DURING

A couple of months ago, on a research trip to Europe, I went to stay with an old friend of mine who teaches English at Cambridge. As it turned out, my visit came at an inconvenient time for him. I arrived during the Faculty's annual examiners' meeting, when undergraduate marks are decided. Traditionally it is a highly charged occasion; these marks don't only determine students' careers, but also whether or not they have (as they still say in Cambridge) 'first-rate minds'. That evening, after the meeting, a stream of apprehensive undergraduates flowed into my friend's rooms to learn their fate. Soon a little party was happening — at least for those whose first-rateness was now assured. Haydn came off the CD player, and David Byrne's Brazilian album went on. The men in particular lingered late and, as the night went on, conversation turned to matters unfamiliar to me. Why were Thomas Harris's thrillers so good, and which was the best of them? As I shuffled off to bed, everyone was crowded around some comic strips from the fifties, discussing their styles with not especially sober erudition and passion.

Visits to Cambridge have always been difficult for me. Even though I was a graduate student there, it is still the place where I feel most positioned as a colonial. This is more than just a personal, slightly paranoid response; the English departments in which I was first trained imitated Cambridge methods. And Cambridge people do have easier access to a larger world than Australians and New Zealanders — they can travel more, British magazines and television are better by almost any standard, they're close to the big museums and art shows, they tend to have a greater command of foreign languages and so on. But, strangely, on this stay my sense of my own provinciality came through my ignorance of what is — too easily — called 'popular culture'. I'd never read a Thomas Harris thriller; I don't know anything about postwar comics. This was especially disquieting because my Cambridge friends are less involved professionally in popular culture than we are at Melbourne, and take quite a different attitude towards it.

This became clear the day after the party. In the absence of students, the conversation turned to the differences between teaching at Melbourne and at Cambridge. Cambridge students study one subject for three years; they have two exams over that period, and written work outside the exam counts for comparatively little. Teaching is much more individualized than in Australia, and an English degree still requires both detailed knowledge of the canon and mastery of the methods of close reading. In Melbourne that just isn't so. Exams have almost completely disappeared. And in certain of my courses students can write on almost anything they want (David Croenenberg's movies or the difference between television and classic

Hollywood film styles . . .). When I defended this, the argument became heated. My host insisted that university English teachers have a responsibility to the literary tradition, and ended the conversation by vehemently declaring that the thought of our pedagogical practices made him sick. Upset myself, I could only feebly and reductively reply that many of our students found it difficult to relate to old books, most of which are, to begin with, anti-democratic, patently sexist and set in places that Australians know, at best, only as tourists.

This somewhat unedifying anecdote is only worth recording because it highlights certain features of important shifts in the academic study of the humanities, and English most of all. These shifts follow the diminution of any firm sense that 'high' culture is of more value than 'mass' or 'popular' culture. This means that academic work is increasingly devoted to topics like, say, film noir rather than eighteenth-century poetry, or the history of nineteenth-century prostitution rather than the organization of patronage in the Georgian House of Commons or, indeed, the influence of popular cultural forms on art previously considered independent of them — magazine illustration on modernist painting, for instance. As a result, whole areas of interest are disappearing from view. Icelandic or Old Norse, for instance, which were taught in most English departments up until about twenty years ago, are now difficult to study at all in Australia. But the new orientation is also methodological: the humanities are moving from *affirming* a more or less rigid cultural canon to *analysing* more localized cultural zones. It has been a long time since culture stood against anarchy (though it can still stand against violence and pornography). 'Culture' is itself broken down into sets of representations, narratives and ways of thinking and acting whose relation to wider social, economic and political formations can be studied. Cultural representations are also analysed in terms of their impact on everyday life: on the way, for instance, that they form people's sense and management of their bodies — their voices, their gestures, their clothes . . . And the channels by which books, pictures, films move from the past into the present, so as to be preserved in the cultural memory as history, have also become objects of analysis and critique.

Here I want to concentrate on the effects of making popular culture central to academic study of the humanities. But some background is necessary. The disciplinary subdivisions of the humanities, which were mainly fixed in their current form during the 1920s, are losing their intellectual legitimacy, despite the fact that they continue to provide the framework for professional associations, certification and university funding and administration. 'Cultural studies' — to give a name to the discipline that is emerging as the embodiment of the shift in the humanities — breaks with the kind of thinking that defined differences between disciplines in terms of media (language, pictures, films . . .) or between the always deeply uncertain distinctions between the political, the social and the cultural. This relaxation of disciplinary divisions leaves cultural studies with problems. How to negotiate its relations with established disciplines? How to be something else than an all-enveloping loose and baggy monster? The last is especially imposing because cultural studies merges the two main senses of the word 'culture' — the humanist meaning (what 'culture' signifies in phrases like 'high culture' or 'the cultural heritage') and the ethnographic meaning (as in 'Polynesian culture'). These different senses of 'culture' have come increasingly to overlap, especially as anthropologists have found it more and more difficult to find colonized societies untouched by the West: societies, that is, unable to tell their own story to the metropolitan centres or to register their own protests against the dominant world order (of which visiting anthropologists are an instrument). This situation in which our culture and other cultures come together is generally called 'postcolonial'. And the other side of the postcolonial moment is the increasing regionalization of the old metropolitan centres: now their cultures don't enter world history as by right either. As my Cambridge experiences show, one way in which the metropolitan centres have defined themselves as such is by their power to grade and preserve cultures for others. What made the Cambridge mastery of thrillers and comics so disquieting was that these popular genres still belong to a huge international system of publication and distribution. So that to claim the right to evaluate *these*, to be their greatest fans, is once again to stake a claim to centrality.

The role of popular culture was by no means simple that night at Cambridge. Although popular genres were sharply distinguished from the texts that my friend taught and examined, they could be shared between teacher and students in a social situation. They provided a field on which a hierarchy of tastes could be established and connoisseurship develop, so that an élite group of students could distinguish themselves from other students outside the official procedures of the university. Popular texts were available for this, of course, because they themselves belong to a highly differentiated field: a literate thriller writer like Thomas Harris is not 'popular' in the way that Jackie Collins is. Any particular popular text may be read in various registers too: the more ironical, the more cultural value. Only in theory is everyone equally armed to appreciate the popular. In fact my friend's authority, charm and intelligence was coming to mould his student's everyday, as well as their formally learned, tastes. I say *his* charm and intelligence but of course these traits also belong to, and are signs of, the university that produced them. The university's power was seeping outwards.

This particular function of the popular needs to be given a little historical depth. When English was established as an academic subject late last century, the relations between cultural zones were quite different from those that prevailed after the emergence of a highly centralized and commodified entertainment sector — the so-called culture industry. In the second half of the nineteenth century, classic texts were discussed in English Associations, in Browning Societies and in numerous courses in noncertifying institutions attended by those who could not go to universities. Great writers, alive and dead, were often discussed in the bourgeois press — especially in the so-called Reviews — as well as in families 'around the fire': literary tastes formed one basis of class and family identities. So university English departments provided their own ways of reading texts that were actively interpreted and distributed outside of them. But in a university literature was taught historically, philologically. As the culture industry became stronger, literary criticism replaced literary history as the dominant form of academic English. Its task was to form tastes that could resist the new mass media, a function that became all the more urgent after the Second World War, when university education was extended to those for whom high literature was not part of a non-pedagogic heritage.

The new orientation in the humanities follows the relative decline of the educational institution's ability to form its pupils' tastes or 'sensibilities' against the media. The media have won — or, at any rate, are winning. Why is this decline stronger in Melbourne than in Cambridge? It's a worthwhile question because it helps us see that the entry of the popular into higher education is not just the expression of some general and progressive will, but the result of particular histories and social conditions. To begin with, in Britain literary high culture still retains stronger bases outside of the education institutions than in Australia. That's obvious — Britain is a society more tolerant of class and other social differences than its colonial offshoots. What is less obvious is that in Britain students tend to leave home to go to university (though recent changes in student financing will help change this). Students live in colleges away from their families and friends, forming strong (and often lifelong) social links with each other and with their teachers. It is in this context that a university education begins to mould not just tastes but also voices, gestures, clothes . . . And in Britain (and the US) the university system is itself more hierarchical than in Australia — which means that to acquire an university (or college) educated manner is itself to gain a widely recognizable form of social capital. These factors enable and dispose such universities to teach material as far as possible from the popular, that is, as far as possible from the market. Though, after 1946, Oxbridge has become more accessible to students from families without high incomes, the university system's hierarchy has not disappeared. Thus, to use one of Pierre Bourdieu's terms, it shelters 'oblates'. In the Middle Ages oblates were children donated to (or abandoned at) the monasteries: modern oblates owe their way of life, their tastes and minds to the institutions that form them. Modern oblates want all their cultural preferences to be formed by the institution that guarantees their first-rateness: that is one reason why it is among them, most of all, that one encounters quasi-institutional discourse about popular culture.

In Australia things are different. Not only is the university system relatively unhierarchical, but most students live at home. This means that their tastes are formed not so much academically as by their families, their secondary schooling, their local social interactions and, most importantly, by the media. And quite small administrative changes can lead to dramatic intellectual shifts — including the transformation of the old humanities into cultural studies. Here university departments tend to be funded by student numbers, which means they must compete for students. Universities themselves actively seek to attract students by making trips into the schools. Unlike their US counterparts, most Australian humanities faculties feel no responsibility to the profession's reproduction: not only are they without graduate schools (through which scholars are directed towards fixed — historical — 'fields') but the conditions of academic employment in general are being increasingly de-professionalized. So it is in a particular department's interest to offer courses that undergraduates will be most likely to choose — these preferences being determined by dispositions established through the media, students' families and social circle and so on. When the Melbourne English Department, in response to such pressures, cancelled core courses that had been based on the canon (Medieval Literature, Renaissance Literature, Romanticism . . .) and replaced them by a 'smorgasbord' of smaller courses, which included topics like 'Popular Fiction', 'The Novel and Film' and 'Postmodernism', enrolments increased sharply — and funding with them. Now students could take what courses they liked: indeed, it became quite possible to acquire a degree in English without having read a single book written before the First World War.

In this case the popular enters the academy as the result of a series of administrative reorganizations connected to Mr Dawkins' policies. But this is not the only way that an institution can be reorganized so that the canon begins to be dethroned. In the United States — despite its professionalism, and its hierarchical tertiary sector — questions of social justice have led to the widespread adoption of affirmative action procedures for student entry. To enter colleges like Stanford, Yale or Harvard, African Americans from the South, for instance, need much lower entry grades than those with East Coast Jewish backgrounds. Under federal and state funding pressure, such colleges welcome students from ethnic minorities. So they change their curriculum (never as radically as in Melbourne), not in response to the market-formed wants of their clientele, but to a sense that the university has a responsibility to other cultural heritages and to social justice (a sense apparently lacking in our university bureaucrats, if not in the Labor government itself).

What happens when popular culture becomes academized? First of all it is processed within the cultural studies tradition already in place — a deeply polarized and unsettled tradition that has not been able to unburden itself from the past or to detach itself from its early policing role. On one side, cultural studies stretches back to the work of Arnold and Leavis; on another to Richard Hoggart, E. P. Thompson and Raymond Williams; and on a third, to the so-called Frankfurt school. For the Frankfurt school (and, much more loosely, for Leavis), popular culture is an instrument of domination rather than an expression of genuine experiences and desires, because it is circulated and produced within a centralized and organized market. To use the terms of Adorno and Horkheimer's famous essay 'The Culture Industry', the widespread 'consent' given to commodified popular entertainment is itself part of the culture industry just because the market offers no alternative to itself. (Adorno and Horkheimer were writing, specifically, of America in the early forties — a society without television or public radio, in which Hollywood's production, distribution and exhibition arms were still vertically integrated, and where art movie houses did not yet exist.) In its 'technological perfection', the culture industry can manufacture narratives and representations powerful enough to substitute for reality so that 'to offer and to deprive [the consumer] of something is one and the same'. What keeps the culture machine going is the constant production of unsatisfiable wants that are simultaneously erotic and consumerist: the desires to look as good as (taking some modern examples) Madonna or Sean Penn, to be as funny as Robin Williams, to fall in love like Debra Winger, to have a house like one in *Dynasty*, or a mouth like Bardot's. Horkheimer and Adorno argue that the culture industry produces increasingly standardized products that form increasingly standardized tastes, values and desires; individuality becomes a floating signifier — as if I am me because I like Cary Grant and you are you because you prefer Spencer Tracy. Here, to prefer Cary Grant to Spencer Tracy is quite different from preferring, say, Frank Sinatra to Mozart — though even Adorno and Horkheimer have a popular canon, Greta Garbo and Betty Boop retaining traces of uncommodified and 'tragic' life in a way that Mickey Rooney and Donald Duck don't.

The British cultural studies tradition never fully detaches itself from the Leavisite and Frankfurt school view of the culture industry: it *cannot*, because the popular is not an expression of unmediated desires and choices. But it has presented a much more nuanced and less dismissive account. For it, popular culture is not a monstrous monolith, but contains many localized 'subcultures', some of which have long histories, often embedded in working-class life, and provide alternatives to hegemonic modes of representation. In writers like Dick Hebdige, the Birmingham School works within a frame where the difference between, say, John Lennon and Paul McCartney matters.

Yet the generation that follows Raymond Williams finds itself in a double bind. For them, high culture becomes increasingly just a marker and instrument of one class or region's domination over another, so that, unlike Leavis or Adorno, they have no set of fixed cultural values, texts and preferences to help them stand outside the cultural market. At the same time their methods and interests do not — cannot — belong to popular culture, which is defined against the academy. In this situation, cultural studies have tended either to read popular texts 'scientifically' — as examples to be analysed within established 'theories' (Lacanian, structuralist, Althusserian) — or symptomatically, as expressions of larger social formations (*The Towering Inferno* might be regarded as an allegory of American insecurity after Vietnam, for instance). Whereas for the old humanities high culture spoke for itself, as it were, through the critic, for cultural studies popular culture has to be interpreted as a sign or an instance of something else. To escape this bind, British cultural studies have taken their task to be a provisional and political one, working to increase the heterogeneity of cultural production, to enhance its connection to the lives that people actually lead. Such politics, however, are almost always gestural, both because they are not connected to any institutions that might actually change the structures of cultural production, and because the power of the market is so strong. More recently cultural studies academics like Hebdige or Constance Penley have attempted to identify with the popular by claiming to combine the role of the critic and the fan. This sounds like a neat solution; indeed it's one that returns us to the early days of English departments. But there are difficulties, not only because the critic (who works in or around academe) and the fan (who does not) must define themselves against each other in order to achieve their own identity, but also because if the critic did not maintain an identity different from the fan, then education — and the educational professions — would have no point.

There are, however, ways in which the popular and the academic do work together non-oppositionally. Teachers of popular culture find that their work bears upon everyday life in a way that it doesn't for those who work on texts that only the academy keeps alive. Their everyday tastes in films and television will be influenced by their critical practices. And as popular culture is increasingly absorbed into the higher education system, as journalists, arts administrators and so on are trained in cultural studies, then reviewing, especially in the up-market press, will move closer to those critical techniques — and vice versa. Equally, relations between teachers and students change in popular culture courses. An undergraduate may know more than an instructor — a lot more, particularly in a field that has not yet become the object of sustained academic research. Sometimes students may have read magazines or books distributed outside the academy, either through the market or through more specialized channels, like fanzine networks. Sometimes students can teach their teachers because they are close to what I'll call 'para-institutions' — computer groups, societies like the Trekkies, film societies even, or para-sciences like Vampirology. (Apparently there is a man on the local lecture circuit claiming a PhD in Vampirology.)

The interruption of the academy by other institutions of learning and connoisseurship is almost wholly productive, but it does induce certain anxieties. What is the difference between teaching or learning in the university and teaching or learning in a para-institution (leaving aside the all-important fact that the first has the power to give official degrees and the second does not)?

This question is complicated because the popular, in its turn, defines (and sells) itself *as* popular against the academic. Negative images of academics and their institutions abound in highly marketed culture, especially where both it and pedagogy are most uniform and far-reaching — where they are directed at children. (The biggest-selling books in Britain during the 1980s were the Adrian Mole series, published by Routledge. They helped Routledge finance the academic journals most engaged in the new orientation in the humanities: *Cultural Studies*, *New Formations* and *Textual Practice*.) Education is demonized and ridiculed, not just in representations of the soullessness and pleasurelessness of schools and universities (see *Ghostbusters*) but in a plethora of images of mad or absent-minded professors and authoritarian or repressed schoolteachers (as in Pink Floyd's *The Wall*). Against this, pedagogical para-institutions are presented positively: the

Ninja masters of the *Teenage Mutant Ninja Turtles* or Ben in the *Star Wars* trilogy, to cite two of many. (And when a movie wants to mark itself as serious and mature — as middlebrow — what better than nostalgia for the days when there were fans for old books and dead poets' societies still existed?) The strategy by which the popular defines itself as popular against the pedagogic can be repeated in 'popular critique', commentary on mass culture within the popular press. A recent article on the *Ninja Turtles* for the Murdoch press by Simon Townsend, for instance, sets 'fun', parental 'instinct' and children's desires against 'anal retentive teachers' who hate pleasure and who instead (how could anybody be so perverted?) 'love theoretical research'.

Popular culture produces mad theorists in two senses. As we have seen, it generates an imagery in which academics are vague, retentive, loopy, arrogant, live in ivory towers and so on. Though this imagery is rarely internalized, it does encourage academic self-doubt, even self-hatred. Certainly it makes the struggle to improve and legitimate education harder. But these popular images are not simply wrong. They are part of the organization of the whole cultural system in (post)modern society: an organization which requires that the popular can never speak for itself in the academy but must be interpreted, theorized, policed. And it is because the grounds for this theory, interpretation and policing are so insecure (partly because the market that carries the popular has more power than the pedagogical institutions) that professors who talk about the popular can begin to enact the popular image of the academic. For instance, in her recent book, *The Future of an Illusion*, Constance Penley, one of the sharpest culture theorists, finds herself writing about *Pee Wee's Playhouse* like this: 'As a giant eyeball, Roger is the metaphorical and metonymical equivalent of what is threatened in the fantasy of castration (an unconscious fear of difference), yet he is also "our new friend Roger" from another planet (a social and conscious wish for the acceptance of difference).' (162) Surely there's a mad professor somewhere here: this is to culture studies what Doc's wild science in *Back to the Future* is to nuclear physics.

To recapitulate a little: in general terms there are three ways that the academy can host the popular. It can do so, as in those Cambridge rooms, in terms of the old tasks of evaluation and taste formation, which help consolidate a centre; or in terms of theories grounded on para-scientific truths (like psychoanalysis); or as part of a struggle against the market in the name of a different kind of popular culture. In my own teaching practices I try to modulate the first through the second towards the third. For me, what a teacher can do is to develop tastes that require political sensitivity, refuse conceptual simplification and retain a historical sense. And the reason why one has a right to attempt to form tastes is that popular critique is politically, historically and conceptually reductive. It does not make enough connections: its notion of pleasure is too detached from the pleasure — and the work — of thought. Saying this though does not help answer the question that has haunted this essay: what responsibility does one have to keep old books alive? It's not an abstract question: it affects decisions on what kind of staff departments hire, for instance. To some degree, the problem answers itself when one begins to historicize the popular. (To give an example: if one is interested in the relation between current 'sensational' reportage of domestic crime and literary fictions, one is soon led back to pre-Shakespearean drama and the 'domestic tragedy' genre.) Today's mass culture can also form tomorrow's cultural heritage, sometimes becoming the object of classical affirmative critical techniques — as in Stanley Cavell's account of the Hollywood 'remarriage' genre in *Pursuits of Happiness*. Nevertheless, for about two hundred years canonical works have been written so as to avoid the obsolescence of the popular: they have consciously worked out strategies that will keep them alive in the future. And yet the struggle between the canon (and its claims on futurity) and the popular (and its claims on the present) is biased towards the latter in the current local organization of culture and pedagogy. After Icelandic, Old English will disappear; after Old English, Middle English; after Middle English . . .

I began with a personal anecdote about appropriating the popular and I want to finish with one about losing the past. After returning from Europe, I took my seven-year-old son, Nicholas, to see *Ninja Turtles*. As much as the movie delighted and amazed me, I soon — inevitably — began to watch it as a theorist. It looked to me like an index of America's current situation: America's fear of a provincialization that it can't avoid, its refusal to recognize the racism that organizes its society and economy; its being torn by tensions between the popular, the pedagogical and the family as they compete to form the minds and manners of children. There may be good Japanese in the movie's narrative line, and the wisdom and technology are imported from Japan, but the only Japanese that we see are baddies. On the other hand, we see almost no blacks or Hispanics at all, though the movie is set on the streets. The gangs and vigilantes are replaced, on one side, by a bunch of middle-class white kids gone wrong, and, on the other, by four happy, anthropomorphized, pizza-guzzling turtles who, though they've never been to school and live in the sewers (literally an under-class), are very smart and have high-cultural icons for names (Raphael, Donatello, Michaelangelo [sic] and Leonardo). Despite these names, the turtles come straight out of patriotic popular knowledge: 'everyone' in America knows that the pizza was invented in New Haven, and that the sewers, rivers of the urban jungle, crawl with reptiles (though this 'information' was first disseminated by the avant-garde novelist Thomas Pynchon). The turtles' violence is beautifully choreographed; it's a party, a dance — they have no guns. The film is magical, and what its magic makes disappear is the difference between what America is and what the American dream would have America be.

Nicholas didn't see it like that. As we came out of the theatre he was already telling me the plot in some detail: for him the popular did not have to speak of something else. We headed into McDonald's, me for a Big Mac, him for a six-pack of Chicken McNuggets. Everyone was talking about the turtles. 'Who was your favourite?' a kid asked me. 'Donatello,' I said without thinking. 'Michaelangelo,' said Nicholas. When we sat down I realized why I'd chosen Donatello as *my* turtle. It had nothing to do with the character, who was hardly any different from the others. For me 'Donatello' is a resonant name: when I was a kid I heard it a lot. My father is a Jewish (in fact, half-Jewish) refugee from the Nazis and, like many such immigrants who came from bourgeois families, he had memories of an economically and culturally richer past. These memories turned into fantasies as the years went by. He often used to tell us that a relation of his had donated his art collection to the Vienna Kunsthistorische Museum and that one of the glories of the collection (which my father believed he should have inherited) was a Donatello. Years later, when I visited the Museum, I found out that the Donatello was in fact a Della Robbia — a very different kettle of fish. Nevertheless for me 'Donatello' signified what we as a family didn't have, *our* culture, lots of money, being like other families. For Nicholas, however, Donatello is a Teenage Mutant Ninja Turtle: for him it is as if the Renaissance sculptor, a source both of Western humanism and of our family's private fantasies, is called Noddy.

So far as I am concerned, that's a welcome change. Especially if his pleasure in the turtles one day comes to be connected to a sense of how that pleasure functions socially and politically. Which requires schooling. And to say that is to speak as a pedagogue rather than a fan or a dad.

Number 2, 1990

What's Left?
Politics in America at the end of the 1980s

Alec McHoul

A bright autumn day in New York City, 1989. Sun reflects back from the used needles lying around Washington Square. Uptown a gigantic neon sign flashes the National Debt in up-to-the-second figures, changing so quickly that I can't read the last five columns. I'm thinking New York warnings: 'Keep your wallet in a front pocket,' 'The latest scam: they squirt you with ketchup and an accomplice cleans you up, and cleans you out,' 'Keep moving if someone asks you for something.'

I'm just off Bleeker Street, Greenwich Village, looking for a coffee shop; looking like a tourist; looking back to the sixties and the incongruity, today, of Paul bloody Simon's lyrics:

> Fog's rolling in off the East River bank
> Like a shroud it covers Bleeker Street
> Fills the alleys where men sleep
> Hides the shepherd from the sheep

On the next corner there's a couple of black guys arguing, New York style, at the top of their voices. So loud. You wonder what they'd do if they really got angry. One of them seems to be a street preacher. Anyhow, he's bringing down a heavy God-message on the other guy. Next thing, the second guy turns to him and says: 'Yo ain't here by the grace of no Higher Authority, brother — yo here by the grace of yowa ass.'

And in some ways, it could finish right here — politics in America, that is, with a non-starter of a difference; with the twin pillars of God and the human soul. With nothing in between. It's an ancient American edifice, a formal structure supporting nothing.

As if in compensation for that lack, that empty space of collective politics, the media are full of gloating details about the fall of socialist regimes in Eastern Europe.

I'm sipping a fourth long black decaf in the Café Florio, watching the woman at the next table compose autobiographical fragments between tall glasses of frothy iced coffee. Someone turns on the wall TV for the CBS news. Wandering the streets of Czechoslovakia, interviewing the celebrants, is Dan Rather, looking bulky as a WWII barrage balloon in his winter gear. His line is the upsurge of the church in Eastern European politics. Poland is the obvious model. He talks to a bishop in full regalia against a stained-glass window. It looks like a fancy-dress party. The bishop has gone to the party as God, and Dan Rather as somebody's ass.

Back in New York, Rather asks that most astute of political experts, Billy Graham: 'From what you've just seen there in Czechoslovakia, would you say that overall in Eastern Europe we're witnessing a triumph of faith over ideology?'

Politics, they presume, is elsewhere, anywhere but America. Here they have only faith. And that, of course, isn't political, is it, Billy?

Flying south on American Airlines, I put down my copy of Baudrillard's eurocentric celebration of America and pick up the in-flight magazine, aptly titled *American Way*. There's a letter I can't begin to understand:

> I enjoy your magazine and look forward to each issue when I fly American Airlines.
>
> It seems paradoxical, however, that you would publicize Mr. Dan Rather ['Rather Redux,' *American Way*, Oct. 1], who symbolizes socialist doctrines, rather than the American ideal that I cherish. Mr. Rather is a master at misinformation, and he distorts truth, which should be the foundation of the news.
>
> Most people of my walk of life abhor that the news media have been so totally captured by the ultraliberal individuals like Mr. Rather and Walter Cronkite.
>
> The one fundamental that has been unique about the American way is the belief that the freedom of the individual is superior to the power of government. I know of no individual (excluding Marx and Lenin) who has done more to subjugate individuals to government than Mr. Rather.
>
> I hope in the future you publicize patriots and those great people who build rather than destroy.
>
> Richard G. Murray
> Perkins, Okla.

In New Orleans, I show this to a learned friend. He tells me Dan Rather was the only TV interviewer to give George Bush anything like a difficult time in the run-up to the last presidential election. That would seem to explain it then. But if giving George a hard time is a case of subjugating individuals to government, then I'm still confused.

A little further on in the magazine is the now ubiquitous photo of the young guy in a white shirt facing down the tanks on the approach to Tiananmen Square — the media archetype of the resistance of individuals to government. As a summary of the passing 80s, it's placed alongside other American triumphs of what are made to look like the same kind: Gorbachev and Reagan's 1987 Geneva summit ('It's the voice of peace'), Springsteen-the-Boss singing 'Born in the USA' ('It's the voice of every man'), the return of the US hostages in 1981 ('It's the voice of hope'), Lech Walesa, a pre-assassination Anwar Sadat (1980), Charles and Di. Charles and Di? And the caption? 'From a distance there is harmony and it echoes through the land . . . God is watching us, from a distance.' The politics of 'God-and-me' is everywhere. It slips by incognito, unrecognized precisely as a politics.

I have to remember hard to find Baudrillard writing, elsewhere, that this 'silence of the masses is . . . obscene'. Obscene because the masses are made of 'useless hyperinformation'. So the information circuits and the masses 'fit one another: the masses have no opinion and information does not inform them'. Both, he goes on, lack 'a scene where the meaning of the social can be enacted'. The social, the political, is forever repressed into the only available and necessarily counter-political discourses. And the most obvious candidates, in fancy dress, are still 'the Higher Authority' and 'yowa ass'.

In a curiously damp and steamy New Orleans December, the wooden shopfronts and verandas of the French Quarter are dripping and sagging with rain and age, trying to lean across the narrow streets to their opposite numbers, as if to whisper some message no longer secret. It's a city predicated on well-known pleasures — where middle-American middle-class mid-Westerners come for vacations, to take drugs, screw, get pissed, throw up and go back home and loudly say how secretly decadent it all was.

My rented mock 'slave quarters' (and this is a selling point for landlords and real-estate agents) is a good way back from the street and I'm walking down from its old pink-painted boards to the kerb. With my garbage: over-packaged Real Superstore remnants, and a pair of jeans. They've had the Higher Authority and the ass shot out of them from belting down the steep slopes of the Rockies. As I reach the kerb, a little black guy with no shoes asks if he can have the garbage bag. He especially wants the jeans. Before the winter sets in. Well, that's certainly OK with me, but why didn't he just wait and take them out of the garbage bin? Turns out some other guys have the de facto rights to scavenge in that neighbourhood but it's OK with them, providing he gets to the garbage before it gets to the bin before they get to it.

A friend of mine, whose political views I've never questioned before now, says it's just a 'cultural' difference. And I start to complain about the industrial and welfare practices I've seen in America and the ones I haven't: the Eastern Airlines pickets confined to a small barricaded rectangle among the vast sprawl of La Guardia Airport. The university tenure system that operates against academic freedom. (They check you out morally and politically for a ten-year period before they let you in, by which time you've forgotten all about axes and how to grind them.) And, in New Orleans in particular, there's the tipping system. Waiters aren't paid salaries; they work for tips, and sometimes they 'hire' under-waiters to work for them for a share of the tips. When business is good, that is. And when it's bad, you don't get to pay the rent. That's why restaurant customers always get a smile; and that's why we must, told or not, add 15 per cent to the bill.

So this friend of mine says I should accept the system: it's no better or worse than the Australian award system, it's just different, and, she adds, at least these guys don't have to stand in line for a roll of toilet paper all day like they do in Moscow.

Next day, I'm shopping at a Schwegmann's supermarket in a poor part of town, between the Mississippi River and a warehouse district. I'm the only white person in the store. Taking my trolley to the checkout, I notice that one register is empty and make a dive for it. The woman asks me if I'm paying cash. This is cash only. Maybe the rest are using credit cards or cheques. But as I leave I see the welfare food coupons: money-sized sheets of various denominations stapled into books. An older woman with a stick buys a single toilet roll.

Meanwhile, throughout December, the media continue to gloat over the events in Eastern Europe. The *New York Times* runs headlines:

> CZECH COMMUNISTS ECLIPSED IN CABINET SWORN INTO OFFICE
> BAKER PRESSES SOVIETS ON LATIN ARMS
> RETIREMENT FOR DEAN OF THE OLD GUARD IN PRAGUE
> HUSSAK SUPPRESSED DISSENT SINCE '68
> TWO BALTIC REPUBLICS VOTE IN TEST OF COMMUNIST RULE
> 50,000 IN BULGARIA DEMAND FASTER MOVE TOWARD DEMOCRACY

The last of these has a 116 by 145 mm photo with the caption: 'Bulgarians at a pro-democracy rally yesterday in Sofia carried a poster showing Stalin with an eye patch and a Nazi armband.' What the eye patch signifies isn't clear. Pirate Nazism perhaps? Surely, given

> JOY AND APPREHENSION AMONG EAST BERLIN'S JEWS

and its ilk, the *NYT* couldn't be referring to Moshe Dayan, could it? This headline is interesting: it gets an entire half page in the international section of the paper, but the article acknowledges its minor importance in the first sentence: 'The handful of citizens who are observant Jews or of Jewish ancestry in this country are viewing the current political upheaval here with a peculiar combination of elation and fear.' Not a mention of the 28,000

Jews in West Germany. And nothing on other minorities in Eastern Europe. Let alone any position from which, for example, Palestinians could speak, except with the (unspeakable) voice called 'terrorism'.

> LENIN STATUE IN MOTHBALLS
> EUROPEANS PRAISING BAKER BLUEPRINT
> CROATIAN COMMUNISTS ENDORSE FREE ELECTION
> COMMUNISTS IN BULGARIA EXPEL ZHIVKOV
> SOVIET LEGISLATORS FAULT GORBACHEV PROGRAM

Again the last one is significant because it prefigures the kinds of paradox America faces in the absence of a clear enemy. If no Other, then no Self, as it were. While Gorbachev has been, by and large, among the heroes of the changes, he remains a Soviet leader and a communist. That is, there is still a space now, albeit a small one, for categories like 'dissenter', 'sceptic', 'minority views' and so on. At the same time, and hence the paradox, several American media outlets have continually urged Gorbachev to take greater control of unruly Soviet populations, especially in the Baltic States, Armenia and Azerbaijan. In the last case, one news commentator suggested that a firm military action would quell dissent and so speed the process of peaceful democratization! Imagine that being said about Afghanistan.

Finally, then:

> FOR PRAGUE'S INSTITUTES, IT'S GOODBYE TO MARXISM

Now students and professors admit how much they lied. And the lying? Well, it's glossed as follows:

> Students agreed cheerfully that they lied in their exams. 'You cram, you say what you don't believe, and you forget it immediately,' said Hanna Hornakova, a 19-year-old second-year student, in a corridor interview. 'It's worthless, so why keep it in your memory?'

No doubt it's a technique Dan Rather might be advised to learn before visiting Perkins, Oklahoma.

I get a real sense that many Americans feel in some way responsible for what's happening: they feel as if their model of individualist freedom has somehow brought about the demise of 'the communist monopoly on power' (to use one phrase that is frequently heard on American TV, not entirely without an element of hypocrisy). A taxi driver tells me that it's all Reagan's doing. 'He told them they were the Evil Empire, and they couldn't take it.' He's not joking.

During a break in the rain, a group of us go off one Sunday afternoon to be counted at a Pro-Choice Rally. It's in a big New Orleans municipal park and the police have set aside a section of the lawns for the rally. We buy T-shirts showing the Statue of Liberty with the caption 'This lady's pro-choice', Catholics-for-choice stickers, and buttons showing a coat-hanger crossed out within a red circle. As we assemble, the Pro-Life crowd begins to group elsewhere in the park. When the rally gets going, they march around the perimeter, chanting, singing hymns and carrying banners. One particularly portly Southern gent is carrying a wooden stake pushed through a baby doll. Fake blood drips down as he walks.

Well, perhaps at last we have here some genuine antagonism, some conflict and opposition? But that idea is soon dissipated by the soap-opera stars, famous names, easily recognizable from American TV in Australia. Their line in the rally goes something like this:

> I grew up in America to respect the rights of the individual and I learnt that only Communists and Nazis were oppressors of my rights and freedom. But today I see another group emerging who want to do the same thing. And here they are [pointing to the Pro-Life crowd]. They say they're religious, but I believe they're dogmatists who are stifling belief. For God distinguished us from the animals by giving us minds to think with and to make our own choices. This is his greatest gift of all to mankind. And these people [again pointing to the Pro-Lifers] want to take away God's gift of choice. They put themselves in the place of God and aspire to nothing but vanity . . .

And so on. No doubt the tactic is a good one. It's certainly a way of winning the local battle in Louisiana; take away the moral and religious ground from under the feet of the opposition, like Hawke's move to the right. But this leaves a negative space — a space for a genuine discourse (party, or institution) of opposition. At least discursively, it confirms reactionary categories as the proper terms and conditions of the struggle. It's probably the only tactic that can win the local battle, but (to continue an obviously masculinist metaphor) it's probably also the very strategy that can lose the war as a whole. Perhaps the ante-bellum South is, in this other sense, already post-bellum. The war for a social-collectivist American self-understanding has already been lost. A single successful lawsuit on behalf of an individual can out-manoeuvre any number of women and men who take to the streets. If this had happened in Europe in the seventeenth century, it could have provoked the search for another new world.

In downtown New Orleans, the statue of Robert E. Lee faces north. Behind him is the red neon sign of the YMCA building. Local wits say it stands for 'Yankees May Come Again'. Maybe they're already here — in fancy dress.

Alone on a beach in Hawaii, waiting for a Qantas 747 to Cairns, drinking a too-warm Foster's, and reading an aerogramme from Melbourne containing a Leunig cartoon about safe sex and romance. I'm watching a group of Japanese girls travelling overseas for the first time, on their first holiday without parents. Everything has to be safely gathered in before they'll be seen in their bathing costumes. One of them has a floatie. I'm thinking about Cottesloe Beach, Perth, on Sunday afternoons.

I'm tired of America now and glad to be on its very edge. From here, you can tour Pearl Harbor and listen to a stock anti-Japanese tourist tape through a headset. Not many Japanese take the trip. No point now. The place has been much more successfully bombed since, with slow and careful droppings of yen. At Pearl Harbor, you're taken over a sunken battleship, the USS *Arizona* — a kind of *in situ* museum. To this day it leaves behind a long spoor of oil on the water. Someone tells me that other things occasionally float up from the wreck. 'Bits of body', they try to hint.

Drifting off on the beach and drifting back, I suddenly see the face of the taxi driver — the one who said that Reagan's 'Evil Empire' speech was what did for communism. By a fantastic sleepy synecdoche, he comes to be America in my dream. I wonder what he's going to think and feel if and when he, America, has no clear world opposition. What terms will be available then? What will be unAmerican? And if nothing is, is he then going to have to think of himself in positive political terms? Will he have to understand himself as political once politics ('ideology', 'government', 'dogma', 'suppression' and the rest) is no longer easily identifiable as being elsewhere? If so: in what terms? What new discourse is about to be born?

The Japanese girls are finally ready and about to take the plunge.

NOTES

Tim Rowse, 'Heaven and a Hills Hoist'

[1] David Thorns, *Suburbia* (Paladin, London, 1973) pp. 149-150.
[2] A. Birch and D. S. Macmillan (eds), *The Sydney Scene 1788-1960* (Melbourne University Press, 1962), p. 166.
[3] Donald Horne, *The Lucky Country* (Penguin, Ringwood, 1971 edition), p. 26.
[4] Nettie to Aileen Palmer, National Library of Australia MS. 1174/1/6750, a reference given me by Humphrey McQueen.
[5] Louis Esson, *The Time Is Not Yet Ripe*, ed. Philip Parsons (Currency/Methuen, Sydney 1973), p. 73.
[6] Vance Palmer, 'Australia's Transformation', *Fellowship*, March 1921, pp. 119-20.
[7] 'The Prophets Downcast: the Palmers and their Nationalism', *Meanjin Quarterly*, 2/1976.
[8] W. K. Hancock, *Australia* (1961 edition), ibid., p. 160.
[9] 'The Australian City', *New Statesman*, 21 January 1928, pp. 454-6.
[10] Hancock ibid. p. 456.
[11] Frederic Eggleston, *State Socialism*, (P. S. King, London 1932), p. 331.
[12] *Australia's Home* (Pelican edition, Ringwood 1968), pp. 12-14.
[13] I have drawn here on a paper given by Jim Davidson on Humphries, at the Australian Cultural History Seminar, Melbourne University, October 1976.
[14] *The Lucky Country*, p. 27.
[15] ibid., p. 29.
[16] 'Businessmen', in P. Coleman (ed.), *Australian Civilisation* (Cheshire, Melbourne, 1962), p. 177.
[17] *The Australian People* (Angus & Robertson, Sydney, 1972), p. 193. The negative image of suburbia is often equally a negative image of women. A rough equation that seems to be employed is: women + domesticity = spiritual starvation. (Men + wide open spaces + achievement = heroism of the Australian spirit.) The female influence in the 'culture' is often taken to amount to an obsession with status and difference. Lady Macbeth has been written into this myth of mateship.
[18] *Profile of Australia* (Hodder & Stoughton, 1966; Penguin, 1968). All references to Penguin edition; see pp. 129-130.
[19] ibid., p. 131.
[20] *People, Politics and Pop: Australians in the Sixties* (Ure Smith, Sydney, 1968), p. 52.
[21] Hugh Stretton, *Ideas For Australian Cities* (published by the author, North Adelaide, 1970), pp. 20-21.
[22] Hugh Stretton, *Capitalism, Socialism and the Environment* (Cambridge University Press, Cambridge, 1976), p. 202.
[23] ibid., p. 192.

Sneja Gunew, 'Migrant Women Writers'

[1] From 'Intellectuals and Power: a conversation between Michel Foucault and Gilles Deleuze' in M. Foucault, *Language, counter-memory, practice* (Cornell University Press, Ithaca, 1977), pp. 206, 209.
[2] Ian Reid, 'What is an Australian Literary Work?' Unpublished paper delivered at ASAL Conference, Adelaide, May 1982.
[3] Edward Said, *Orientalism* (Vintage Books, New York, 1979), p. 54.
[4] Maria Lewitt, *Come Spring* (Scribe, Fitzroy, 1980), p. 268.
[5] See for example *Orientalism*, pp. 207, 309.
[6] *The Island* (to be published by Hale & Iremonger in 1983).
[7] P. Lumb and A. Hazell (ed), *Diversity and Diversion: an Annotated Bibliography of Australian Ethnic Minority Literature* (Hodja Press, Richmond, 1983).
[8] Published by Saturday Centre Books, Cammeray NSW, 1981.

[9] Nelly Furman, 'Textual Feminism' in *Women and Language in Literature and Society*, ed. by S. McConnell-Ginet *et al.* (Praeger, New York, 1980), p. 50.
[10] 'A Preface to Transgression' in *Language, counter-memory, practice*, pp. 34-35.
[11] Ania Walwicz, 'I' in *Mattoid*, 13, p. 22 (available from the School of Humanities, Deakin University, Victoria 3217).
[12] M. Loh, *With Courage in their Cases* (F.I.L.E.F. Coburg, 1980). W. Lowenstein and M. Loh, *The Immigrants* (Penguin Australia, 1977).
[13] Jacques Lacan, *Ecrits: a Selection* (Tavistock, London, 1980).
[14] A. Walwicz, *Writing* (Rigmarole, Melbourne, 1982), p. 27.
[15] A. Couani, *Italy* (Rigmarole, Melbourne, 1977), p. 11.
[16] A. Couani, *Were all women sex-mad?* (Rigmarole, Melbourne, 1982), p. 20.
[17] Walwicz, *Mattoid*, 13, p. 14.
[18] A. Kefala, *The First Journey* (Wild & Woolley, Sydney, 1975), p. 27.
[19] 'Alexia' in *Mattoid*, 13, pp. 38-43.
[20] M. Jürgensen (ed), *Ethnic Australia* (Phoenix, Brisbane, 1981).
[21] *Mattoid*, 13, p. 19.
[22] S. Gunew (ed), *Displacements: Migrant Storytellers* (Deakin University, Victoria, 1982), p. 2.
[23] D. White and A. Couani (ed), *Island in the Sun 2* (Sea Cruise Books, Glebe, 1981), pp. 58-9.
[24] Walwicz, *Writing*, pp. 20-21.
[25] Walwicz in *Island in the Sun 2*, pp. 90-91.
[26] Walwicz, *Mattoid*, 13, pp. 16-17.

Graeme Smith, 'Making Folk Music'

[1] Charles Keil, 'Who needs the "Folk"?', *Journal of the Folklore Institute*, Vol. 15, No. 3 (1978), p. 263.
[2] *Folklife and the Australian Government: A Guide to Commonwealth Activities and Resources* (Australian Government Publishing Service, Canberra, 1985).
[3] János Marthy, *Music and the Bourgeois, Music and the Proletarian* (Akadémiai Kiad, Budapest, 1974), pp. 132, 257-8.
[4] Cecil Sharp, *English Folksong, Some Conclusions* (Methuen, London, 1954 [1907]). For commentary upon the first English Folksong revival, see Dave Harker, 'May Cecil Sharp be Praised?', *History Workshop* No. 14 (1982), pp. 44-62, and Vic Gammon, 'Folksong Collecting in Sussex and Surrey, 1843-1914', *History Workshop*, No. 10 (1980).
[5] Carl Sands, 'A Program for Proletarian Composers', *Daily Worker* (New York, 16 January 1934), p. 5.
[6] Charles Seeger, 'On Proletarian Music', *Modern Music*, Vol. 11, No. 3 (1934), p. 122, and 'Grass Roots for American Composers', *Modern Music*, Vol. 16, No. 3 (1939), pp. 143-9.
[7] Wendy Lowenstein, Editorial, *Australian Tradition*, No. 37 (1975).
[8] Percy Jones, 'Australia's Folk Songs', *Twentieth Century: An Australian Quarterly Review*, Vol. 1, No. 1 (1946), p. 41.
[9] Vance Palmer and Margaret Sutherland, *Old Australian Bush Ballads* (Allen & Co., Melbourne, 1950).
[10] For correspondence between Sutherland and Edwards concerning Sutherland's 'restoration', see Ron Edwards, *The Big Book of Australian Folk Song* (Rigby, Adelaide, 1976), p. 414.
[11] Ron Edwards and John Manifold, *Bandicoot Ballads* (Rams Skull Press, Melbourne, 1951-5).
[12] J. D. Blake, 'Folk Culture and the People's Movement', *Communist Review*, No. 116 (August 1951), pp. 872-5.
[13] John Docker, 'Culture, Society and the Communist Party', in Ann Curthoys and John Merritt, *Australia's First Cold War, 1945-1953*, Vol. 1 (George Allen & Unwin, Sydney, 1984), pp. 183-212.
[14] See Eric Watson, *Country Music in Australia* (Rodeo Productions, Eastlake, 1975).

[15] Lawrence Zion, 'Pop Music and Australian Culture. Some Considerations', *Melbourne Historical Journal* No. 14, pp. 18-33.
[16] Simon Frith, '"The magic that can set you free": The Ideology of Folk and the Myth of the Rock Community', *Popular Music I* (Cambridge University Press, 1981).
[17] *Draft Paper No. 2. The Problem of Allocation of Music Board Funds Between Competing Uses* (Music Board, Australia Council, 1984).
[18] Tim Rowse, 'Doing Away With Ordinary People', *Meanjin*, Vol. 44, No. 2 (1985), pp. 161-169.

Author index

Page references in italics are to correspondence or other unpublished matter.